Theme

KU-009-890

Thematic Guide

NB This is a broad thematic guide – inevitably a number of the categories overlap.

Within each theme the organisations are listed alphabetically by key word as in the main listing.

Activity Holidays and Placements

Africa & Asia Venture

Archaeology Abroad

Backpackers Club

BAPA - Activity Providers

Brathay Exploration Group

BSES Expeditions - Exploration

Calvert Trust

CHICKS - Country Holidays for Inner City Children

Commonwealth Youth Exchange Council

Environment (Young People's Trust for the)

Farms for City Children

Forest School Camps

Girls Venture Corps Air Cadets

IVS GB - International Voluntary Service

Jubilee Sailing Trust

Lattitude Global Volunteering

Marine Leisure Association (MLA)

National Trust Volunteering

National Trust Working Holidays

Outward Bound Trust

Prince's Trust - Pembrokeshire Adventure Centre

Project Trust

Quaker Voluntary Action

Raleigh International

Scientific Exploration Society

Venture Trust

Volunteer Action for Peace

Waterway Recovery Group

Wind Sand & Stars

World Challenge Expeditions

WWOOF UK - Opportunities on Organic Farms UK

YHA - Youth Hostel Association

Youth Cancer Trust

Addiction

Addaction

Addiction (Action on)

ADFAM

Al-Anon Alateen

Alcohol Concern

Alcoholics Anonymous

Blenheim CDP

Children of Alcoholics (National Association for)

Cocaine Anonymous UK

Drink Helpline (National)

Families Anonymous

Frank

Freshfield Service

Gam-Anon UK & Ireland

Gamblers Anonymous

Gamblers Anonymous Scotland

GAMCARE

Help - For a life without tobacco

London Drug & Alcohol Network

Narcotics Anonymous UK

Tranquillisers, Antidepressants and Painkillers (Council for Information on)

Adoption & Fostering

AAA-NORCAP - Adults affected by adoption

Adoption and Fostering Information Line

Adoption records

Adoption UK

BAAF Adoption and Fostering (British Association for)

Coram

Fostering Network

Intercountry Adoption Centre

National Records of Scotland (NRS)

OASIS

PACT (Parents and Children Together)

Post-Adoption Centre

Register Office for Northern Ireland (General)

TACT - The Adolescent and Children's Trust

Talk Adoption

Alcohol

Addaction

Addiction (Action on)

ADFAM

Al-Anon Alateen

Alcohol Concern

Alcohol Education and Research Council

Alcohol Focus Scotland

Alcohol Studies (Institute of)

Alcoholics Anonymous

BNTL-Freeway: British National

Temperance League

CADD- Campaign Against Drinking & Driving

CAMRA - Campaign for Real Ale

Children of Alcoholics (National Association for)

Drink Helpline (National)

Drinkaware

London Drug & Alcohol Network

Portman Group

Roofie Foundation

Science in the Public Interest (Center for)

Turning Point

Animals

ACT – Animal Cancer Trust

African Conservation Experience

Animal Aid

Animal Aid Youth

Animal Defenders International

Animal Health (National Office of)

Animal Health Trust

Animal Rescue (International)

Animal Rescuers (UK)

Animal Welfare Trust (National)

Anti Snaring Campaign (National)

Anti-Vivisection Society (National)

Ape Alliance

ARKive

Avicultural Society

Badger Trust

Bat Conservation Trust

Battersea Dogs Home

Bird Council (British)

Blue Cross

Born Free Foundation

Brooke

Animals continued

BUAV - British Union for the Abolition of Vivisection

Budgerigar Society

Butterfly Conservation

Canine Partners

Captive Animals' Protection Society

Care for the Wild International

Cat Fancy (Governing Council of the)

Cats Protection

Cinnamon Trust

City Farms & Community Gardens (Federation of)

Companion Animal Studies (Society for)

Compassion in World Farming Trust

Cruel Sports Ltd (League Against)

Crufts Dog Show

David Sheldrick Wildlife Trust

Deer Society (British)

Divers Marine Life Rescue (British)

DogLost

Dogs for the Disabled

Dogs Trust

Donkey Breed Society

Donkey Sanctuary

Dr Hadwen Trust for Humane Research

Dragonfly Society (British)

Entomologists' Society (Amateur)

Environmental Investigation Agency

Eurogroup for Animals

Farm Animal Welfare Committee

Farms for City Children

Fauna & Flora International

Feline Advisory Bureau

FRAME - Fund for the Replacement of Animals in Medical Experiments

Freshfields Donkey Village

Froglife

Gambia Horse and Donkey Trust

Gorilla Organization

Guide Dogs for the Blind Association

Hamster Council (National)

HAPPA - Horses and Ponies Protection Association

Hawk and Owl Trust

Hearing Dogs for Deaf People

Hedgehog Preservation Society (British)

Horse Society (British)

Humane Slaughter Association

Hunt Saboteurs Association

IFAW - International Fund for Animal Welfare

IPPL (UK) - International Primate Protection League

Kennel Club

Lord Dowding Fund

Marine Conservation Society

Marine Life Study Society (British)

Naturewatch

Ocean Mammal Institute

Onekind

Orangutan Foundation

Ornithology (British Trust for)

PDSA - People's Dispensary for Sick Animals

People's Trust for Endangered Species

Pet Advisory Committee

Pet Behaviour Counsellors (Association of)

Pet Care Trust

Pet Health Council

Pet Month (National)

PETA Foundation - People for the Ethical Treatment of Animals

PetLog Database (National)

Pets as Therapy

Pony Club

Rabbit Council (British)

Rare Breeds Survival Trust

Red List of Endangered Species

Redwings Horse Sanctuary

Respect for Animals

Royal College of Veterinary Surgeons

RSPB - Royal Society for the Protection of Birds

RSPCA - Royal Society for the Prevention of Cruelty to Animals

Scottish SPCA - Scottish Society for the Prevention of Cruelty to Animals

Shark Alliance

Small Animal Veterinary Association (British)

Support Dogs

Uncaged Campaigns

Understanding Animal Research

Viva! - Vegetarians International Voice for Animals

Whale & Dolphin Conservation Society

Wildlife Aid

Wildlife Trusts (Royal Society of)

Wood Green Animal Shelters

World Horse Welfare

WSPA International - World Society for the Protection of Animals

WWF-UK

ZSL- Zoological Society of London

Ancient Buildings (Society for the Protection of)

Archiseek

Architects (Royal Institute of British)

Architectural Heritage Fund

Architecture Foundation

Design Council

Friends of Friendless Churches

Georgian Group

GreatBuildings

Landscape Institute

Open-City

Royal Scottish Academy

SALVO - Architectural Salvage Listings

Twentieth Century Society

Victorian Society

Access Art

Access London Theatre

Access Space

Action Transport Theatre

Age Exchange

Apples & Snakes

Arc Theatre

Architects (Royal Institute of British)

Architecture Foundation

Ariel Studios

Art and Design (National Society for Education in)

Art Fund

Art Library (National)

Art Therapists (British Association of)

Artists Against Racism

Arts (National Campaign for the)

Arts & Business

Arts Council England

Arts Council of Northern Ireland

Arts Council of Wales

Arts in Therapy & Education (Institute for)

Arts Marketing Association

Artsline

Artswork

ArtWatch UK

Ashmolean

Authors' Licensing and Collecting Society

Arts continued

Ballet Organization (British)

BBC Studio Audiences

Benesh Institute

Birmingham Royal Ballet

Bolshoi Ballet

Book Trust (Scottish)

Books Council (Welsh)

Booktrust

BRIT School for Performing Arts and Technology

British Film Institute

British Library Sound Archive

Brontë Parsonage Museum & Brontë Society

Cambridge Past, Present & Future

Cello Society (Internet)

Children's Literature (National Centre for Research in)

Chinese Arts Centre

Circus Sensible/Circus School

Circus Space

Classical Association

Contemporary Art Society

Courtauld Institute of Art

Crafts Council

Creative Scotland

Dance UK

Danceconsortium

Design and Artists Copyright Society

Design and Technology Association

Disability Arts Cymru

Drama Association of Wales

Drama UK

Dramatic Need

Drawing (The Campaign for)

Edinburgh International Book Festival

Edinburgh International Festival

Engage - The National Association for Gallery Education

English National Ballet

English National Opera

English PEN

English Touring Theatre

ENYAN - English National Youth Arts Network

European Youth Music Week

Festivals (British & International Federation of)

Finnish Institute

Folger Shakespeare Library

France: culture and communications website

Frankfurt Book Fair

Georgian Group

Headlong Theatre

Henry Moore Foundation

History of Cinema & Popular Culture (The Bill Douglas Centre for the)

Hull Truck Theatre

ICON - Institute of Conservation

Imaginate

Italian Cultural Institute in London

IXIA

Live Theatre

London Charity Orchestra

London Theatre (Official)

London theatres: online

Lowry Theatre and Art Gallery

Mousetrap Theatre Projects

Movie Review Query Engine

Museums (International Council of)

Music Council (National)

National Drama

National Opera Studio

National Theatre

National Youth Ballet of Great Britain

NODA - National Operatic & Dramatic Association

Northern Ballet

Northern Broadsides

Northern Stage

Open College of the Arts

Open-City

Out of Joint

Performing Arts Medicine (British Association for)

Poetry Library

Poetry Society

Polka Theatre

Project Gutenberg

PRS for Music - Performing Rights Society

Public Monuments & Sculpture Association

Queen's House

RADA - Royal Academy of Dramatic Art

Rambert Dance Company

Roundhouse

Royal Academy of Arts

Royal Academy of Dance

Royal Ballet

Royal Opera

Royal Scottish Academy

RSA - Royal Society for the Encouragement of Arts, Manufactures and Commerce

RSC - Royal Shakespeare Company

Science, Technology & the Arts (National Endowment for)

Scottish Ballet

Scottish Opera

Scottish Youth Theatre

SCRAN

Shakespeare Association (British)

Shakespeare at the Tobacco Factory

Shakespeare Birthplace Trust

Shakespeare Schools Festival

Shakespeare's Globe Theatre

Shared Experience

Skylight Circus Arts

Sound Sense

Southbank Centre

SPIT - Signed Performances in Theatre

Storytelling (Society for)

Student Drama Festival (National)

Studies in British Art (Paul Mellon Centre for)

Teaching of Drama (National Association for the)

Theatre Council (Independent)

Théâtre de Complicité

Theatre for Children and Young People (International Association of)

Theatre Network (The Amateur)

Theatrenet

Theatres Trust

Twentieth Century Society

UK Theatre Web

Unicorn Theatre for Children

Venice in Peril Fund

Visual Arts & Galleries Association

Voluntary Arts Network

Welsh National Opera

Women in Publishing

Writers in Education (National Association of)

Writers' Guild of Great Britain

Youth Arts Wales (National)

Youth Music Theatre (National)

Youth Opera (British)

Youth Orchestra (National of GB)

Youth Theatre of GB (National)

Youth Theatres (National Association of)

Care/Carers

4Children
Action for Children
Action for Children Northern Ireland
Action for Children Scotland
Action for Children Wales
Alzheimer Scotland
Alzheimer's Society
Anchor Trust
Anxiety Care UK
Assisted Dying (Healthcare Professionals for)
Attend
Baby Lifeline
Breast Cancer Care
CACHE - Council for Awards in Children's Care and Education
Care Council for Wales
Care Quality Commission
Carers Trust
CarersUK
Chance UK
Childminding Association (National)
Christian Lewis Trust
CLICSargent
Contact a Family
Counsel and Care
Cruse Bereavement Care
Daycare Trust
Disability Law Service
Disabled Living Foundation
Early Years
Elder Abuse (Action on)
Epilepsy Society
Freedom from Torture
Half the Sky Foundation

Help the Hospices
Home-Start
Hyperactive Children's Support Group
Life
Macmillan Cancer Support
Marie Curie Cancer Care
Muslim Welfare House
PACT (Prison Advice & Care Trust)
Palliative Care (National Council for)
Pastoral Care in Education (National Association for)
Pituitary Foundation
Pre-school Learning Alliance
Pre-school Play Association (Scottish)
Pre-School Providers Association (Wales)
Sick Children (Action for)
Sickle Cell Society
Skills for Care
Social Care Association
Solicitors for the Elderly
Treloar Trust
Twins & Multiple Births Association
Voice
Who Cares? Trust

Censorship

ARTICLE 19
Film Classification (British Board of)
Freedom of Information (Campaign for)
Index on Censorship
Information Commissioner's Office
Internet Watch Foundation
Press and Broadcasting Freedom (Campaign for)
Video Standards Council

Charities (general)

Big Lottery Fund

Charities Aid Foundation

CharitiesDirect.com

Charity Choice

Charity Commission for England & Wales

Children in Need Appeal

Comic Relief

Computers 4 Africa

Disasters Emergency Committee

Giving Nation

Jane Tomlinson Appeal

Justgiving

Medical Research Charities (Association of)

ShareGift

Children & Young People

100 Black Men of London

4Children

Access to Industry

Action for Children

Action for Children Northern Ireland

Action for Children Scotland

Action for Children Wales

Action Transport Theatre

Additives (Action on)

Adoption and Fostering Information Line

Adoption records

Adoption UK

Adventure Activities Licensing Authority

Afasic

Africans Unite Against Child Abuse

Al-Anon Alateen

Alone in London

Ambition

Anti-Bullying Alliance

Anti-Bullying Network

Ariel Studios

Army Cadet Force

Artswork

Aspect

Athletic Association (English Schools')

BAAF Adoption and Fostering (British Association for)

Baby Milk Action

Babyworld

Baobab Centre for Young Survivors in Exile

Barnardo's

BASPCAN - British Association for the Study and Prevention of Child Abuse and Neglect

Beatbullying

Big Read (The)

BNTL-Freeway: British National Temperance League

Boarding Concern

Bolton Lads & Girls Club

Boys' Brigade

Brainwave

Brandon Centre

Brazil's Children Trust (Action for)

Bully Free Zone

Bullying UK

Butterfly Project

CACHE - Council for Awards in Children's Care and Education

Cafcass

Camp Mohawk

Cardiac Risk in the Young

Cards for Little Lives

Catch22

Chain of Hope

Chance UK

Chernobyl Children's Life Line

Children and Young people continued

CHICKS - Country Holidays for Inner City Children

Child & Woman Abuse Studies Unit

Child Accident Prevention Trust

Child and Adolescent Mental Health (Association for)

Child Bereavement Charity

Child Brain Injury Trust

Child Contact Centres (National Association of)

Child Growth Foundation

Child Poverty Action Group

Child Protection in Sport Unit

Child Soldiers

Childhood (Alliance for)

Childhood Bereavement Network

ChildHope

ChildLine

Childminding Association (National)

CHILDREN 1ST

Children are unbeatable! Alliance

Children in Need Appeal

Children in Scotland

Children of Alcoholics (National Association for)

Children with Cancer

Children's Book Groups (Federation of)

Children's Commissioner for England (Office of the)

Children's Heart Federation

Children's Hope Foundation

Children's Legal Centre

Children's Literature (National Centre for Research in)

Children's Orchestra (National)

Children's Rights Alliance for England

Children's Scrapstore

Children's Society

Christian Lewis Trust

Church Lads' and Church Girls' Brigade

Church of England Education Division

Cirdan Sailing Trust

CLICSargent

Communication Trust

Coram

Council of Europe Youth

CRAC - Careers Research & Advisory Centre

CRIN - Child Rights Information Network

CyberMentors

Dad

Dad Talk

Dads House

Daneford Trust

Daycare Trust

Deaf Children's Society (National)

Depaul International

Depaul Nightstop UK

Down Syndrome Education International

Dramatic Need

Duke of Edinburgh's Award

Early Education

Early Years

Education (Department for)

Education and Culture (Directorate General for)

Education for Choice

Ellen MacArthur Cancer Trust

End violence against women

Endeavour Training Limited

England Athletics

ENYAN - English National Youth Arts Network

Epilepsy (National Centre for Young People with)

ERIC - Education and Resources for Improving Childhood Continence

European Youth Card Association

European Youth Forum

European Youth Information and Counselling Agency

Every Child a Chance Trust

EveryChild

Fair Play for Children Association

Families Need Fathers

Find a Parent or Child

First Light

Foundation For Peace (Tim Parry Johnathan Ball)

Foyer Federation

Free the Children

Get connected

Gifted Children (National Association for)

Gifted Children's Information Centre

Girlguiding UK

Girls Venture Corps Air Cadets

Girls' Brigade England & Wales

Giving Nation

Grandparents Plus

Half the Sky Foundation

Handsel Trust

Headliners

Heart Programme

Hideout

Hope UK

Hyperactive Children's Support Group

Imaginate

Include

Independent Safeguarding Authority

IntoUniversity

Jeans for Genes

Jewish Lads' & Girls' Brigade (JLGB)

Just for Kids Law

Kids Company

Kids for Kids

Kidscape

Lavender Trust

Leap Confronting Conflict

Learning Outside the Classroom (Council for)

Lesbian Information Service

likeitis.org

Live Music Now

London Children's Ballet

London Youth

Magic Breakfast

Marine Society and Sea Cadets

MATCH - Mothers Apart from Their Children

Maternal & Childhealth Advocacy International

Mermaids

Methodist Children & Youth

Midi Music Company

Missing Children website

Montessori Centre

Mousetrap Theatre Projects

Mumsnet

Music for Youth

Mydaughter.co.uk

NABSS - National Association of Black Supplementary Schools

National Youth Ballet of Great Britain

NBCS - National Blind Children's Society

NCB - National Children's Bureau

NSPCC - National Society for the Prevention of Cruelty to Children

Nurture Group Network

Ocean Youth Trust

Out of trouble

PACT (Parents & Abducted Children Together)

Parenting UK

Pastoral Care in Education (National Association for)

Philip Lawrence Awards Network

Children and Young people continued

Plan UK

Play England

Play Wales

PLAYLINK

Pod Charitable Trust

Pre-school Learning Alliance

Pre-school Play Association (Scottish)

Pre-School Providers Association (Wales)

Prince's Trust (Head Office)

Pyramid

Quality in Study Support and Extended Services

Railway Children

Raw Material

React - Rapid Effective Assistance for Children with Potentially Terminal illness

Restless Development

reunite

Rona Sailing Project

Roundhouse

Runaway Helpline

Save the Children UK

School Food Trust

Scottish Youth Theatre

Scout Association

Sea Ranger Association

SEBDA - Social, Emotional & Behavioural Difficulties Association

Seven Stories

Shared Parenting Information Group

Sick Children (Action for)

Siobhan Dowd Trust

Skylight Circus Arts

Smallpeice Trust

SOS Children's Villages

Sparks

Tall Ships Youth Trust

Teenage Cancer Trust

Theatre for Children and Young People (International Association of)

Thesite.org

Trackoff

UK Parents Lounge

UK Youth

UNICEF UK

United Reformed Church

University of the First Age

Urban Saints

Values Education for Life (The Collegiate Centre for)

Venture Trust

Voice

Voluntary Arts Network

Voluntary Youth Services (National Council for)

What About The Children?

Whizz-Kidz

Who Cares? Trust

Willow Foundation

Winston's Wish

Wired Safety

Woodcraft Folk

Working on Wheels

WorldWide Volunteering

Year Out Group

YMCA England

Young Christian Workers

Young Concert Artists Trust

Young Fathers Initiative

Young People in Focus

Young People with ME (Association of)

Young Scot

YoungMinds

Youth Access

Youth Advocacy Service (National)

Youth Agency (National)

Youth Arts Wales (National)

Youth at Risk

Youth Choir of Great Britain (National)

Youth Council (British)

Youth Council for Northern Ireland

Youth for Christ

Youth in Action

Youth Information

Youth Music

Youth Music Theatre (National)

Youth Orchestra (National of GB)

Youth Sport Trust

Youth Theatre of GB (National)

Youth Theatres (National Association of)

Youthhealthtalk

YouthNet UK

Citizenship & Community Issues

Advocacy Resource Exchange

Arthur Rank Centre

Better Transport (Campaign for)

Bevan Foundation

Black Environment Network

Blenheim CDP

British Legion (Royal)

Business in the Community

Certificate ordering service

Changemakers

Citizens UK

Citizenship and the Law (National Centre for)

Citizenship Foundation

Citizenship Teaching (Association for)

City Farms & Community Gardens (Federation of)

Common Ground

Common Purpose

Commonwealth Youth Exchange Council

Communities and Local Government (Department for)

Communities in Rural England (Action with)

Community Composting Network

Community Dance (Foundation for)

Community Foundation Network

Community Matters

Community Media Association

Community Rail Partnerships (Association of)

Community Safety Network (National)

Community Service Volunteers

Courts and Tribunal Service (HM)

Crimestoppers

Crown Prosecution Service

Data Archive (UK)

DirectGov

Family Names Profiling (GB)

Forgiveness Project

Foundation For Peace (Tim Parry Johnathan Ball)

Friends, Families and Travellers

Get Global!

GFS Platform for Young Women - Girls Friendly Society

Groundwork UK

Gun Control Network

Gypsy Association

Habitat for Humanity Great Britain

Homeless Link

Immigrants (Joint Council for the Welfare of)

Immigration Aid Unit (Greater Manchester)

Integrated Education (N. Ireland Council for)

Intermix

IVS GB - International Voluntary Service

Lattitude Global Volunteering

Citizenship and Community Issues continued

Leap Confronting Conflict

Legal Services Commission

Letslink UK

Local Government Association

Local Government Ombudsman (England)

Missing People

Peace Alliance

Pensioners Convention (National)

Pet Advisory Committee

Philip Lawrence Awards Network

Placement Survival Guide

Project Trust

Public Services Ombudsman (Scottish)

Quaker Voluntary Action

Raleigh International

RAPt - Rehabilitation for Addicted Prisoners Trust

Registering life events

Republic

Runaway Helpline

Science in the Public Interest (Center for)

Show Racism the Red Card

Skills for Justice

Social Care Association

Social Issues Research Centre

Social Workers (British Association of)

Squatters (Advisory Service for)

Transforming Conflict

UK Border Agency

UK New Citizen

Undercurrents

Venture Trust

Voluntary and Community Action (National Association for)

Volunteers For Rural India

Working with men

WRVS (Women's Royal Voluntary Service)

Complementary Medicine

Acupuncture Council (British)

Acupuncture Society (British Medical)

Alexander Teachers (Professional Association of)

Alexander Technique (Society of Teachers of the)

Bach Centre

Chiropractic (Anglo-European College of)

Chiropractic Association (British)

Chiropractic Patients' Association

Complementary and Natural Medicine (Institute for)

Healing Organisations (Confederation of)

Herb Society

Holistic Therapists (Federation of)

Homeopathic Association (British)

Homeopaths (Society of)

Medical Herbalists (National Institute of)

Osteopathic Council (General)

Paul's Cancer Support Centre

Reflexology Association (British)

Shiatsu Society (UK)

Consumers, Commerce & Business

ABTA - The Travel Association

Adbusters

Advertising Association

Advertising Standards Authority

Arts & Business

ATM locator

Banana Link

Bankruptcy Advisory Service Limited

Blind in Business

British Standards Institute

Building Societies Members Association

Bus Users UK

Business & Professional Women UK Ltd

Business Gateway

Business in Sport & Leisure

Buy Nothing Day (UK)

CAMRA - Campaign for Real Ale

Chambers of Commerce (British)

Chartered Management Institute

Chartered Surveyors (Royal Institute of)

Chartered Surveyors Training Trust

Chartered Surveyors Voluntary Service

Citizens Advice

Competition Commission

Consumer Credit Counselling Service

Consumer Focus

Consumer Focus Post

Consumers International

Corporate Watch

Credit Unions Ltd. (Association of British)

Crown Estates

Dairy Council (The)

Direct Marketing Association

Directors (Institute of)

Economics, Business and Enterprise Association

Education Business Excellence (Institute for)

Effective Dispute Resolution (Centre for)

Egg Information Service (British)

EIRIS - Experts in Responsible Investment Solutions

Ethical Consumer Research Association (ECRA)

European Central Bank

European Investment Bank

Facsimile Preference Service

Fair Trade Shops (British Association for)

Fair Trading (Office of)

Fairtrade Foundation

Farmers' Markets (Scottish Association of)

Farmers' Retail & Markets Association (National)

Financial Ombudsman Service

Financial Services Authority

Fiscal Studies (Institute for)

Food & Drink Federation

Food Commission (UK)

Fredericks Foundation

Freecycle

Freegle

Home Business Alliance

Homeworking

Howtocomplain.com

Information Management (Association for)

Intellectual Property Office

Lorna Young Foundation

Mailing Preference Service

Marine Stewardship Council

Mentoring and Befriending Foundation

Moneysavingexpert.com

My Supermarket

National Debtline

Naturewatch

OFCOM

Ofgem

Patent Office (European)

Payplan

Personnel & Development (Chartered Institute of)

Phonebrain

Phonepay Plus

Pipedown

Post Office

Postcode Finder

Rail Regulation (Office of)

Road Haulage Association

Consumers, Commerce and Business continued

Shared Interest Society Ltd

Simple Free Law Advisor

Sleep Council

Small Businesses (Federation of)

Social Entrepreneurs (School for)

Stock Exchange (London)

SustainAbility

TaxAid

Telephone Directories On Web

Telephone Preference Service

Tour Operators (Association of Independent)

Trading Standards Institute

Traidcraft

Trainline

Unite

Water Services (Office of)

We Are What We Do

Which?

Women Entrepreneurs (British Association of)

Work & Pensions (Department for)

World Trade Organization

Contraception, Pregnancy & Birth

Abortion Rights

Action of Postpartum Psychosis Network

Active Birth Centre

AIMS - Association for Improvements in the Maternity Services

ARC - Antenatal Results and Choices

Baby Lifeline

Babyworld

Birth Trauma Association

BirthChoice UK

Bliss - For babies born too soon, too small or too sick

Bliss Scotland

Bounty Healthcare Fund

BPAS - British Pregnancy Advisory Service

Brandon Centre

Brook

COTS - Childlessness overcome through surrogacy

Dad

Donor Conception Network

Education for Choice

Family Planning Association

Fertility Friends

Fertility UK

Gamete Donation Trust (National)

Human Fertilisation & Embryology Authority

Infertility Counselling Association (British)

Infertility Network UK

Interact Worldwide

La Leche League GB

Life

likeitis.org

Margaret Pyke Centre

Marie Stopes International

Midwives UK (Independent)

Miscarriage Association

Multiple Births Foundation

Mumsnet

National Childbirth Trust

Netmums

Newlife Foundation for Disabled Children

Nursing & Midwifery Council

Pathfinder International

Planned Parenthood Federation (International)

Post Natal Illness

Post-Natal Illness (Association for)

SANDS - Stillbirth & Neonatal Death Charity

Sex Education Forum

Tommy's, the baby charity

Twins & Multiple Births Association

UK Parents Lounge

Unborn Children (Society for the Protection of)

Voice for Choice

White Ribbon Alliance

Your Life

Counselling

AAA-NORCAP - Adults affected by adoption

AdviceUK

Advocacy Resource Exchange

Ahimsa

Albany Trust

Anxiety Care UK

Arbitrators (Chartered Institute of)

Barnardo's

BEAT - Beating Eating Disorders

Befrienders Worldwide

Bereavement Network (London)

Birmingham Settlement

BPAS - British Pregnancy Advisory Service

Brandon Centre

Broken Rainbow UK

Brook

CALM - Campaign Against Living Miserably

Changing Faces

ChildLine

Citizens Advice

Communities Empowerment Network

Concord Media

Counsel and Care

Counselling & Psychotherapy (British Association for)

Crisis Counselling for Alleged Shoplifters

Cruse Bereavement Care

Cry-sis

Dial UK

Donor Conception Network

Down's Heart Group

Eating Problems Service

ENABLE Scotland

Everyman Project

Family Lives

Family Rights Group

Frank

Freshfield Service

Gamete Donation Trust (National)

Handsel Trust

Hereditary Breast Cancer Helpline (National)

Hideout

Infertility Counselling Association (British)

Karma Nirvana

Kids Company

Lesbian and Gay Switchboard (London)

Life

Marie Stopes International

Medical Advisory Service

Men's Advice Line

Miracles

Mosac

NHS Direct

No Panic

NSPCC - National Society for the Prevention of Cruelty to Children

PACE

Paul's Cancer Support Centre

Post-Adoption Centre

Prisoners' Advice Service

Public Concern at Work

Rape Crisis

Relate

Counselling continued

Relationships Scotland

Respect

RoadPeace

Roofie Foundation

Samaritans

SAMM - Support After Murder & Manslaughter

SANE

Seasonal Affective Disorder Association

SEBDA - Social, Emotional & Behavioural Difficulties Association

Survivors of Bereavement by Suicide

SurvivorsUK

Talk Adoption

Teacher Support Network

The Survivors Trust

Triumph over Phobia (TOP UK)

Victim Support

Wessex Cancer Trust

Who Cares? Trust

Youth Access

Youth Advocacy Service (National)

Dance

Refer also to the section on Dance, Drama, Music & Performing Arts Schools

Ballet Organization (British)

Benesh Institute

Birmingham Royal Ballet

Bolshoi Ballet

Ceroc

Community Dance (Foundation for)

Dance Council (British)

Dance Education & Training (Council for)

Dance UK

Danceconsortium

Dancesport UK

Dancing and Kindred Arts (United Kingdom Alliance of Professional Teachers of)

English National Ballet

Festivals (British & International Federation of)

IDTA - International Dance Teachers Association

ISTD - Imperial Society of Teachers of Dancing

London Children's Ballet

Men's Morris & Sword Dance Clubs (National Association of)

Morris Federation

National Youth Ballet of Great Britain

Northern Ballet

Rambert Dance Company

Royal Academy of Dance

Royal Ballet

Scottish Ballet

Death and Bereavement

Advocacy After Fatal Domestic Abuse

Assisted Dying (Healthcare Professionals for)

Bereavement Network (London)

Cardiac Risk in the Young

Care Not Killing

Child Bereavement Charity

Child Death Helpline

Childhood Bereavement Network

Compassionate Friends

Cremation Society of Great Britain

Cruse Bereavement Care

Dignity in Dying

Dying Matters

Friends at the end

Help the Hospices

Infant Deaths (Foundation for the Study of)

INQUEST

Lone Twin Network

Natural Death Centre

Palliative Care (National Council for)

React - Rapid Effective Assistance for Children with Potentially Terminal illness

SAMM - Support After Murder & Manslaughter

Survivors of Bereavement by Suicide

Winston's Wish

Developing World

ActionAid

ADD International (Action on Disability and Development)

Afghanaid

Africa & Asia Venture

Africa Centre

African Initiatives

Africans Unite Against Child Abuse

Anti-Slavery International

Baby Milk Action

Banana Link

Bond

Book Aid International

Brazil's Children Trust (Action for)

Broadcasting Trust (International)

Brooke

Burma Campaign UK

CAFOD - Catholic Overseas Development Agency

CAMFED International - Campaign for Female Education

Canon Collins Trust

CARE International UK

Chain of Hope

Christian Aid

Comic Relief

Commonwealth Education Trust

Commonwealth Scholarship Commission in the UK

Commonwealth Society (Royal)

Computer Aid International

Computers 4 Africa

Concern Worldwide

Conflict Minerals

Cross Cultural Solutions

Development Education Project

Dramatic Need

Ethiopiaid

Fair Trade Shops (British Association for)

Fairtrade Foundation

Forest Peoples Programme

Gambia Horse and Donkey Trust

Global Crop Diversity Trust

Global Dimension

Global Eye

HALO Trust

HIV InSite

HIV/Aids Alliance (International)

Homeless International

Hunger Education Service (World) & Hunger Notes

International Development (Department for)

International Monetary Fund

International Service

Islamic Relief Worldwide

Jubilee Debt Campaign

Kids for Kids

Kiva

Labour Behind the Label

Lorna Young Foundation

Developing World continued

Malaria No More UK

Mary's Meals

Médecins sans Frontières (UK)

Media for Development

Medical Trust (Britain-Nepal)

Mercy Corps

Nicaragua Solidarity Campaign

ONE International

Operation Smile UK

Opportunity International UK

Overseas Development Institute

Oxfam

Panos Institute

Pathfinder International

People & Planet

Plan UK

Practical Action

Restless Development

Room to Read

Samaritans International

Save the Children UK

SCIAF - Scottish Catholic International Aid Fund

Shine a Light

Sightsavers

Skillshare International

SOS Children's Villages

Stakeholder Forum

Survival International

TAPOL

Tearfund

Tools for Self Reliance

Tourism Concern

Traidcraft

TRóCAIRE

UNICEF UK

United Nations Association of the UK

Vision Aid Overseas

VSO - Voluntary Service Overseas

War on Want

Water Aid

Womankind Worldwide

World Bank

World Development Movement

World Food Programme (United Nations)

World Health Organisation

World Vision UK

Y Care International

Disability & Special Needs

1 Voice

Access London Theatre

Accessible Environments (Centre for)

Action on Hearing Loss

ADD International (Action on Disability and Development

Afasic

Artsline

Asian People's Disability Alliance

Back-up Trust

BASIC - Brain & Spinal Injury Centre

Bibic

Bikers with a Disability (National Association for)

Blind (Royal National Institute of the)

Blind Golf Association (English)

Blind in Business

Blind of the United Kingdom (National Federation of the)

Blind People (Action for)

Blind Sport (British)

Blue Badge Network

Braille Chess Association

Calvert Trust

Camp Mohawk

Canine Partners

Carers Trust

Changing Faces

Child Growth Foundation

Children's Hope Foundation

CLAPA - Cleft Lip & Palate Association

ClearVision Project

Conductive Education (The National Institute of)

Connect

Contact a Family

CP Sport England and Wales (cerebral palsy)

Cued Speech Association UK

Cycling Projects

Deaf Association (British)

Deaf Children's Society (National)

Deaf Education Through Listening and Talking

Deafblind International

Deafblind Scotland

Deafblind UK

Deafness Research UK

Dial UK

Disability Action

Disability Arts Cymru

Disability Law Service

Disability Pregnancy & Parenthood International

Disability Rights UK

Disability Snowsport UK

Disability Sport (English Federation of)

Disability Sport (English Federation of)

Disabled Living Foundation

Disabled Motoring UK

Disabled Parents Network

Disabled People's Council (UK)

Disfigurement Guidance Centre

Dogs for the Disabled

Douglas Bader Foundation

Down's Syndrome Association

Down's Syndrome Scotland

Dyslexia Action

Dyslexia Association (British)

Dyspraxia Foundation

ENABLE Scotland

Equality and Human Rights Commission

Equality Britain

Freshfields Donkey Village

Gateway Award

Guide Dogs for the Blind Association

Hairline International

Handsel Trust

HEADWAY

Hearing Dogs for Deaf People

Hypermobility Syndrome Association

Inclusion (National Development Team for)

Inclusive Education (Alliance for)

Inclusive Education (Centre for Studies on)

Independent Living Alternatives

IPSEA - Independent Parental Special Education Advice

Jubilee Sailing Trust

Learning Disabilities (British Institute of)

Let's Face It

Limbless Association

Listening Books

Makaton Charity

Mencap

Mental Health Foundation

Multiple Sclerosis Society

Multiple Sclerosis Therapy Centres (National)

Music and the Deaf

Music Therapy (British Association for)

NBCS - National Blind Children's Society

Network 81

Disability & Special Needs continued

Newlife Foundation for Disabled Children

NOAH - National Organization for Albinism and Hypopigmentation

Norwood

Not Dead Yet UK

Operation Smile UK

Papworth Trust

Paralympic GB

Parents for Inclusion

Partially Sighted Society

People First

Phab - Physically Disabled & Able Bodied

Rathbone

REMAP

Remploy

Ricability

Riding for the Disabled Association

RNIB - Royal National Institute of Blind People

Rona Sailing Project

RYA Sailability

Saving Faces

Scope

SeeAbility

Self Unlimited

Sense

Shine

Shopmobility (National Federation of)

Short Persons Support

Sibs

Sightsavers

Signature

Skills for Care

Sound Seekers

Sound Sense

Speakability

Special Educational Needs (National Association for)

Special Needs Education (European Agency for Development in)

Special Olympics

Special Olympics Great Britain

SPIT - Signed Performances in Theatre

Sports Association for People with Learning Disability (UK)

Stammering Association (British)

Stammering Children (Michael Palin Centre for)

Support Dogs

Swimming Clubs for people with Disabilities (National Association for)

TACT - The Adolescent and Children's Trust

Talking Newspapers and Magazines (National)

Thalidomide Society (UK)

Thrive

Tourism for All

Transport for London

Treloar Trust

Tuberous Sclerosis Association UK

UPDATE

Voice UK

VoiceAbility

Volunteer Reading Help

WheelPower

Whizz-Kidz

Winvisible (Women with visible & invisible disabilities)

Wireless for the Blind Fund (British)

Drugs and Substance Abuse

Addaction
Addiction (Action on)
ADFAM
Advisory Council on the Misuse of Drugs
Blenheim CDP
BNTL-Freeway: British National Temperance League
CADD- Campaign Against Drinking & Driving
Cocaine Anonymous UK
Drug Education Forum
Drugs and Crime (UN Office on)
Drugs Forum (Scottish)
DrugScope
Families Anonymous
Frank
Freshfield Service
Hope UK
Know Cannabis
London Drug & Alcohol Network
Narcotics Anonymous UK
RAPt - Rehabilitation for Addicted Prisoners Trust
Release
ReSolv
Roofie Foundation
Thesite.org
Tranquillisers, Antidepressants and Painkillers (Council for Information on)
Transform Drug Policy Foundation
Turning Point

Economics

Adam Smith Institute
Audit Commission
Audit Office (National)
Bank of England
Bankruptcy Advisory Service Limited
Citizens Income Trust
CLES - Centre for Local Economic Strategies
Credit Unions Ltd. (Association of British)
Currency converter
Economic & Social Research (National Institute of)
Extreme Inequality
Foreign Policy Centre
HM Treasury
International Monetary Fund
Letslink UK
Local Economy Policy Unit
Monetary Justice (Christian Council for)
MyBnk
New Economics Foundation
Pensions Ombudsman
Public Management and Policy Association
Shared Interest Society Ltd
Smith Institute
Social & Economic Research (Institute for)
unbiased.co.uk

Education

100 Black Men of London

Access Art

Access to Industry

Alcohol Education and Research Council

Alexander Teachers (Professional Association of)

Alexander Technique (Society of Teachers of the)

Anne Frank Trust UK

Antidote

AQA

Art and Design (National Society for Education in)

Arvon Foundation

ASDAN

Asiatic Society of Great Britain and Ireland (Royal)

ASPE - Association for the Study of Primary Education

Aspect

Associated Board of the Royal Schools of Music

Association of Colleges

Athletic Association (English Schools')

AV Foundation (Africa Asia Venture)

Awesome Library

BBC Schools

Bibliomania

Big Bus

Big Read (The)

Bilingualism & Literacies Education Network

Bitesize: BBC revision web site

BKA - British Kodály Academy

Black Training & Enterprise Group

Boarding Concern

Book Aid International

Books Council (Welsh)

Booktrust

Brainwave

BRIT School for Performing Arts and Technology

British Council

Business in the Community

CACHE - Council for Awards in Children's Care and Education

CAMFED International - Campaign for Female Education

Canon Collins Trust

Cards for Little Lives

Career Development Loans

Catholic Education Service

Chartered Surveyors Training Trust

Chess Association (English Primary Schools)

Children's Book Groups (Federation of)

Chinese Arts Centre

Choir Schools' Association

Christian Education/International Bible Reading Association (IBRA)

Christian Teachers (Association of)

CILT

Citizenship Foundation

Citizenship Teaching (Association for)

City and Guilds

Classical Association

Clear Vision Trust

ClearVision Project

Coleg Harlech (WEA)

CollegesWales

Common Purpose

Commonwealth Education Trust

Commonwealth Scholarship Commission in the UK

Commonwealth Society (Royal)

Communication Trust

Communities Empowerment Network

Conductive Education (The National Institute of)

Countryside Foundation for Education

CRAC- Careers Research & Advisory Centre

CREST Awards

Cult Information Centre

Dance Education & Training (Council for)

Daneford Trust

Dark Skies (Campaign for)

Deaf Education Through Listening and Talking

Debt Advice Foundation

Design and Technology Association

Development Education Project

Down Syndrome Education International

Drama UK

Drug Education Forum

Dyslexia Action

Dyslexia Association (British)

e-Learning Foundation

Early Education

Early Years

Eco-Schools

Economics, Business and Enterprise Association

Edexcel

Education (Department for)

Education (Global Campaign for)

Education & Industry (Centre for)

Education and Culture (Directorate General for)

Education and Training (Centre for the Study of)

Education Business Excellence (Institute for)

Education Consultants (Society of)

Education for Choice

Education Index (British)

Education of Adults (European Association for the)

Education Otherwise

Education Scotland

Education Statistics (National Center for)

Educational Psychologists (Association of)

Educational Recording Agency

EMI Music Sound Foundation

Employment & Learning (Department for) Northern Ireland

Engage - The National Association for Gallery Education

England Athletics

English and Media Centre

English Association

English Heritage

English Speaking Union

Enterprise Education Trust

Environment (Young People's Trust for the)

Erasmus

ESU - European Students' Union

Eurodesk

Every Child a Chance Trust

Fair Access (Office for)

Farming & Countryside Education

Field Studies Council

Film & Television Archive (Northern Region)

Film and Television School (National)

Film Education

Findhorn Foundation

Football Association (English Schools)

Forest School Camps

Fulbright Commission (The US-UK)

GCSE Revision

Geographical Association

Geological Society

Get Global!

Gifted Children (National Association for)

Gifted Children's Information Centre

Education continued

GLE - Greater London Enterprise

Global Action Plan

Global Dimension

Global Eye

Governors' Association (National)

Headliners

Healthy Schools

Heartstone

Higher Education Funding Council for England

Historical Association

History World

HMRC Education Zone

Holocaust Educational Trust

Homework High

Hope UK

Human Rights Education Association

Human Scale Education Movement

IATEFL - International Association of Teachers of English as a Foreign Language

IDTA - International Dance Teachers Association

Imaginate

Include

Inclusion (National Development Team for)

Inclusive Education (Alliance for)

Inclusive Education (Centre for Studies on)

Independent Schools Council

Innovation in Mathematics Teaching (Centre for)

Integrated Education (N. Ireland Council for)

International Baccalaureate Organization

IntoUniversity

IPPL (UK) - International Primate Protection League

IPSEA - Independent Parental Special Education Advice

ISTD - Imperial Society of Teachers of Dancing

JANET

Japan Foundation, London

Kid Info

Kids in Museums

Language Awareness (Association for)

Language Learning (Association for)

Languages (Scotland's National Centre for)

learndirect

Learning (Campaign for)

Learning (Institute for)

Learning and Skills Improvement Service

Learning Disabilities (British Institute of)

Learning Outside the Classroom (Council for)

Learning Zone

Left 'n' Write

Life Science Centre

Lifelong Learning

Linguists (Chartered Institute of)

Listening Books

Literacy Association (National)

Literacy Association (UK)

Literacy in Primary Education (Centre for)

Literacy Trust (National)

Local History (British Association for)

Makaton Charity

Mathematical Association

Mentoring and Befriending Foundation

Met Office

Montessori Centre

Mousetrap Theatre Projects

Music Council (National)

Music Educators (National Association of)

Muslim Schools UK (Association of)

My World of Work

Mydaughter.co.uk

NAACE - National Association of Advisers for Computers in Education

NABSS - National Association of Black Supplementary Schools

NAPE - National Association for Primary Education

National Drama

National Extension College

Network 81

NFER - National Foundation for Educational Research

NHS Health Scotland

NIACE - National Institute of Adult Continuing Education

NUS - National Union of Students

OCR/Oxford Cambridge and RSA Examinations

Ofqual

Ofsted

Open & Distance Learning Quality Council

Open College of the Arts

Open University

Orangutan Foundation

Outdoor Learning (Institute for)

Parents for Inclusion

Parliamentary Education Unit

Pastoral Care in Education (National Association for)

Personal Finance Education Group

Pharmaceutical Society (Royal)

Physical Education (Association for)

Physics (Institute of)

Placement Survival Guide

Pre-school Learning Alliance

Pre-school Play Association (Scottish)

Pre-School Providers Association (Wales)

Prospects

PTA-UK

Pyramid

Quality in Study Support and Extended Services

RADA - Royal Academy of Dramatic Art

RE Today Services

Real Education (Campaign for)

REonline

Room to Read

Royal Academy of Arts

Royal College of Veterinary Surgeons

Royal Geographical Society

Royal Society

RSA - Royal Society for the Encouragement of Arts, Manufactures and Commerce

Ruskin College

School Councils UK

School Food Trust

School Journey Association

School Librarianship (International Association of)

School Library Association

Schools Adjudicator (Office of the)

Schools Health Education Unit

Schools Music Association of Great Britain

SCIcentre

Science Education (Association for)

Science Education (Centre for)

Scottish Qualifications Authority

SCRAN

Sex Education Forum

Shakespeare Schools Festival

Simon Wiesenthal Centre

Skills Funding Agency

Smallpeice Trust

Social Entrepreneurs (School for)

Social Sciences (Association for the Teaching of the)

Spanish Embassy Education Office

Spartacus Educational

Special Educational Needs (National Association for)

Specialist Schools and Academies Trust

Spelling Society (The English)

Education continued

State Education (Campaign for)

Steel Can Recycling Information Bureau

Steiner Waldorf Education (European Council for)

Steiner Waldorf Schools Fellowship

Stephen Lawrence Charitable Trust

Storytelling (Society for)

Student Awards Agency for Scotland

Student Drama Festival (National)

Sundial Society (British)

Surname Profiler

Swimming

Teacher Support Network

Teachers of Mathematics (Association of)

Teachers of Religious Education (National Association of)

Teaching Council for Wales (General)

Teaching English & Other Community Languages to Adults (National Association for)

Teaching of Drama (National Association for the)

Teaching of English (National Association for the)

Teenage Cancer Trust

Telescope (Bradford Robotic)

The Sikh Way

Think Global

Third Age Trust

Topmarks

Transforming Conflict

Treloar Trust

UCAS

UJIA - United Jewish Israel Appeal

UK Youth

UNESCO - United Nations Educational, Scientific & Cultural Organisation

Uni4me

Unistats

University of the First Age

Values Education for Life (The Collegiate Centre for)

Victorian Society

Voices Foundation

Volunteer Reading Help

We Are What We Do

Winston Churchill Memorial Trust

Workers Educational Association

Working Men's College for Women & Men

WorkLife Support Limited

World Challenge Expeditions

Writers in Education (National Association of)

Year Out Group

Young Engineers

Young Enterprise

Youth Choir of Great Britain (National)

Youth in Action

Emergency aid

CAFOD - Catholic Overseas Development Agency

Christian Aid

Concern Worldwide

Disasters Emergency Committee

ECHO

Islamic Relief Worldwide

Médecins sans Frontières (UK)

Mercy Corps

MERLIN

Oxfam

Plan UK

Red Cross (International Committee of the)

Save the Children UK

SCIAF - Scottish Catholic International Aid Fund

Tearfund

UNICEF UK

World Health Organisation

World Jewish Relief

World Vision UK

Environment & Countryside

Access Space

ACT ON CO2

AirportWatch

Allotment and Leisure Gardeners Ltd. (National Society of)

Alternative Technology (Centre for)

Aluminium Packaging Recycling Organisation

An Taisce

Ancient Tree Forum

Arthur Rank Centre

Basel Action Network (BAN)

Bat Conservation Trust

Biological Diversity (Convention on)

Body Shop Foundation

Born Free Foundation

Botanic Garden of Wales (National)

BTCV - British Trust for Conservation Volunteers

Butterfly Conservation

Byways & Bridleways Trust

Cadw

Canal & River Trust

Carbon Neutral Company

Carbon Trust

CEH - Centre for Ecology & Hydrology

Choose Climate

·Churches Conservation Trust

Civic Voice

CLA - Country Land and Business Association

Climate Change (Committee on)

Climate Change (Intergovernmental Panel on)

Climate Parliament

Common Ground

Communities in Rural England (Action with)

Community Composting Network

Conservation of Energy (Association for the)

Conservation of Plants & Gardens (National Council for the)

Conservation Volunteers Northern Ireland

Corporate Watch

Countryside Alliance

Countryside Council for Wales

Countryside Foundation for Education

CPRE - Campaign to Protect Rural England

CTC - Cyclists' Touring Club

Cycling Campaign (London)

Dark Skies (Campaign for)

Deer Society (British)

Defra - Department for Environment Food & Rural Affairs

Divers Marine Life Rescue (British)

Down to Earth

Earth First! Worldwide

EarthAction

Earthquake Locator (World Wide)

Earthwatch Institute

Eco-Schools

Ecological Society (British)

Ecology Building Society

Ecotourism Society (The International)

Eden Project

Energy Association (International)

Energy Foundation (National)

Environment & Countryside continued

Energy Saving Trust

Environment (Young People's Trust for the)

Environment Agency

Environment and Development (International Institute for)

Environment Council

Environment Protection Agency (Scottish)

Environmental Investigation Agency

Environmental Law Foundation

Environmental Noise Maps

Environmental Protection UK

Environmental Transport Association

FareShare

Farming & Countryside Education

Fauna & Flora International

FIELD - Foundation for International Environmental Law & Development

Field Studies Council

Findhorn Foundation

Floodline

Forestry Commission Great Britain

Forestry Society (Royal)

Forum for the Future

Friends of the Earth

Friends of the Earth International

Friends of the Earth Scotland

Froglife

Furniture Re-use Network

Gaia Foundation

Galapagos Conservation Trust

Garden History Society

Gardens Scheme (National)

Geographic Society (National)

Geographical Association

Geological Society

Global Action Plan

Global Witness

Go4awalk

Green Alliance

Green Mark

Green Party

GreenMoves

Greenpeace

Groundwork UK

Hawk and Owl Trust

Heat is Online

Hurricane Center (National)

Indigenous Tribal Peoples of the Tropical Forests (International Alliance of)

INK - Independent News Collective

Inland Waterways Association

IPPL (UK) - International Primate Protection League

IUCN - International Union for Conservation of Nature

Joint Nature Conservation Committee

Keep Britain Tidy

Lake District (Friends of the)

Lake District National Park Authority

Lake District Weather Line

Landlife

Landmark Trust

Landscape Institute

Living Earth Foundation

Living Streets

London Green Belt Council

Marine Conservation Society

Marine Stewardship Council

Maritime & Coastguard Agency

Met Office

Meteorological Organization (World)

Meteorological Society (Royal)

Millennium Seed Bank

Mongabay.com

National Energy Action

National Forest Company

National Parks (Campaign for)

National Tidal and Sea Level Facility

National Trust

National Trust for Scotland

National Trust Working Holidays

Natural Death Centre

Natural England

Natural Environment Research Council

Natural Heritage (Scottish)

Noise Abatement Society

Northern Ireland Environment Link

Nuclear Society (European)

Nuclear Tourist (Virtual)

Open Spaces Society

Orangutan Foundation

Ordnance Survey

Our Dynamic Earth

People & Planet

People's Trust for Endangered Species

Permaculture Association (Britain)

Pesticide Action Network UK

Pipedown

Plantlife

Port of London Authority

Preservation Trusts (UK Association of)

Protection of Rural Wales (Campaign for the)

Rainforest Concern

Rainforest Foundation

Re-Cycle

Recycle for London

recycle more

RecycleNow

Recycling Appeal

Red List of Endangered Species

RenewableUK

Rising Tide

Royal Geographical Society

Royal Horticultural Society

Royal Parks

Rural Communities (Commission for)

Rural Research (Centre for)

Rural Scotland (Association for the Protection of)

Schumacher UK

Scientific Exploration Society

Scottish Canals

Scottish Environment LINK

Shark Alliance

Snow and Ice Data Center (National)

Soil Association

Stakeholder Forum

State of the Ocean (International Programme on the)

Steel Can Recycling Information Bureau

STEPS Centre - Social Technological and Environmental Pathway to Sustainability

Stop Climate Chaos Coalition

Stop Climate Chaos Scotland

Surfers Against Sewage

SustainAbility

Telework Association

Think Global

Thrive

Town & Country Planning Association

Town Planning Institute (Royal)

Transport (Department for)

Transport & Environment (European Federation for)

Tree Council

UK Climate Projections

United Nations Environment Programme

Wales Environment Link

WalkScotland

Waste Watch

We Are What We Do

Weather Centre (BBC Online)

Whale & Dolphin Conservation Society

Wild Flower Society

Wildfowl & Wetlands Trust (WWT)

Environment & Countryside continued

Wildlife and Countryside Link

Wildlife Trusts (Royal Society of)

Wind Energy Association (European)

Women's Environmental Network

Woodland Trust

World Land Trust

World Monuments Fund Britain

WRAP

WSPA International - World Society for the Protection of Animals

WWF-UK

Equality issues

Black Training & Enterprise Group

Citizens Income Trust

Education (Global Campaign for)

Equality and Human Rights Commission

Equality Britain

Extreme Inequality

Fawcett Society

Friends, Families and Travellers

Left 'n' Write

ManKind Initiative

Migration Policy Group

Minority Rights Group International

Peace & Freedom (Women's International League for)

Race Equality Foundation

Room to Read

Runnymede Trust

Short Persons Support

Stonewall

Tall Persons Club (GB & Ireland)

UKRC

UNLOCK

Europe

AIRE Centre - Advice on Individual Rights in Europe

Council of Europe

Council of Europe Youth

Education of Adults (European Association for the)

Erasmus

ESU - European Students' Union

EU in the United Kingdom

Eurodesk

Europa

Europe in the UK

European Central Bank

European Commission Agriculture and Rural Development

European Investment Bank

European Movement UK

European Parliament Information Office in Edinburgh

European Parliament Information Office in the United Kingdom

European Parliamentary Labour Party

European Trade Union Confederation

European Union (Court of Justice of the)

European Union Committee of the Regions

European Youth Card Association

European Youth Forum

European Youth Information and Counselling Agency

European Youth Music Week

France: culture and communications website

Franco British Council

Franco-Scottish Society of Scotland

Freedom Association

Friedrich Ebert Foundation

Golf Association (European)

Rail Europe

Special Needs Education (European Agency for Development in)

Wind Energy Association (European)

Family

4Children

AAA-NORCAP - Adults affected by adoption

Action for Children

Action for Children Northern Ireland

Action for Children Scotland

Action for Children Wales

Adoption and Fostering Information Line

Adoption records

Adoption UK

Afasic

Ahimsa

ARC - Antenatal Results and Choices

BAAF Adoption and Fostering (British Association for)

Barnardo's

Birth Trauma Association

Bounty Healthcare Fund

Certificate ordering service

Chance UK

Child Contact Centres (National Association of)

CHILDREN 1ST

Compassionate Friends

Contact a Family

Cry-sis

Dad

Dad Talk

Dads House

Daycare Trust

Disability Pregnancy & Parenthood International

Disabled Parents Network

Donor Conception Network

Donor Family Network

Down's Heart Group

Elder Abuse (Action on)

Families Need Fathers

Family Action

Family and Parenting Institute

Family Holiday Association

Family Lives

Family Planning Association

Family Rights Group

Family Search

Family Therapy (Institute of)

Fatherhood Institute

Fathers4justice Ltd

Find a Parent or Child

FreeBMD

Friendship Works

Gamete Donation Trust (National)

Gingerbread

Grandparents Plus

Grandparents' Association

Half the Sky Foundation

HELP - Holiday Endeavour for Lone Parents

Home-Start

Karma Nirvana

Lone Twin Network

Lucy Faithfull Foundation

ManKind Initiative

MATCH - Mothers Apart from Their Children

Mosac

Mothers at home Matter

Mothers' Union

Mydaughter.co.uk

Family continued

National Childbirth Trust

National Records of Scotland (NRS)

NCB - National Children's Bureau

Netmums

One Plus One

PACT (Parents & Abducted Children Together)

PACT (Parents and Children Together)

Parenting UK

Planned Parenthood Federation (International)

Prisoners' Families (Action for)

Prisoners' Families & Friends Service

Register Office for Northern Ireland (General)

Registering life events

Relate

Relationships Scotland

Resolution

Respect

reunite

Sibs

Twins & Multiple Births Association

Working Families

Working with men

Young Fathers Initiative

Farming & Agriculture

Allotment and Leisure Gardeners Ltd. (National Society of)

City Farms & Community Gardens (Federation of)

CLA - Country Land and Business Association

Compassion in World Farming Trust

Countryside Alliance

Countryside Foundation for Education

Dairy Council (The)

Defra - Department for Environment Food & Rural Affairs

Environment Agency

European Commission Agriculture and Rural Development

Farm Animal Welfare Committee

Farmers' Markets (Scottish Association of)

Farmers' Retail & Markets Association

Farming & Countryside Education

Farms for City Children

Food & Agricultural Organisation (UN)

Garden Organic

Global Crop Diversity Trust

Natural England

Organic Research Centre

Rare Breeds Survival Trust

Rural Communities (Commission for)

Rural Research (Centre for)

Soil Association

Sustain

Viva! - Vegetarians International Voice for Animals

Women's Food & Farming Union

WWOOF UK - Opportunities on Organic Farms UK

Young Farmers' Clubs

Food

Additives (Action on)

Agriculture and Horticulture Development Board

Anaphylaxis Campaign

Chocolate Society

Dairy Council (The)

Defra - Department for Environment Food & Rural Affairs

Dietetic Association (British)

Egg Information Service (British)

FareShare

Farmers' Markets (Scottish Association of)

Farmers' Retail & Markets Association (National)

Food & Agricultural Organisation (United Nations)

Food & Drink Federation

Food & Drug Administration (US)

Food Commission (UK)

Food Standards Agency

GM Freeze

Herb Society

IFST - Institute of Food Science & Technology

Magic Breakfast

Mary's Meals

Nutrition Foundation (British)

Nutrition Society

Optimum Nutrition (Institute for)

Overeaters Anonymous of Great Britain

School Food Trust

Seafish

Slow Food UK

Sustain

Tea Council (UK) Ltd.

Vegan Society

Vegetarian & Vegan Foundation

Vegetarian Society

Viva! - Vegetarians International Voice for Animals

Women's Food & Farming Union

World Food Programme (United Nations)

Government

10 Downing Street Website

Advisory Council on the Misuse of Drugs

Attorney General's Office

Audit Commission

Audit Office (National)

Business, Innovation & Skills (Department for)

Cabinet Office

Cafcass

Charity Commission for England & Wales

CIA - Central Intelligence Agency

Climate Change (Committee on)

Climate Parliament

Communities and Local Government (Department for)

Competition Commission

COSLA - Convention of Scottish Local Authorities

Criminal Cases Review Commission

Criminal Injuries Compensation Authority

Crown Estates

Defence (Ministry of)

DirectGov

Education (Department for)

Energy Association (International)

EU in the United Kingdom

Europa

European Parliament Information Office in the United Kingdom

Government continued

Fair Access (Office for)

Fair Trading (Office of)

FBI - Federal Bureau of Investigation

Financial Ombudsman Service

Foreign and Commonwealth Office

Foreign and Commonwealth Office Travel Advice

Government Actuary's Department

Greater London Authority

Health (Department of)

Health, Social Services and Public Safety (N. Ireland Department of)

Hear From Your MP

HM Revenue and Customs

HM Treasury

HMRC Education Zone

Home Office

House of Lords

Housing Ombudsman Service

Human Rights Commission (N. Ireland)

Identity & Passport Service

Intellectual Property Office

International Development (Department for)

Joint Nature Conservation Committee

Justice

Land Registry

legislation.gov.uk

Local Economy Policy Unit

Local Government Association

Local Government Information Unit

Local Government Ombudsman (England)

Low Pay Commission

Maritime & Coastguard Agency

National Archives

National Archives of Scotland (NAS)

National Records of Scotland (NRS)

Northern Ireland Executive

Northern Ireland Office

Northern Ireland Ombudsman

Office for National Statistics

Ofsted

Parliament

Parliamentary and Health Service Ombudsman

Parliamentary Education Unit

Parliaments (Websites of National)

Pensions Ombudsman

Privacy International

Public Services Ombudsman (Scottish)

Public Whip

Register Office for Northern Ireland (General)

Republic

Schools Adjudicator (Office of the)

Scotland Office

Scottish Government

Scottish Parliament

Serious Fraud Office

TheyWorkForYou.com

Trading Standards Institute

Transparency International

Transport (Department for)

UK Border Agency

US Department of State

Wales Office

Welsh Government

Work & Pensions (Department for)

WriteToThem.com

Health and Medicine

Abortion Rights

Active Birth Centre

Acupuncture Council (British)

Acupuncture Society (British Medical)

Additives (Action on)

AIDS Trust (National)

Albinism Fellowship

Alcohol Studies (Institute of)

Allergy UK

Alzheimer Scotland

Alzheimer's Research Trust

Alzheimer's Society

Anaphylaxis Campaign

Anthony Nolan

Anxiety UK

ARC - Antenatal Results and Choices

Art Therapists (British Association of)

Arthritic Association

Arthritis Care

Arthritis Research UK

Arts in Therapy & Education (Institute for)

ASH - Action on Smoking and Health

Aspire

Assisted Dying (Healthcare Professionals for)

Asthma UK

Ataxia UK

Attend

Autistic Society (National)

AVERT

Baby Lifeline

Baby Milk Action

Bach Centre

BackCare

BASIC - Brain & Spinal Injury Centre

BBC Health

BEAT - Beating Eating Disorders

Behavioural & Cognitive Psychotherapies (British Association for)

Better Seating (Campaign for)

Bibic

Bioethics (Nuffield Council on)

BirthChoice UK

Bladder and Bowel Foundation (B&BF)

Blood Pressure Association

Bob Champion Cancer Trust

Bounty Healthcare Fund

Bowel Cancer UK

Brain & Spine Foundation

Breakthrough Breast Cancer

Breast Cancer Care

British Heart Foundation

British Medical Association

Brittle Bone Society

Butterfly Project

Cancer Research UK

Cancer Society (American)

CancerHelp UK

Cardiac Risk in the Young

Care Quality Commission

Carers Trust

CarersUK

Casualties Union

Chain of Hope

Chernobyl Children's Life Line

Child Brain Injury Trust

Child Growth Foundation

Childhood Eye Cancer Trust

Children with Cancer

Children's Heart Federation

Chiropodists & Podiatrists (Institute of)

Chiropodists and Podiatrists (The Society of)

Chiropractic (Anglo-European College of)

Chiropractic Association (British)

Health and Medicine continued

Chiropractic Patients' Association

Christian Lewis Trust

Cinnamon Trust

CLAPA - Cleft Lip & Palate Association

Cleanair

CLICSargent

Climb

Colitis & Crohn's UK

Complementary and Natural Medicine (Institute for)

Concord Media

Connect

Core

COTS - Childlessness overcome through surrogacy

Cystic Fibrosis Trust

Daisy Network

DebRA

Dental Association (British)

Dental Association (Scotland)

Dental Council (General)

Depression Alliance

Dermatologists (British Association of)

Diabetes UK

Diabetes.co.uk

Dietetic Association (British)

Different Strokes

Disfigurement Guidance Centre

Donor Family Network

Down's Heart Group

Down's Syndrome Association

Down's Syndrome Medical Interest Group

Down's Syndrome Scotland

Dr Hadwen Trust for Humane Research

Drinking Water Inspector - Northern Ireland

Drinking Water Inspectorate

Drinking Water Quality Regulator For Scotland

Dyspraxia Foundation

Eating Problems Service

Eczema Society (National)

Ellen MacArthur Cancer Trust

Embarrassing Problems

Endometriosis UK

Epilepsy (National Centre for Young People with)

Epilepsy Action

Epilepsy Scotland

Epilepsy Society

ERIC - Education and Resources for Improving Childhood Continence

ETCO - European Transplant Coordinators Organisation

Eyecare Trust

Fertility Friends

Fertility UK

FirstSigns

Fit for Travel

Food & Drug Administration (US)

Forward

Fragile X Society

Freedom from Torture

Friends at the end

GASP

General Medical Council

Genetic Alliance UK

GM Freeze

Gulf Veterans & Families Association (National)

Haemochromatosis Society

Haemophilia Society

Hairline International

HEADWAY

Health (Department of)

Health & Safety Executive

Health Information Resources

Health Professions Council

Health Protection Agency

Health, Social Services and Public Safety (N. Ireland Department of)

Healthtalkonline

Healthy Schools

Heart Research UK

Help - For a life without tobacco

Help for Heroes

Help the Hospices

Hereditary Breast Cancer Helpline (National)

Herpes Viruses Association

HIV InSite

HIV/Aids Alliance (International)

Holistic Therapists (Federation of)

Hospital Broadcasting Association

Human Fertilisation & Embryology Authority

Humane Research Trust

Hunger Education Service (World) & Hunger Notes

Huntington's Disease Association

Hyperactive Children's Support Group

Hypermobility Syndrome Association

IBS Network

Infant Deaths (Foundation for the Study of)

Infertility Network UK

Interact Worldwide

Jane Tomlinson Appeal

Jeans for Genes

Jo's Cervical Cancer Trust

Kidney Patient Association (British)

Kidney Research UK

King's Fund

Lavender Trust

Learning Disabilities (The Foundation for People with)

LEPRA

Let's Face It

Leukaemia and Lymphoma Research

Liver Trust (British)

Lung Foundation (British)

Lupus UK

Macmillan Cancer Support

Malaria No More UK

Marfan Association UK

Marie Curie Cancer Care

MASTA - Medical Advisory Services for Travellers Abroad

Maternal & Childhealth Advocacy International

MDF The Bipolar Organisation

ME (Action for)

ME Association

Médecins sans Frontières (UK)

Medical Accidents (Action Against)

Medical Advisory Service

Medical Aid for Palestinians

Medical Conditions at School

Medical Helpline (General)

Medical Research Charities (Association of)

Medical Research Council

Medical Trust (Britain-Nepal)

MedicAlert Foundation

Medicines & Healthcare products Regulatory Agency

Men's Health Helpline

Meningitis Research Foundation

Meningitis Trust

Mental Health (Scottish Association for)

MERLIN

Migraine Action Association

Migraine Trust

Miscarriage Association

Motor Neurone Disease Association

Mouth Cancer Foundation

Multiple Sclerosis Society

Health and Medicine continued

Multiple Sclerosis Therapy Centres (National)

Multiple Sclerosis Trust

Muscular Dystrophy Campaign

Musculoskeletal Medicine (British Institute of)

Music Therapy (British Association for)

Narcolepsy UK

National Institute for Health and Clinical Excellence

NBCS - National Blind Children's Society

Netdoctor

Neuro Foundation UK

Newlife Foundation for Disabled Children

NHS Blood and Transplant

NHS Careers

NHS Confederation

NHS Direct

NHS Health Scotland

NHS Support Federation

NICON - Northern Ireland Confederation

Not Dead Yet UK

Nursing & Midwifery Council

Nutrition Foundation (British)

Obesity (International Association for the Study of) & Obesity TaskForce (International)

Obesity Forum (National)

Occupational Hygiene Society (British)

Orchid Cancer Appeal

Organ Donation

Organ Donation and Transplantation (International Registry of)

Osteopathic Council (General)

Osteoporosis Society (National)

Overeaters Anonymous of Great Britain

PACE

Pain Relief Foundation

Pain Society (British)

Pain Support

Palliative Care (National Council for)

Papworth Trust

PAPYRUS - Prevention of young suicide

Parkinson's Disease Society

Parliamentary and Health Service Ombudsman

Pathfinder International

Patient UK

Patients Association

Paul's Cancer Support Centre

Performing Arts Medicine (British Association for)

Personal Injury Lawyers (Association of)

Pets as Therapy

Physiotherapy (Chartered Society of)

Pilates Foundation

Pituitary Foundation

Pod Charitable Trust

Polio Fellowship (British)

Population Services International

Positively UK

Post Natal Illness

Premenstrual Syndrome (National Association for)

Prostate Cancer Charity

Psoriasis Association

Psychiatrists (Royal College of)

Psychotherapists (British Association of)

Psychotherapy (UK Council for)

Public Health Agency

PWSA (UK) - Prader-Willi Syndrome Association

QUIT

Raynaud's & Scleroderma Association

React - Rapid Effective Assistance for Children with Potentially Terminal illness

Red Cross (British)

Relatives & Residents Association

Restricted Growth Association

Roy Castle Lung Cancer Foundation

Royal Society of Medicine

Safer Medicines Campaign

SANDS - Stillbirth & Neonatal Death Charity

Schools Health Education Unit

Scoliosis Association (UK)

Sexual Advice Association

Shiatsu Society (UK)

Shine

Shingles Support Society

Sick Children (Action for)

Sickle Cell Society

Sightsavers

Skills for Care

Skin Care Campaign

Skin Foundation (British)

Sleep Council

Smokefree (NHS)

Social Workers (British Association of)

Socialist Health Association

Sparks

Speakability

Speech and Language Therapists (Royal College of)

Spinal Injuries Association

St John Ambulance

Stress Management Association UK (International)

Stroke Association

SunSmart Campaign

Surgery Door

Tampon Alert (Alice Kilvert)

TB Alert

Teenage Cancer Trust

Tenovus

Terrence Higgins Trust

Thalidomide Society (UK)

Tinnitus Association (British)

Tommy's, the baby charity

Tranquillisers, Antidepressants and Painkillers (Council for Information on)

Tropical Diseases (Hospital for)

Tuberous Sclerosis Association UK

Vision Aid Overseas

Vitiligo Society

Voice for Choice

Wellbeing of Women

Wessex Cancer Trust

White Ribbon Alliance

Williams Syndrome Foundation (UK)

Willow Foundation

World AIDS Day

World Cancer Research Fund International

World Health Organisation

Yoga (Iyengar Institute)

Young People with ME (Association of)

Your Life

Youth Cancer Trust

Youthhealthtalk

Heritage

1901 Census for England & Wales

An Taisce

Ancient Buildings (Society for the Protection of)

Ancient Monument Society

Ancient Tree Forum

Antiquaries of London (Society of)

Archaeology (Council for British)

Archaeology Abroad

Archaeology Scotland

Archiseek

Architectural Heritage Fund

Arms and Armour Society

Heritage continued

Army Museum (National)

ArtWatch UK

Black History Month

Brontë Parsonage Museum & Brontë Society

Byways & Bridleways Trust

Cadw

Cambridge Past, Present & Future

Churches Conservation Trust

Civic Voice

Crown Estates

Culture, Media & Sport (Department for)

Cutty Sark Trust

English Heritage

Family Names Profiling (GB)

Family Search

FreeBMD

Friends of Friendless Churches

Garden History Society

Gardens Scheme (National)

Genealogists (Society of)

Georgian Group

Heraldry Society

Heraldry Society of Scotland

Heritage Lottery Fund

Heritage Railway Association

Historic Houses Association

Historic Scotland

Historical Association

Historical Maritime Society

History World

ICON - Institute of Conservation

Landmark Trust

Local History (British Association for)

Museums (International Council of)

National Archives

National Archives of Scotland (NAS)

National Churches Trust

National Trust

National Trust for Scotland

Natural Heritage (Scottish)

Open-City

Oral History Society

Preservation Trusts (UK Association of)

Public Monuments & Sculpture Association

Quilters' Guild of the British Isles

Royal Airforce Museum

Royal Naval Museum

Royal Parks

Scottish Canals

SCRAN

Sealed Knot Ltd

Shakespeare Birthplace Trust

St Fagans: National History Museum

Sundial Society (British)

Theatres Trust

Twentieth Century Society

Vatican

Venice in Peril Fund

Victorian Society

Waterfront Museum (National)

Weights & Measures Association (British)

Women's Archive of Wales

Woodland Trust

Working Class Movement Library

World Monuments Fund Britain

Homeless and Housing

Albert Kennedy Trust

Alone in London

Big Issue

Borderline

Broadway

Building & Social Housing Foundation
Centrepoint
ChildHope
CIH - Chartered Institute of housing
Crisis (UK)
Depaul International
Depaul Nightstop UK
Eaves
Ecology Building Society
Elderly Accommodation Counsel
Emmaus
Empty Homes Agency
GreenMoves
Habitat for Humanity Great Britain
Homeless International
Homeless Link
Housing (Confederation of Co-operative)
Housing Advice
Housing Federation (National)
Housing Justice
Housing Ombudsman Service
Housing Policy (Centre for)
HousingCare.org
Joseph Rowntree Foundation
Llamau
Nethouseprices
Poppy Project
Refuge
Salvation Army
Scarlet Centre
Shelter
Shine a Light
Simon Community
Squatters (Advisory Service for)
Tenant Participation Advisory Service for England
Town Planning Institute (Royal)

Human Rights

African Initiatives
Africans Unite Against Child Abuse
AIRE Centre - Advice on Individual Rights in Europe
AMAR
Amnesty International UK
Anti-Slavery International
ARTICLE 19
ATD Fourth World
BIHR - British Institute of Human Rights
Body Shop Foundation
Burma Campaign UK
Canon Collins Trust
Children are unbeatable! Alliance
Children's Rights Alliance for England
Children's Society
Colombia Solidarity Campaign
Conscience
CRIN - Child Rights Information Network
Disability Action
Elders (The)
EveryChild
Fair Trials International
Foreign Policy Centre
Forest Peoples Programme
Free the Children
Free Tibet
Freedom from Torture
Freedom of Information (Campaign for)
Global Witness
Gypsy Association
Howard League for Penal Reform
Human Dignity Trust
Human Fertilisation & Embryology Authority

Human Rights continued

Human Rights (European Court of)

Human Rights Commission (N. Ireland)

Human Rights Education Association

Human Rights Policy (International Council on)

Human Rights Watch

IKWRO - Iranian and Kurdish Women's Rights Organisation

Inclusive Education (Centre for Studies on)

Indigenous Tribal Peoples of the Tropical Forests (International Alliance of)

Interact Worldwide

Interights

Islamic Human Rights Commission

JUSTICE

Kurdish Human Rights Project

Laogai Research Foundation

Liberty

Lilith Research and Development

Medical Aid for Palestinians

Minority Rights Group International

Music Freedom Day

No Sweat

Ombudsman Association

Overseas Development Institute

Peace & Freedom (Women's International League for)

Peace Brigades International

Peace Pledge Union

Penal Reform International

People & Planet

Poppy Project

Prisoners Abroad

Prisoners of Conscience Appeal Fund

Privacy International

Red Cross (British)

REDRESS

Refugee Council

Release

Reporters Without Borders

Simon Wiesenthal Centre

Sojourner Project

Solidar

Southall Black Sisters

Statewatch

Stonewall

Survival International

TAPOL

Tibet Society UK

Tibetan Nuns Project

Torture (Association for the Prevention of)

Torture (The World Organisation Against)

Transforming Conflict

UN High Commissioner for Human Rights (Office of the)

Unborn Children (Society for the Protection of)

UNHCR

United Nations Development Programme

Unlock Democracy

Volunteer Action for Peace

War Resisters League

Womankind Worldwide

Women living under Muslim laws

World Development Movement

World Land Trust

Industry and Employment

Acas - Advisory, Conciliation and Arbitration Service

Acas Scotland

Acas Wales

Access to Industry

Architects (Royal Institute of British)

British Standards Institute

Business, Innovation & Skills (Department for)

Centre for Economic & Social Inclusion

Certification Officer

Co-operatives UK

Community and Youth Workers in Unite

Directors (Institute of)

Directory of Social Change

Education & Industry (Centre for)

Education and Training (Centre for the Study of)

Effective Dispute Resolution (Centre for)

Employment & Learning (Department for) Northern Ireland

Employment Research (Warwick Institute for)

Employment Rights (Institute of)

Employment Solicitors

Employment Studies (Institute for)

Endeavour Training Limited

Engineering Council

Enterprise Education Trust

European Trade Union Confederation

Fawcett Society

Fitness Industry Association

Fredericks Foundation

GLE - Greater London Enterprise

Homeworking

Independent Safeguarding Authority

Industrial Injuries Advisory Council

International Labour Organization

Jobcentre Plus

Labour Behind the Label

Labour Research Department

learndirect

Mechanics' Institute

Motor Manufacturers and Traders Ltd. (Society of)

My World of Work

NHS Careers

No Sweat

Opportunity Now

Personnel & Development (Chartered Institute of)

Practical Action

Public Concern at Work

Public Service Excellence (Association for)

Rathbone

Reach

Recycle-IT!

Remploy

Seafish

Simon Jones Memorial Campaign

Slivers of Time

Solidar

Tea Council (UK) Ltd.

Trade Union Confederation (International)

Trade Union Rights (International Centre for)

Trades Union Congress

Travel and Tourism (Institute of)

Unite

Women and Manual Trades

Women's Engineering Society

Woodworking Federation (British)

Work & Pensions (Department for)

Work Foundation

Workaholics Anonymous

Workers Educational Association

Working Families

WorkLife Support Limited

Young Engineers

Young Enterprise

Language

Alliance Française

Apples & Snakes

Arab-British Understanding (Council for)

Bilingualism & Literacies Education Network

British Council

CILT

Communication Trust

Connect

Cymdeithas yr Iaith Gymraeg

Daiwa Anglo-Japanese Foundation

English Association

English Speaking Union

Esperanto Association of Britain

Franco British Council

Franco-Scottish Society of Scotland

Gaelic Books Council

Goethe-Institut

Hispanic & Luso Brazilian Council

IATEFL - International Association of Teachers of English as a Foreign Language

Italian Cultural Institute in London

Japan Foundation, London

Language Awareness (Association for)

Language Learning (Association for)

Languages (Scotland's National Centre for)

Linguists (Chartered Institute of)

Literacy in Primary Education (Centre for)

Makaton Charity

Plain English Campaign

Scots Language Centre

Spanish Embassy Education Office

Spanish Institute

Speakability

Speakers Clubs (Association of)

Speech and Language Therapists (Royal College of)

Spelling Society (The English)

Teaching English & Other Community Languages to Adults (National Association for)

Teaching of English (National Association for the)

Welsh Language Board (Bwrdd yr Iaith Gymraeg)

Law

Advicenow

AdviceUK

Advocacy After Fatal Domestic Abuse

Advocacy Resource Exchange

AIRE Centre - Advice on Individual Rights in Europe

All Wales Domestic Abuse and Sexual Violence Helpline

Arbitrators (Chartered Institute of)

Ask The Police

Attorney General's Office

Bar Council

Bar Pro Bono Unit

Black Police Association (National)

Cafcass

Catch22

Children are unbeatable! Alliance

Children's Legal Centre

Citizenship and the Law (National Centre for)

Coram

Courts and Tribunal Service (HM)

Crime and Justice Studies (Centre for)

Crimestoppers

Criminal Cases Review Commission

Criminal Injuries Compensation Authority

Crisis Counselling for Alleged Shoplifters

Crown Prosecution Service

Dignity in Dying

Disability Law Service

Domestic Violence (Campaign Against)

Drugs and Crime (UN Office on)

DVLA - Driver and Vehicle Licensing Agency

Employment Solicitors

Environmental Law Foundation

European Union (Court of Justice of the)

Fair Trials International

Fathers4justice Ltd

FIELD - Foundation for International Environmental Law & Development

Friends at the end

Gun Control Network

Heart Programme

Howard League for Penal Reform

Human Dignity Trust

Human Rights (European Court of)

Immigration & Asylum Tribunals Service

Immigration Law Practitioners' Association

Immigration Services Commissioner (Office of the)

Independent Police Complaints Commission

Interights

International Criminal Court

Interpol

Just for Kids Law

Justice

JUSTICE

Law Centres Federation

Law Commission

Law Society of England & Wales

Legal Action Group

Legal Services Commission

legislation.gov.uk

Liberty

Magistrates' Association

Metropolitan Police

Money Claim Online

Most Wanted (UK)

Not Dead Yet UK

Old Bailey, London (Proceedings of) 1674 to 1834

Ombudsman Association

Out of trouble

PACT (Prison Advice & Care Trust)

Peace Alliance

Penal Reform International

Personal Injury Lawyers (Association of)

Police Federation (Scottish)

Police Federation of England & Wales

Prison Reform Trust

Prison Studies (International Centre for)

Prisons and Probation Ombudsman for England and Wales

Release

Resolution

Rights of Women

Serious Fraud Office

Simple Free Law Advisor

Skills for Justice

SOCA - Serious Organised Crime Agency

Solicitors for the Elderly

SOVA - Supporting Others Through Volunteer Action

St Giles Trust

Statewatch

This is abuse

Trackoff

UNLOCK

Voice UK

Women Solicitors (Association of)

Libraries, Books & Publishing

American Library Association

Antiquaries of London (Society of)

ARKive

Art Library (National)

Authors' Licensing and Collecting Society

Bartleby.com

Big Read (The)

Bodleian Library

Book Aid International

Book Trust (Scottish)

BookCrossing

Books Council (Welsh)

Booktrust

British Library

British Library Sound Archive

Buddhist Society

Children's Book Groups (Federation of)

CILIP - Chartered Institute of Library and Information Professionals

ClearVision Project

Demos

Edinburgh International Book Festival

Editors and Proofreaders (Society for)

English PEN

Feminist Archive

Folger Shakespeare Library

Frankfurt Book Fair

Gaelic Books Council

Hay Festival

Health Information Resources

Heartstone

Indexers (Society of)

Information Management (Association for)

INK - Independent News Collective

ipl2

Libraries for Life for Londoners

Library Campaign

Library of France (National)

Listening Books

Literacy Association (UK)

London Library

Marx Memorial Library

Music Publishers Association

National Libraries (Friends of the)

National Library of Scotland

National Library of Wales

New Internationalist

Newspaper Library (British Library)

Nobel Prize Internet Archive

People's Network

Poetry Library

Project Gutenberg

Psychical Research (Society for)

Questionpoint

Read

School Librarianship (International Association of)

School Library Association

Searchlight Magazine Ltd

Seven Stories

Siobhan Dowd Trust

Storytelling (Society for)

Women in Publishing

Women's Archive of Wales

Women's Library

Working Class Movement Library

Writers' Guild of Great Britain

Media

Adbusters

Advertising Association

Advertising Standards Authority

Al Jazeera

APRS

BBC

BBC Backstage Tours

BBC News

BBC Online

BBC Schools

BBC Studio Audiences

BBC World Service

Blogger

British Film Institute

Broadcasting Trust (International)

Channel 4

Commonwealth Broadcasting Association

Community Media Association

Concord Media

Creative Scotland

Editors and Proofreaders (Society for)

Educational Recording Agency

English and Media Centre

Extreme Inequality

Film & Television Archive (Northern
    Region)

Film and Television School (National)

Film Classification (British Board of)

Film Education

Film London

First Light

Five

Headliners

History of Cinema & Popular Culture (The
    Bill Douglas Centre for the)

Hospital Broadcasting Association

Index on Censorship

Indexers (Society of)

INK - Independent News Collective

ITN - Independent Television News

Learning Zone

Media Center (Independent)

Media for Development

Media Trust

MediaWise Trust

Movie Review Query Engine

New Internationalist

Newspaper Library (British Library)

Nominet UK

OFCOM

Paperboy

Phonepay Plus

photoLondon

Press and Broadcasting Freedom
    (Campaign for)

Press Association

Press Association Ireland

Press Association Scotland

Press Complaints Commission

Radio Society of Great Britain

Raw Material

Reporters Without Borders

S4C

Sense about Science

Sky

Talking Newspapers and Magazines
    (National)

Undercurrents

Video Standards Council

Voice of the Listener and Viewer

Wireless for the Blind Fund (British)

Mental Health

Action of Postpartum Psychosis Network

Albany Trust

Anxiety Care UK

Anxiety UK

Behavioural & Cognitive Psychotherapies (British Association for)

Blurt Foundation

Brainwave

Butterfly Project

CALM - Campaign Against Living Miserably

Care Quality Commission

Child and Adolescent Mental Health (Association for)

Combat Stress

Depression Alliance

Down Syndrome Education International

Educational Psychologists (Association of)

Journeys

Learning Disabilities (The Foundation for People with)

MDF The Bipolar Organisation

Mencap

Mental Health (Scottish Association for)

Mental Health Foundation

Mental Welfare Commission for Scotland

MIND

No Panic

OCD Action

PAPYRUS - Prevention of young suicide

Psychological Society (British)

Psychotherapists (British Association of)

Psychotherapy (UK Council for)

Rethink

SANE

Scarlet Centre

Seasonal Affective Disorder Association

SEBDA - Social, Emotional & Behavioural Difficulties Association

Time to change

Triumph over Phobia (TOP UK)

Turning Point

Women's Therapy Centre

Workaholics Anonymous

YoungMinds

Money

Bank of England (Damaged and Mutilated Banknotes)

Career Development Loans

Debt Advice Foundation

European Central Bank

Heritage Lottery Fund

HM Revenue and Customs

International Monetary Fund

Jubilee Debt Campaign

Low Pay Commission

Money Advice Service

Moneysavingexpert.com

My Supermarket

MyBnk

Nethouseprices

Personal Finance Education Group

Slivers of Time

Student Loans Company Ltd

Turn2us

Museums & Galleries

Antiquaries of London (Society of)

Apsley House Wellington Museum

Army Museum (National)

Ashmolean

BALTIC

Bank of England Museum

Barbican

Beamish

Big Pit

British Monarchy (The official website of)

British Museum

Brontë Parsonage Museum & Brontë Society

Bugatti Trust

Burrell Collection

Childhood (Museum of) V&A

Churchill War Rooms

Courtauld Institute of Art

Culture24

Cutty Sark Trust

Design Museum

Dulwich Picture Gallery

Eureka!

Exploratorium

Fitzwilliam Museum

Football Museum (National)

Football Museum (Scottish)

Gallery of Modern Art

Glasgow Museums Resource Centre

Glass Centre (National)

GreatBuildings

Hayward Gallery

Henry Moore Foundation

HMS Belfast

Imperial War Museum

Imperial War Museum London

Institute of Contemporary Arts

Ironbridge Gorge Museum

Jewish Museum

Kelvingrove Art Gallery and Museum

Kids in Museums

Lady Lever Art Gallery

Life Science Centre

Liverpool (Museum of)

Liverpool (National Museums)

London (Museum of)

London Transport Museum

Lowry Theatre and Art Gallery

Magna: science adventure centre

Manchester Museum

Maritime Museum (Merseyside)

Maritime Museum (National)

Mining Museum (National)

MOSI - Museum of Science & Industry

Museum Net

Museum of London

Museum of Scotland (National)

Museums (International Council of)

National Gallery

National Gallery (Scottish)

National Gallery of Modern Art (Scottish)

National Media Museum

National Museum Cardiff

National Portrait Gallery

National Portrait Gallery (Scottish)

Natural History Museum

Open Museum

People's History Museum

People's Palace and Winter Gardens

Provands Lordship

Queen's House

Railway Museum (National)

Riverside Museum: Scotland's Museum of Transport and Travel

Roman Legion Museum (National)

Museums and Galleries continued

Royal Academy of Arts
Royal Airforce Museum
Royal Armouries Museum
Royal Institution of Great Britain
Royal Naval Museum
Royal Observatory, Greenwich
Royal Scottish Academy
Science Centre (Glasgow)
Science Museum
Scotland Street School Museum
Scottish National Gallery
Scottish National Gallery of Modern Art
Seven Stories
Slate Museum (National)
Slavery Museum (International)
Space Centre (National)
St Fagans: National History Museum
St Mungo Museum of Religious Life and Art
Sudley House
Tate Britain
Tate Liverpool
Tate Modern
Tate St Ives
The Deep
Vatican Museums & Sistine Chapel
Walker Art Gallery
Waterfront Museum (National)
Waterways Museum (National)
Wool Museum (National)
World Museum
World Rugby Museum

Music

Refer also to the section on Dance, Drama, Music & Performing Arts Schools

Associated Board of the Royal Schools of Music
Barbershop Singers (British Association of)
BASCA - British Academy of Songwriters, Composers and Authors
BKA - British Kodály Academy
Cello Society (Internet)
Children's Orchestra (National)
Choir Schools' Association
CoMA - Contemporary Music-making for Amateurs
EMI Music Sound Foundation
English National Opera
European Youth Music Week
Festivals (British & International Federation of)
Guitar Foundation (International)
Live Music Now
London Charity Orchestra
London Symphony Orchestra
Making Music
Midi Music Company
Music and the Deaf
Music Council (National)
Music Educators (National Association of)
Music for Youth
Music Freedom Day
Music Publishers Association
Music Therapy (British Association for)
Musicians (Incorporated Society of)
Musicians Union
Natural Voice Practitioners' Network
NODA - National Operatic & Dramatic Association
Orchestras (Association of British)
Passion for Jazz
PRS for Music - Performing Rights Society

Raw Material
Royal Academy of Music
Royal Opera
Schools Music Association of Great Britain
Scottish Opera
Sound and Music
Sound Sense
SoundJunction
Southbank Centre
Suzuki Institute (British)
Voices Foundation
Welsh National Opera
Young Concert Artists Trust
Youth Choir of Great Britain (National)
Youth Music
Youth Music Theatre (National)
Youth Opera (British)
Youth Orchestra (National of GB)

Older People

Accessible Environments (Centre for)
Age Exchange
Age UK
Anchor Trust
Contact the Elderly
Counsel and Care
Elder Abuse (Action on)
Elderly Accommodation Counsel
Grandparents Plus
HousingCare.org
Pensioners Convention (National)
Policy on Ageing (Centre for)
Relatives & Residents Association
Ricability
Solicitors for the Elderly
Third Age Trust
WRVS (Women's Royal Voluntary Service)

Politics

10 Downing Street Website
ACTSA - Action for Southern Africa
Adam Smith Institute
Baobab Centre for Young Survivors in Exile
Bevan Foundation
Cabinet Office
Christian Socialist Movement
Civitas
Co-operative Party
Colombia Solidarity Campaign
Conscience
Conservative Party
Cuba Solidarity Campaign
Democracy and Electoral Assistance
    (International Institute for)
Demos
Elders (The)
Electoral Reform Services
Electoral Reform Society
European Parliamentary Labour Party
Fabian Society
Free Tibet
Freedom Association
Green Party
Hansard Society
Hear From Your MP
House of Lords
IPPR - Institute for Public Policy Research
Labour Party
Labour Research Department
Labour Women's Network
Law Society of Scotland
Liberal Democrats
Martin Luther King Jr. Center
Marx Memorial Library

Politics continued

Media Center (Independent)
Monetary Justice (Christian Council for)
Nicaragua Solidarity Campaign
No candidate deserves my vote
Operation Black Vote
Parliament
Plaid Cymru - The Party of Wales
Policy Studies (Centre for)
Policy Studies Institute
Political Studies Association
Public Whip
Republic
Schumacher UK
Searchlight Magazine Ltd
Smith Institute
SNP - Scottish National Party
Social Democratic & Labour Party
Social Market Foundation
Socialist Health Association
Socialist Labour Party
TheyWorkForYou.com
Tibet Society UK
Unborn Children (Society for the Protection of)
Unite Against Fascism
Unlock Democracy
Voice for Choice
Welsh Government
White House
WriteToThem.com

Poverty

ActionAid
Afghanaid
ATD Fourth World
Birmingham Settlement
Brazil's Children Trust (Action for)
CARE International UK
Child Poverty Action Group
Church Action on Poverty
Comic Relief
Concern Worldwide
e-Learning Foundation
Ethiopiaid
Family Holiday Association
FareShare
Hunger Education Service (World) &
    Hunger Notes
International Development (Department for)
Islamic Relief Worldwide
Kiva
Magic Breakfast
Maternal & Childhealth Advocacy
    International
National Debtline
ONE International
Practical Action
Shine a Light
Sustain
Taskforce for the Rural Poor (International)
TaxAid
Traidcraft
VSO - Voluntary Service Overseas
War on Want
Water Aid
World Bank
World Development Movement

Prisoners

Race

Amnesty International UK

Crime and Justice Studies (Centre for)

English PEN

Hibiscus

Howard League for Penal Reform

Human Writes

INQUEST

Nacro

New Bridge Foundation

Out of trouble

PACT (Prison Advice & Care Trust)

Penal Reform International

Prison Reform Trust

Prison Service NI

Prison Studies (International Centre for)

Prison Visitors (National Association of Official)

Prisoners Abroad

Prisoners of Conscience Appeal Fund

Prisoners' Advice Service

Prisoners' Families (Action for)

Prisoners' Families & Friends Service

Prisons and Probation Ombudsman for England and Wales

RAPt - Rehabilitation for Addicted Prisoners Trust

SACRO - Safeguarding Communities - Reducing Offending in Scotland

Sentencing, prison and probation

St Giles Trust

UNLOCK

Women in Prison

100 Black Men of London

Anne Frank Trust UK

Artists Against Racism

Asian People's Disability Alliance

Black Environment Network

Black History Month

Black Police Association (National)

CEMVO (Scotland) - Council of Ethnic Minority Voluntary Sector Organisations

Equality and Human Rights Commission

Equality Britain

Football Unites, Racism Divides

Heartstone

Intermix

Kick It Out

Martin Luther King Jr. Center

NABSS - National Association of Black Supplementary Schools

Operation Black Vote

Race Equality Foundation

Race Relations (Institute of)

Runnymede Trust

Show Racism the Red Card

Stephen Lawrence Charitable Trust

UK New Citizen

Refugees and Immigration

AMAR

Asylum Aid

Baobab Centre for Young Survivors in Exile

Immigrants (Joint Council for the Welfare of)

Immigration & Asylum Tribunals Service

Immigration Advice Service

Immigration Aid Unit (Greater Manchester)

Immigration Law Practitioners' Association

Immigration Services Commissioner (Office of the)

Medical Aid for Palestinians

Refugee Council

Refugees (Student Action for)

Refugees (US Committee for)

Refugees and Exiles (European Council on)

UK Border Agency

UNHCR

Relationships

All Wales Domestic Abuse and Sexual Violence Helpline

Broken Rainbow UK

Commonwealth Youth Exchange Council

Dads House

Divorced & Separated (National Council for the)

Domestic Violence (Campaign Against)

Family Therapy (Institute of)

Fatherhood Institute

Grandparents' Association

Heart Programme

Intermix

Karma Nirvana

Leap Confronting Conflict

ManKind Initiative

Men's Advice Line

Relate

Relationships Scotland

Respect

Shared Parenting Information Group

Solo Clubs (National Federation of)

Southall Black Sisters

The Survivors Trust

Young Fathers Initiative

Religion and Beliefs

Arthur Rank Centre

Astrological and Psychic Society (British)

Bible Society

British Jews (Board of Deputies of)

Buddhist Centre (North London)

Buddhist Information Network

Buddhist Society

Catholic Education Service

Christian Education/International Bible Reading Association (IBRA)

Christian Socialist Movement

Christian Teachers (Association of)

Christians and Jews (Council of)

Church Army

Church Mission Society

Church of England

Church of England Education Division

Churches Together in Britain and Ireland

Clear Vision Trust

Cult Information Centre

Day One Christian Ministries

Evangelical Alliance

Findhorn Foundation

Hindu Universe - Hindu Resource Center

Humanist Association (British)

Inform

Integrated Education (N. Ireland Council for)

Inter Faith Network for the UK

Islamic Human Rights Commission

Jewish Women (League of)

Methodist Children & Youth

Methodist Church

Muslim Schools UK (Association of)

Muslim Welfare House

National Churches Trust

Nil by Mouth

Pax Christi

Quakers in Britain

RE Today Services

Reform Judaism (Movement for)

REonline

Richard Dawkins Foundation for Reason and Science

Salvation Army

Secular Society (National)

Sikh Organisations (Network of)

Teachers of Religious Education (National Association of)

Tearfund

The Sikh Way

Tibetan Nuns Project

Time for God

United Reformed Church

Urban Saints

Vatican

Women living under Muslim laws

Young Christian Workers

Youth for Christ

Research

1901 Census for England & Wales

ACT – Animal Cancer Trust

Adam Smith Institute

Alcohol Education and Research Council

Atmospheric Research (National Center for)

Australian Bureau of Statistics

AVERT

Biotechnology & Biological Sciences Research Council

Bob Champion Cancer Trust

Brain & Spine Foundation

British Heart Foundation

BSES Expeditions - Exploration

Cancer Research UK

CEH - Centre for Ecology & Hydrology

Childhood Eye Cancer Trust

Children with Cancer

Climb

Data Archive (UK)

Dr Hadwen Trust for Humane Research

Economic & Social Research (National Institute of)

Education Index (British)

Education Statistics (National Center for)

Ergonomics & Human Factors (Institute of)

Feminist Archive

Fiscal Studies (Institute for)

Folger Shakespeare Library

Football Industry Group

Forward

FRAME - Fund for the Replacement of Animals in Medical Experiments

Friedrich Ebert Foundation

Garden Organic

Government Actuary's Department

Research continued

History of Cinema & Popular Culture (The Bill Douglas Centre for the)

Humane Research Trust

Indian Census

International Affairs (Royal Institute of)

IPPR - Institute for Public Policy Research

JANET

Jeans for Genes

Jodrell Bank Observatory and Discovery Centre

Joseph Rowntree Foundation

King's Fund

Leukaemia and Lymphoma Research

Linnean Society of London

Liver Trust (British)

Lord Dowding Fund

Lucy Faithfull Foundation

Marine Life Study Society (British)

Medical Research Charities (Association of)

Medical Research Council

Meningitis Research Foundation

Mouth Cancer Foundation

Mycological Society (British)

National Archives

National Archives of Scotland (NAS)

Natural Environment Research Council

New Economics Foundation

NFER - National Foundation for Educational Research

NOAH - National Organization for Albinism and Hypopigmentation

Nobel Prize Internet Archive

Ocean Mammal Institute

Office for National Statistics

Old Bailey, London (Proceedings of) 1674 to 1834

Optimum Nutrition (Institute for)

Orchid Cancer Appeal

Organic Research Centre

Overseas Development Institute

Pain Relief Foundation

PETA Foundation - People for the Ethical Treatment of Animals

Policy Studies (Centre for)

Policy Studies Institute

Political Studies Association

Prostate Cancer Charity

Psychical Research (Society for)

Public Management and Policy Association

Royal Institution of Great Britain

Rural Research (Centre for)

Saving Faces

Snow and Ice Data Center (National)

Social & Economic Research (Institute for)

Social Issues Research Centre

Social Market Foundation

Soil Association

Stammering Children (Michael Palin Centre for)

Statistics New Zealand

Suzy Lamplugh Trust

Tenovus

Tommy's, the baby charity

Understanding Animal Research

Unistats

Vitiligo Society

Wellbeing of Women

Wessex Cancer Trust

What About The Children?

World Cancer Research Fund International

World Gazetteer

Worldometers

Young People in Focus

Safety, Accidents & Injury

Airsafe.com

Arson Prevention Bureau

Aspire

Back-up Trust

BASIC - Brain & Spinal Injury Centre

Bibic

Bicycle Helmet Initiative Trust

Brake

Casualties Union

Child Accident Prevention Trust

Child Brain Injury Trust

Consumers International

Criminal Injuries Compensation Authority

Drinking Water Inspector - Northern Ireland

Drinking Water Inspectorate

Drinking Water Quality Regulator For Scotland

Ergonomics & Human Factors (Institute of)

Fire Brigade (London)

Fire Protection Association

Floodline

Food Commission (UK)

Foreign and Commonwealth Office Travel Advice

Get Safe Online

HEADWAY

Health & Safety Executive

Heritage Railway Association

Industrial Injuries Advisory Council

Infant Deaths (Foundation for the Study of)

Internet Watch Foundation

Kidscape

Let's Face It

Lifeguard Skills

Lifesavers

Living Streets

London Hazards Centre

Make Roads Safe

Medical Accidents (Action Against)

Medicines & Healthcare products Regulatory Agency

Navigation (Royal Institute of)

Occupational Safety & Health (Institution of)

PC David Rathband's Blue Lamp Foundation

Personal Injury Lawyers (Association of)

Pesticide Action Network UK

Placement Survival Guide

Refuge

RoadPeace

RoSPA

Royal National Lifeboat Institution

Safety Council (British)

Simon Jones Memorial Campaign

Spinal Injuries Association

sportscotland Avalanche Information Service

Surf Life Saving GB

Sustrans

Suzy Lamplugh Trust

Traffic Statistics (Global)

Transport Safety (Parliamentary Advisory Council for)

Science

Animal Health Trust

Anthropological Institute of Great Britain and Ireland (Royal)

Astronomical Association (British)

Atmospheric Research (National Center for)

BCS - Chartered Institute for IT

Bioethics (Nuffield Council on)

Biological Diversity (Convention on)

Biology (Society of)

Biotechnology & Biological Sciences Research Council

Botanical Society of the British Isles

BSES Expeditions - Exploration

CaSE - Campaign for Science & Engineering in the UK

Chemistry (Royal Society of)

Climate Change (Intergovernmental Panel on)

Computing Centre (National)

CREST Awards

Earthwatch Institute

Eden Project

Energy Foundation (National)

FRAME - Fund for the Replacement of Animals in Medical Experiments

Genetic Alliance UK

Geological Survey (British)

Geological Survey (US)

Geologists Association

GM Freeze

Heat is Online

IFST - Institute of Food Science & Technology

Intellect

Jodrell Bank Observatory and Discovery Centre

Life Science Centre

Linnean Society of London

Magna: science adventure centre

Met Office

Meteorological Organization (World)

Meteorological Society (Royal)

Millennium Seed Bank

Mongabay.com

MOSI - Museum of Science & Industry

Mycological Society (British)

Nuclear Society (European)

Nuclear Tourist (Virtual)

Nutrition Society

Our Dynamic Earth

Pharmaceutical Society (Royal)

Physics (Institute of)

Popular Astronomy (Society for)

Psychical Research (Society for)

Richard Dawkins Foundation for Reason and Science

Royal Botanic Garden Edinburgh

Royal Botanic Gardens, Kew

Royal Institution of Great Britain

Royal Observatory, Greenwich

Royal Society

SCIcentre

Science Association (British)

Science Centre (Glasgow)

Science Education (Association for)

Science Education (Centre for)

Science in the Public Interest (Center for)

Science Museum

Science, Technology & the Arts (National Endowment for)

Scientific Exploration Society

Scientists for Global Responsibility

Sense about Science

Solar Energy Society

Space Agency (European)

Space Agency (UK)

Space Centre (National)

STEPS Centre - Social Technological and Environmental Pathway to Sustainability

Telescope (Bradford Robotic)

UK Climate Projections

UNESCO - United Nations Educational, Scientific & Cultural Organisation

Weights & Measures Association (British)

Women Into Science & Engineering (WISE)

World Space Week

Sexual Advice Association

Stonewall

SurvivorsUK

Terrence Higgins Trust

The Survivors Trust

Thesite.org

This is abuse

Your Life

Sexual issues

AIDS Trust (National)

Albany Trust

Albert Kennedy Trust

AVERT

BASPCAN - British Association for the Study and Prevention of Child Abuse and Neglect

Beaumont Society

Child Protection in Sport Unit

ChildLine

Crossroads Women's Centre

HIV/Aids Alliance (International)

Human Dignity Trust

Justin Campaign

Lesbian and Gay Switchboard (London)

Lesbian Information Service

Lesbians & Gays (Families & Friends of)

likeitis.org

Lucy Faithfull Foundation

Mankind UK

Marie Stopes International

Mermaids

PACE

Positively UK

Sport and Leisure

Adventure Activities Licensing Authority

Aikido Board (British)

Allotment and Leisure Gardeners Ltd. (National Society of)

Amateur Boxing Association of England Ltd.

Amateur Boxing Scotland Ltd.

Ambition

Angling Trust

Archery GB

Arms and Armour Society

Army Cadet Force

Artistic Roller Skating (Federation of)

Athletic Association (English Schools')

Athletics Federations (International Association of)

Backpackers Club

Badminton England

Balloon and Airship Club (British)

BAPA - Activity Providers

Basketball Association (English)

BBC Backstage Tours

Bike Events

Bike Express (European)

Blind Golf Association (English)

Blind Sport (British)

Bowling Association Ltd (English Indoor)

Sport and Leisure continued

Bowling Federation (English)

Boys' Brigade

Braille Chess Association

British Cycling

British Rowing

Business in Sport & Leisure

Camping and Caravanning Club

Canoe Association (Scottish)

Canoe Association of Northern Ireland

Canoe Union (British)

Canoe Wales

Caravan Club

Caving Association (British)

Ceroc

Chess Association (English Primary Schools)

Chess Federation (English)

Chess Scotland

Chess Union (Ulster)

Chess Union (Welsh)

Child Protection in Sport Unit

Church Lads' and Church Girls' Brigade

Circus Sensible/Circus School

Circus Space

Cirdan Sailing Trust

Commonwealth Games Federation

Countryside Alliance

CP Sport England and Wales (cerebral palsy)

Cricinfo

Cricket Board (England & Wales)

Croquet Association

Crown Green Bowling Association (British)

Crufts Dog Show

Cruising Association

CTC - Cyclists' Touring Club

Culture, Media & Sport (Department for)

Cyclenation

Cycling Association (Welsh)

Cycling Centre (National)

Cycling Projects

Cycling Union (International)

Cyclists' Federation (European)

Dancesport UK

Disability Snowsport UK

Disability Sport (English Federation of)

Disability Sport (English Federation of)

Elastic Rope Sports Association (British)

Ellen MacArthur Cancer Trust

EMDP - Exercise, Movement and Dance Partnership

England Athletics

England Golf

England Hockey

England Netball

England Squash & Racketball

Family Holiday Association

Fell Runners Association

Fencing (British Academy of)

Fencing Association (British)

Fields in Trust - FIT

FIFA

Fitness Industry Association

Fitness League

Fitness Northern Ireland

Flower Arrangement Societies (National Association of)

Football Association

Football Association (English Schools)

Football Association (Irish)

Football Association (Scottish)

Football Foundation

Football Industry Group

Football League

Football League (Scottish)

Football Museum (National)

Football Supporters' Federation

Football Unites, Racism Divides

Footy4kids

Girlguiding UK

Girls Venture Corps Air Cadets

Girls' Brigade England & Wales

Glasgow Life

Gliding Association (British)

Go4awalk

Golf Association (European)

Gymnastics (British)

Handball Association (England)

Handball Association (Scottish)

Hang Gliding and Paragliding Association (British)

HELP - Holiday Endeavour for Lone Parents

Hostelling International

Hostelling International (N. Ireland)

Hostels.com

Human Power Club (British)

Ice Hockey UK

Ice Skating Association of Great Britain and N.I. (National)

International Olympic Committee

Jewish Lads' & Girls' Brigade (JLGB)

Ju Jitsu Association GB National Governing Body (British)

Judo Association (British)

Judo Scotland

Justin Campaign

Karate and Kickboxing Association (World)

Karate Board (N. Ireland)

Karate England

Karate Governing Body Ltd (Welsh)

Keep Fit Association

Kennel Club

Kick It Out

Kite Society of Great Britain

Lacrosse Association (English)

Ladies' Golf Union

Lake District Weather Line

Lawn Tennis Association

Lifesavers

London Marathon (Virgin)

Long Distance Walkers Association

Marine Leisure Association (MLA)

Marine Society and Sea Cadets

Martial Association (Amateur)

MCC - Marylebone Cricket Club

Medau

Mountain Leader Training England

Mountaineering Council (British)

Mountaineering Council of Scotland

NAKMAS - National Association of Karate and Martial Art Schools

National Trust Holiday Cottages

Ocean Youth Trust

Olympic Association (British)

Orienteering Federation (British)

Outdoor Learning (Institute for)

Outward Bound Trust

Parachute Association (British)

Paralympic GB

Photographic Society (Royal)

Physical Education (Association for)

Pilates Foundation

Play England

PLAYLINK

Plus

Pony Club

Pool Association (English)

Professional Footballers Association

Professional Golfers' Association

Quilters' Guild of the British Isles

Ramblers

Riding for the Disabled Association

Rifle Association (National) of United Kingdom

Sport and Leisure continued

Road Runners Club

Roller Hockey (England)

Rona Sailing Project

Royal Botanic Garden Edinburgh

Royal Botanic Gardens, Kew

Royal Mint (British)

Rugby Football League

Rugby Football Union

Rugby Football Union for Women

RYA Sailability

Sand & Land Yacht Clubs (British Federation of)

Scottish Cycling

scottishathletics

Scout Association

Scrum.com

Sea Ranger Association

Sealed Knot Ltd

Show Jumping Association (British)

Show Racism the Red Card

Ski Club of Great Britain

Skylight Circus Arts

Sparks

Speakers Clubs (Association of)

Special Olympics

Special Olympics Great Britain

Sport & Recreation Alliance

Sport England

Sport Northern Ireland

Sport Wales

Sports Association for People with Learning Disability (UK)

Sports Centre (Lilleshall National)

Sports Coach UK

Sports Leaders UK

SportsAid

sportscotland

sportscotland Avalanche Information Service

Sub Aqua Club (British)

Surf Life Saving GB

Surfers Against Sewage

Swimming

Swimming Clubs for people with Disabilities (National Association for)

SYHA Hostelling Scotland

Table Tennis Association (English)

Tai Chi Finder

Tai Chi Union for Great Britain

Tall Ships Youth Trust

Tandem Club

Tour de France

Tourism for All

Triathlon Association (British)

UEFA

UK Sport

UK Youth

Universities and Colleges Sport (British)

Venuemasters

Volleyball Association (English)

Volleyball Association (Scottish)

Walking Federation (British)

Walkit

WalkScotland

Water Ski & Wakeboard (British)

Welsh Athletics

Welsh Cycling

WheelPower

Wimbledon

Wind Sand & Stars

Windsurfing Association (UK)

Women's Bowling Federation (English)

Women's Sports & Fitness Foundation

Woodcraft Folk

World Cup

World Ju-Jitsu Federation (Ireland)

World Travel & Tourism Council

Yachting Association (Royal)

YHA - Youth Hostel Association

YMCA England

Yoga (British Wheel of)

Yoga (Iyengar Institute)

Young Farmers' Clubs (National Federation of)

Youth Sport Trust

Technology

Access Space

Alternative Technology (Centre for)

APRS

BCS - Chartered Institute for IT

Bibliomania

Blogger

Computer Aid International

Computers 4 Africa

Computing Centre (National)

CyberMentors

Data Archive (UK)

Design and Technology Association

e-Learning Foundation

Get Safe Online

IFST - Institute of Food Science & Technology

Information Commissioner's Office

Intellect

Internet Watch Foundation

ipl2

JANET

Jodrell Bank Observatory and Discovery Centre

My Supermarket

Nominet UK

OFCOM

People's Network

Popular Astronomy (Society for)

Science, Technology & the Arts (National Endowment for)

Scientists for Global Responsibility

Space Agency (European)

Space Centre (National)

Specialist Schools and Academies Trust

STEPS Centre - Social Technological and Environmental Pathway to Sustainability

Telescope (Bradford Robotic)

Telework Association

Wired Safety

World Space Week

Transport

Aeronautical Society (Royal)

AirportWatch

Airsafe.com

Automobile Association (AA)

Balloon and Airship Club (British)

Better Transport (Campaign for)

Bicycle Helmet Initiative Trust

Bikers with a Disability (National Association for)

Blue Badge Network

Brake

Bus Users UK

CAA - Civil Aviation Authority

CADD- Campaign Against Drinking & Driving

Choose Climate

Community Rail Partnerships (Association of)

Community Transport Association UK

Cyclenation

Cycling Campaign (London)

Transport continued

Cycling Projects

Disabled Motoring UK

DVLA - Driver and Vehicle Licensing Agency

Environmental Transport Association

Heritage Railway Association

Human Power Club (British)

Inland Waterways Association

Liftshare.com Ltd

Light Rail Transit Association

Living Streets

Logistics and Transport in the UK (Chartered Institute of)

Make Roads Safe

Navigation (Royal Institute of)

Passenger Focus

Passenger Transport UK (Confederation of)

Port of London Authority

RAC

Rail Enquiries (National)

Rail Europe

Rail Regulation (Office of)

Railfuture

Road Haulage Association

RoadPeace

School Journey Association

Shopmobility (National Federation of)

Sustrans

Traffic Statistics (Global)

Trainline

Transport & Environment (European Federation for)

Transport for London

Transport Safety (Parliamentary Advisory Council for)

WalesRails

Waterway Recovery Group

Working on Wheels

Travel & Tourism

ABTA - The Travel Association

Berlin info

Berlin International

Bike Express (European)

Brathay Exploration Group

Choose Climate

Couch Surfing

Currency converter

Cycling Union (International)

Ecotourism Society (The International)

Fit for Travel

Foreign and Commonwealth Office Travel Advice

Geographic Society (National)

Hostelling International

Hostelling International (N. Ireland)

Hostels.com

Identity & Passport Service

Journeywoman.com

MASTA - Medical Advisory Services for Travellers Abroad

Ordnance Survey

Royal Parks

SYHA Hostelling Scotland

Tour Operators (Association of Independent)

Tourism Concern

Tourism Offices Worldwide Directory

Travel and Tourism (Institute of)

Travel Warnings (US State Department)

Tropical Diseases (Hospital for)

Visit London

Visit Wales

VisitBritain

VisitEngland

VisitScotland

WalesRails

Winston Churchill Memorial Trust

World Tourism Organization

World Travel & Tourism Council

YHA - Youth Hostel Association

Volunteers

Africa & Asia Venture

African Conservation Experience

An Taisce

Army Cadet Force

AV Foundation (Africa Asia Venture)

Bond

BTCV - British Trust for Conservation Volunteers

Casualties Union

CEMVO (Scotland) - Council of Ethnic Minority Voluntary Sector Organisations

Chartered Surveyors Voluntary Service

Children in Need Appeal

Cinnamon Trust

Community Service Volunteers

Community Transport Association UK

Conservation Volunteers Northern Ireland

Contact the Elderly

Couch Surfing

Cross Cultural Solutions

Depaul Nightstop UK

Directory of Social Change

Do-it

Friendship Works

Get connected

Girlguiding UK

Habitat for Humanity Great Britain

International Service

IVS GB - International Voluntary Service

Jewish Lads' & Girls' Brigade (JLGB)

Jewish Women (League of)

Lattitude Global Volunteering

Lesbians & Gays (Families & Friends of)

Mercy Corps

National Trust Volunteering

NOAH - National Organization for Albinism and Hypopigmentation

Pets as Therapy

Prince's Trust (Head Office)

Prison Visitors (National Association of Official)

Project Trust

Quaker Voluntary Action

Raleigh International

Reach

REMAP

Restless Development

Retired and Senior Volunteer Programme

Royal National Lifeboat Institution

Self Unlimited

Simon Community

SOVA - Supporting Others Through Volunteer Action

Time for God

Toc H

Tools for Self Reliance

United Nations Volunteers

Voluntary Agencies (International Council of)

Voluntary and Community Action (National Association for)

Voluntary Arts Network

Voluntary Organisations (National Council for) (NCVO)

Voluntary Organisations (Scottish Council for)

Voluntary Youth Services (National Council for)

Volunteer Action for Peace

Volunteer Development Scotland

Volunteer Now

Volunteers continued

Volunteer Reading Help

Volunteering England

Volunteers For Rural India

VSO - Voluntary Service Overseas

Waterway Recovery Group

WCVA - Wales Council for Voluntary Action

Women's Institutes (National Federation of)

Working For A Charity

WorldWide Volunteering

WRVS (Women's Royal Voluntary Service)

WWOOF UK - Opportunities on Organic Farms UK

Year Out Group

Young Enterprise

Youth Council (British)

Youth Council for Northern Ireland

Youth in Action

War & Conflict

Abolition of War (Movement for the)

Action on Armed Violence (AOAV)

Aegis Trust

Army (British)

British Legion (Royal)

Campaign Against Arms Trade

Child Soldiers

Churchill War Rooms

CND - Campaign for Nuclear Disarmament

Combat Stress

Conflict Minerals

Conscience

Control Arms

Defence (Ministry of)

E-MINE

ECHO

Elders (The)

Forgiveness Project

Gulf Veterans & Families Association (National)

HALO Trust

Help for Heroes

Imperial War Museum

International Criminal Court

Landmines (International Campaign to Ban)

Mines Advisory Group

Miracles

Navy (US)

Pax Christi

Peace Brigades International

Peace Pledge Union

Royal Air Force

Royal Navy

Saferworld

War Resisters League

Women

Abortion Rights

Action of Postpartum Psychosis Network

Birth Trauma Association

Black Women for Wages for Housework

Black Women's Rape Action Project

Bowling Association Ltd (English Indoor)

Breakthrough Breast Cancer

Breast Cancer Care

Business & Professional Women UK Ltd

CAMFED International - Campaign for Female Education

Child & Woman Abuse Studies Unit

Crossroads Women's Centre

Daisy Network

Eaves

End violence against women

Endometriosis UK

Feminist Archive

Forward

GFS Platform for Young Wome - Girls Friendly Society

Hibiscus

IKWRO - Iranian and Kurdish Women's Rights Organisation

Jewish Women (League of)

Jo's Cervical Cancer Trust

Journeywoman.com

Labour Women's Network

Ladies' Golf Union

Lavender Trust

Lilith Research and Development

Llamau

Margaret Pyke Centre

MATCH - Mothers Apart from Their Children

Mothers at home Matter

Mothers' Union

Netmums

Opportunity Now

Peace & Freedom (Women's International League for)

Platform 51

Poppy Project

Positively UK

Post-Natal Illness (Association for)

Premenstrual Syndrome (National Association for)

Rape Crisis

Refuge

Rights of Women

Rugby Football Union for Women

Scarlet Centre

Sea Ranger Association

Sojourner Project

Southall Black Sisters

Tampon Alert (Alice Kilvert)

White Ribbon Alliance

Winvisible (Women with visible & invisible disabilities)

Womankind Worldwide

Women (National Assembly of)

Women and Manual Trades

Women Entrepreneurs (British Association of)

Women in Prison

Women in Publishing

Women Into Science & Engineering (WISE)

Women living under Muslim laws

Women of Great Britain (National Council of)

Women Solicitors (Association of)

Women Working Worldwide

Women's Aid (Scottish)

Women's Aid (Welsh)

Women's Aid Federation (N. Ireland)

Women's Aid Federation of England

Women's Archive of Wales

Women's Bowling Federation (English)

Women's Clubs (National Association of)

Women's Engineering Society

Women's Environmental Network

Women's Food & Farming Union

Women's Institutes (National Federation of)

Women's Library

Women's Register (National)

Women's Resource Centre

Women's Sports & Fitness Foundation

Women's Therapy Centre

Organisations

Before contacting an organisation, check first whether your library has information. Most organisations which include British, National, International, Association, Society etc in their names have been placed in order by the key word in the name except where such a change would make the name unfamiliar or more difficult to find.

1 Voice Communicating together
Network and support for children and families using communication aids
PO Box 600 Chorley PR6 6JR
Tel: 0845 330 7862
info@1voice.info
www.1Voice.info

10 Downing Street Website
Interactive information from Prime Minister's Department
www.number10.gov.uk

10:10
A movement of people, schools, businesses and organisations cutting their carbon - 10% at a time
PO Box 64749 London NW1W 8HE
Tel: 020 7388 6688
hello@1010global.org
www.1010global.org
www.1010uk.org

100 Black Men of London
Charity dedicated to the education, development and uplifting of our youth and the wider community
The Bridge 12-16 Clerkenwell Road London EC1M 5PQ
Tel: 0870 1214100
info@100bmol.org.uk
www.100bmol.org.uk

1901 Census for England & Wales
Search over 400 million people living in England and Wales between 1841-1901 and view images of the original documents
www.1901censusonline.com

24 hour museum now see Culture24

4Children
National charity that promotes out of school hours child care
City Reach 5 Greenwich View Place London E14 9NN
Information helpline: 020 7512 2100
Tel: 020 7512 2112 (switchboard)
info@4children.org.uk
www.4children.org.uk

A

AAA-NORCAP
Supporting adults affected by adoption. Home to the UK's longest established Contact Register: finding, making contact, making it work
112 Church Rd Wheatley Oxon OX33 1LU
Tel: 01865 875000
enquiries@norcap.org
www.norcap.org.uk

ABA see Amateur Boxing Association of England Ltd.

ABCUL see Credit Unions Ltd. (Association of British)

Abolition of War (Movement for the)
11 Venetia Road London N4 1EJ
Tel: 01908 511 948
email via website
www.abolishwar.org.uk

Abortion see also ARC – Antenatal Results & Choices, BPAS, Education for Choice, Life, Marie Stopes International, Unborn Children (Society for the Protection of), Pathfinder International, Voice for Choice

Abortion Campaign (National) now see Abortion Rights

Abortion Law Reform Association now see Abortion Rights

Abortion Rights
The national pro-choice campaign. Campaigns for equal access to safe, legal, free abortion on request
18 Ashwin Street London E8 3DL
Tel: 020 7923 9792
email via website
www.abortionrights.org.uk

ABSA now see Arts & Business

ABTA The Travel Association
Aims to ensure high standards of trading practice for the benefit of the travel industry and the consumers that they serve
30 Park Street London SE1 9EQ
Consumer Affairs: 0901 201 5050
email via website
www.abta.com

Acas Advisory, Conciliation and Arbitration Service
Industrial relations and employment enquiries
Euston Tower 286 Euston Road London NW1 3JJ
Helpline: 08457 47 47 47
Customer services: 08457 38 37 36
Text Relay: 18001 08457 47 47 47
www.acas.org.uk

Acas Scotland Advisory, Conciliation and
Arbitration Service
151 West George Street Glasgow G2 2JJ
Helpline: 08457 47 47 47
Customer services: 08457 38 37 36
Text Relay: 18001 08457 47 47 47
www.acas.org.uk

Acas Wales Advisory, Conciliation and
Arbitration Service
Third Floor Fusion Point 2 Dumballs Road
Cardiff CF10 5BF
Helpline: 08457 47 47 47
Customer services: 08457 38 37 36
Text Relay: 18001 08457 47 47 47
www.acas.org.uk

Access Art
Online workshops & arts educational
activities for all ages
email via website
www.accessart.org.uk

Access London Theatre
www.officiallondontheatre.co.uk

Access Space
Sustainable free, open access media lab.
People interested in art, design, computers,
recycling, music, electronics, photography
and more meet like minded people, share
and develop skills and work on creative,
enterprising and technical projects
Unit 1, AVEC Building 3-7 Sidney Street
Sheffield S1 4RG
Tel: 0114 249 5522
access-space.org

Access to Industry Reducing barriers to
further education and employment
To move excluded people into education
and onto employment across the South East
of Scotland
156 Cowgate Edinburgh EH1 1RP
& 15 Blair Street Edinburgh EH1 1QR
Tel: 0131 260 9721
Tel: 0131 226 3006
mail@accesstoindustry.co.uk
www.accesstoindustry.co.uk

Accessible Environments (Centre for) CAE
Advise on access to the built environment/
inclusive design
70 South Lambeth Road London SW8 1RL
Tel: 020 7840 0125
info@cae.org.uk
www.cae.org.uk

ACRE see Communities in Rural England
(Action with)

ACT Animal Cancer Trust
Fighting cancer in our pets
5 Flag Business Exchange Vicarage Farm Road
Peterborough Cambridgeshire PE1 5TX
Tel: 08701 644225
info@animalcancertrust.org.uk
www.animalcancertrust.org.uk

ACT ON CO2
Email via website
www.direct.gov.uk/enEnvironment
andgreenerliving/Thewiderenvironment

Action for Children
Supports and speaks out for the most
vulnerable children and young people in
the UK
3 The Boulevard Ascot Road
Watford WD18 8AG
Tel: 030 123 2112
Tel: 01923 361500
ask.us@actionforchildren.org.uk
www.actionforchildren.org.uk

Action for Children Northern Ireland
10 Heron Road Belfast BT3 9LE
Tel: 030 123 2112
Tel: 028 9046 0500
ask.us@actionforchildren.org.uk
www.actionforchildren.org.uk

Action for Children Scotland
City Park 368 Alexandra Parade Glasgow
G31 3AU
Tel: 030 123 2112
Tel: 0141 550 9010
ask.us@actionforchildren.org.uk
www.actionforchildren.org.uk

Action for Children Wales
St David's Court 68a Cowbridge Road East
Cardiff CF11 9DN
Tel: 030 123 2112
Tel: 029 2022 2127
ask.us@actionforchildren.org.uk
www.actionforchildren.org.uk

Action for ME see M.E. (Action for)

Action for Sick Children see Sick Children
(Action for)

Action for Southern Africa see ACTSA

Action for Victims of Medical Accidents
see Medical Accidents (Action Against)

Action on Postpartum Psychosis Network
Provides information to women and their
families on Postpartum Psychosis – a severe
mental illness which has a sudden onset in
the first few weeks following childbirth
FREEPOST RSGT-YJEY-ZRREE Room 225
Monmouth House Dept. of Psychological
Medicin Heath Park Cardiff CF14 4XW
Tel: 029 2074 2038
info@app-network.org
www.app-network.org

Action on Addiction see Addiction (Action on)

Action on Armed Violence (AOAV) Formerly
Landmine Action
Working to reduce the incidence of armed
violence and its impact on vulnerable
populations around the world.
5th Floor Epworth House 25 City Road
London EC1Y 1AA
Tel: 020 7256 9500
info@aoav.org.uk
www.aoav.org.uk

Action on Disability and Development
now see ADD International

Action on Elder Abuse see Elder Abuse (Action on)

Action on Hearing Loss Formerly RNID -
Royal National Institute for Deaf People
Largest charity in the UK tackling hearing
loss and making hearing matter
19-23 Featherstone St London EC1Y 8SL
Information Line: 0808 808 0123
Tel: 0808 808 9000 (text phone)
informationline@hearingloss.org.uk
www.actiononhearingloss.org.uk/

Action Transport Theatre
Action Transport Theatre Company is an arts
and ideas company creating work for, by and
with young people
Whitby Hall Stanney Lane Ellesmere Port
CH65 9AE
Tel: 0151 357 2120
info@actiontransporttheatre.org
www.actiontransporttheatre.org

ActionAid
Help and support for the poorest and most
vulnerable people worldwide
33-39 Bowling Green Lane London EC1R OBJ
Tel: 0120 3122 0561
mail@actionaid.org
www.actionaid.org.uk

Active Birth Centre
Education for active birth, professional
training, water birth pool hire & sales
25 Bickerton Rd London N19 5JT
Tel: 020 7281 6760
info@activebirthcentre.com
www.activebirthcentre.com

ACTSA Action for Southern Africa
Campaigns for peace, democracy and
development in Southern Africa
231 Vauxhall Bridge Road London SW1V 1EH
Tel: 020 3263 2001
actsa@actsa.org
www.actsa.org

Acupuncture Council (British)
Self-regulatory body for acupuncturists in
the UK
63 Jeddo Road London W12 9HQ
Tel: 020 8735 0400
email via website
www.acupuncture.org.uk

Acupuncture Society (British Medical)
BMAS
Professional organisation
BMAS House 3 Winnington Court Northwich
Cheshire CW8 1AQ
Tel: 01606 786782
admin@medical-acupuncture.org.uk
www.medical-acupuncture.co.uk

Adam Smith Institute
Free market think-tank
23 Great Smith St London SW1P 3BL
Tel: 020 7222 4995
Email via website
www.adamsmith.org

Adbusters
Website providing a critical look at
advertising
www.adbusters.org

ADD International
Charity working in Africa and Asia to help
people with disabilities
Vallis House 57 Vallis Rd Frome Somerset
BA11 3EG
Tel: 01373 473064
Email via website
www.add.org.uk

Addaction
Helping individuals and communities
manage the effects of drug and alcohol
misuse
67-69 Cowcross St London EC1M 6PU
Tel: 020 7251 5860
info@addaction.org.uk
www.addaction.org.uk

Addiction (Action on)
Charity seeking out the causes of nicotine,
alcohol and drug addiction
East Knoyle Salisbury Wiltshire SP3 6BE
Tel: 0300 330 0659
admin@actiononaddiction.org.uk
www.actiononaddiction.org.uk

Additives (Action on)
Aims to list all the foods, drinks and
medicines which contain the additives linked
to hyperactivity in susceptible children
94 White Lion Street
London N1 London N1 9PF
info@actiononadditives.com
www.actiononadditives.com

ADFAM

National charity working with families affected by drugs & alcohol
25 Corsham Street London N1 6DR
Tel: 020 7553 7640
admin@adfam.org.uk
www.adfam.org.uk

Adoption and Fostering Information Line

204 Stockport Road Altrincham WA157UA
Tel: 0800 883 8887
office@adoption.org.uk
www.adoption.org.uk

Adoption records

Adoption certificates & access to birth records. Contact Register for adoptions in England and Wales
www.direct.gov.uk/en/
Governmentcitizensandrights/
Registeringlifeevents/index.htm

Adoption UK

Supporting adoptive families before, during and after adoption
Linden House 55 The Green South Bar Street Banbury Oxon OX16 9AB
Helpline: 0844 848 7900
Tel: 01295 752240 (Admin)
email via website
www.adoptionuk.org

& Scotland
172 Leith Walk Edinburgh EH6 5EA
Helpline: 0844 848 7900
Tel: 0141 5555 111
email via website
www.adoptionuk.org

& Wales
Penhevad Studios Penhevad Street Grangetown Cardiff CF11 7LU
Helpline: 0844 848 7900
Tel: 02920 230319
email via website
www.adoptionuk.org

& Northern Ireland
545 Antrim Road Belfast BT15 3BU
Helpline: 0844 848 7900
Tel: 028 9077 5211
email via website
www.adoptionuk.org

Adult Continuing Education (National Institute of) see NIACE

Adult Education see also NIACE, learndirect, My World of Work, Open University, Third Age Trust, Workers Educational Association

Advancing Gender Equality in Science, Engineering and Technology see UKRC

Adventure Activities Licensing Authority

Inspects providers of adventure activities 44 Lambourne Crescent Llanishen Cardiff CF14 5GG
Tel: 029 20 755 715
info@aala.org.uk
www.aala.org.uk

Advertising Association

Federation of trade bodies. Promoting and protecting the role, rights and responsibilities of advertising
7th Floor North Artillery House 11-19 Artillery Row London SW1P 1RT
Tel: 020 7340 1100
aa@adassoc.org.uk
www.adassoc.org.uk

Advertising Standards Authority

Regulates content of non-broadcast advertisements
Mid City Place 71 High Holborn London WC1V 6QT
Tel: 020 7492 2222
email via website
www.asa.org.uk

Advice see thematic guide - Counselling

Advice on Individual Rights in Europe see AIRE Centre

Advicenow

Comprehensive legal information from a variety of leading services
www.advicenow.org.uk

AdviceUK

Umbrella organisation. Membership organisation of independent social welfare law advice centres
WB1 PO Box 70716 London EC1P 1GQ
Tel: 020 7469 5700
mail@adviceuk.org.uk
www.adviceuk.org.uk

Advisory Council on the Misuse of Drugs

Independent expert body that advises government on drug related issues in the UK
Home Office 3rd Floor Seacole Building 2 Marsham Street London SW1P 4DF
Tel: 020 7035 0454
ACMD@homeoffice.gsi.gov.uk
www.homeoffice.gov.uk/agencies-public-bodies/acmd/

Advocacy After Fatal Domestic Abuse

AAFDA
Practical and emotional support after fatal domestic abuse incidents
PO Box 3636 Swindon SN3 9BG
Helpline: 07768 386922 if you need immed Domestic violence Helpline: 0808 2000 247
www.aafda.org.uk

Advocacy Resource Exchange ARX
A resource agency supporting local
advocacy schemes by providing training,
information and advice
Portman House 53 Millbrook Road East
Southampton SO15 1HN
Tel: 02380 234 904
enquiries@advocacyresource.org.uk
www.advocacyresource.org.uk

Advocates for Animals see Onekind

Aegis Trust
Campaigns against crimes against humanity
and genocide
Acre Edge Road, Laxton Newark,
Nottinghamshire NG22 0PA
Tel: 01623 836 627
office@aegistrust.org
www.aegistrust.org

AENA now see England Netball

Aeronautical Society (Royal)
A professional institution dedicated to the
Global Aerospace Community
4 Hamilton Place London W1J 7BQ
Tel: 020 7670 4300
raes@aerosociety.com
www.aerosociety.com

Afasic
Representing children & young adults with
speech, language and communication
impairments
1st Floor, 20 Bowling Green La London EC1R
0BD
Helpline: 0845 355 5577
Tel: 020 7490 9410
email via website
www.afasic.org.uk

Afghanaid
UK based charity working alongside Afghan
communities
56 - 64 Leonard Street London EC2A 4LT
Tel: 020 7065 0825
info@afghanaid.org.uk
www.afghanaid.org.uk

Africa & Asia Venture
UK-based volunteering organisation
specialising in volunteering opportunities
and gap year projects for 18 - 25 year olds in
the developing world
10 Market Place Devizes Wiltshire SN10 1HT
Tel: 01380 729009
av@aventure.co.uk
www.aventure.co.uk

Africa Centre
Promoting African arts, culture, opinion and
business. Undergoing refurbishment. See
website for details
Tel: 020 7836 1973
email via website
www.africacentre.org.uk

African Conservation Experience
Gives volunteers the opportunity for
conservation work in Southern Africa and to
provide financial support and information for
conservation projects
Unit 1, Manor Farm Churchend Lane
Charfield Wotton-under-edge GL12 8LJ
Tel: 01454 269 182
email via website
www.conservationafrica.net

African Initiatives
Promotes right to participate in decisions
affecting communities in Africa
Brunswick Court Brunswick Square Bristol
BS2 8PE
Tel: 0117 915 0001
info@african-initiatives.org.uk
www.african-initiatives.org.uk

Africans Unite Against Child Abuse
Promoting the rights and welfare of African
children
Unit 3D/F Leroy House 436 Essex Road
London N1 3QP
Tel: 0844 660 8607
email via website
www.afruca.org

Age Cymru
Charity working for older people in Wales
Ty John Pathy 13-14 Neptune Court
Vanguard Way Cardiff CF24 5PJ
 Age UK Advice line: 0800 169 6565
Tel: 029 20 431555
enquiries@agecymru.org.uk
www.ageuk.org.uk/cymru

Age Exchange
Works with older people to improve their
quality of life by valuing their reminiscences
The Reminiscence Centre 11 Blackheath
Village London SE3 9LA
Tel: 020 8318 9105
administrator@age-exchange.org.uk
www.age-exchange.org.uk

Age NI
Charity working for older people in Northern
Ireland
3 Lower Cres Belfast BT7 1NR
Age UK Advice line: 0800 169 6565
Tel: 028 9024 5729
info@ageni.org
www.ageuk.org.uk/northern-ireland

Age Scotland
Charity working for older people in Scotland
Causewayside House 160 Causewayside
Edinburgh EH9 1PR
Age UK Advice line: 0800 169 6565
Tel: 0845 125 9732
info@agescotland.org.uk
www.ageuk.org.uk/scotland

Age UK

Age UK is the new force combining Age Concern and Help the Aged
Tavis House 1-6 Tavistock Square London WC1H 9NA
Advice: 0800 169 6565
Tel: 0800 169 8787
contact@ageuk.org.uk
www.ageuk.org.uk

Ageing (Centre for Policy on) see Policy on Ageing (Centre for)

Ageing (Research Info) now see Age Cymru, Age UK, Age NI, Age Scotland

Agriculture and Horticulture Development Board

Helps improve the efficiency and competitiveness of various agriculture and horticulture sectors within the UK
Stoneleigh Park Kenilworth Warwickshire CV8 2TL
Tel: 0247 669 2051
info@ahdb.org.uk
www.ahdb.org.uk

Ahimsa Safer Families

Specialist help for men with a history of violence. Support for their partners
1 Bridge Court Kingsmill Road Saltash PL12 6LS
Tel: 01752 848248
mail@ahimsa-saferfamilies.co.uk
www.ahimsasaferfamilies.co.uk

AIDS Trust (National)

The UK's leading independent policy and campaigning voice on HIV and AIDS
New City Cloisters 196 Old St London EC1V 9FR
Tel: 020 7814 6767
info@nat.org.uk
www.nat.org.uk

AIDS/HIV see also AVERT, HIV/Aids Alliance (International), HIV InSite, ONE International, PACE, Positively UK, Terrence Higgins Trust

Aikido Board (British) BAB

Governing body for Aikido in the United Kingdom
general@bab.org.uk
www.bab.org.uk

AIMS Association for Improvements in the Maternity Services

Advice and information network for parents' choices in childbirth
Helpline: 0300 365 0663
helpline@aims.org.uk
www.aims.org.uk

Air Cadets see Girls' Venture Corps Air Cadets

Air Transport Users' Council now see CAA

AIRE Centre Advice on Individual Rights in Europe

3rd Floor 17 Red Lion Square London WC1R 4QH
Advice Line: 020 7831 3850
Tel: 020 7831 4276
info@airecentre.org
www.airecentre.org

AirportWatch

Opposes airport expansion across the UK
Broken Wharf House 2 Broken Wharf
London EC4V 3DT
Tel: 020 7248 2227
info@airportwatch.org.uk
www.airportwatch.org.uk

Airsafe.com Safety information for the airline passenger
www.airsafe.com

AITO see Tour Operators (Association of Independent)

Al Jazeera

English language web site of the Arab news service, based in Qatar
english.aljazeera.net

Al-Anon Alateen Family Groups (UK & Eire)

Al-Anon offers understanding & support for families & friends of problem drinkers. Alateen is for 12 & 20 year olds who have been affected by someone else's drinking, usually that of a parent
61 Great Dover St London SE1 4YF
Confidential Helpline: 020 7403 0888
Tel: 020 7407 0215
enquiries@al-anonuk.org.uk
www.al-anonuk.org.uk

& Scotland
Al-Anon Information Centre Mansfield Park Building Unit 6 22 Mansfield Street Patrick Glasgow G11 5QP
Helpline: 0141 339 8884
enquiries@al-anonuk.org.uk
www.al-anonuk.org.uk

& Republic of Ireland
Al-Anon Information Centre Room 5, 5 Capel Street Dublin 1 Republic of Ireland
Helpline: 01 873 2699
enquiries@al-anonuk.org.uk
www.al-anonuk.org.uk

& Northern Ireland
Al-Anon Information Centre Peace House 224 Lisburn Road Belfast BT9 6GE Northern Ireland
Helpline: 02890 68 2368
enquiries@al-anonuk.org.uk
www.al-anonuk.org.uk

Albany Trust
A professional therapy service offering emotional, sexual and/or psychological help
239a Balham High Road London SW17 7BE
Tel: 020 8767 1827
info@albanytrust.org
www.albanytrust.org.uk

Albert Kennedy Trust
Supporting lesbian, gay and bisexual young people who are homeless or living in hostile environments
Unit 203 Hatton Square Busines 16/16a Baldwins Gardens London EC1N 7RJ
Tel: 020 7831 6562 (London)
Tel: 0161 228 3308 (Manchester)
contact@akt.org.uk
www.akt.org.uk

Albinism see also NOAH - National Organization for Albinism and Hypopigmentation

Albinism Fellowship
Advice and support
PO Box 77 Burnley BB11 5GN
Tel: 01282 771900
info@albinism.org.uk
www.albinism.org.uk

Alcohol Concern
Provides information and comment on alcohol issues
Suite B5 West Wing New City Cloisters 196 Old Street London EC1V 9FR
National Drink Helpline: 0800 917 8282
Tel: 0207 566 9800
email via website
www.alcoholconcern.org.uk

Alcohol Education and Research Council
AERC
Develops research based evidence to inform and influence policy and practice and help people and organisations to address alcohol issues
Willow House 4th Floor 17-23 Willow Place London SW1P 1JH
Tel: 0207 821 7880
email via website
www.alcoholresearchuk.org

Alcohol Focus Scotland
Dedicated to raising awareness of, and reducing the significant health and social harm caused by alcohol
2nd Floor 166 Buchanan Street Glasgow G1 2LW
Tel: 0141 572 6700
enquiries@alcohol-focus-scotland.org.uk
www.alcohol-focus-scotland.org.uk

Alcohol Studies (Institute of)
Increasing awareness of alcohol related issues in society
Alliance House 12 Caxton St
London SW1H 0QS
Tel: 020 7222 4001
info@ias.org.uk
www.ias.org.uk

Alcoholics Anonymous
PO Box 1 10 Toft Green York YO1 7NJ.
Helpline: 0845 7697 555
Tel: 01904 644026 (office hours only)
help@alcoholics-anonymous.org.uk
www.alcoholics-anonymous.org.uk

Alexander Teachers (Professional Association of)
Room 706 The Big Peg 120 Vyse St
Birmingham B18 6NF
Tel: 01743 241478
info@paat.org.uk
www.paat.org.uk

Alexander Technique (Society of Teachers of the)
1st Floor Linton House 39-51 Highgate Rd London NW5 1RS
Tel: 020 7482 5135
office@stat.org.uk
www.stat.org.uk

Alice Kilvert Tampon Alert see Tampon Alert (Alice Kilvert)

All Wales Domestic Abuse and Sexual Violence Helpline
Helpline: 0808 80 10 800
email via website
www.allwaleshelpline.org.uk

Allergies see also Anaphylaxis Campaign

Allergy UK
Medical charity for people with allergy, food intolerance and chemical sensitivity
Planwell House LEFA Business Park Edgington Way Sidcup DA14 5BH
Tel: 01322 619898
info@allergyuk.org
www.allergyuk.org

Alliance for Inclusive Education see Inclusive Education (Alliance for)

Alliance Française
French classes/diplomas in French as a foreign language & language skills consultancy, some social and cultural activities
1 Dorset Square London NW1 6PU
Tel: 020 7723 6439
email via website
www.alliancefrancaise.org.uk

Allotment and Leisure Gardeners Ltd. (National Society of)

National representative body for the allotment movement in the UK. Managed and funded by its members to protect, promote and preserve allotments for future generations to enjoy
O'Dell House Hunters Road Corby NN17 5JE
Tel: 01536 266 576
natsoc@nsalg.org.uk
www.nsalg.org.uk

Alone in London

Assists the single young homeless under 26 in London
Unit 6 48 Provost Street N1 7SU
Tel: 020 7278 4224
enquiries@als.org.uk
www.aloneinlondon.org

Alopecia see Hairline International

Alternative Technology (Centre for)

Environmental demonstration centre open to visitors
Machynlleth Powys SY20 9AZ
Tel: 01654 705950
www.cat.org.uk

Aluminium Packaging Recycling Organisation

Info packs, educational materials
1 Brockhill Court Brockhill Lane Redditch B97 6RB
Tel: 01527 597757
info@alupro.org.uk
www.alupro.org.uk

Alzheimer Scotland

Helping people with dementia and their carers and families in Scotland
22 Drumsheugh Gardens Edinburgh EH3 7RN
Helpline: 0808 808 3000
Tel: 0131 243 1453
alzheimer@alzscot.org
www.alzscot.org

Alzheimer's Research Trust Defeating Dementia

Leading UK research charity for Alzheimer's disease and related dementias. Provides free information on dementia
The Stables Station Road Great Shelford Cambridge CB22 5LR
Tel: 01223 843899
enquiries@alzheimersresearchuk.org
www.alzheimers-research.org.uk

Alzheimer's Society Leading the fight against dementia

Provides local information and services across England, Wales & N. Ireland to people affected by dementia in their communities. Provides day care and home care for people with dementia, as well as support and befriending services to help partners and families cope with the demands of caring
Devon House 58 St Katharine's Way London E1W 1LB
Helpline: 0845 300 0336
Tel: 020 7423 3500
enquiries@alzheimers.org.uk
www.alzheimers.org.uk

AMAR International Charitable Foundation

Works to create and to sustain professional services in medicine, public health, education and basic need provision within refugee and other communities living under stress in war zones or in areas of civil disorder and disruption
Hope House 45 Great Peter Street London SW1P 3LT
Tel: 020 7799 2217
london@amarfoundation.org
www.amarfoundation.org

Amateur Boxing Association of England Ltd. ABA

National governing body
EIS Sheffield Coleridge Road Sheffield S9 5DA
Tel: 0114 223 5654
email via website
www.abae.co.uk

Amateur Boxing Scotland Ltd.

Promotes boxing as physical exercise for boys and girls
5 Nasmyth Court Houston Industrial Estate Livingston EH54 5EG
Tel: 0845 241 7016
enquiries@abs-ltd.org.uk
www.amateurboxingscotland.co.uk

Amateur Theatre Network see Theatre Network (The Amateur)

Ambition formerly Clubs for Young People

Helps young people to achieve their potential through social and personal development opportunities
371 Kennington Lane London SE11 5QY
Tel: 020 7793 0787
via website
www.ambitionuk.org

American Library Association

www.ala.org

Amnesty International UK

Campaigns for prisoners of conscience, against the use of torture & the death penalty
17-25 New Inn Yard London EC2A 3EA
Tel: 020 7033 1500
Textphone 020 7033 1664
sct@amnesty.org.uk
www.amnesty.org.uk

An Taisce National Trust for Ireland
An environmental voluntary organisation
concerned with the preservation of
buildings, landscapes and natural heritage
Tailor's Hall Back Lane Dublin 8
Tel: 00 353 1 454 1786
info@antaisce.org
www.antaisce.org

Anaphylaxis Campaign
Fighting for people with life-threatening
allergies, providing education, information
and support
PO Box 275 Farnborough Hants GU14 6SX
Helpline: 01252 542029
Tel: 01252 546100
info@anaphylaxis.org.uk
www.anaphylaxis.org.uk/

Anchor Trust
Working with older people and providing
residential care homes
2nd Floor 25 Bedford Street
London WC2E 9ES
Tel: 0845 140 2020
email via website
www.anchor.org.uk

**Ancient Buildings (Society for the
Protection of)** SPAB
Campaigns to save threatened buildings,
gives advice on repair and runs courses
37 Spital Sq London E1 6DY
Tel: 020 7377 1644
Fax : 020 7247 5296
info@spab.org.uk
www.spab.org.uk

Ancient Monument Society
Study and conservation of historic buildings
of all ages and types
St Ann's Vestry Hall 2 Church Entry London
EC4V 5HB
Tel: 020 7236 3934
office@ancientmonumentssociety.org.uk
www.ancientmonumentssociety.org.uk

Ancient Tree Forum
c/o Woodland Trust Autumn Park Dysart
Road Grantham NG32 6LL
Tel: 01476 581135
ancient-tree-forum@woodland-trust.org.uk
www.woodland-trust.org.uk/ancient-tree-
forum

Angling Trust
Represent all game, coarse and sea anglers
and angling in England
Eastwood House 6 Rainbow Street
Leominster Herefordshire HR6 8DQ
Tel: 0844 7700616
admin@anglingtrust.net
www.anglingtrust.net

Animal Aid
Campaigns against animal abuse and for a
cruelty-free lifestyle
The Old Chapel Bradford St Tonbridge Kent
TN9 1AW
Tel: 01732 364546
info@animalaid.co.uk
www.animalaid.org.uk

Animal Aid Youth
Youth section of Animal Aid
www.animalaid.org.uk/h/n/YOUTH/HOME/

Animal Defenders International
Works globally with the National Anti-
Vivisection Society and the Lord Dowding
Fund for Humane Research for the protection
of animals
Millbank Tower Millbank London SW1P 4QP
Tel: 020 7630 3340
info@ad-international.org
www.ad-international.org

Animal Health (National Office of)
Represents the UK animal medicines industry
3 Crossfield Chambers Gladbeck Way
Enfield EN2 7HF
Tel: 020 8367 3131
noah@noah.co.uk
www.noah.co.uk

Animal Health Trust
Registered charity that aims to advance
veterinary science
Lanwades Park Kentford Newmarket
Suffolk CB8 7UU
Tel: 01638 751000
info@aht.org.uk
www.aht.org.uk

Animal Rescue (International)
Charity for the rescue and rehabilitation of
suffering animals
Lime House Regency Close Uckfield East
Sussex TN22 1DS
Tel: 01825 767688
info@internationalanimalrescue.org
www.iar.org.uk

Animal Rescuers (UK)
Directory of UK rescue centres
www.animalrescuers.co.uk

Animal Research (Understanding) see
Understanding Animal Research

Animal Welfare Trust (National)
Operates rescue centres for unwanted, ill-
treated and abandoned animals and birds.
No healthy animal is ever put to sleep
Tyler's Way Watford-By-Pass Watford Herts
WD25 8WT
Tel: 020 8950 0177
email via web
www.nawt.org.uk

Animals in Medical Experiments (Fund for the Replacement of) see FRAME

Anne Frank Trust UK
Exhibitions and educational programmes on citizenship and social responsibility to counter bigotry and racism. Organises the Anne Frank Awards for Moral Courage
Star House 104-108 Grafton Road London NW5 4BA
Tel: 020 7284 5858
info@annefrank.org.uk
www.annefrank.org.uk

Antenatal Results and Choices see ARC

Anthony Nolan
Co-ordinates donation of bone marrow for treatment of disease
2 Heathgate Place 75-87 Agincourt Rd London NW3 2NU
Tel: 0303 303 0303
email via website
www.anthonynolan.org.uk

Anthropological Institute of Great Britain and Ireland (Royal) RAI
World's longest-established scholarly association dedicated to the study of humankind
50 Fitzroy St London W1T 5BT
Tel: 020 7387 0455
admin@therai.org.uk
www.therai.org.uk

Anti Snaring Campaign (National) NASC
Campaigns against the sale and manufacture of animal snares in the UK
PO BOX 3058 Littlehampton West Sussex BN16 3LG
Tel: 05601 716524
email via website
www.antisnaring.org.uk

Anti-Bullying Alliance
The ABA brings together over 130 organisations into one network. Promotes annual Anti-Bullying Week
National Children's Bureau 8 Wakley Street London EC1V 7QE
aba@ncb.org.uk
www.anti-bullingalliance.org.uk

Anti-Bullying Network
Network set up by The Scottish Executive so that teachers, parents and young people in Scotland could share ideas about how bullying should be tackled
Simpson House 52 Queen Street Edinburgh EH2 3NS
info@antibullying.net
www.antibullying.net

Anti-Nazi League now see Unite Against Fascism

Anti-Slavery International Today's fight for tomorrow's freedom
Campaigns for the elimination of slavery, child labour, debt bondage, forced labour, trafficking people. Educational materials available
Thomas Clarkson House The Stableyard Broomgrove Road London SW9 9TL
Tel: 020 7501 8920
info@antislavery.org
www.antislavery.org

Anti-Vivisection Society (National)
Campaigns to end all animal experiments
Millbank Tower Millbank London SW1P 4QP
Tel: 020 7630 3340
email via website
www.navs.org.uk

Antidote Promising Progress
Developed The PROGRESS Programme to help schools shape dynamic learning environments
3rd Floor, Cityside House 40 Adler St London E1 1EE
Tel: 020 7247 3355
admin@antidote.org.uk
www.antidote.org.uk

Antiquaries of London (Society of)
Fellowship of antiquaries. Has a library for scholars to which access is by appointment
Burlington House Piccadilly London W1J 0BE
Tel: 020 7479 7080
Tel: 020 7479 7084 (Library - to make a
Tel: 020 7479 7088 (Museum - collection
admin@sal.org.uk
www.sal.org.uk

Anxiety Care UK
Deals with anxiety, phobias and obsessive compulsive disorders
98-100 Ilford Lane Ilford Essex IG1 2LD
Tel: 07552 877219
admin@anxietycare.org.uk
www.anxietycare.org.uk

Anxiety UK
Provides information & support for people suffering from anxiety disorders
Zion Community Resource Centre 339 Stretford Rd Hulme Manchester M15 4ZY
Tel: 0844 4775 774
Tel: 0161 226 7727
info@anxietyuk.org.uk
www.anxietyuk.org.uk

Ape Alliance
An international coalition of organisations and individuals, working for the conservation and welfare of apes
30 Lansdown Stroud GL5 1BG
via web
www.4apes.com

Aphasia see Connect, Speakability

Apples & Snakes
Promotes performance poetry as a social and cross-cultural activity
The Albany Douglas Way Deptford London SE8 4AG
Tel: 0845 521 3460
info@applesandsnakes.org
www.applesandsnakes.org

APRS see Rural Scotland (Association for the Protection of)

APRS The professional recording association
Representing audio professionals
PO Box 22 Totnes TQ9 7YZ
Tel: 01803 868600
email via website
www2.aprs.co.uk

Apsley House Wellington Museum
One of London's finest Georgian buildings, former home of the Duke of Wellington
Hyde Park Corner 149 Piccadilly London W1J 7NT
Tel: 020 7499 5676
www.apsleyhouseguide.co.uk/

AQA Assessment and Qualifications Alliance
Largest A-level and GCSE awarding body in the UK
31-33 Springfield Av Harrogate HG1 2HW
Exam support: 0844 209 6614
Tel: 0161 953 1180
mailbox@aqa.org.uk
www.aqa.org.uk

& Devas St Manchester M15 6EX
Tel: 0161 953 1180
www.aqa.org.uk

& Stag Hill House Guildford GU2 7XJ
Tel: 01483 506 506
www.aqa.org.uk

Arab-British Understanding (Council for)
CAABU
1 Gough Square London EC4A 3DE
Tel: 020 7832 1321
info@caabu.org
www.caabu.org

Arbitration see Acas

Arbitrators (Chartered Institute of) CIArb
Professional organisation for arbitrators, mediators and adjudicators
CIArb 12 Bloomsbury Square London WC1A 2LP
Tel: 020 7421 7444
info@ciarb.org
www.ciarb.org

ARC Antenatal Results and Choices
Information and support to parents throughout antenatal testing
345 City Road London EC1V 1LR
Helpline: 0845 077 2290
Tel: 020 7713 7356
info@arc-uk.org
www.arc-uk.org

Arc Theatre
Specialise in creating and performing theatre that challenges assumptions and causes real change in the way that people relate to one another at work, at school and in the community
1st Floor, The Malthouse Studi 62-76 Abbey Road Barking IG11 7BT
Tel: 020 8594 1095
email via website
www.arctheatre.com

Archaeology (Council for British)
St Mary's House 66 Bootham York YO30 7BZ
Tel: 01904 671417
email via website
www.britarch.ac.uk

Archaeology Abroad
Information about fieldwork opportunities outside the UK. The annual edition of Archaeology Abroad includes comprehensive guidance notes and advice about joining a dig abroad
31-34 Gordon Sq London WC1H 0PY
Tel: 020 8537 0849
arch.abroad@ucl.ac.uk
www.britarch.ac.uk/archabroad

Archaeology Scotland
Suite 1a Stuart House Station Road Eskmills Musselburgh EH21 7PB
Tel: 0845 872 3333
info@archaeologyscotland.org.uk
www.archaeologyscotland.org.uk

Archery GB
The governing body for the sport of archery in Great Britain and Northern Ireland
Lilleshall National Sports Cen Nr Newport Shropshire TF10 9AT
Tel: 01952 677 888
enquiries@archerygb.org
www.archerygb.org

Archiseek
Website dedicated to the promotion of Irish architecture
www.archiseek.com

Architects (Royal Institute of British) RIBA
66 Portland Place London W1B 1AD
Tel: 020 7580 5533
info@inst.riba.org
www.architecture.com

Architectural Heritage Fund
Loans and grants to charities to preserve historic buildings
Alhambra House 27-31 Charing Cross Road London WC2H 0AU
Tel: 020 7925 0199
ahf@ahfund.org.uk
www.ahfund.org.uk

Architecture Foundation
Aims to promote the importance of high quality contemporary architecture & urban design
Ground Floor East 136-148 Tooley Street London SE1 2TU
Tel: 020 7084 6767
mail@architecturefoundation.org.uk
www.architecturefoundation.org.uk

Ariel Studios
Studio/rehearsal space and digital recording studio
Mullacott Cross Ilfracombe Devon EX34 8ND
Tel: 01271 862701
www.ariel.org.uk

ARKive
Images of life on earth. The world's centralised digital library of films, photographs and associated recordings of species
Wildscreen Ground Floor The Rackhay Queen Charlotte Street Bristol BS1 4HJ
Tel : 0117 328 5950
arkive@wildscreen.org.uk
www.arkive.org

Arms and Armour Society
A learned society for the study and preservation of arms and armour
PO Box 10232 London SW19 2ZD
armsandarmour.soc@btinternet.com
www.armsandarmour.net

Army (British)
www.army.mod.uk

Army Cadet Force
National voluntary youth organisation
Holderness House 51-61 Clifton Street London EC2A 4DW
www.armycadets.com

Army Museum (National)
Royal Hospital Road Chelsea London SW3 4HT
Tel: 020 7881 6606 (information line)
Tel: 020 7730 0717 (switchboard)
info@nam.ac.uk
www.nam.ac.uk

Arson Prevention Bureau
Funded by UK insurers to reduce the incidence and costs of arson
www.arsonpreventionbureau.org.uk

Art and Design (National Society for Education in)
For gallery educators, artists in residence, parents and all those with an interest in arts education
3 Masons Wharf Potley Lane Corsham Wiltshire SN13 9FY
Tel: 01225 810134
info@nsead.org
www.nsead.org

Art Fund
The UK's leading art charity, it enriches museums and galleries with works of art
Millais House 7 Cromwell Place London SW7 2JN
Tel: 020 7225 4800
info@artfund.org
www.artfund.org

Art Library (National)
A major public reference library & the V&A's curatorial department for the art, craft & design of the book
Victoria and Albert Museum South Kensington Cromwell Road London SW7 2RL
Tel: 020 7942 2000
vanda@vam.ac.uk
www.vam.ac.uk/nal

Art Therapists (British Association of)
24-27 White Lion Street London N1 9PD
Tel: 020 7686 4216
info@baat.org
www.baat.org

Arthritic Association
Offers a natural drug free Home Treatment programme to help arthritis sufferers
One Upperton Gardens Eastbourne East Sussex BN21 2AA
Tel: 01323 416550
Freephone: 0800 652 3188
info@arthriticassociation.org.uk
www.arthriticassociation.org.uk

Arthritis Care
Supporting people with arthritis
18 Stephenson Way London NW1 2HD
Helpline: 0808 800 4050
Tel: 020 7380 6500
info@arthritiscare.org.uk
www.arthritiscare.org.uk

Arthritis Research UK
Aims to advance the understanding, prevention and treatment of arthritis & related conditions
Copeman House St Mary's Gate Chesterfield Derbyshire S41 7TD
Tel: 0300 790 0400
enquiries@arthritisresearchuk.org
www.arthritisresearchuk.org

Arthur Rank Centre
National rural resources unit for the churches
Stoneleigh Park Warwickshire CV8 2LG
Tel: 024 7685 3060
admin@arthurrankcentre.org.uk
www.arthurrankcentre.org.uk

ARTICLE 19 The Global Campaign for Free Expression
Human rights organisation which campaigns globally for freedom of expression and information
Free Word Centre 60 Farringdon Road
London EC1R 3GA
Tel: 020 7324 2500
info@article19.org
www.article19.org

Artistic Roller Skating (Federation of)
Terence House 24 London Road Thatcham
Berkshire RG18 4LQ
Tel: 01635 877322
office@fars.co.uk
www.fars.co.uk

Artists Against Racism
www.artistsagainstracism.com

Arts (National Campaign for the)
17 Tavistock Street London WC2E 7PA
tel 0207 240 4698
nca@artscampaign.org.uk
www.artscampaign.org.uk

Arts (Royal Academy of) see Royal Academy of Arts

Arts & Business
Helps business people support the arts & the arts inspire business people
137 Shepherdess Walk London N1 7RQ
020 7566 6650
contactus@artsandbusiness.org.uk
www.artsandbusiness.org.uk

Arts Council England
National development agency for the arts in England, distributing public money from government & the national lottery
14 Great Peter Street SW1P 3NQ
Tel: 0845 300 6200
Textphone: 020 7973 6564
Email via website
www.artscouncil.org.uk

Arts Council of Northern Ireland
77 Malone Road Belfast BT9 6AQ
Tel: 028 9038 5200
info@artscouncil-ni.org
www.artscouncil-ni.org

Arts Council of Wales Cyngor Celfyddydau Cymru
Distributes Welsh Assembly, Government and National Lottery funding to the arts in Wales
Bute Place Cardiff CF10 5AL
Tel: 0845 8734 900
Minicom: 029 2045 1023
info@artswales.org.uk
www.artswales.org.uk

Arts in Therapy & Education (Institute for)
Qualification in integrative arts psychotherapy and child therapy
2-18 Britannia Row London N1 8PA
Tel: 020 7704 2534
info@artspsychotherapy.org
www.artspsychotherapy.org

Arts Marketing Association
Works to improve professional development and the status of arts professionals
7a Clifton Court Clifton Rd Cambridge CB1 7BN
Tel: 01223 578078
info@a-m-a.co.uk
www.a-m-a.org.uk

Artsline
Advice service for disabled people on access to the arts and entertainment
21 Pine Court Wood Lodge Gardens
Bromley BR1 2WA
Tel: 020 7388 2227
ceo@artsline.org.uk
www.artsline.org.uk

Artswork National Youth Arts Development Agency
National, independent youth arts development agency, committed to making a difference to the lives of young people at risk
Unit 26, Bargate Shopping Centre, East Bargate Southampton SO14 1HF
02380 332491
info@artswork.org.uk
www.artswork.org.uk

ArtWatch UK
Campaigning body of artists & art historians opposed to the damaging effects of modern, invasive restorations on our artistic heritage
Tel: 0208 216 3492
artwatch.uk@gmail.com
www.artwatch.org.uk

Arvon Foundation The Foundation for Writing
Runs residential creative writing courses for adults and groups of young people at centres in Devon, Shropshire, W. Yorkshire and Inverness
Free Word 60 Farringdon Road London EC1R 3GA
Tel: 020 7324 2554
london@arvonfoundation.org
www.arvonfoundation.org

ASBAH now see Shine

ASDAN
Curriculum development organisation and internationally recognised awarding body, offering programmes and qualifications that explicitly grow skills for learning, skills for employment and skills for life
Wainbrook House Hudds Vale Rd St George Bristol BS5 7HY
Tel : 0117 941 1126
info@asdan.org.uk
www.asdan.org.uk

ASH Action on Smoking and Health
First Floor 144-145 Shoreditch High Street London E1 6JE
Tel: 0207 739 5902
enquiries@ash.org.uk
www.ash.org.uk

ASH Scotland Action on Smoking and Health
Working for a tobacco-free Scotland
8 Frederick St Edinburgh EH2 2HB
Tel: 0131 225 4725
ashscotland@ashscotland.org.uk
www.ashscotland.org.uk

ASH Wales Action on Smoking and Health
Towards a tobacco free Wales
2nd Floor, 8 Museum Place Cardiff CF10 3BG
Tel: 029 2064 1101
email via website
www.ashwales.org.uk

Ashmolean Museum of Art and Archaeology
Beaumont St Oxford OX1 2PH
Tel: 01865 278002
www.ashmolean.org/

Asian People's Disability Alliance APDA
Alric Avenue off Bruce Road London NW10 8RA
Tel: 020 8459 1030
apdmcha@aol.com
www.apda.org.uk

Asiatic Society of Great Britain and Ireland (Royal)
Provides a forum for those who are interested in the history, languages, cultures and religions of Asia to meet and exchange ideas. It offers lectures and seminars and it provides facilities for research and publishing
14 Stephenson Way London NW1 2HD
Tel: 020 7388 4539
email via website
www.royalasiaticsociety.org

Ask The Police
Access to the Police National Legal Database with an a-z of frequently asked questions. Intended to reduce the number of non-emergency calls to police forces by providing the answers direct to the public via the Internet
www.askthe.police.uk/content

Aslib see Information Management (Association for)

ASPE Association for the Study of Primary Education
Aims to promote and foster the development of informed and reflective study of Early Years and Primary Education
The Swallow Barn Brandon Court Station Road Long Marston Herts HP23 4RA
mary@swallowbarn.fsnet.co.uk
www.aspe-uk.eu

Aspect The Association of Professionals in Education and Children's Trusts
Professional association and trade union
Woolley Hall Woolley Wakefield West Yorkshire WF4 2JR
Tel: 01226 383 428
info@aspect.org.uk
www.aspect.org.uk

Aspire Supporting people with spinal injury
Offers practical support to people living with a spinal cord injury in the UK so that they can lead fulfilled and independent lives in their homes, with their families, in work places and in leisure time
National Training Centre Wood Lane Stanmore HA7 4AP
Tel: 020 8954 5759
info@aspire.org.uk
www.aspire.org.uk

Assessment and Qualifications Alliance see AQA

Assisted Dying (Healthcare Professionals for) HPAD
Supporting greater patient choice at the end of life
email via website
www.hpad.org.uk

Associated Board of the Royal Schools of Music
24 Portland Place London W1B 1LU
Tel: 020 7636 5400
email via website
www.abrsm.org

Association for the Protection of Rural Scotland see Rural Scotland (Association for the Protection of)

Association of Colleges AOC
Promotes the interests of further education colleges in England and Wales.
2-5 Stedham Place London WC1A 1HU
Tel: 020 7034 9900
enquiries@aoc.co.uk
www.aoc.co.uk

Asthma UK
Independent UK charity
Summit House 70 Wilson Street London
EC2A 2DB
Advice Line: 0800 121 62 44
Tel: 0800 121 62 55
info@asthma.org.uk
www.asthma.org.uk

Astrological and Psychic Society (British)
Communications House 26 York Street,
London, W1U 6PZ
Tel: 0207 111 0912
enquiries@baps.uk.com
www.baps.uk.com

Astronomical Association (British)
Burlington House Piccadilly London W1J
0DU
Tel: 0207 734 4145
Email via website
www.britastro.org

Astronomy see Dark Skies (Campaign for),
Popular Astronomy (Society for)

Asylum see also Immigration & Asylum
Tribunals Service

Asylum Aid
Free advice & legal representation to
refugees and asylum-seekers. Campaigns for
their rights
Club Union House 253-254 Upper Street
London N1 1RY
Advice line number: 0207 354 9264
Tel: 0207 354 9631
info@asylumaid.org.uk
www.asylumaid.org.uk

Ataxia UK
National charity working with and for people
affected by Friedreich's and other cerebellars
ataxias
Lincoln House Kennington Park 1-3 Brixton
Road London SW9 6DE
Helpline: 0845 644 0606
Tel: 020 7582 1444
office@ataxia.org.uk
www.ataxia.org.uk

ATD Fourth World
Aims to eradicate extreme poverty.
Organises summer volunteering
opportunities in Europe and long term
volunteer work worldwide
48 Addington Sq London SE5 7LB
Tel: 0207 703 3231
atd@atd-uk.org
www.atd-uk.org

Athletic Association (English Schools')
ESAA
Governing body of schools athletics in
England
email via website
www.esaa.net

Athletics see also England Athletics,
scottishathletics, UK Sport, Welsh Athletics

Athletics Federations (International Association of) IAAF
Email via website
www.iaaf.org

ATM locator
Search facility to find ATMs worldwide
visa.via.infonow.net/locator/global

Atmospheric Research (National Center for) NCAR
www.ncar.ucar.edu

ATSS see Social Sciences (Association for the
Teaching of the)

Attend
Independent local charities which care
for and support people disadvantaged by
illness, age or disability
11-13 Cavendish Square London W1G 0AN
Tel: 0845 450 0285
info@attend.org.uk
www.attend.org.uk

Attorney General's Office
20 Victoria Street London SW1H 0NF
Tel: 020 7271 2492
correspondenceunit@attorneygeneral.gsi.
gov.uk
www.attorneygeneral.gov.uk

Audit Commission
Helps to improve public services and
promotes the best use of public money
1st Floor Millbank Tower Millbank London
SW1P 4HQ
Textphone (minicom): 020 7630 0421
Tel: 020 7828 1212
Tel: 0844 798 1212
email via website
www.audit-commission.gov.uk

Audit Office (National)
Monitors central government spending
157-197 Buckingham Palace Road London
SW1W 9SP
Helpdesk: 020 7798 7264
Tel: 020 7798 7000
enquiries@nao.gsi.gov.uk
www.nao.gov.uk

Australian Bureau of Statistics
www.abs.gov.au

Authors' Licensing and Collecting Society
The Writers' House 13 Haydon Street
EC3N 1DB
Tel: 020 7264 5700
alcs@alcs.co.uk
www.alcs.co.uk

Autistic Society (National)
Helpline, information service and support services
393 City Rd London EC1V 1NG
Helpline: 0808 800 4104
Tel: 020 7833 2299
nas@nas.org.uk
www.autism.org.uk

Automobile Association (AA)
www.theaa.com

AV Foundation Helping Transform Lives Through Education
Channels funds into the rural areas to which it sends volunteers. Objective is to boost the quality of school education in the communities served by AV (Africa Asia Venture) volunteers
10 Market Place Devizes Wiltshire SN10 1HT
Tel: 01380 729009
av@aventure.co.uk
www.avfoundation.org

Avalanche Information Service see
sportscotland Avalanche Information Service

AVERT
Charity involved in HIV/AIDS education, research and care projects worldwide
4 Brighton Rd Horsham West Sussex RH13 5BA
Tel: 01403 210202
info@avert.org
www.avert.org

Avicultural Society
Covers the keeping and breeding of all types of birds other than domesticated varieties
Sheraton Lodge Station Road Southminster Essex CM0 7EW
admin@avisoc.co.uk
www.avisoc.co.uk

Award Scheme now see ASDAN

Awesome Library
American educational website
www.awesomelibrary.org

B

BAAF Adoption and Fostering (British Association for)
Saffron House 6-10 Kirby Street
London EC1N 8TS
Tel: 0207 421 2600
mail@baaf.org.uk
www.baaf.org.uk

BAB see Aikido Board (British)

BABCP see Behavioural & Cognitive Psychotherapies (British Association of)

Baby Lifeline
Supports the care of pregnant mothers & newborn babies
Empathy Enterprise Building Bramston Crescent Tile Hill Coventry CV4 9SW
Tel: 024 7642 2135
info@babylifeline.org.uk
www.babylifeline.org.uk

Baby Milk Action
Aims to save infant lives & end avoidable suffering caused by inappropriate infant feeding
34 Trumpington Street Cambridge CB2 1QY
Tel: 01223 464420
email via website
www.babymilkaction.org

Babyworld
Online magazine and discussion group
www.babyworld.co.uk

Baccalaureate see International Baccalaureate Organization

Bach Centre
Home of Dr Edward Bach and the Bach flower based remedies, information, education & manufacture. Referral to practitioners
Mount Vernon Bakers Ln
Brightwell-cum-Sotwell Oxon OX10 0PZ
Consultation line: 01491 832 877
Tel: 01491 834 678
email via website
www.bachcentre.com

Back-up Trust Transforming lives after spinal cord injury
Works with people paralysed through spinal cord injury to rebuild self confidence and independence
Jessica House Red Lion Square 191 Wandsworth High Street London SW18 4LS
Tel: 020 8875 1805
admin@backuptrust.org.uk
www.backuptrust.org.uk

BackCare
National charity that aims to reduce the impact of back pain on society. Provides information and support
16 Elmtree Rd Teddington TW11 8ST
Helpline: 0845 130 2704
Tel: 020 8977 5474
email via website
www.backcare.org.uk

Backpackers Club
A club for the lightweight camper, who travels on foot, by bicycle, canoe or cross-country ski
inforequest@backpackersclub.co.uk
www.backpackersclub.co.uk

Badger Trust
Promotes the conservation and welfare of badgers and the protection of their setts and habitats for the public benefit
PO Box 708 East Grinstead RH19 2WN
Tel: 08458 287878
email via website
www.badgertrust.org.uk

Badminton England
National Badminton Centre
Milton Keynes MK8 9LA
Tel: 01908 268400
enquiries@badmintonengland.co.uk
www.badmintonengland.co.uk

Ballet see also Birmingham Royal Ballet, Bolshoi Ballet, English National Ballet, London Children's Ballet, National Youth Ballet of Great Britain, Northern Ballet, Royal Academy of Dance, Royal Ballet, Scottish Ballet & see thematic guide Dance and also section on Dance, Drama, Music & Performing Arts Schools

Ballet Organization (British)
A teaching and examining society for ballet, jazz, modern and tap
Woolborough House 39 Lonsdale Rd Barnes London SW13 9JP
Tel: 020 8748 1241
info@bbo.org.uk
www.bbo.org.uk

Balloon and Airship Club (British)
Cushy Dingle Watery Lane Llanishen Monmouthshire NP16 6QT
information@bbac.org
www.bbac.org

BALTIC The Centre for Contemporary Art
Gateshead Quays South Shore Rd
Gateshead NE8 3BA
Tel: 0191 478 1810
Text phone: 0191 440 4944
info@balticmill.com
www.balticmill.com

Banana Link
Working towards a fair and sustainable banana industry
.42-58 St George's Street Norwich NR3 1AB
Tel: 01603 765670
email via website
www.bananalink.org.uk

Bank of England
Threadneedle St London EC2R 8AH
Tel: 020 7601 4444 (switchboard)
Tel: 020 7601 4878 (public enquiries)
enquiries@bankofengland.co.uk
www.bankofengland.co.uk

Bank of England (Damaged and Mutilated Banknotes)
The Manager, Dept MN, Bank of England
King Street Leeds LS1 1HT
Tel: 0113 244 1711
www.bankofengland.co.uk/banknotes/damaged_banknotes.htm

Bank of England Museum
Free presentations for groups
Threadneedle St London EC2R 8AH
Tel: 020 7601 5545
museum@bankofengland.co.uk
www.bankofengland.co.uk/museum

Banking Ombudsman see Financial Ombudsman Service

Bankruptcy Advisory Service Limited
PO Box 155 Knaresborough North Yorkshire HG5 0UE
Tel 01423 862114
gill@bankruptcyadvisoryservice.co.uk
www.bankruptcyadvisoryservice.co.uk

Baobab Centre for Young Survivors in Exile
Specialises in therapeutic services to children, adolescents and young people who arrive in Britain each year fleeing from the trauma of political violence
6-9 Manor Gardens London N7 6LA
Tel: 020 7263 1301
email via website
www.baobabsurvivors.org

BAPA Activity Providers Association (British)
Trade association for private sector providers of activity holidays and courses in the UK.
Tel: 01746 769982
info@thebapa.org.uk
www.thebapa.org.uk

Bar Council
Regulatory & representative body for barristers in England & Wales
289-293 High Holborn London WC1V 7HZ
Tel: 020 7242 0082
ContactUs@BarCouncil.org.uk
www.barcouncil.org.uk

Bar Pro Bono Unit
Free legal advice and representation in deserving cases where Legal Aid is not available
48 Chancery Lane London WC2A 1JF
Tel: 020 7092 3960
enquiries@barprobono.org.uk
www.barprobono.org.uk

Barbershop Singers (British Association of)
Promoting the enjoyment of harmony singing
www.singbarbershop.com

Barbican
Silk Street London EC2Y 8DS
Tel: 020 7638 4141 (switchboard)
Tel: 020 7382 7211 (Group Bookings)
Tel: 020 7638 8891 (Box Office & members
email via website
www.barbican.org.uk

Barnardo's
Campaigning, lobbying and research to improve outcomes for children young people and families. Works with families
Tanners Lane Barkingside Ilford IG6 1QG
Tel: 020 8550 8822
email via website
www.barnardos.org.uk

Bartleby.com
Hundreds of out-of-copyright books, all digitised and free
www.bartleby.com

BASCA Songwriters, Composers and Authors (British Academy of)
Membership organisation for music writers of all genres
British Music House 26 Berners St
London W1T 3LR
email via website
www.basca.org.uk

Basel Action Network (BAN)
Confronting the toxic trade (toxic wastes, products and technologies) and its devastating impacts.
contact@ban.org
www.ban.org

BASIC Brain & Spinal Injury Centre
Provides counselling, information and support to patients and their families following brain or spinal injury
554 Eccles New Rd Salford M5 5AP
National Helpline: 0870 750 0000
Tel: 0161 707 6441
enquiries@basiccharity.org.uk
www.basiccharity.org.uk

Basketball Association (English)
Governing body
PO Box 3971 Sheffield S9 9AZ
Tel: 0114 284 1060
info@englandbasketball.co.uk
www.englandbasketball.co.uk

BASPCAN British Association for the Study and Prevention of Child Abuse and Neglect
Registered charity that aims to prevent physical, emotional and sexual abuse and neglect of children by promoting the physical, emotional, and social well-being of children. Aims to promote the rights of children as citizens, through multi-disciplinary collaboration, education, campaigning etc
17 Priory St York YO1 6ET
Tel: 01904 613605
baspcan@baspcan.org.uk
www.baspcan.org.uk

Bat Conservation Trust
5th Floor Quadrant House 250 Kennington Lane London SE11 5RD
Helpline: 0845 1300 228
enquiries@bats.org.uk
www.bats.org.uk

Battersea Dogs Home
4 Battersea Park Rd London SW8 4AA
Tel: 020 7622 3626
email via website
www.battersea.org.uk

BBC
www.bbc.co.uk

BBC Backstage Tours
www.bbc.co.uk/showsandtours/tours

BBC Health
Access to information about a wide range of illnesses and conditions
www.bbc.co.uk/health/conditions

BBC News
http://news.bbc.co.uk

BBC Online
Covers all BBC programmes plus sections on business, health, lifestyle, science
www.bbc.co.uk

BBC Schools
Email via website
www.bbc.co.uk/schools

BBC Studio Audiences
Apply for free tickets to watch live & recorded TV shows
www.bbc.co.uk/tickets/

BBC World Service
www.bbc.co.uk/worldservice

BCS - Chartered Institute for IT
Promotes the global IT profession and the interests of individuals engaged in that profession for the benefit of all
1st Floor, Block D North Star House North Star Ave Swindon SN2 1FA
Tel: 01793 417424
Tel: 0845 300 4417 (lo-call rate)
Email via website
www.bcs.org/

BDA see Dyslexia Association (British)

Beamish Museum
Recreates Northern life in the early 1800s and 1900s.
Beamish Museum Beamish Co. Durham DH9 0RG
Tel: 0191 370 4000
museum@beamish.org.uk
www.beamish.org.uk

BEAT Beating Eating Disorders
Raises awareness & offers support to people affected by eating disorders
103 Prince of Wales Rd Norwich NR1 1DW
Helpline: 0845 634 1414
Youthline:0845 634 7650
Tel: 01603 619090
Head Office: 0300 123 3355
help@b-eat.co.uk
fyp@b-eat .co.uk
www.b-eat.co.uk

Beatbullying Shaping attitudes, changing behaviours
Empowers people to understand, recognise, and say no to bullying, violence and harassment by giving them the tools to transform their lives and the lives of their peers. Working with families, schools, and communities
Rochester House Units 1, 4 & 5 4 Belvedere Road London SE19 2AT
Tel: 0208 771 3377
info@beatbullying.org
www.beatbullying.org

Beaumont Society
Transgender support group
27 Old Gloucester St London WC1N 3XX
Information Line: 01582 412 220
enquiries@beaumontsociety.org.uk
www.beaumontsociety.org.uk

Befrienders Worldwide with Samaritans
Work worldwide to provide emotional support, and reduce suicide
www.befrienders.org

Behavioural & Cognitive Psychotherapies (British Association for) BABCP
Imperial House Hornby Street Bury BL9 5BN
Tel: 0161 705 4304
babcp@babcp.com
www.babcp.com

Benefits Agency see Work & Pensions (Department for)

Benesh Institute
Training organisation and governing body of Benesh movement notation system
c/o Royal Academy of Dance 36 Battersea Sq London SW11 3RA
Tel: 020 7326 8000
info@rad.org.uk
www.rad.org.uk

Bereavement Network (London)
Forum for bereavement issues in Greater London. Referral line for bereavement support
61 Philpot Street London E1 2JH
info@bereavement.org.uk
www.bereavement.org.uk

Berlin info
Comprehensive information about Berlin
www.berlin-info.de/en/index

Berlin International
Berlin's official Internet site
www.berlin.de/international/index.en.php

Better Seating (Campaign for)
Information about the importance of chair design
22 Leys Avenue Cambridge, CB4 2AW
cambetseat@msn.com
www.betterseating.org

Better Transport (Campaign for)
Sustainable transport campaign aiming to reduce car dependence
16 Waterside 44-48 Wharf Road
London N1 7UX
Tel: 020 7566 6480
info@bettertransport.org.uk
www.bettertransport.org.uk

Bevan Foundation
Radical Welsh think tank concerned with social justice
FREEPOST RSHC-XZZU-UTUU
Innovation Centre Festival Drive Ebbw Vale Blaenau Gwent NP23 8XA
Tel: 01495 356 702
info@bevanfoundation.org
www.bevanfoundation.org

BFI see British Film Institute

BHF see British Heart Foundation

Bibic
Works to maximise the potential of children with conditions affecting behaviour, sensory processing, communication, social, motor and learning abilities.
Knowle Hall Bridgwater Somerset TA7 8PJ
Tel: 01278 684060
info@bibic.org.uk
www.bibic.org.uk

Bible Society
Involved in translation and retranslation projects worldwide. Work to change the public's perception of the Bible in England & Wales
Stonehill Green Westlea Swindon SN5 7DG
Tel: 01793 418 222
email via website
www.biblesociety.org.uk

Bibliomania
Literary texts (particularly those set for exams) available online
www.bibliomania.com

Bibliothèque Nationale de France see
Library of France (National)

Bicycle Helmet Initiative Trust
Promoting and educating about the need to wear bicycle helmets
71 Milford Rd Reading RG1 8LG
Tel: 0118 958 3585
BHIT@dial.pipex.com
www.bhit.org

Big Bus
Fun interactive learning for 3-11 year-olds
Sherston Software Angel House Sherston
Wiltshire SN16 0LH
Tel: 01666 843200
info@sherston.com
www.thebigbus.com

Big Issue
Exists to offer homeless and vulnerably housed people the opportunity to earn a legitimate income by selling the weekly magazine. This selling opportunity is planned to extend to long term unemployed and other vulnerable groups
1-5 Wandsworth Road Vauxhall
LondonSW8 2LN
Tel: 020 7526 3200
info@bigissue.com
www.bigissue.com

Big Lottery Fund
Lottery distribution organisation awarding funds for community projects
1 Plough Place London EC4A 1DE
BIG advice line: 0845 410 2030
Tel: 020 7211 1800
Tel: 0300 500 5050
Textphone: 0845 602 1659
general.enquiries@biglotteryfund.org.uk
www.biglotteryfund.org.uk

Big Pit
National Coal Museum
Blaenafon Torfaen NP4 9XP
Tel: 01495 790 311
Email via website
www.museumwales.ac.uk/en/bigpit

Big Read (The)
Campaign against illiteracy and for a decent education for all
info@campaignforeducation.org
www.campaignforeducation.org/bigread/

BIHR British Institute of Human Rights
School of Law Queen Mary University of Londo Mile End Road London E1 4NS
Tel: 020 7882 5850
info@bihr.org.uk
www.bihr.org.uk

Bike Events
Organises fund raising and recreational cycle rides
PO Box 2127 Bristol BS99 7LN
Email via website
www.bike-events.com

Bike Express (European)
Offer bike transport for you and your bike into Europe
3 Newfield Lane South Cave Hull HU15 2JW
Tel: 01430 422 111
info@bike-express.co.uk
www.bike-express.co.uk

Bike Links see Cycling Projects

Bikers with a Disability (National Association for)
Helps disabled people to enjoy the freedom and independence of motorcycling
Unit 20 The Bridgewater Centre Robson Avenue Urmston Manchester M41 7TE
Tel: 0844 415 4849
office@nabd.org.uk
www.nabd.org.uk

Bilingualism & Literacies Education Network blen
35 Connaught Rd London N4 4NT
Tel: 020 7281 8686
ask@blen-education.org.uk
www.blen-education.org.uk

Bill Douglas Centre for the History of Cinema & Popular Culture see History of Cinema & Popular Culture (The Bill Douglas Centre for the)

Bioethics (Nuffield Council on)
Examining ethical issues around developments in medicine and biology
28 Bedford Square London WC1B 3JS
Tel: 020 7681 9619
bioethics@nuffieldbioethics.org
www.nuffieldbioethics.org

Biological Diversity (Convention on)
International treaty to sustain the rich diversity of life on Earth
www.cbd.int

Biology (Society of)

Advising Government and influencing policy. Advancing education and professional development, supporting our members, and engaging and encouraging public interest in the life sciences
12 Roger Street London WC1N 2JU
020 7685 2550
email via website
www.societyofbiology.org

Biotechnology & Biological Sciences Research Council BBSRC

Explores the science & issues of modern biological research
Polaris House North Star Avenue Swindon Wiltshire SN2 1UH
Tel: 01793 413200
General enquires press.office@bbsrc.ac.uk
www.bbsrc.ac.uk/life

Bird Council (British)

Hampstead House Condover Road West Heath Birmingham B31 3QY
Tel: 0121 476 5999
info@britishbirdcouncil.com
www.britishbirdcouncil.com

Birmingham Royal Ballet

Thorp St Birmingham B5 4AU
Tel: 0121 245 3500
info@brb.org.uk
www.brb.org.uk

Birmingham Settlement

A multi-purpose inner city charity tackling social disadvantage
Units 4-7 Alma House Newtown Shopping Centre Birmingham B19 2AB
Tel: 0121 250 3000
info@bsettlement.org.uk
www.birminghamsettlement.org.uk

Birth Defects Foundation see Newlife
Foundation for Disabled Children

Birth Trauma Association Helping people
traumatised by childbirth

Support for people suffering from Post Natal Post Traumatic Stress Disorder (PTSD) or birth trauma
PO Box 671 Ipswich Suffolk IP1 9AT
enquiries@birthtraumaassociation.org.uk
www.birthtraumaassociation.org.uk

BirthChoice UK

To help make the right decisions about where to have a baby
www.birthchoiceuk.com

BIS see Business Innovation & Skills
(Department for)

Bitesize: BBC revision web site

For KS2, 3 & 4 / Standard Grade
www.bbc.co.uk/schools/bitesize/

BKA British Kodály Academy

Musical literacy through singing
c/o 10 Lapwing Close South Croydon Surrey CR2 8TD
Tel: 020 8651 3728
enquiries@britishkodalyacademy.org
www.britishkodalyacademy.org

Black Environment Network

Networking organisation working for full ethnic participation in the built & natural environment
1st Floor 60 High St Llanberis LL55 4EU
Tel: 0207 9214339
email via website
www.ben-network.org.uk

Black History Month

www.black-history-month.co.uk

Black Police Association (National)

PO Box 15690
Tamworth Staffordshire B77 9HZ
Tel: 07971 162821
Email via website
www.nationalbpa.com

Black Training & Enterprise Group

Seeks to ensure fair access and outcomes for black communities in employment, enterprise and regeneration
2nd Floor 200a Pentonville Road London, N1 9JP
Tel: 0207 832 5800
info@bteg.co.uk
www.bteg.co.uk

Black Women for Wages for Housework

contact Crossroads Women's Centre
www.allwomencount.net

Black Women's Rape Action Project contact
Crossroads Women's Centre
www.allwomencount.net

Bladder and Bowel Foundation (B&BF)

The UK's largest advocacy charity providing information and support for all types of bladder and bowel related problems, including incontinence, prostate problems, constipation and Diverticular Disease, for patients, their families, carers and healthcare professionals
SATRA Innovation Park Rockingham Road Kettering Northants NN16 9JH
Helpline: 0845 345 0165
Tel: 01536 533255
info@bladderandbowelfoundation.org
www.bladderandbowelfoundation.org

Blenheim CDP The London Drug Agency
Substance misuse charity working across
London to reduce the harm caused by
drug misuse to individuals and the public.
Provides opportunity and help for people to
end their dependency on drugs
66 Bolton Crescent London SE5 0SE
Tel: 020 7582 2200
info@blenheimcdp.org.uk
www.blenheimcdp.org.uk

Blind see also Braille Chess Association,
ClearVision Project, Deafblind UK, Deafblind
Scotland, Guide Dogs for the Blind Association,
Listening Books, Partially Sighted Society,
Sense, RNIB, SeeAbility, Sightsavers, Talking
Newspapers and Magazines (National), Wireless
for the Blind Fund (British)

Blind (Royal National Institute of the) RNIB
Supporting blind and partially sighted
people
105 Judd St London WC1H 9NE
Helpline: 0303 123 9999
Tel: 020 7388 1266
helpline@rnib.org.uk
www.rnib.org.uk

Blind Golf Association (English)
email via website
www.blindgolf.co.uk

Blind in Business
Helping blind and partially sighted people
into work
4th floor 1 London Wall Buildings London
EC2M 5PG
Tel: 020 7588 1885
info@blindinbusiness.org.uk
www.blindinbusiness.co.uk

**Blind of the United Kingdom (National
Federation of the)**
Campaigning organisation for a better
quality of life for blind and partially sighted
people
Sir John Wilson House 215 Kirkgate
Wakefield WF1 1JG
Tel: 01924 291 313
nfbuk@nfbuk.org
www.nfbuk.org

Blind People (Action for)
Employment support, hotels, supported
housing, out-of-school clubs for visually
impaired children, grants, information and
advice
14-16 Verney Rd London SE16 3DZ
Helpline: 0303 123 9999
Tel: 020 7635 4800
Email via website
www.actionforblindpeople.org.uk

Blind Sport (British)
Encourages blind and partially sighted
children and adults to take part in sport and
recreation
Pure Offices, Plato Close Tachbrook Park
Leamington Spa Warwickshire CV34 6WE
Tel: 01926 424247
info@britishblindsport.org.uk
www.britishblindsport.org.uk

Bliss For babies born too soon, too small or
too sick
National charity dedicated to improving
both the survival and long-term quality of
life for babies born too soon, too small or too
sick to cope on their own
9 Holyrood Street London Bridge
London SE1 2EL
Family Support Helpline: 0500 618 140
Tel: 020 7378 1122
RNID typetalk 018001 0500 618140
information@bliss.org.uk
www.bliss.org.uk

Bliss Scotland
PO Box 29198 Dunfermline KY12 2BB
Tel: 0845 157 0077
scotland@bliss.org.uk
www.bliss.org.uk

Blogger
A site to help you create and manage a
weblog
www.blogger.com

Blood Pressure Association
Information and support to the general
public on problems of high blood pressure
60 Cranmer Terrace London SW17 0QS
Blood Pressure Information Line: 0845 241
0989
Tel: 020 8772 4994
info@bpassoc.org.uk
www.bpassoc.org.uk

Blood Service (National) see NHS Blood and
Transplant

Blue Badge Network
Assists disabled people, and their families to
integrate with society to overcome access
problems. Seeks to maintain the integrity
and validity of the concessionary parking
permit
11 Parson's Street Dudley DY1 1JJ OR 198
Wolverhampton Street Dudley DY1 1DZ
Tel: 01384 257001
headoffice@bluebadgenetwork.org.uk
www.bluebadgenetwork.org

Blue Cross
Animal welfare charity
Shilton Rd Burford Oxon OX18 4PF
Tel: 0300 777 1897
info@bluecross.org.uk
www.bluecross.org.uk

Blue Lamp Foundation see PC David Rathband's Blue Lamp Foundation

Blurt Foundation
Tackling the stigma of depression, one word at a time
18 The Business Centre 2 Cattedown Road Plymouth PL4 0EG
info@blurtitout.org
blurtitout.org

BMA see British Medical Association

BMAS see Acupuncture Society (British Medical)

BNTL-Freeway British National Temperance League
The 'Freeway' newsletter provides drug and alcohol resources based around the national curriculum
30 Keswick Road Worksop S81 7PT
Tel: 01909 477882
bntl@btconnect.com
www.bntl.org

Boarding Concern
Represents people who have concerns about the practice of boarding education for the young and the effect on these people as adults. This website offers a voice and provides information and support to ex-boarders, current boarders and those thinking of boarding
email via website
www.boardingconcern.org.uk

Boardsailing Association (UK) now see Windsurfing Association

Bob Champion Cancer Trust
Aims to identify cancer genes and ultimately eradicate male cancers
6 Old Garden House The Lanterns Bridge Lane London SW11 3AD
Tel: 020 7924 3553
info@bobchampion.org.uk
www.bobchampion.org.uk

Bodleian Library
Main research library of the University of Oxford and copyright deposit library
Main Enquiry Desk Bodleian Library Broad Street Oxford OX1 3BG
Tel: 01865 277162
reader.services@bodleian.ox.ac.uk
www.bodleian.ox.ac.uk/bodley

Body Shop Foundation
Human/civil rights projects, animals & environment. No unsolicited requests for support
Watersmead Littlehampton West Sussex BN17 6LS
Tel: 01903 844 039
bodyshopfoundation@thebodyshop.com
www.thebodyshopfoundation.org

Bolshoi Ballet
www.bolshoi.ru/en

Bolton Lads & Girls Club
The UK's biggest youth centre
18 Spa Road Bolton BL1 4AG
Tel: 01204 540 100
info@blgc.co.uk
www.boltonladsandgirlsclub.co.uk

Bond
Network of voluntary organisations working in international development
Regent's Wharf 8 All Saints Street London N1 9RL
Tel: 020 7837 8344
advocacy@bond.org.uk
www.bond.org.uk

Bone Marrow donation see Anthony Nolan, NHS Blood and Transplant

Book Aid International
Works in partnership with organisations in developing countries to support their work in literacy, education, training and publishing
39-41 Coldharbour Lane Camberwell London SE5 9NR
Tel: 020 7733 3577
info@bookaid.org
www.bookaid.org

Book Fair see Frankfurt Book Fair

Book Festival see Edinburgh International Book Festival, Hay Festival

Book Trust (Scottish)
Scotland's national agency for readers and writers. Provides key services to readers, writers and the educational sector
Sandeman House Trunk's Close 55 High St Edinburgh EH1 1SR
Tel: 0131 524 0160
info@scottishbooktrust.com
www.scottishbooktrust.com

BookCrossing
Encourages readers to leave books for others in a public place and tracks their progress via the web
www.bookcrossing.com

Books Council (Welsh)
National body which provides a focus for the publishing industry in Wales
www.wbc.org.uk
www.wbc.org.uk/gwales

Booktrust
Book information service, reading resource centre, book prizes, projects and National Children's Book Week
Book House 45 East Hill London SW18 2QZ
Tel: 020 8516 2977
query@booktrust.org.uk
www.booktrust.org.uk
www.booktrustchildrensbooks.org.uk

Border and Immigration Agency now see
UK Border Agency

Borderline
Advice, information & support to homeless
Scots in London
22 City Road London EC1Y 2AJ
Tel: 0845 456 2190
Tel: 0800 174047
email via website
www.borderline-uk.org

Born Free Foundation
Animal welfare and conservation charity.
Works to prevent individual animal suffering,
protect threatened species and keep wildlife
in the wild
3 Grove House Foundry Lane Horsham
RH13 5PL
Tel: 01403 240 170
info@bornfree.org.uk
www.bornfree.org.uk

Botanic Garden of Wales (National)
Llanarthne Carmarthenshire SA32 8HG
Tel: 01558 668 768
info@gardenofwales.org.uk
www.gardenofwales.org.uk

Botanic Gardens see Royal Botanic Gardens,
Edinburgh & Kew

Botanical Society of the British Isles
Botany Department The Natural History
Museum Cromwell Rd London SW7 5BD
email via website
www.bsbi.org.uk

Bounty Healthcare Fund
Raises funds for good causes which make
family life easier
www.bounty.com/charity

Bowel Cancer UK
National charity. Aims to save lives by raising
awareness of bowel cancer, campaigning
for best treatment and care and providing
practical support and advice.
7 Rickett St London SW6 1RU
Helpline: 0800 8 40 35 40
Tel: 020 7381 9711
admin@bowelcanceruk.org.uk or advisory@
bowelcanceruk.org.uk
www.bowelcanceruk.org.uk

Bowling see also Crown Green Bowling
Association (British), Women's Bowling
Federations (English)

Bowling Association Ltd (English Indoor)
National governing body for indoor level
green bowls in England
David Cornwell House Bowling Green
Melton Mowbray LE13 0FA
Tel: 01664 481900
enquiries@eiba.co.uk
www.eiba.co.uk

Bowling Federation (English)
www.fedbowls.co.uk

Boxing see Amateur Boxing Association of
England Ltd., Amateur Boxing Scotland Ltd.

Boys' Brigade
Uniform youth organisation for children and
young people
Felden Lodge Hemel Hempstead HP3 0BL
Tel: 01442 231 681
enquiries@boys-brigade.org.uk
www.boys-brigade.org.uk

BPAS British Pregnancy Advisory Service
Non-profit making charity offering advice
and treatment for unplanned pregnancy and
fertility control
20 Timothys Bridge Road Stratford
Enterprise Park Stratford-upon-Avon CV37
9BF
Advice: 08457 30 40 30
Tel: 0845 365 5050
info@bpas.org
www.bpas.org

Braille Chess Association
Promoting and supporting visually impaired
chess players in the UK
customerservices@braillechess.org.uk
www.braillechess.org.uk

Brain & Spinal Injury Centre see BASIC

Brain & Spine Foundation
A registered charity supporting neuroscience
research projects. Offers information service
and education
3.36 Canterbury Court Kennington Park 1-3
Brixton Road London SW9 6DE
Helpline: 0808 808 1000
Tel: 020 7793 5900
info@brainandspine.org.uk
www.brainandspine.org.uk

Brain Injuries see BASIC, BIBIC, Child Brain
Injury Trust, HEADWAY

Brainwave Unlocking Children's Potential
Therapy & rehabilitation for children with
special needs
Huntworth Gate Bridgwater Somerset TA6
6LQ
Tel: 01278 429 089
Email via website
www.brainwave.org.uk

Brake
Road safety organisation
PO Box 548 Huddersfield HD1 2XZ
Helpline: 0845 603 8570
Tel: 01484 559 909
helpline@brake.org.uk
www.brake.org.uk

Brandon Centre
Free counselling, psychotherapy and contraceptive advice for 12-21 year olds
26 Prince of Wales Rd London NW5 3LG
Tel: 020 7267 4792
reception@brandoncentre.org.uk
www.brandon-centre.org.uk

Brathay Exploration Group
Expeditions in wild parts of the world for 16-25 year olds
Brathay Hall Ambleside Cumbria LA22 0HP
Tel: 015394 33942
admin@brathayexploration.org.uk
www.brathayexploration.org.uk

Brazil's Children Trust (Action for)
Aims to relieve suffering, maintain and educate deprived, children, young people and their families
Level 4, 53 Frith Street London W1D 4SN
Tel: 020 7494 9344
info@abctrust.org.uk
www.abctrust.org.uk

Breakthrough Breast Cancer
Research, campaigning and education - removing the fear of breast cancer
Weston House 246 High Holborn London WC1V 7EX
Freephone Info Line: 08080 100 200
Tel: 020 7025 2400
info@breakthrough.org.uk
www.breakthrough.org.uk

Breast Cancer Care
National organisation offering support and information
5-13 Great Suffolk Street London SE1 0NS
Helpline: 0808 800 6000
Textphone: 0808 800 6001
info@breastcancercare.org.uk
www.breastcancercare.org.uk

Breastfeeding see La Leche League GB

BRIT School for Performing Arts and Technology
Britain's only FREE Performing Arts and Technology School. Dedicated to education and vocational training for the performing arts, media, art and design and the technologies that make performance possible
60 The Crescent Croydon CR0 2HN
Tel: 020 8665 5242
admin@brit.croydon.sch.uk
www.brit.croydon.sch.uk

British Association for the Advancement of Science (BA) now see Science Association (British)

British Council
Cultural, educational & technical co-operation between Britain & other countries
Bridgewater House 58 Whitworth Street Manchester M1 6BB
Tel: 0161 957 7755
general.enquiries@britishcouncil.org
www.britishcouncil.org/

British Cycling
National Governing Body for cycling in the UK whose aim is to inspire participation in cycling as a sport, recreation and sustainable transport through achieving worldwide success
Stuart St Manchester M11 4DQ
Tel: 0161 274 2000
info@britishcycling.org.uk
www.britishcycling.org.uk

British Film Institute BFI
Belvedere Road South Bank Waterloo London SE1 8XT
Tel: 020 7928 3232
Email via website
www.bfi.org.uk

British Heart Foundation
Leading heart research charity
Greater London House 180 Hampstead Road London NW1 7AW
Heart HelpLine: 0300 330 3311
Tel: 020 7554 0000
via website
www.bhf.org.uk

British Jews (Board of Deputies of)
Elected representative body of the British Jewish community.
6 Bloomsbury Square London WC1A 2LP
Tel: 020 7543 5400
info@bod.org.uk
www.bod.org.uk

British Legion (Royal)
Safeguarding the welfare, interests and memory of those who have served in the Armed Forces
199 Borough High Street London SE1 1AA
Legionline: 08457 725 725
Tel: 020 3207 2100
email via website
www.britishlegion.org.uk

British Library
Hold 14 million books, 920,000 journal and newspaper titles, 58 million patents and 3 million sound recordings
St Pancras 96 Euston Rd London NW1 2DB
Tel: 0843 2081144
Minicom: 01937 546860
Customer-Services@bl.uk
www.bl.uk

British Library Sound Archive
Holds recordings of popular, classical & world and traditional music, oral history, drama and literature and wildlife sounds
96 Euston Rd London NW1 2DB
Tel: 020 7412 7831
email via website
www.bl.uk/soundarchive

British Medical Association BMA
Voluntary professional association for doctors
BMA House Tavistock Sq London WC1H 9JP
Tel: 020 7387 4499
Email via website
www.bma.org.uk

British Monarchy (The official website of)
email via website
www.royal.gov.uk

British Museum
Great Russell St London WC1B 3DG
Tel: 020 7323 8299
Tel: 020 7323 8000
information@britishmuseum.org
www.britishmuseum.org

British Overseas NGOs for Development
see Bond

British Pregnancy Advisory Service see
BPAS

British Rowing
Governing body for rowing in GB
6 Lower Mall Hammersmith London W6 9DJ
Tel: 020 8237 6700
info@britishrowing.org
www.britishrowing.org

British Standards Institute BSI
Produces standards and technical regulations for industry and small businesses
389 Chiswick High Rd London W4 4AL
Tel: 020 8996 9001
cservices@bsigroup.com
www.bsigroup.com

Brittle Bone Society
Promotes research & supports people with osteogenesis imperfecta and their families
Grant-Paterson House 30 Guthrie St Dundee DD1 5BS
Tel: 01382 204446
contact@brittlebone.org
www.brittlebone.org

Broadcasting Trust (International)
Educational charity & independent TV production company specialising in development, environment and human rights issues
CAN Mezzanine 32-6 Loman Street London SE1 0EH
Tel: 020 7922 7940
mail@ibt.org.uk
www.ibt.org.uk

Broadway
Support & rehousing services to homeless people in London
15 Half Moon Court Bartholomew Close London EC1A 7H
Tel: 020 7710 0550
reception@broadwaylondon.org
www.broadwaylondon.org

Broken Rainbow UK
Support for lesbian, gay, bisexual and transgender (LGBT) people experiencing domestic violence
J414 Tower Bridge Business Com 100 Clements Rd London SE16 4DG
Helpline: 0300 999 5428
Tel: 08452 60 55 60
mail@broken-rainbow.org.uk
www.broken-rainbow.org.uk

Brontë Parsonage Museum & Brontë Society
Haworth Keighley West Yorkshire BD22 8DR
Tel: 01535 642 323
info@bronte.org.uk
www.bronte.info

Brook
Free sexual health & contraceptive advice service for young people under 25
421 Highgate Studios 53-79 Highgate Rd London NW5 1TL
Tel: 0808 802 1234 (Free & confidential information for under 25s)
Tel: 020 7284 6040
admin@brook.org.uk
www.brook.org.uk

Brooke
Aims to improve the lives of horses, donkeys and mules in some of the world's poorest communities: Africa, Asia & Latin America
30 Farringdon Street London EC4A 4HH
Tel: 0203 012 3456
Email via website
www.thebrooke.org

BSES British Schools Exploring Society
Runs adventure and research expeditions for 16-20 year olds
Royal Geographical Society 1 Kensington Gore London SW7 2AR
Tel: 020 7591 3141
info@bses.org.uk
www.bses.org.uk

BSI see British Standards Institute

BTCV British Trust for Conservation Volunteers
Working to bring about positive environmental change
Sedum House Mallard Way Doncaster DN4 8DB
Tel: 01302 388883
information@tcv.org.uk
www2.btcv.org.uk

BTCV Scotland
Balallan House 24 Allan Park Stirling FK8 2QG
Tel: 01786 479697
scotland@tcv.org.uk
www2.btcv.org.uk/display/btcv_scotland

BTCV Wales
Scottish environmental conservation charity
The Conservation Centre Forest Farm Road
Whitchurch Cardiff CF14 7JJ
Tel: 029 2052 0990
wales@btcv.org.uk
www2.btcv.org.uk/display/btcv_wales

BTEC see Edexel

BUAV British Union for the Abolition of Vivisection
Campaigns peacefully to create a world where nobody wants or believes we need to experiment on animals
16A Crane Grove London N7 8NN
Tel: 020 7700 4888
info@buav.org
www.buav.org

Buddhist Centre (North London)
72 Holloway Rd London N7 8JG
Tel: 020 7700 1177
email via website
www.northlondonbuddhistcentre.com

Buddhist Information Network
www.buddhanet.net

Buddhist Society
Centre teaching Buddhism and meditation.
Also large Buddhist library and bookshop
58 Eccleston Sq London SW1V 1PH
Tel: 020 7834 5858
info@thebuddhistsociety.org
www.thebuddhistsociety.org

Budgerigar Society
Spring Gardens Northampton NN1 1DR
Tel: 01604 624549
www.budgerigarsociety.com

Bugatti Trust
To preserve and make available for study the works of Ettore Bugatti
Prescott Hill Gotherington Cheltenham Gloucestershire GL52 9RD
Tel: 01242 677201
Email via website
www.bugatti-trust.co.uk

Building & Social Housing Foundation
BSHF
Carries out research into low cost housing around the world
Memorial Square Coalville Leicestershire LE67 3TU
Tel: 01530 510444
bshf@bshf.org
www.bshf.org

Building Societies see also Ecology Building Society, Financial Ombudsman Service

Building Societies Members Association
Fighting to maintain mutuality & accountability of the building societies to their members
49 Clifford Avenue Taunton
Somerset TA2 6DL
Tel: 01823 321 304
Info@building-societies-members.org.uk
www.building-societies-members.org.uk

Bully Free Zone
Provides a service for children and young people who have issues around bullying
50 Chorley New Road
Bolton BL1 4AP
Tel: 01204 454 958
office@bullyfreezone.co.uk
www.bullyfreezone.co.uk

Bullying see also Anti-Bullying Alliance, Anti-Bullying Network, Beatbullying, Childline, CyberMentors, Kidscape

Bullying UK
Part of Family Lives, a national charity providing help and support in all aspects of family life. Offers advice to young people and parents and guidance for schools
CAN Mezzanine 49-51 East Road
London N1 6AH
Parentline: 0808 800 2222 (free)
Tel: 020 7553 3080
parentsupport@familylives.org.uk
www.bullying.co.uk

Bungee Jumping see Elastic Rope Sports Association (British)

Burma Campaign UK
Human rights & democracy in Burma
28 Charles Square London N1 6HT
Tel: 020 73244710
info@burmacampaign.org.uk
www.burmacampaign.org.uk

Burrell Collection
A unique art collection including medieval art, tapestries and stained glass
Pollok Country Park 2060 Pollokshaws Rd
Glasgow G43 1AT
Tel: 0141 287 2550
Text Phone: 0141 287 0047
museums@glasgowlife.org.uk
www.glasgowlife.org.uk

Bus Users UK
To give bus passengers a voice
PO Box 119 Shepperton TW17 8UX
Tel: 01932 232574
enquiries@bususers.org
www.bususers.org

Business & Professional Women UK Ltd
Lobbying training and networking
organisation for working women
74 Fairfield Rise Billericay Essex CM12 9NU
Tel: 01277 623 867
hq@bpwuk.co.uk
www.bpwuk.co.uk

Business & Technology Education Council (BTEC) see Edexel

Business Gateway
Practical help, advice and support for new
and growing businesses in Scotland
Tel: 0845 609 6611
www.bgateway.com

Business in Sport & Leisure BISL
Umbrella organisation for private sector
companies
Tel: 020 8255 3782
email via website
www.bisl.org

Business in the Community
Companies across the UK committed to
improving their positive impact on society
137 Shepherdess Walk London N1 7RQ
Tel: 020 7566 8650
information@bitc.org.uk
www.bitc.org.uk

Business, Enterprise and Regulatory Reform (Department for) now see Business Innovation & Skills (Department for)

Business, Innovation & Skills (Department for) BIS
1 Victoria St London SW1H 0ET
Tel: 020 7215 5000
Minicom: 020 7215 6740
email via website
www.bis.gov.uk/

Butterfly Conservation
UK charity taking action to save butterflies,
moths and their habitats
Manor Yard East Lulworth Wareham Dorset
BH20 5QP
Tel: 01929 400 209
info@butterfly-conservation.org
www.butterfly-conservation.org

& N. Ireland
3 New Line Crossgar Downpatrick BT30 9EP
Tel: 07584 597690
bcni@btconnect.com

& Scotland
Balallan House Allan Park Stirling FK8 2QG
Tel: 01786 447753
scotland@butterfly-conservation.org

& Wales
10 Calvert Terrace Swansea SA1 6AR
Tel: 01792 642972
wales@butterfly-conservation.org

Butterfly Project
Created for self-harmers who feel they are
ready to stop and need the motivation or
support to do so
Magdalen House 3 Magdalen Street Eye
Suffolk IP23 7AJ
www.recoveryourlife.com

Buy Nothing Day (UK)
Challenges consumer culture. Takes place on
the last Saturday in November
www.buynothingday.co.uk

Byways & Bridleways Trust
Registered charity, formed to protect the
public rights that exist over the many ancient
lanes that form part the British landscape
and, our traditional means of travel
PO Box 117 Newcastle upon Tyne NE3 5YT
editor@bbtrust.org.uk
www.bbtrust.org.uk

C

CAA Civil Aviation Authority
Responsible for air safety, economic regulation, airspace regulation, consumer protection, environmental research and consultancy
CAA House 45-59 Kingsway London WC2B 6TE
Tel: 020 7379 7311
infoservices@caa.co.uk
www.caa.co.uk

CAAT see Campaign Against Arms Trade

CABE now see Design Council

Cabinet Office
70 Whitehall
London SW1A 2AS
Tel: 020 7276 3000
Email via website
www.cabinetoffice.gov.uk

CACHE Council for Awards in Children's Care and Education
Apex House 81 Camp Road St Albans Hertfordshire AL1 5GB
Tel: 0845 347 2123
info@cache.org.uk
www.cache.org.uk

CADD Campaign Against Drinking & Driving
Provide support for the families of victims killed and injured by drunk or drugged motorists
PO Box 62 Brighouse West Yorkshire HD6 3YY
Helpline: 0845 123 5542
Tel: 0845 1235541
Tel: 0845 1235543
cadd@scard.org.uk
www.cadd.org.uk

Cadw
Protects and conserves the ancient monuments and historic buildings in Wales
Welsh Government Plas Carew Unit 5/7 Cefn Coed Parc Nantgarw Cardiff CF15 7QQ
Tel: 01443 336000
cadw@wales.gsi.gov.uk
www.cadw.wales.gov.uk

CAF see Charities Aid Foundation

Cafcass Children and Family Court Advisory and Support Service
Looks after the interests of children involved in family proceedings. Work with children and their families, and then advise the courts on what is considered to be in the best interests of individual children
6th Floor Sanctuary Buildings Great Smith Street London SW1P 3BT
Tel: 0844 353 3350
webenquiries@cafcass.gsi.gov.uk
www.cafcass.gov.uk

CAFOD Catholic Overseas Development Agency
The official Catholic aid agency for England and Wales
Romero House 55 Westminster Bridge Road London SE1 7JB
Tel: 020 7733 7900
cafod@cafod.org.uk
www.cafod.org.uk

CALM Campaign Against Living Miserably
Encourages young men aged 15 to 35 in Manchester, Merseyside and Bedfordshire to open up and talk about their problems. Helpline open to all ages and sexes
PO Box 68766, London SE1P 4JZ.
Tel: 0800 58 58 58
via website
www.thecalmzone.net

Calvert Trust Kielder
Challenging disability through outdoor adventure
Kielder Water & Forest Park Hexham Northumberland NE48 1BS
Tel: 01434 250232
email via website
www.calvert-trust.org.uk/kielder/kielder

Calvert Trust Exmoor
Wistlandpound Kentisbury Barnstaple Devon EX31 4SJ
Tel: 01598 763221
email via website
www.calvert-trust.org.uk/exmoor/exmoor

Calvert Trust Lake District
Little Crosthwaite Keswick Cumbria CA12 4QD
Tel: 01768 772255
email via website
www.calvert-trust.org.uk/lake-district

Cambridge Past, Present & Future
Aims to protect the character, amenities, historic buildings and settings of Cambridge and its surroundings.
Wandlebury Ring Gog Magog Hills Babraham Cambridge CB22 3AE
Tel: 01223 243830
email via website
www.cambridgeppf.org

CAMFED International
Supporting the education of girls in Africa
24 Castle Street Cambridge CB3 0AJ
Tel: 01223 362648
info@camfed.org
www.camfed.org

Camp Mohawk
A unique and very caring camp offering day care for brain damaged and autistic children from all over England.
Highfield Lane Crazies Hill Wargrave Berkshire RG10 8PU
Tel: 0118 940 4045
info@campmohawk.org.uk
www.campmohawk.org.uk

Campaign Against Arms Trade CAAT
Unit 4, 5-7 Wells Terrace, London, N4 3JU.
Tel: 020 7281 0297
enquiries@caat.org.uk
www.caat.org.uk

Campaign Against Drinking & Driving see
CADD

Campaign Against Living Miserably see
CALM

Campaign for Nuclear Disarmament see
CND, CND (Scottish)

**Campaign for the Protection of Rural
Wales** see Protection of Rural Wales (Campaign
for the)

Campaign to Protect Rural England see
CPRE

Camping and Caravanning Club
The largest and longest established
membership organisation for all types of
camping and caravanning
Greenfields House Westwood Way Coventry
CV4 8JH
Tel: 0845 130 7631
Tel: 024 7647 5448
email via website
www.campingandcaravanningclub.co.uk

CAMRA Campaign for Real Ale
To promote and preserve full-flavoured,
distinctive beers, ciders and perries and the
best features of the pub
230 Hatfield Rd St Albans AL1 4LW
Tel: 01727 867201
camra@camra.org.uk
www.camra.org.uk

Canal & River Trust formerly Waterways
(British)
Developing the potential of canals and rivers
and ensuring their longterm survival
Head Office First Floor North Station House
500 Elder Gate Milton Keynes MK9 1BB
Tel: 0303 040 4040
customer.services@canalrivertrust.org.uk
canalrivertrust.org.uk

Canals see also Inland Waterways Association,
Scottish Canals

Cancer see also ACT – Animal Cancer Trust,
Bob Champion Cancer Trust, Bowel Cancer UK,
Breakthrough Breast Cancer, Breast Cancer
Care, Childhood Eye Cancer Trust, Children
with Cancer, Christian Lewis Trust, CLICSargent,
Core, Ellen MacArthur Trust, Hereditary Breast
Cancer Helpline (National), Jo's Cervical Cancer
Trust, Lavender Trust, Let's Face It, Leukaemia
& Lymphoma Research, Macmillan Cancer
Support, Marie Curie Cancer Care, Mouth
Cancer Foundation, Orchid Cancer Appeal,
Paul's Cancer Support Centre, Prostate Cancer
Charity, Roy Castle Lung Cancer Foundation,
Saving Faces, Teenage Cancer Trust, Tenovus,
Wessex Cancer Trust, World Cancer Research
Fund International, Youth Cancer Trust

Cancer and Leukaemia in Childhood see
CLICSargent

Cancer BACUP now see Macmillan Cancer
Support

Cancer Research Fund see World Cancer
Research Fund International

Cancer Research UK
Angel Building 407 St John Street London
EC1V 4AD
Supporter Services: 0300 123 1861
Tel: 020 7242 0200
email via website
www.cancerresearchuk.org

Cancer Resource Centre now see Paul's
Cancer Support Centre

Cancer Society (American)
www.cancer.org

Cancerbackup now see Macmillan Cancer
Support

CancerHelp UK
Information website from Cancer Research
UK
Nurse: 0808 800 4040
email via website
www.cancerhelp.org.uk

Canine Defence League see Dogs Trust

Canine Partners
Trains assistance dogs for disabled people
Mill Lane Heyshott Midhurst West Sussex
GU29 0ED
Tel: 08456 580 480
email via website
www.caninepartners.co.uk

Canoe Association (Scottish)
Volunteer led, membership based
organisation working to support canoeing
and kayaking in Scotland and the recognised
Governing Body for the sport
Caledonia House 1 Redheughs Rigg
Edinburgh EH12 9DQ
Tel: 0131 317 7314
email via website
www.canoescotland.org

Canoe Association of Northern Ireland
Governing body for canoeing in Northern
Ireland
Unit 2, Rivers Edge 13-15 Ravenhill Road
Belfast BT6 8DN
Tel: 02890 738884
office@cani.org.uk
www.cani.org.uk

Canoe Union (British)
Governing body of sport for canoe & kayak in the UK
18 Market Place Bingham Nottingham NG13 8AP
Tel: 0845 370 9500
Tel: 0300 0119 500
Info@bcu.org.uk
www.bcu.org.uk

Canoe Wales
National governing body for paddle sport in Wales
National White Water Centre Frongoch Bala Gwynedd LL23 7NU
Tel: 01678 521199
admin@canoewales.com
www.canoewales.com

Canon Collins Trust Education for Southern Africa
22 The Ivories 6 Northampton St London N1 2HY
Tel: 020 7354 1462
info@canoncollins.org.uk
www.canoncollins.org.uk

Captive Animals' Protection Society
Campaigns against use of animals in circuses & zoos
PO Box 540 Salford M5 0DS
Tel: 0845 330 3911
info@captiveanimals.org
www.captiveanimals.org

Caravan Club
East Grinstead House East Grinstead West Sussex RH19 1UA
Tel: 01342 326944
enquiries@caravanclub.co.uk
www.caravanclub.co.uk

Caravanning see also Camping & Caravanning Club

Carbon Neutral Company
Plants trees to offset carbon emissions
Bravington House 2 Bravington Walk Regent Quarter Kings Cross London N1 9AF
Tel: 020 7833 6000
email via website
www.carbonneutral.com

Carbon Trust
Provides specialist support to business and the public sector to help cut carbon emissions, save energy and commercialise low carbon technologies
4th Floor,Dorset House, 27-45 Stamford Street, London SE1 9NT
Tel: 0800 085 2005
customer centreTel: 020 7170 7000
email via website
www.carbontrust.co.uk

Cardiac Risk in the Young CRY
Raises awareness of conditions that can lead to Young Sudden Cardiac Death (YSCD), Sudden Death Syndrome (SDS) and Sudden Arrhythmic Death Syndrome (SADS)
Unit 7 Epsom Downs Metro Centre Waterfield, Tadworth Surrey KT20 5LR
Tel: 01737 363 222
cry@c-r-y.org.uk
www.c-r-y.org.uk

Cards for Little Lives
Unique resource for primary schools. Learning for well-being through prompted discussion in PSHE
8 Wakley Street London EC1V 7QE
tel: 020 78431160
fcrow@ncb.org.uk
www.cardsforlittlelives.org.uk

CARE now see Self Unlimited

Care Council for Wales Cyngor Gofal Cymru
South Gate House Wood Street Cardiff CF10 1EW
Tel: 0300 30 33 444
info@ccwales.org.uk
www.ccwales.org.uk

Care for the Wild International
Charity dedicated to protecting wild animals
72 Brighton Road Horsham West Sussex RH13 5BU
Tel: 01403 249832
info@careforthewild.com
www.careforthewild.com

CARE International UK
Development charity helping world's poorest and most vulnerable people
9th Floor 89 Albert Embankment London SE1 7TP
Tel: (0) 20 7091 6000
email via website
www.careinternational.org.uk

Care Not Killing
Promoting palliative care, opposing euthanasia and assisted suicide
6 Marshalsea Road London SE1 1HL
Tel: 020 7234 9680
info@carenotkilling.org.uk
www.carenotkilling.org.uk

Care Quality Commission
Independent regulator of health and social care in England. Aims to make sure better care is provided for everyone, whether that's in hospital, in care homes, in people's own homes, or elsewhere
Citygate Gallowgate Newcastle upon Tyne NE1 4PA
Tel: 03000 616161
email via website
www.cqc.org.uk

Career Development Loans
A deferred repayment loan providing individuals with help to fund vocational education or learning
www.direct.gov.uk/cdl

Careers Research & Advisory Centre see CRAC

Carers Trust formerly Crossroads Care & Princess Royal Trust for Carers
Support for carers and the people they care for
32-36 Loman Street London SE1 0EH
Tel: 0844 800 4361
info@carers.org
www.carers.org

& Wales Office
Third Floor 33-35 Cathedral Road Cardiff CF11 9HB
Tel: 0292 009 0087
info@carers.org
www.carers.org

& Glasgow Office
Charles Oakley House 125 West Regent Street Glasgow G2 2SD
Tel: 0141 221 5066
info@carers.org
www.carers.org
NB The Glasgow office has retained the name 'Princess Royal Trust for Carers"

Carers UK
Information and advice on all aspects of caring
20 Great Dover Street London SE1 4LX
Adviceline: 0808 808 7777
Tel: 020 7378 4999
email via website
www.carersuk.org

& Northern Ireland
58 Howard Street Belfast BT1 6JP
Adviceline: 0808 808 7777
Tel: 028 9043 4700
email via website
www.carersuk.org

& Scotland
The Cottage 21 Pearce Street Glasgow G51 3UT
Adviceline: 0808 808 7777
Tel: 0141 445 3070
email via website
www.carersuk.org

& Wales
River House Ynys Bridge Court Cardiff CF15 9SS
Adviceline: 0808 808 7777
Tel: 02920 811 370
email via website
www.carersuk.org

CaSE - Campaign for Science & Engineering in the UK
An independent campaign for effective policies for science, engineering, technology and medicine and a proper appreciation of their cultural and economic importance
Gordon House 29 Gordon Square London WC1H 0PP
Tel: 020 7679 4994/5
info@sciencecampaign.org.uk
www.sciencecampaign.org.uk

Cash machines see ATM locator

Casualties Union
Recruits volunteers to act as casualties in first aid and rescue practice
PO Box 1942 London E17 6YU
Tel: 08700 780590
hq@casualtiesunion.org.uk
www.casualtiesunion.org.uk

Cat Fancy (Governing Council of the)
Registers pedigree cats
5 King's Castle Business Park The Drove Bridgewater Somerset TA6 4AG
Tel: 01278 427 575
info@gccfcats.org
www.gccfcats.org

Catch22
National charity that works with young people who find themselves in difficult situations
Churchill House 142-146 Old Street London EC1V 9BW
Tel: 020 7336 4800
information@catch-22.org.uk
www.catch-22.org.uk

Catholic Education Service Promoting & Supporting Catholic Education in England & Wales
Negotiates on behalf of all bishops, with Government, and other national bodies on legal, administrative, and religious education matters
39 Eccleston Square London SW1V 1BX
Tel: 0207 901 1900
email via website
www.cesew.org.uk

Cats Protection
UK's oldest and largest feline charity offering rescue, rehabilitation and rehoming services
National Cat Centre Chelwood Gate Sussex RH17 7TT
National helpline: 03000 12 12 12
Tel: 08707 708 649
helpline@cats.org.uk
www.cats.org.uk

Caving Association (British)
The Old Methodist Chapel Great Hucklow Buxton SK17 8RG
www.british-caving.org.uk

CCETSA see Canon Collins Trust

CEH Centre for Ecology & Hydrology
Environmental research
Maclean Building Benson Lane Crowmarsh
Gifford Wallingford Oxfordshire OX10 8BB
Tel: 01491 838800
Tel: 01491 692371 (enquiries)
enquiries@ceh.ac.uk
www.ceh.ac.uk

Cello Society (Internet)
International cyber-community of cellists,
seeks to advance the knowledge and joy of
cello playing around the world
www.cello.org

CEMVO (Scotland) Council of Ethnic Minority
Voluntary Sector Organisations
Charity for the social regeneration of Black &
Minority Ethnic Communities
Lancefield House 1st Floor, 95 - 107
Lancefield Street Glasgow G3 8HZ
Tel: 0141 248 4830
email via website
www.cemvoscotland.org.uk

Census see 1901 Census for England & Wales,
Family Search, FreeBMD, Indian Census,
National Archives, National Records of Scotland
(NRS), Office for National Statistics, Register
Office for N. Ireland (General)

Centre for Alternative Technology see
Alternative Technology (Centre for)

Centre for Economic & Social Inclusion
Promoting social inclusion in the labour
market
3rd Floor Camelford House 89 Albert
Embankment London SE1 7TP
Tel: 020 7582 7221
info@cesi.org.uk
www.cesi.org.uk

Centrepoint
Runs emergency shelters and
accommodation in Greater London for
homeless young people (16-25)
Central House 25 Camperdown Street
London E1 8DZ
Tel: 0845 466 3400
email via website
www.centrepoint.org.uk

Ceroc
Biggest dance club in the world. Dance style
sometimes referred to as 'Modern Jive' - a
fusion of Salsa, Ballroom, Hip Hop, Tango
and Jive
77 Fernhead Road London W9 3EA
Tel: 020 8969 4401
email via website
www.ceroc.com

Certificate ordering service
General Register Office for England and
Wales online ordering service and official
information on births, marriages and deaths
www.gro.gov.uk/gro/content/certificates/
default.asp

Certification Officer
Maintains a list of trade unions and
employers' associations
22nd Floor Euston Tower 286 Euston Road
London NW1 3JJ
Tel: 020 7210 3734
info@certoffice.org
www.certoffice.org

Chain of Hope
Chain of Hope exists to provide children
suffering from life-threatening disease with
the corrective surgery and treatment to
which they do not have access
South Parade Chelsea London SW3 6NP
Tel: 020 7351 1978
email via website
www.chainofhope.org

Chambers of Commerce (British)
65 Petty France London SW1H 9EU
Tel: 020 7654 5800
info@britishchambers.org.uk
www.britishchambers.org.uk

Chance UK
Early intervention in the lives of vulnerable
children, to build a brighter future. Provides
mentoring programmes for children aged
5-11 years with behavioural difficulties
2nd Floor, London Fashion Cent 89-93
Fonthill Rd London N4 3JH
Tel: 020 7281 5858
admin@chanceuk.com
www.chanceuk.com

Changemakers
A charity which encourages young people
to tackle issues of concern to themselves,
their community and to the world in which
they live
22 Upper Woburn Place London WC1H 0TB
Tel: 020 7554 2840
info@changemakers.org.uk
www.changemakers.org.uk

Changing Faces
Advice & counselling for children and adults
with disfigurements and promotion of public
awareness
The Squire Centre 33-37 University Street
London WC1E 6JN
Tel: 0207 391 9270
Tel: 0845 4500 275
info@changingfaces.org.uk
www.changingfaces.org.uk
www.iface.org.uk

Channel 4
www.channel4.com

Channel 5 see Five

Charities Aid Foundation CAF
Not for profit organisation which is
committed to effective giving, providing
a range of specialist services to donors,
companies and charities in the UK and
internationally
25 Kings Hill Avenue Kings Hill West Malling
Kent ME19 4TA
Tel: 03000 123 000
enquiries@cafonline.org
www.cafonline.org

CharitiesDirect.com
A guide to UK charities
www.charitiesdirect.com

Charity Appointments see CF Appointments

Charity Choice
Online Guide to Charities in the UK
www.charitychoice.co.uk

Charity Commission for England & Wales
Registers, supervises and advises charities.
Provides free publications and runs an
outreach and education programme
PO Box 1227 Liverpool L69 3UG
Tel: 0845 300 0218
email via website
www.charity-commission.gov.uk

Charter 88 now see Unlock Democracy

Chartered Management Institute
Professional organisation
2 Savoy Court London WC2R 0EZ
Tel: 020 7497 0580
Tel: 01536 204222
enquiries@managers.org.uk
www.managers.org.uk

Chartered Surveyors (Royal Institute of)
RICS
Professional body for surveyors
Parliament Square London SW1P 3AD
Tel: 0870 333 1600
contactrics@rics.org
www.rics.org

Chartered Surveyors Training Trust
Encourages young people to become
chartered surveyors via other routes than
university
6-8 Gunnery Terrace The Royal Arsenal
London SE18 6SW
Tel: 0207 871 0454
info@cstt.org.uk
www.cstt.org.uk

Chartered Surveyors Voluntary Service
contact Chartered Surveyors (Royal Institute of)
Works with Citizen's Advice Bureaux when a
chartered surveyor can't be afforded

Chemistry (Royal Society of)
The largest organisation in Europe for
advancing the chemical sciences
Burlington House Piccadilly
London W1J 0BA
Tel: 020 7437 8656
email via website
www.rsc.org

Chernobyl Children's Life Line
Supports child victims of radioactivity and
organises recuperative visits to the UK
Courts 61 Petworth Rd Haslemere Surrey
GU27 3AX
Tel: 01428 642 523
email via website
www.chernobylchildlifeline.org

Chess see also Braille Chess Association

Chess Association (English Primary Schools)
Exists to advance the education of
primary school aged children by teaching,
supervising and developing the playing of
chess by those children
www.epsca.org.uk

Chess Federation (English)
Governing body for chess in England
The Watch Oak Chain Lane Battle East
Sussex TN33 0YD
Tel: 01424 775222
office@englishchess.org.uk
www.englishchess.org.uk

Chess Scotland
www.chessscotland.com

Chess Union (Ulster)
www.ulsterchess.org

Chess Union (Welsh)
www.welshchessunion.org.uk

CHICKS Country Holidays for Inner City
Children
Children's charity that provides free respite
breaks for disadvantaged children aged
between 8 and 15 regardless of race or
religion
Moorland Retreat Bonnaford Brentor
Tavistock Devon PL19 0LX
Tel: 01822 811020
info@chicks.org.uk
www.chicks.org.uk

Child & Woman Abuse Studies Unit
Centre for independent research, evaluation,
training, consultancy and networking from a
feminist perspective
London Metropolitan University Ladbroke
House 62-66 Highbury Grove
London N5 2AD
Tel: 020 7133 5014
email via website
www.cwasu.org

Child Abuse see also Africans Unite Against Child Abuse, Barnardo's, Chance UK, Child Protection in Sport Unit, ChildLine, Children 1st, NSPCC

Child Abuse and Neglect (British Association for the Study and Prevention of) see BASPCAN

Child Accident Prevention Trust
Committed to reducing the number of children and young people killed, disabled or seriously injured in accidents
Canterbury Court 1-3 Brixton Road London SW9 6DE
Tel: 020 7608 3828
safe@capt.org.uk
www.capt.org.uk

Child Advocacy International now see Maternal & Childhealth Advocacy International

Child and Adolescent Mental Health (Association for)
Professional organisation
St Saviour's House 39-41 Union St London SE1 1SD
Tel: 020 7403 7458
email via website
www.acamh.org.uk

Child Bereavement Charity
Helps bereaved families by providing training, resources and support to professionals
The Saunderton Estate Wycombe Road Saunderton Bucks HP14 4BF
Support & Info Line: 1494 568900
enquiries@childbereavement.org.uk
www.childbereavement.org.uk

Child Brain Injury Trust
Information, support and training to anyone affected by childhood acquired brain injury
Unit 1 The Great Barn Baynards Green Farm
Nr Bicester Oxfordshire OX27 7SG
Helpline: 0845 6014939
Tel: 01869 341075
info@cbituk.org or helpline@cbituk.org
www.cbituk.org

Child Contact Centres (National Association of)
Supports Child Contact Centres, where children of separated families can have contact with family members
1 Heritage Mews High Pavement Nottingham NG1 1HN
Tel: 0845 4500 280
Tel: 0115 948 4557
contact@naccc.org.uk
www.naccc.org.uk

Child Death Helpline
Helpline is staffed by volunteers, all of them bereaved parents. Provide support not only at times of crisis but also for ongoing needs of callers over their lifetime
Helpline: 0800 282 986
contact@childdeathhelpline.org
www.childdeathhelpline.org.uk

Child Growth Foundation
Supports sufferers of growth disorders and their families
21 Malvern Drive Sutton Coldfield B76 1PZ
Tel: 020 8995 0257
info@childgrowthfoundation.org
www.childgrowthfoundation.org

Child Poverty Action Group CPAG
Information about low-income families and the policies that affect them. Monitor official poverty statistics and carry out research
94 White Lion St London N1 9PF
Tel: 020 7837 7979
info@cpag.org.uk
www.cpag.org.uk

Child Protection in Sport Unit CPSU
Offers advice to sports professionals, volunteers, parents and children as part of a long-term strategy for ending child abuse
NSPCC National Training Centre 3 Gilmour Close Beaumont Leys Leicester LE4 1EZ
Tel: 0116 234 7278
cpsu@nspcc.org.uk
www.thecpsu.org.uk

& Scotland
Unit 9, Ladywell 94 Duke Street Glasgow G4 0UW
Tel: 0141 552 3303
staff@cpagscotland.org.uk
www.cpag.org.uk

& Northern Ireland
NSPCC Block 1 Jennymount Business Park
North Derby Street Belfast BT15 3HN
Tel: 0203 222 4246
cpsu@nspcc.org.uk
www.thecpsu.org.uk

Child Protection in Sport Unit Cymru/Wales
Diane Engelhardt House, Treglown Court, Dowlais Road Cardiff CF24 5LQ
Tel: 0844 892 0290
cpsuwales@nspcc.org.uk
www.thecpsu.org.uk

Child Protection in Sport Unit Scotland
CHILDREN 1ST Sussex House 61 Sussex Street Kinning Park Glasgow G41 1DY
Tel: 0141 418 5674
safeguardinginsport@children1st.org.uk
www.safeguardinginsport.org.uk

Child Rights Information Network see CRIN

Child Soldiers
Working to stop the use of child soldiers worldwide
4th Floor, 9 Marshalsea Road London SE1 1EP
Tel: 020 7367 4110/4129
info@child-soldiers.org
www.child-soldiers.org

Childbirth Trust see National Childbirth Trust

Childcare see Daycare Trust, Directgov

Childhood (Alliance for)
Partnership of individuals and organisations committed to each child's inherent right to a healthy, developmentally appropriate childhood
Kidbrooke Park Forest Row East Sussex RH18 5JA
Tel: 01342 827792
info@alliancechildhood.org
www.alliancechildhood.org

Childhood (Museum of) V&A
Cambridge Heath Road London E2 9PA
Tel: 020 8983 5200
Group Bookings: 020 8983 5205
mocbookings@vam.ac.uk
www.vam.ac.uk/moc

Childhood Bereavement Network
A national, multi-professional federation of organisations and individuals working with bereaved children and young people.
8 Wakley Street London EC1V 7QE
Tel: 020 7843 6309
cbn@ncb.org.uk
www.childhoodbereavementnetwork.org.uk

Childhood Eye Cancer Trust CHECT
UK wide charity for families and individuals affected by retinoblastoma. We offer support and information, fund research and raise public awareness of this rare cancer
The Royal London Hospital Whitechapel Road London E1 1BB
Tel: 020 7377 5578
info@chect.org.uk
www.chect.org.uk

ChildHope
International development charity supporting street and working children
Development House 56/64 Leonard Street London EC2A 4LT
Tel: 0207 065 0950
info@childhope.org.uk
www.childhope.org.uk

ChildLine
Confidential counselling service for children and young people
Weston House 42 Curtain Road London EC2A 3NH
Helpline: 0800 1111
email via website
www.childline.org.uk

Childlink Adoption Society now see PACT (Parents and Children Together)

Childminding Association (National)
Helping every child reach their full potential
Offers help and advice on a wide range of issues related to home-based childcare
Royal Court 81 Tweedy Road Bromley Kent BR1 1TG
Tel: 0845 880 0044
info@ncma.org.uk
www.ncma.org.uk

CHILDREN 1ST Royal Scottish Society for
Prevention of Cruelty to Children
Support families under stress, protect children from harm and neglect, help them to recover from abuse and promote children's rights and interests
83 Whitehouse Loan Edinburgh EH9 1AT
Tel: 0131 446 2300
info@children1st.org.uk
www.children1st.org.uk

Children and Family Court Advisory Support Service see Cafcass

Children and peace see Peace Pledge Union

Children are unbeatable! Alliance
To satisfy human rights obligations by modernising the law on assault to afford children the same protection as adults
94 White Lion Street London N1 9PF
Tel: 020 7713 0569
info@endcorporalpunishment.org
www.childrenareunbeatable.org.uk

& Northern Ireland
Unit 9, 40 Montgomery Road Belfast BT6 9HL
Tel: 028 9040 1290
www.childrenareunbeatable.org.uk

& Scotland
c/o ChildLine in Scotland 2nd Floor Tara House 46 Bath St Glasgow G2 1HG
www.childrenareunbeatable.org.uk

& Wales/Cymru
Children in Wales 25 Windsor Place Cardiff CF10 3BZ
029 20 342434
www.childrenareunbeatable.org.uk

Children in Need Appeal BBC
www.bbc.co.uk/pudsey

Children in Scotland
National agency for voluntary, statutory and professional organisations and individuals working with children and their families in Scotland
Princes House 5 Shandwick Place Edinburgh EH2 4RG
Tel: 0131 228 8484
info@childreninscotland.org.uk
www.childreninscotland.org.uk

Children of Alcoholics (National Association for) NACOA
Support and advice to children of alcoholics and to professionals
PO Box 64 Fishponds Bristol BS16 2UH
Helpline: 0800 358 3456
Tel: 0117 924 8005
admin@nacoa.org.uk
www.nacoa.org.uk

Children with Cancer Formerly Children with Leukaemia
Fighting Britain's biggest childhood cancer
51 Great Ormond St London WC1N 3JQ
Tel: 020 7404 0808
info@childrenwithcancer.org.uk/
www.childrenwithcancer.co.uk

Children with Leukaemia Now see Children with Cancer

Children's Book Groups (Federation of)
Parents, teachers, librarians and publishers promoting good children's books
Hampton Farm Bowerhill Melksham Wiltshire SN12 6QZ
Tel: 01225 353710
info@fcbg.org.uk
www.fcbg.org.uk

Children's Bureau (National) see NCB

Children's Care & Education (Council for Awards in) see CACHE

Children's Commissioner for England (Office of the)
Promoting the views and best interests of all children and young people
33 Greycoat Street London SE1P 2QF
Tel: 020 77883 8330
info.request@childrenscommissioner.gsi.gov.uk
www.childrenscommissioner.gov.uk

Children's Express now see Headliners

Children's Heart Federation
For families of children with heart conditions
Level One
2-4 Great Eastern Street London EC2A 3NW
Helpline: 0808 808 5000
Tel: 020 7422 0630
Email via website
www.childrens-heart-fed.org.uk

Children's Hope Foundation
Caring for children with special needs
15 Palmer Place London N7 8DH
Tel: 020 7700 6855
info@childrenshopefoundation.org
www.childrenshopefoundation.org.uk

Children's Legal Centre
Free and confidential legal advice on issues affecting children
University of Essex Wivenhoe Park Colchester Essex CO4 3SQ
Child Law Advice Line Freephone:
0808 802 0008
Tel: 01206 877 910
clc@essex.ac.uk
www.childrenslegalcentre.com
www.lawstuff.org.uk

Children's Literature (National Centre for Research in) NCRCL
Department of English & Creative Writing
Roehampton University Roehampton Lane London SW15 5PH
Tel: 020 8392 3000
email via website
www.roehampton.ac.uk/Research-Centres/National-Centre-for-Research-in-Childrens-Literature

Children's Medical Research Charity now see Sparks

Children's Orchestra (National)
For children between the ages of 7-14 years
57 Buckingham Road Weston-Super-Mare BS24 9BG
Tel: 01934 418855
mail@nco.org.uk
www.nco.org.uk

Children's Play Initiative now see Play England

Children's Rights Alliance for England CRAE
Promoting the fullest implementation of the UN convention on rights of the child.
94 White Lion St London N1 9PF
Tel: 020 7278 8222
info@crae.org.uk
www.crae.org.uk

Children's Scrapstore
Clean and safe waste products from industry as a resource for children's art and play activities. Directory of scrapstores.
Scrapstore House 21 Sevier Street Bristol BS2 9LB
Tel: 0117 908 5644
enquiries@childrensscrapstore.co.uk
www.childrensscrapstore.co.uk

Children's Society
A Christian, social justice organisation for children at risk on the streets, in trouble with the law, disabled children & young refugees
Edward Rudolf House Margery St London WC1X 0JL
Tel: 020 7841 4400
Tel: 0300 303 7000
supportercare@childrenssociety.org.uk
www.childrenssociety.org.uk

Chinese Arts Centre
UK agency for Chinese arts, culture and creativity
Market Buildings Thomas Street Manchester M4 1EU
Tel: 0161 832 7271
Email via website
www.chinese-arts-centre.org

Chiropodists & Podiatrists (Institute of)
27 Wright St Southport PR9 0TL
Tel: 01704 546141
secretary@iocp.org.uk
www.iocp.org.uk

Chiropodists & Podiatrists (The Society of)
Professional Body and Trade Union for registered podiatrists. The Society represents around 10,000 private practitioners, NHS podiatrists and students
1 Fellmonger's Path Tower Bridge Rd London SE1 3LY
Tel: 020 7234 8620
Email via website
www.feetforlife.org

Chiropractic (Anglo-European College of)
13-15 Parkwood Rd Bournemouth BH5 2DF
Tel: 01202 436200
email via website
www.aecc.ac.uk

Chiropractic Association (British)
59 Castle Street Reading RG1 7SN
Tel: 0118 950 5950
enquiries@chiropractic-uk.co.uk
www.chiropractic-uk.co.uk

Chiropractic Patients' Association
Supports chiropractic patients and seeks to make treatment more widely available
Twingley Centre The Portway Winterbourne Gunner Salisbury SP4 6JL
Tel: 01980 610218
cpa@centreonesarum.com
www.chiropatients.org.uk

Chocolate Society
Promotes the consumption and enjoyment of the finest chocolates
Unit 10 Lower Charlton Trading Estate Shepton Mallet Somerset BA4 5QE
Tel: 01749 342884
email via website
www.chocolate.co.uk

Choir Schools' Association
Provides advice to prospective pupils and bursary help where applicable
The Information Officer Windrush, Church Road Market Weston Diss Norfolk IP22 2NX
Tel: 01359 221333
info@choirschools.org.uk
www.choirschools.org.uk

Choirs see also Youth Choir of Great Britain (National)

Choose Climate
Details the science of climate change & the effects of air travel
www.chooseclimate.org

Christian Aid
35 Lower Marsh Waterloo London SE1 7RL
Tel: 020 7620 4444
via website
www.christianaid.org.uk

& Cardiff
5 Station Road Radyr Cardiff CF15 8AA
Tel: 029 2084 4646
cardiff@christian-aid.org
www.christianaid.org.uk

& Glasgow
First floor Sycamore House 290 Bath Street
Glasgow G2 4JR
Tel: 0141 221 7475
glasgow@christian-aid.org
www.christianaid.org.uk

& Belfast
Linden House Beechill Business Park 96 Beechill Road Belfast BT8 7QN
Tel: 028 9064 8133
belfast@christian-aid.org
www.christianaid.org.uk

& Cork
Hill View Bandon Co Cork
Tel: (+353) 238 841 468
cork@christian-aid.org
www.christianaid.org.uk

& Dublin
17 Clanwilliam Terrace Grand Canal Quay
Dublin 2
Tel: (+353) 1 611 0801
dublin@christian-aid.org
www.christianaid.org.uk

Christian Education/International Bible Reading Association (IBRA)
Provides Christian resources for use by individuals, families and churches
1020 Bristol Road Selly Oak Birmingham B29 6LB
Tel: 0121 472 4242
sales@christianeducation.org.uk
www.christianeducation.org.uk

Christian Lewis Trust Children's Cancer Charity
62 Walter Road Swansea SA1 4PT
Tel: 01792 480 500
enquiries@christianlewistrust.org
www.christianlewistrust.org.uk

Christian Socialist Movement CSM
PO Box 65108 London SW1P 9PQ
Tel: 020 7783 1590
info@thecsm.org.uk
www.thecsm.org.uk

Christian Teachers (Association of)
23 Billing Road Northampton NN1 5AT
Tel: 01604 632046
act@christians-in-education.org.uk
www.christian-teachers.org.uk

Christians and Jews (Council of)
Godliman House
21 Godliman Street
London EC4V 5BD
Tel: 0207 015 5160
cjrelations@ccj.org.uk
www.ccj.org.uk

Church Action on Poverty
Aiming to raise awareness about the causes,
extent and impact of poverty in the UK
Dale House 35 Dale Street Manchester M1
2HF
Tel: 0161 236 9321
info@church-poverty.org.uk
www.church-poverty.org.uk

Church Army
Sharing the gospel in a variety of situations
right across the UK and Ireland
Wilson Carlile Centre 50 Cavendish Street
Sheffield S3 7RZ
Tel: 0300 123 2113
info@churcharmy.org.uk
www.churcharmy.org.uk

Church Lads' and Church Girls' Brigade
A uniformed young people and children's
organisation within the Church of England
2 Barnsley Rd Wath-upon-Dearne
Rotherham S63 6PY
Tel: 01709 876 535
brigadesecretary@clcgb.org.uk
www.clcgb.org.uk

Church Mission Society
Sends UK personnel to other countries, in
partnership with churches
Watlington Road Oxford OX4 6BZ
Tel: 01865 787400
info@cms-uk.org
www.cms-uk.org

Church of England
www.churchofengland.org

Church of England Education Division
www.churchofengland.org/education.aspx

Churches Conservation Trust
National charity protecting historic churches
at risk
1 West Smithfield London EC1A 9EE
Tel: 020 7213 0660
central@tcct.org.uk
www.visitchurches.org.uk

Churches Together in Britain and Ireland
39 Eccleston Square London SW1V 1BX
Tel: 0845 680 6851
info@ctbi.org.uk
www.ctbi.org.uk

Churchill War Rooms part of the Imperial War
Museum
Clive Steps King Charles Street London
SW1A 2AQ
Tel: 020 7930 6961
Textphone: 020 7839 4906
cwr@iwm.org.uk
cwr.iwm.org.uk
www.iwm.org.uk

CIA Central Intelligence Agency
Independent US Government agency
responsible for providing national security
intelligence to senior US policymakers
www.cia.gov

CIH
The professional body for people working in
the field of social housing
Octavia House Westwood Way Coventry
CV4 8JP
Tel: 024 7685 1700
customer.services@cih.org
www.cih.org

& Cymru
4 Purbeck House Lambourne Crescent
Cardiff Business Park Llanishen Cardiff CF14
5GJ
Tel: 029 2076 5760
cymru@cih.org
www.cih.org

& Northern Ireland
Carnmoney House Edgewater Office Park
Dargan Road Belfast BT3 9JQ
Tel: 028 9077 8222
ni@cih.org
www.cih.org

& Scotland
4th Floor 125 Princes Street Edinburgh EH2
4AD
Tel: 0131 225 4544
scotland@cih.org
www.cih.org

CILIP Chartered Institute of Library and
Information Professionals
Professional body for Information Managers
and Librarians.
7 Ridgmount St London WC1E 7AE
Tel: 020 7255 0500
Textphone: 020 7255 0505
info@cilip.org.uk
www.cilip.org.uk

CILIPS Chartered Institute of Library and
Information Professionals in Scotland
151 West George Street, Glasgow G2 2JJ
Tel: 0141 228 4790
cilips@slainte.org.uk
www.cilips.org.uk

CILT National Centre for Languages
Works to convince people of the benefits of learning and using more than one language Operating as part of the CfBT Education Trust
CfBT Education Trust 60 Queens Road
Reading RG1 4BS
Tel: 0118 902 1000
www.cilt.org.uk

Cinema see British Film Institute, Film Classification (British Board of), Film Education, Film & Television Archive (Northern Region), Film and Television School (National), Film London, History of Cinema & Popular Culture (The Bill Douglas Centre for the)

Cinnamon Trust
National charity for the elderly, the terminally ill and their pets
10 Market Square Hayle Cornwall TR27 4HE
Tel: 01736 757 900
admin@cinnamon.org.uk
www.cinnamon.org.uk

Circus see also Skylight Circus Arts

Circus Sensible/Circus School
Britain's smallest tented circus. Performance & teaching of circus skills in schools, youth clubs etc.
4 The Moorings Mossley Lancs OL5 9BZ
Mobile: 07958 780246
via website
www.circussensible.co.uk

Circus Space
Circus training & production venue offering the only BA circus degree in the UK
Coronet St London N1 6HD
Tel: 020 7613 4141
info@thecircusspace.co.uk
www.thecircusspace.co.uk

Cirdan Sailing Trust
Adventure sailing for groups of all abilities of 10 years+
Bradwell Marina Waterside Bradwell-on-Sea
Essex CM0 7RB
Tel: 01621 851 433
via website
www.cirdansailing.com

Citizens Advice
Independent advice, policy and campaigning charity. For local CAB, see phone book or websites
Myddelton House 115-123 Pentonville Rd
London N1 9LZ
www.citizensadvice.org.uk
www.adviceguide.org.uk

Citizens Income Trust
Research and education on the feasibility of a citizen's income: an unconditional income for every citizen
37 Becquerel Court West Parkside
London SE10 0QQ
Tel: 020 8305 1222
info@citizensincome.org
www.citizensincome.org

Citizens UK
Alliance of active citizens and community leaders organising for change
112 Cavell Street London E1 2JA
Tel: 020 7043 9881
josephine.mukanjira@citizensuk.org.uk
www.citizensuk.org

Citizenship and the Law (National Centre for)
Runs learning programmes
Galleries of Justice High Pavement The Lace Market Nottingham NG1 1HN
Tel: 0115 952 0555
learning@nccl.org.uk
www.nccl.org.uk

Citizenship Foundation
Educational charity promoting citizenship education
50 Featherstone Street London EC1Y 8RT.
Tel: 020 7566 4141
info@citizenshipfoundation.org.uk
www.citizenshipfoundation.org.uk

Citizenship Teaching (Association for) ACT
Professional subject association for those involved in citizenship education
63 Gee Street London EC1V 3RS
Tel: 020 7253 0051
info@teachingcitizenship.org.uk
www.teachingcitizenship.org.uk

City and Guilds
Awarding body for vocational qualifications, NVQs and GNVQs
1 Giltspur St London EC1A 9DD
Tel: 0844 543 0000
via website
www.cityandguilds.com

City Farms & Community Gardens (Federation of)
Supports, promotes and represents city farms and community gardens throughout the UK
The GreenHouse Hereford St Bristol BS3 4NA
Tel: 01179 231 800
admin@farmgarden.org.uk
www.farmgarden.org.uk

Civic Voice
National charity for the civic movement in England. Making places more attractive, enjoyable and distinctive and promoting civic pride
Unit 101 82 Wood Street The Tea Factory Liverpool L1 4DQ
Tel: 0151 708 9920
info@civicvoice.org.uk
www.civicvoice.org.uk

Civil Aviation Authority see CAA

Civil Liberties see also thematic guide Human Rights

Civil Liberties (National Council for) see Liberty

Civitas Institute for the Study of Civil Society
Independent health, education and social policy think tank
First Floor 55 Tufton Street Westminster London SW1P 3QL
Tel: 0207 799 6677
info@civitas.org.uk
www.civitas.org.uk

CLA Country Land and Business Association
A membership organisation and lobby group representing rural land and business owners
16 Belgrave Sq London SW1X 8PQ
Tel: 020 7235 0511
mail@cla.org.uk
www.cla.org.uk

CLAPA Cleft Lip & Palate Association
Information and support for all those with and affected by cleft lip and/or palate
First Floor Green Man Tower 332B Goswell Road London EC1V 7LQ
Tel: 020 7833 4883
info@clapa.com
www.clapa.com

Classical Association
To promote the development and maintain the well-being of classical studies. Unites the interests of all who value the study of the languages, literature and civilisation of ancient Greece and Rome
Senate House Malet St London WC1E 7HU
Tel: 020 7862 8706
office@classicalassociation.org
www.classicalassociation.org

Clean Air & Environmental Protection (National Society for) see Environmental Protection UK

Cleanair Campaign for a Smoke Free Environment
Raises awareness about the dangers of smoking
33 Stillness Rd London SE23 1NG
Tel: 0181 690 4649
www.ezme.com/cleanair

Clear Vision Trust
Supports the teaching of Buddhism in schools
16-20 Turner Street Manchester M4 1DZ
Tel: 0161 839 9579
clearvision@clear-vision.org
www.clear-vision.org

ClearVision Project
Postal lending library of children's books suitable for sharing by sighted and visually impaired
Linden Lodge School 61 Princes Way London SW19 6JB
Tel: 020 8789 9575
info@clearvisionproject.org
www.clearvisionproject.org

Cleft Lip & Palate Association see Clapa

CLES
Independent think-doing organisation, with charitable status, involved in regeneration, local economic development and local governance
Express Networks 1 George Leigh St Manchester M4 5DL
Tel: 0161 236 7036
info@cles.org.uk
www.cles.org.uk

CLICSargent
Offers professional, practical and financial help to young people up to 21 years diagnosed with cancer, and their families
Horatio House 77-85 Fulham Palace Road London W6 8JA
Child Cancer Helpline: 0800 197 0068
Tel: 0300 330 0803
via website
www.clicsargent.org.uk

Climate see also Choose Climate, Global, Met Office, Meteorological Organization (World), Meteorological Society (Royal), Rising Tide, Stop Climate Chaos Coalition

Climate Change (Committee on) CCC
Independent advisors to the UK Government on tackling and preparing for climate change
7 Holbein Place London SW1W, 8NR
Tel: 0207 591 6262
enquiries@theccc.gsi.gov.uk
www.theccc.org.uk

Climate Change (Intergovernmental Panel on) IPCC
Assessment of factual information on all aspects of climate change
c/o World Meteorological Organ 7bis Avenue de la Paix C.P. 2300 CH- 1211 Geneva 2, Switzerland
Tel: 00 41 22 730 8208 / 54 / 84
ipcc-sec@wmo.int
www.ipcc.ch

Climate Parliament
Legislators working worldwide to combat climate change
www.climateparl.net

Climate projections see UK Climate projections

Climb Children Living with Inherited Metabolic Diseases
Support and information for families and professionals covering over 700 metabolic disorders
Climb Building 176 Nantwich Rd Crewe CW2 6BG
Tel: 0845 241 2173
adm.svcs@climb.org.uk
www.climb.org.uk

Clubs for Young People now see Ambition

CND Campaign for Nuclear Disarmament
Non-political, peace educational material & speakers
Mordechai Vanunu House 162 Holloway Rd London N7 8DQ
Tel: 020 7700 2393
enquiries@cnduk.org
www.cnduk.org

CND (Scottish)
77 Southpark Avenue Glasgow G12 8LE
Tel: 0141 357 1529
scnd@banthebomb.org
www.banthebomb.org

Co-operative Party
Political wing of co-operative movement
77 Weston Street London SE1 3SD
Tel: 020 7367 4150
Email via website
www.party.coop

Co-operatives UK
Information and advice on employee ownership, innovative co-operatives, social enterprise and mutual businesses
Holyoake House Hanover St Manchester M4 4AH
Tel: 0161 246 2978
Email via website
www.uk.coop

Coaching Foundation (National) see Sports Coach UK

Coal Museum (National) see Big Pit

Cocaine Anonymous UK
Fellowship of men and women who share their experience, strength and hope so that they may solve their common problem and help others to recover from their addiction
204-226 Imperial Way Rayners Lane Harrow HA2 7HH
Tel: 0800 612 0225
Tel: 0208 429 5924
info@cauk.org.uk
www.cauk.org.uk

Coleg Harlech (WEA)
Adult education residential college. Full time & short courses
Harlech Gwynedd LL46 2PU
Tel: 01766 781900
email via website
www.harlech.ac.uk

Colitis & Crohn's UK
Aims to improve life for everyone affected by Inflammatory Bowel Disease (IBD)
4 Beaumont House Sutton Rd St Albans Herts AL1 5HH
Tel: 0845 130 2233
Tel: 01727 844296
info@ChronsAndColitis.org.uk
www.nacc.org.uk

CollegesWales
Raises the profile of further education with key decision-makers to improve opportunities for learners in Wales
7 Cae Gwyrdd, Tongwynlais Cardiff CF15 7AB
Tel: 029 2052 2500
hello@collegeswales.ac.uk
www.collegeswales.ac.uk

Colombia Solidarity Campaign Fighting for peace with justice
Campaigns for a socially just and sustainable peace in Colombia based on respect for the human rights and diversity of the Colombian people
PO Box 8446 London N17 6NZ
info@colombiasolidarity.org.uk
www.colombiasolidarity.org.uk

CoMA Contemporary Music-making for Amateurs
Promotes participation in contemporary music through commissions, music ensembles and training
35 - 47 Bethnal Green Road London E1 6LA
Tel: 020 7739 4680
admin@coma.org
www.coma.org

Combat Stress
Treatment and support to Ex-Service men and women with conditions such as Post Traumatic Stress Disorder (PTSD), depression and anxiety disorders
Tyrwhitt House Oaklawn Road Leatherhead Surrey KT22 0BX
Tel: 01372 587 000
contactus@combatstress.org.uk
www.combatstress.org.uk

Comic Relief
89 Albert Embankment London SE1 7TP
Tel: 020 7820 2000
Minicom: 0207 820 2005
info@comicrelief.com
www.comicrelief.com

Common Ground

Environmental charity; encourages people to value everyday places and local distinctiveness
Gold Hill House 21 High St Shaftesbury Dorset SP7 8JE
Tel: 01747 850820
info@commonground.org.uk
www.commonground.org.uk
www.england-in-particular.info

Common Purpose

Independent not-for-profit organisation that runs leadership development courses which mix people from the private, public and not-for-profit sectors
Discovery House 28-42 Banner St London EC1Y 8QE
Tel: 020 7608 8100
enquiries@commonpurpose.org.uk
www.commonpurpose.org.uk

Commonwealth Broadcasting Association

Working for quality broadcasting throughout the Commonwealth
17 Fleet St London EC4Y 1AA
Tel: 020 7583 5550
Email via website
www.cba.org.uk

Commonwealth Education Trust

Principal objective is to advance education in the Commonwealth
6th Floor New Zealand House 80 Haymarket London SW1Y 4TE
Tel: 020 7024 9822
information@cet1886.org
www.cet1886.org/

Commonwealth Games Federation

The organisation that is responsible for the direction and control of the Commonwealth Games - a unique, world class, multi-sports event which is held once every four years. It is often referred to as the 'Friendly Games'
2nd Floor 138 Piccadilly London W1J 7NR
Tel: 020 7491 8801
info@thecgf.com
www.thecgf.com

Commonwealth Institute now see

Commonwealth Education Trust

Commonwealth Scholarship Commission in the UK

Offers opportunities to Commonwealth citizens to study in the UK and to identify UK citizens to study overseas
Woburn House 20-24 Tavistock Square London WC1H 9HF
Tel: 0207 380 6700
email via website
cscuk.dfid.gov.uk

Commonwealth Society (Royal) RCS

Promotes and educates about the Commonwealth. Provides a multicultural meeting place. Does not give out grants or sponsorship
25 Northumberland Ave London WC2N 5AP
Tel: 020 7766 9200
info@thercs.org
www.thercs.org

Commonwealth Society for the Deaf see

Sound Seekers

Commonwealth Youth Exchange Council

Promotes educational exchanges for 15-25 year olds from Britain and their partners in the Commonwealth
7 Lion Yard Tremadoc Road London SW4 7NQ
Tel: 020 7498 6151
Email via website
www.cyec.org.uk

Communication Trust

Highlights the importance of speech, language and communication to enable practitioners to access the best training and expertise to support the communication needs of all children
8 Wakley Street London EC1V 7QE
Tel: 0207 843 2526
enquiries@thecommunicationtrust.org.uk
www.thecommunicationtrust.org.uk

Communities and Local Government (Department for)

Helping to create a free, fair and responsible Big Society by putting power in the hands of citizens, neighbourhoods and councils
Eland House Bressenden Place London SW1E 5DU
Tel: 0303 444 0000
contactus@communities.gov.uk
www.communities.gov.uk

Communities Empowerment Network

Provides support for people experiencing mistreatment and disadvantage in education
Unit 104 Shakespeare Business Centre 245a Coldharbour Lane Brixton SW9 8RR
Tel: 0207 7330297
post@compowernet.org
www.compowernet.org

Communities in Rural England (Action with) ACRE

A national charity supporting sustainable rural community development
Somerford Court Somerford Rd Cirencester GL7 1TW
Tel: 01285 653477
acre@acre.org.uk
www.acre.org.uk

Community and Youth Workers in Unite
Trade union for youth, community, play workers, mentors and personal advisers. Part of Unite the Union, the biggest trade union in Europe
Transport House 211 Broad Street
Birmingham B15 1AY
Tel: 0121 643 6221
Email via website
www.cywu.org.uk

Community Composting Network
Advice & support
67 Alexandra Rd Sheffield S2 3EE
Tel: 0114 258 0483
info@communitycompost.org
www.communitycompost.org

Community Dance (Foundation for)
Professional organisation for anyone involved in creating opportunities for people to experience and participate in dance
LCB Depot 31 Rutland Street Leicester LE1 1RE
Tel: 0116 253 3453
info@communitydance.org.uk
www.communitydance.org.uk

Community Foundation Network
National network linking, promoting and supporting over 60 community foundations throughout the UK
12 Angel Gate
320-326 City Road London EC1V 2PT
Tel: 020 7713 9326
network@communityfoundations.org.uk
www.communityfoundations.org.uk

Community Fund see Big Lottery Fund

Community Justice National Training Organisation see Skills for Justice

Community Matters
National federation of community organisations
12-20 Baron St Islington London N1 9LL
Tel: 020 7837 7887
Advice: 0845 847 4253
Email via website
www.communitymatters.org.uk

Community Media Association
UK representative body for the community broadcasting sector. Committed to promoting access to the media for people and communities
15 Paternoster Row Sheffield S1 2BX
Tel: 0114 279 5219
cma@commedia.org.uk
www.commedia.org.uk

Community Rail Partnerships (Association of)
Association of organisations promoting links between railways and local communities
Rail and River Centre, Canal Side Civic Hall 15a New Street Slaithwaite Huddersfield HD7 5AB
Tel: 01484 847790
office@acorp.uk.com
www.acorp.uk.com

Community Safety Network (National)
Involved in crime reduction and community safety
1 Hunters Walk Canal Street Chester CH1 4EB
Tel: 01244 322314
enquiries@community-safety.net
www.community-safety.net/

Community Service Volunteers CSV
Creates opportunities for everyone to play an active part in their community
237 Pentonville Rd London N1 9NJ
Tel: 020 7278 6601
information@csv.org.uk
www.csv.org.uk

Community Transport Association UK
Co-ordinating body for voluntary and community transport
Central Support Office Highbank Halton St Hyde SK14 2NY
Tel: 0845 130 6195
Tel: 0161 351 1475
info@ctauk.org
www.ctauk.org

Community Transport Association UK
London Office
Co-ordinating body for voluntary and community transport
CAN Mezzanine 45-51 East Road Old Street London N1 6AH
Tel: 020 7250 8362
info@ctauk.org

& Northern Ireland Office
Co-ordinating body for voluntary and community transport
109-112 CityEast 68-72 Newtownards Road Belfast BT4 1GW
Tel: 028 9094 1661

& Scotland Office
Co-ordinating body for voluntary and community transport
54 Manor Place Edinburgh EH3 7EH
Tel: 0131 220 0052

& South Wales Office
Co-ordinating body for voluntary and community transport
Room 10, Forge Fach Hebron Road Clydach Swansea SA6 5EJ
Tel: 01792 844 290

& North Wales Office
Co-ordinating body for voluntary and community transport
Unit 17, Morfa Hall Bath Street Rhyl Denbighshire LL18 3EB
Tel: 01745 356 751

Companion Animal Studies (Society for)
SCAS
Education charity working to support and promote the health and social benefits of interactions between people and companion animals. Works in partnership with the Blue Cross
The Blue Cross Shilton Rd Burford Oxon OX18 4PF
Tel: 01993 867214
info@scas.org.uk
www.scas.org.uk

Compassion in World Farming Trust
Campaign to end cruel factory farming
River Court Mill Lane Godalming Surrey GU7 1EZ
Tel: 01483 521 953
Email via website
www.ciwf.org

Compassionate Friends
Support and friendship for bereaved parents and their families, through the loss of a child of any age and through any circumstance
53 North St Bristol BS3 1EN
Helpline: 0845 123 2304 (UK)
0288 77 88 016 (N Ireland)
Tel: 0845 120 3785
info@tcf.org.uk
www.tcf.org.uk

Competition Commission
independent public body which conducts in-depth inquiries into mergers, markets and the regulation of the major regulated industries, ensuring healthy competition between companies in the UK for the benefit of companies, customers and the economy
Victoria House Southampton Row London WC1B 4AD
Tel: 020 7271 0100
Tel: 020 7271 0243 (Public enquiries)
info@cc.gsi.gov.uk
www.competition-commission.org.uk

Complementary and Natural Medicine (Institute for)
Provides register of practitioners' names and a list of courses
Can-Mezzanine 32-36 Loman Street London SE1 0EH
Tel: 0207 922 7980
info@icnm.org.uk
www.icnm.org.uk

Complementary Medicine Association (British)
Umbrella organisation. Has a practitioners register
PO Box 5122 Bournemouth BH8 0WG
Tel: 0845 345 5977
office@bcma.co.uk
www.bcma.co.uk

Computer Aid International
Recycles computer equipment for use in developing world
Unit 10 Brunswick Industrial Park Brunswick Way London N11 1JL
Tel: 020 8361 5540
info@computeraid.org
www.computeraid.org

Computer Society (British) now see BCS - Chartered Institute for IT

Computers see also Intellect, NAACE, Recycle-IT!

Computers 4 Africa
Encourages schools, businesses, and individuals to give used PCs and laptops to charity for onward delivery to Africa
Unit 4 Priory Park Mills Road Aylesford Kent ME20 7PP
Tel: 03000 112233
Tel: 01622 808897
contact-us@computers4africa.org.uk
www.computers4africa.org.uk

Computing Centre (National)
2nd Floor, Lexham House 14a Hill Avenue Amersham Bucks HP6 5BW
Tel: 0870 908 8767
info@ncc.co.uk
www.ncc.co.uk

Concern Worldwide England & Wales
Working with the world's poorest people to transform their lives
13/14 Calico House Clove Hitch Quay London SW11 3TN
Tel: 020 7801 1850
Email via website
www.concern.net

& Republic of Ireland
52-55 Lower Camden Street Dublin 2 Ireland
Tel: ++353 1 417 7700

& Northern Ireland
47 Frederick Street Belfast BT1 2LW
Tel: 028 9033 1100

& Scotland
40 St. Enoch Square Glasgow G1 4DH
Tel: 0141 221 3610

Concord Media (Concord Video & Film Council)
Hires & sells videos concerned with social welfare, counselling, health & medical education and domestic violence
22 Hines Road Ipswich IP3 9BG
Tel: 01473 726012
sales@concordmedia.org.uk
www.concordmedia.co.uk

Conductive Education (The National Institute of)
Teaches children and adults with movement disabilities the skills and practical techniques they need to control their bodies
www.conductive-education.org.uk

Conflict Minerals
Aims to share the truth about the historic exploitation of Congo and the role that Western nations continue to play in fomenting conflict, breeding dependency and keeping the Congolese people impoverished
conflictminerals.org

Connect The communication disability network
Charity for people living with aphasia, a communication disability which usually occurs after stroke or brain injury
16-18 Marshalsea Road London SE1 1HL
Tel: 020 7367 0840
info@ukconnect.org
www.ukconnect.org

Connect Youth now see Youth in Action

Connexions Direct now see Directgov

Conscience
Campaigns for the right for those ethically opposed to war to have the military part of their taxes spent on peace-building initiatives
Archway Resource Centre 1a Waterlow Rd
London N19 5NJ
Tel:0 20 3515 9132
info@conscienceonline.org.uk
www.conscienceonline.org.uk

Conservation see thematic guide - Environment and Countryside & Heritage

Conservation (Institute of) see ICON

Conservation of Energy (Association for the)
Aims to reduce overall energy demand to ensure a secure and sustainable energy future
Westgate House 2A Prebend St
London N1 8PT
Tel: 020 7359 8000
Email via website
www.ukace.org

Conservation of Plants & Gardens (National Council for the)
Charity responsible for National Plant Collection Scheme - 'living libraries' of individual species, cared for by dedicated specialist growers
Plant Heritage 12 Home Farm Loseley Park
Guildford GU3 1HS
Tel: 01483 447 540
info@plantheritage.org.uk
www.nccpg.com

Conservation Volunteers see also BTCV

Conservation Volunteers Northern Ireland (BTCV)
Beech House 159 Ravenhill Road Belfast BT6 0BP Cardiff CF14 7JJ
Tel: 028 9064 5169
cvni@btcv.org.uk
www2.btcv.org.uk/display/btcv_wales

Conservative Party
30 Millbank London SW1P 4DP
Tel: 020 7222 9000
email via website
www.conservatives.com

Consumer Affairs (Research Institute for) see Ricability

Consumer Council (National) now see Consumer Focus

Consumer Credit Counselling Service
Charity funded by the financial services industry specialising in debt management plans
Wade House Merrion Centre Leeds LS2 8NG
Helpline: 0800 138 1111
Email via website
www.cccs.co.uk

Consumer Focus Campaigning for a fair deal
Tackles the issues that matter to consumers, and aims to give people a stronger voice.
Victoria House
Southampton Row
London
WC1B 4AD
Tel: 020 7799 7900
contact@consumerfocus.org.uk
www.consumerfocus.org.uk

& Scotland's Consumer Council
Royal Exchange House 100 Queen Street
Glasgow G1 3DN
Consumer Direct: 08454 04 05 06
Tel: 0141 226 5261
mail@consumerfocus-scotland.org.uk
www.consumerfocus.org.uk/scotland

& Wales' Consumer Council
Portcullis House 21 Cowbridge Road East
Cardiff CF11 9SR
Consumer Direct: 08454 04 05 06
Tel: 029 2078 7100
contactwales@consumerfocus.org.uk
www.consumerfocus.org.uk/wales

Consumer Focus Post Campaigning for a fair deal
Champion for postal consumers in Northern
Ireland
Elizabeth House 116 Holywood Road
Belfast BT4 1NY
Consumer Direct: 08454 04 05 06
Tel: 028 9067 4833
contact.post@consumerfocus.org.uk
www.consumerfocus.org.uk/northern-
ireland/

Consumers International
Defends the rights of all consumers,
especially the poorest, by international
campaigning
24 Highbury Cres Islington London N5 1RX
Tel: 020 7226 6663
consint@consint.org
www.consumersinternational.org

Consumers' Association see Which?

Contact a Family
Supporting families who care for children
with any disability or health condition
including rare disorders
209-211 City Rd London EC1V 1JN
Helpline: 0808 808 3555
Tel: 020 7608 8700
Textphone: 0808 808 3556
helpline@cafamily.org.uk
www.cafamily.org.uk

Contact the Elderly
Links volunteers with isolated elderly people
for monthly outings
15 Henrietta St Covent Garden
London WC2E 8QG
Freephone: 0800 716543
Tel: 020 7240 0630
info@contact-the-elderly.org.uk
www.contact-the-elderly.org.uk

Contemporary Art Society
Promotes collection of contemporary art
and acquires works by living artists for gift to
public collections in UK
11-15 Emerald Street London WC1N 3QL
Tel: 020 7831 1243
info@contemporaryartsociety.org
www.contemporaryartsociety.org

Continence Foundation now see Bladder
and Bowel Foundation

ContinYou Changing lives through learning
Works in education, health, economic and
community regeneration nationally and
internationally
Unit C1 Grovelands Court Grovelands Estate
Longford Rd Exhall Coventry CV7 9NE
Tel: 024 7658 8440
email via website
www.continyou.org.uk

Control Arms
Control Arms is a campaign jointly run by
Amnesty International, IANSA and Oxfam
www.controlarms.org

Coram Better chances for children since 1739
Supports the UK's most vulnerable children,
young people and families
Coram Community Campus 49
Mecklenburgh Square London WC1N 2QA
Tel: 020 7520 0300
chances@coram.org.uk
www.coram.org.uk

Core
Information for people with digestive
problems from food poisoning to bowel
cancer. Medical research
Freepost
LON4268 London NW1 0YT
Tel: 020 7486 0341
info@corecharity.org.uk
www.corecharity.org.uk

Corporate Watch
Research into corporate behaviour &
structure
c/o Freedom Press Angel Alley 84b
Whitechapel High Street London E1 7QX
Tel: 0207 426 0005
contact@corporatewatch.org
www.corporatewatch.org.uk

COSLA
National voice for local government in
Scotland
Verity House 19 Haymarket Yards
Edinburgh EH12 5BH
Tel: 0131 474 9200
info@cosla.gov.uk
www.cosla.gov.uk

Cot Death see Infant Deaths (Foundation for
the Study of)

COTS Childlessness overcome through
surrogacy
Providing advice, help and support to
surrogates and intended parents
Moss Bank Manse Road Lairg IV27 4EL
Tel: 0844 414 0181
Tel: 01549 402777
info@surrogacy.org.uk
www.surrogacy.org.uk

Cottage and Rural Enterprises Ltd. now see Self Unlimited

Couch Surfing
Helping to make connections around the world by offering some sort of accommodation to travellers
www.couchsurfing.com

Council for Advancement of Communication with Deaf People now see Signature

Council of Ethnic Minority Voluntary Sector Organisations see CEMVO

Council of Europe
Head Office Avenue de l'Europe F - 67075 Strasbourg Cedex
France
Tel. +33 (0)3 88 41 20 00
email via website
www.coe.int

Council of Europe Youth
An international meeting place for youth organisations
www.coe.int/youth

Counsel and Care
Advice for older people & their carers, research & campaigns about ageing and quality of care in care homes
6 Avonmore Road Kensington Olympia London W14 8RL
Advice Line: 0845 300 7585 (Mon-Fri 10am
Tel: 020 7605 4200 (Admin)
advice@counselandcare.org.uk
www.counselandcare.org.uk

Counselling & Psychotherapy (British Association for)
Promotion of counselling & training of counsellors
BACP House 15 St John's Business Park Lutterworth Leicestershire LE17 4HB
Client Info Helpdesk: 01455 8833316
Tel: 01455 883300
bacp@bacp.co.uk
www.bacp.co.uk

Country Holidays for Inner City Children see CHICKS

Country Landowners Association see CLA

Countryside Alliance
Campaigning organisation on rural issues. Defends and promotes country sports and rural life at Parliament, in the media and on the ground
The Old Town Hall 367 Kennington Rd London SE11 4PT
Tel: 020 7840 9200
info@Countryside-Alliance.org
www.countryside-alliance.org.uk

Countryside Council for Wales
Advises the government on conservation matters in Wales
Maes y Ffynnon Penrhosgarnedd Bangor Gwynedd LL57 2DW
Tel: 0845 1306229
email via website
www.ccw.gov.uk

Countryside Foundation for Education
Promotes an understanding of the countryside as a living, working environment and the problems facing those responsible for its management
PO Box 8 Hebden Bridge West Yorkshire HX7 5YJ
Tel: 01422 885566
info@countrysidefoundation.org.uk
www.countrysidefoundation.org.uk

Courtauld Institute of Art
Somerset House The Strand London WC2R 0RN
24-hour Gallery information line: 020 7848 2526
Tel: 020 7872 0220
email via website
www.courtauld.ac.uk

Courts and Tribunal Service (HM)
Works with a range of Government departments and justice agencies to ensure access to justice is provided in the most timely and effective way possible
www.justice.gov.uk

CP Sport England and Wales
Provides opportunities for people with cerebral palsy
5 Heathcoat Building Nottingham Science Park University Boulevard Nottingham NG7 2QJ
Tel: 0115 925 7027
info@cpsport.org
www.cpsport.org

CPRE Campaign to Protect Rural England
Campaigning charity that promotes the beauty, tranquility and diversity of rural England
5-11 Lavington Street London SE1 0NZ
Tel: 020 7981 2800
info@cpre.org.uk
www.cpre.org.uk

CPSU see Child Protection in Sport Unit

CPT see Passenger Transport UK (Confederation of)

CRAC Careers Research & Advisory Centre
2nd Floor Sheraton House Castle Park Cambridge CB3 0AX
Tel: 01223 460277
email via website
www.crac.org.uk

CRAE see Children's Rights Alliance for England

Crafts Council
Promotes British contemporary crafts and provides services to craftspeople and the public
44A Pentonville Rd London N1 9BY
Tel: 0207 806 2500
email via website
www.craftscouncil.org.uk

Creative Scotland
Develop the arts, screen and creative industries of Scotland
Waverley Gate 2-4 Waterloo Place
Edinburgh EH1 3EG
Tel: 0845 603 6000 (enquiries)
Tel: 0330 333 2000 (office)
enquiries@creativescotland.com
www.creativescotland.com

Credit Unions Ltd. (Association of British)
ABCUL
Main trade association for credit unions (financial co-operatives)
Holyoake House Hanover St Manchester M60 0AS
Tel: 0161 832 3694
info@abcul.org
www.abcul.org

Cremation Society of Great Britain
Promotion of cremation
1st Floor Brecon House 16/16a Albion Place
Maidstone Kent ME14 5DZ
Tel: 01622 688292/3
info@cremation.org.uk
www.cremation.org.uk

CREST Awards
Awards for creativity in science and technology
c/o The British Science Associ Wellcome Wolfson Building 165 Queen's Gate London SW7 5HD
Tel: 0870 770 7101
email via website
www.britishscienceassociation.org/web/ccaf/CREST

Cricinfo
Cricket information website
www.espncricinfo.com/

Cricket see also Cricinfo, MCC

Cricket Board (England & Wales) ECB
Governing body
Lord's Cricket Ground London NW8 8QZ
Tel: 020 7432 1200
www.ecb.co.uk

Crime and Justice Studies (Centre for)
Non-campaigning body for all concerned with criminal justice
2 Langley Lane London SW8 1GB
Tel: 020 7840 6110
info@crimeandjustice.org.uk
www.crimeandjustice.org.uk

Crime Concern now see Catch22

Crimestoppers
Only charity in the UK helping to solve crimes
PO Box 324 Wallington SM6 6BG
Tel: 0800 555 111 (for public to give in
email via website
www.crimestoppers-uk.org

Criminal Cases Review Commission
Independent public body set up to investigate possible miscarriages of justice in England, Wales and Northern Ireland. Assesses whether convictions or sentences should be referred to a court of appeal.
5 St Philip's Place Birmingham B3 2PW
Tel: 0121 233 1473
info@ccrc.gov.uk
www.ccrc.gov.uk

Criminal Defence Service Legal Services Commission

Criminal Injuries Compensation Authority
Government organisation that can pay money (compensation) to people who have been physically or mentally injured because they were the blameless victim of a violent crime
Tay House 300 Bath Street Glasgow G2 4LN
Helpline: 0300 003 3601
email via website
www.justice.gov.uk/guidance/compensation-schemes/cica/index.htm

Criminal Justice System now see Directgov

CRIN Child Rights Information Network
Global network coordinating information and promoting action on child rights
East Studio 2 Pontypool Place London SE1 8QF
Tel: 020 7401 2257
info@crin.org
www.crin.org

Crisis (UK)
National charity for single homeless people
66 Commerical St London E1 6LT
Tel: 0300 636 1967
enquiries@crisis.org.uk
www.crisis.org.uk

Crisis Counselling for Alleged Shoplifters
PO Box 147 Stanmore Middlesex HA7 4PQ
Tel: 020 8954 8987

Croquet Association
National governing body for the sport of Croquet in England, Wales, Northern Ireland, the Channel Islands and the Isle of Man
c/o Cheltenham Croquet Club Old Bath Rd Cheltenham GL53 7DF
Tel: 01242 242318
caoffice@croquet.org.uk
www.croquet.org.uk

Cross Cultural Solutions
Operates international volunteer programmes
Tower Point 44 North Road Brighton BN1 1YR
Tel: 0845 458 2781 / 2782
Tel: 01273 666392
infouk@crossculturalsolutions.org
www.crossculturalsolutions.org

Crossroads Care now see Carers Trust

Crossroads Women's Centre
Base for a number of organisations covering a wide range of women's issues
230a Kentish Town Road London NW5 2AB
or PO Box 287 London NW6 5QU
Tel: 020 7482 2496 (voice/minicom) (mann
allwomencount@crossroadswomen.net
www.allwomencount.net

Crown Estates
Manages land belonging to the Crown
16 New Burlington Place London W1S 2HX
Tel: 020 7851 5000
email via website
www.crownestate.co.uk

& 6 Bell's Brae Edinburgh EH4 3BJ
Tel: 0131 260 6070

Crown Green Bowling Association (British)
94 Fishers Lane Pensby Wirral CH61 8SB
Tel: 0151 648 5740
email via website
crowngreenbowls.sharepoint.com

Crown Prosecution Service
Rose Court 2 Southwark Bridge London SE1 9HS
Tel: 020 3357 0000
email via website
www.cps.gov.uk

Cruel Sports Ltd (League Against)
Campaigning for the welfare of animals involved in sport
New Sparling House Holloway Hill
Godalming
Surrey GU7 1QZ
Tel: 01483 524 250
info@league.org.uk
www.league.org.uk

Crufts Dog Show
Annual canine spectacular
The Kennel Club 1-5 Clarges St Piccadilly
London W1J 8AB
Tickets: 0844 444 9944
Tel: 0844 463 3980
Email via website
www.crufts.org.uk

Cruising Association
A worldwide association of cruising boaters with headquarters in London containing an extensive library
CA House 1 Northey St Limehouse Basin
London E14 8BT
Tel: 020 7537 2828
email via website
www.cruising.org.uk

Cruse Bereavement Care
Support groups, advice & practical information. Link to RD4U website designed for young people by young people
PO Box 800 Richmond Surrey TW9 1RG
Helpline: 0844 477 9400
Tel: 020 8939 9530
info@cruse.org.uk
www.crusebereavementcare.org.uk
www.rd4u.org.uk

CRY see Cardiac Risk in the Young

Cry-sis
Support for families with excessively crying, sleepless & demanding children
BM Cry-sis London WC1N 3XX (please send stamped addressed envelope)
Helpline: 08451 228 669
info@cry-sis.org.uk
www.cry-sis.org.uk

CSET see Education and Training (Centre for the Study of)

CTC The UK's national cyclists' organisation
Protecting and promoting the rights of cyclists
Parklands Railton Rd Guildford GU2 9JX
Tel: 0844 736 8450
Direct line: 01483 238 337
cycling@ctc.org.uk
www.ctc.org.uk

Cuba Solidarity Campaign
Campaigns in the UK against the US blockade of Cuba
c/o UNITE Woodberry 218 Green Lanes
London N4 2HB
Tel: 020 8800 0155
office@cuba-solidarity.org.uk
www.cuba-solidarity.org.uk

Cued Speech Association UK Complete spoken language through vision
Cued Speech overcomes the problems of lip-reading and thus enables deaf children and adults to understand full spoken language
9 Jawbone Hill Dartmouth Devon TQ6 9RW
Tel: 01803 832 784 (voice and textphone)
info@cuedspeech.co.uk
www.cuedspeech.co.uk

Cult Information Centre

Help and information for families and friends of people involved in cults. Gives talks and offers information to media and researchers
BCM Cults London WC1N 3XX
Tel: 0845 4500 868
www.cultinformation.org.uk

Culture, Media & Sport (Department for)

2-4 Cockspur St London SW1Y 5DH
Tel: 020 7211 6000
enquiries@culture.gov.uk
www.culture.gov.uk

Culture24

Latest news, exhibition reviews, links, event listings and education resources from thousands of UK museums, galleries, archives and libraries, all in one place
Office 4 28 Kensington Street Brighton BN1 4AJ
Tel: 01273 623266
info@culture24.org.uk
www.culture24.org.uk

Currency converter

www.xe.com/ucc/

Curvature of the spine see Scoliosis Association (UK)

Customs and Excise see HM Revenue and Customs

Cutty Sark Trust

To conserve and display the clipper ship 'Cutty Sark'
2 Greenwich Church Street Greenwich London SE10 9BG
Tel: 020 8858 2698
enquiries@cuttysark.org.uk
www.rmg.co.uk/cuttysark

CyberMentors

Supports all young people affected by bullying and uses social networking to allow young people at different levels to mentor each other.
Beatbullying Units 1 + 4 Belvedere Road London SE19 2AT
Tel: 0208 771 3377
admin@beatbullying.org
www.cybermentors.org.uk

Cyclenation

In support of cycling
54-57 Allison Street Digbeth Birmingham B5 5TH
email via website
www.cyclenation.org.uk

Cycling see also Bike Events, Bike Express (European), British Cycling, CTC, Cyclenation, Scottish Cycling, Sustrans, Tandem Club, Welsh Cycling

Cycling Association (Welsh)

www.welshcycling.org

Cycling Campaign (London)

The voice of cyclists in Greater London, working to create a better city for all
2 Newhams Row London SE1 3UZ
Tel: 020 7234 9310
info@lcc.org.uk
www.lcc.org.uk

Cycling Centre (National)

Centre for training in track racing cycling and other sports events
Stuart St Manchester M11 4DQ
Tel: 0161 223 2244
admin@nationalcyclingcentre.com
www.nationalcyclingcentre.com

Cycling Projects

Cycling related training, bringing cycling to disabled people, encouraging people with poor health to take up cycling and working with excluded communities to help them make cycling part of their lives. Runs Health on Wheels and Wheels for All projects
3 Priory Court Buttermarket Street Warrington WA1 2NP
Tel: 01925 234 213
ian.tierney@cycling.org.uk
www.cycling.org.uk

Cycling Union (International) Union Cycliste Internationale
Develops and promotes all aspects of cycling
International Cycling Union (UCI) Ch. de la Mêlée 12 1860 Aigle Switzerland
Tel: 00 41 24 468 5811
admin@uci.ch
www.uci.ch

Cyclists Touring Club now see CTC

Cyclists' Federation (European)

Promoting and encouraging cycling throughout Europe and abroad
Rue Franklin, 28 1000 Brussels, Belgium
Tel: 0032 2 880 92 74
office@ecf.com
www.ecf.com

Cymdeithas Clychoedd Chwarae Cynysgol Cymru see Pre-School Providers Association (Wales)

Cymdeithas Ddrama Cymru see Drama Association of Wales

Cymdeithas y Cerddwyr see Ramblers Association Wales

Cymdeithas yr Iaith Gymraeg Welsh Language Society
Ystafell 5 Y Cambria Rhodfa'r Mor Aberystwyth SY23 2AZ
Tel: 01970 624501
swyddfa@cymdeithas.org
cymdeithas.org

Cyngor Celfyddydau Cymru see Arts Council of Wales

Cyngor Gofal Cymru see Care Council for Wales

Cystic Fibrosis Trust
11 London Rd Bromley Kent BR1 1BY
Support helpline: 0300 373 1000
Tel: 020 8464 7211
enquiries@cftrust.org.uk
www.cftrust.org.uk

D

Dad
To give dads a free and permanent source of the information they're likely to need - from pregnancy, birth and babies to financial, legal and education info - from a dad's perspective
Via website
www.dad.info

Dad Talk
Community of men promoting fatherhood and exploring what it is to be a dad in 21st Century Britain
Via website
www.dadtalk.co.uk

Dads House
Homes for Fathers and Families (HOFF) project aimed at providing the same degree of support for single fathers as is available for single mothers in the UK
5 Kensington Square London W8 5EP
07765 183504
info@dadshouse.co.uk
www.dadshouse.co.uk

Dairy Council (The)
Provides science based information on the role of dairy foods as part of a healthy balanced diet and lifestyle and provides evidenced based information to health professionals, the media, industry and consumers
93 Baker Street London W1U 6QQ
Tel: 020 7467 2629
info@dairycouncil.org.uk
www.milk.co.uk

Daisy Network
Nationwide support group for women who have suffered a premature menopause
PO Box 183   Rossendale BB4 6WZ
daisy@daisynetwork.org.uk
www.daisynetwork.org.uk

Daiwa Anglo-Japanese Foundation
Charity supporting links between Britain & Japan. Scholarships, grant-giving and cultural events
13/14 Cornwall Terrace London NW1 4QP
Tel: 020 7486 4348
office@dajf.org.uk
www.dajf.org.uk

DAN see Disabled People's Council (UK)

Dance Council (British)
Governing body for ballroom dancing in Great Britain
Terpsichore House 240 Merton Road South Wimbledon SW19 1EQ
Tel: 020 8545 0085
secretary@british-dance-council.org
www.british-dance-council.org

Dance Education & Training (Council for)
Provides a list of accredited dance courses & can offer advice on obtaining grants & careers advice
Old Brewer's Yard
17-19 Neal Street Covent Garden
London WC2H 9UY
Tel: 020 7240 5703
info@cdet.org.uk
www.cdet.org.uk

Dance UK
Membership organisation for professional dancers, choreographers, teachers and dance managers
The Urdang The Old Finsbury Town Hall
Rosebery Avenue London EC1R 4QT
Tel: 020 7713 0730
info@danceuk.org
www.danceuk.org

Danceconsortium
Group of 18 large theatres located across the UK sharing a passion for engaging people with contemporary dance from different parts of the world
www.danceconsortium.com

Dancesport UK
Resource on competitive ballroom and Latin dancing
www.dancesport.uk.com

Dancing and Kindred Arts (United Kingdom Alliance of Professional Teachers of) UKA
Centenary House 38/40 Station Rd
Blackpool FY4 1EU
info@ukadance.co.uk
www.ukadance.co.uk

Daneford Trust International Youth Exchange Educational & working exchanges for 18-28 year olds (from London only) in Africa, Asia & the Caribbean
45-47 Blythe St London E2 6LN
Tel: 020 7729 1928
info@danefordtrust.org
www.danefordtrust.org

Dark Skies (Campaign for)
The British Astronomical Association's campaign explores the issues about light pollution and includes educational projects
www.britastro.org/dark-skies

DATA see Design and Technology Association

Data Archive (UK)
The UK's largest collection of digital research data in the social sciences and humanities
data-archive.ac.uk

Data Protection Registrar see Information Commissioner's Office

David Sheldrick Wildlife Trust
Dedicated to the preservation and protection of Africa's wilderness and its denizens, particularly endangered species
2nd Floor 3 Bridge Street Leatherhead KT22 8BL
Tel: 01372 378 321
infouk@sheldrickwildlifetrust.org
www.sheldrickwildlifetrust.org

Day One Christian Ministries
Ryelands Road Leominster Herefordshire HR6 8NZ
Tel: 01568 613740
info@dayone.co.uk
www.lordsday.co.uk

Daycare Trust
Campaigns for quality, accessible, affordable childcare for all
2nd Floor Novas Contemporary Urban Centr
73-81 Southwark Bridge Road London SE1 0NQ
Tel: 0845 872 6260 (020 7940 7510)
info@daycaretrust.org.uk
www.daycaretrust.org.uk

Deaf see also Action on Hearing Loss, Cued Speech Association UK, Hearing Dogs for Deaf People, Music and the Deaf, Sense, Signature, SPIT, TAG

Deaf (Commonwealth Society for the) see Sound Seekers

Deaf Association (British)
18 Leather Lane London EC1N 7SU
Tel: 0207 405 0090
bda@bda.org.uk
www.bda.org.uk

Deaf Children's Society (National) NDCS
Campaign to break down barriers faced by deaf children and young people
15 Dufferin St London EC1Y 8UR
Freephone Helpline & minicom: 0808 800 8880
Tel: 020 7490 8656
Minicom: 020 7490 8656
ndcs@ndcs.org.uk
helpline@ndcs.org.uk
www.ndcs.org.uk

& Northern Ireland
38-42 Hill Street Belfast BT1 2LB
Tel: 028 9031 3170
Minicom: 028 9027 8177
nioffice@ndcs.org.uk

& Scotland
Second Floor Empire House 131 West Nile Street Glasgow G1 2RX
Tel: 0141 354 7850
Textphone: 0141 332 6133
ndcs.scotland@ndcs.org.uk

& Wales
4 Cathedral Road Cardiff CF11 9LJ
Tel: 029 2037 3474
Minicom: 029 2023 2739
ndcswales@ndcs.org.uk

Deaf Education Through Listening and Talking DELTA
Members are parents of deaf children, teachers of the Deaf, etc. Provides information and advice on the Natural Aural Approach to the education of deaf children
The Con Powell Centre Alfa House Molesey Road Walton on Thames Surrey KT12 3PD
Tel: 0845 108 1437
enquiries@deafeducation.org.uk
www.deafeducation.org.uk

Deaf-Blind & Rubella Association (National) see Sense

Deafblind International Dbl
World association promoting services for deafblind people
www.deafblindinternational.org

Deafblind Scotland
21 Alexandra Avenue Lenzie Glasgow G66 5BG
Tel: 0141 777 6111 (voice/text)
info@deafblindscotland.org.uk
www.deafblindscotland.org.uk

Deafblind UK
Assists people who are losing their sight and hearing and raises awareness of deafblindness through educational programmes
National Centre for Deafblindness John & Lucille van Geest Place Cygnet Rd Hampton Peterborough PE7 8FD
Information and Advice Line: 0800 132 320
Tel/Minicom: 01733 358 100
info@deafblind.org.uk
www.deafblind.org.uk

Deafness Research UK
National medical research charity
330/332 Gray's Inn Rd London WC1X 8EE
Freephone: 0808 808 2222
Tel: 020 7164 2290
contact@deafnessresearch.org.uk
www.deafnessresearch.org.uk

DebRA
Supports people living with all forms of epidermolysis bullosa (EB) and funds research into the condition
DebRA House 13 Wellington Business Park Dukes Ride Crowthorne Berks RG45 6LS
Tel: 01344 771961
debra@debra.org.uk
www.debra.org.uk

Debt Advice Foundation
Free and impartial debt advice fromm a UK charity
Free debt advice: 0800 043 40 50
email via website

Deer Society (British)
The Walled Garden Burgate Manor Fordingbridge Hampshire SP6 1EF
Tel: 01425 655434
h.q@bds.org.uk
www.bds.org.uk

Defence (Ministry of) MoD
Main Building Whitehall London SW1A 2HB
Tel: 020 7218 9000
email via website
www.mod.uk

Defra Department for Environment Food & Rural Affairs
Nobel House 17 Smith Square London SW1P 3JR
Tel: 08459 33 55 77
defra.helpline@defra.gsi.gov.uk
www.defra.gov.uk/

Delinquency (Institute for the Study and Treatment of) see Crime and Justice Studies (Centre for)

Dementia see Alzheimer's Research Trust, Alzheimer Scotland, Alzheimer's Society

Democracy and Electoral Assistance (International Institute for) IDEA
An intergovernmental organisation aiming to help build and support democracy
Email via website
www.idea.int

Demos
Political think-tank & publisher
3rd Floor Magdalen House 136 Tooley Street London SE1 2TU
Tel: 0845 458 5949
hello@demos.co.uk
www.demos.co.uk

Dental Association (British)
National professional association for dentists
64 Wimpole St London W1G 8YS
Helpline: 0845 063 1188
Tel: 020 7935 0875
enquiries@bda.org
www.bda.org

& Wales
4th Floor, 2 Caspian Point Caspian Way Cardiff Bay CF10 4DQ
Tel: 029 2049 6174

& Northern Ireland
The Mount 2 Woodstock Link Belfast BT6 8DD
Tel: 02890 735 856

& Scotland
Forsyth House Lomond Court Castle
Business Park Stirling FK9 4TU
Tel: 01786 476040

Dental Council (General)
37 Wimpole St London W1G 8DQ
Tel: 020 7887 3800
Tel: 0845 222 4141
email via website
www.gdc-uk.org

Depaul International
Largest charity for young homeless people in
the UK. Affiliated body for over 50 Nightstop
schemes nationwide
291-299 Borough High Street
London SE1 1JG
Tel: 0207 939 1220
depaul@depauluk.org
www.depauluk.org

Depaul Nightstop UK
Provides safe emergency accommodation for
homeless young people aged 16-25 in the
homes of approved volunteers
www.depaulnightstopuk.org

Depression see also Blurt Foundation,
Journeys, MDF The Bipolar Organisation

Depression (Action on)
Scotland's national charity for depression
11 Alva Street Edinburgh EH2 4PH
Helpline: 0808 802 2020
Tel: 0131 467 3050
info@actionondepression.org
www.dascot.org

Depression Alliance
Information and support
20 Great Dover Street London SE1 4LX
Tel: 0845 1232 320
information@depressionalliance.org
www.depressionalliance.org

Depression Alliance Cymru now see
Journeys

Dermatologists (British Association of)
Professional organisation
Willan House 4 Fitzroy Square
London W1T 5HQ
Tel: 020 7383 0266
admin@bad.org.uk
www.bad.org.uk

Design see also Art & Design (National Society
for Education in), Better Seating (Campaign for)

Design and Artists Copyright Society DACS
By artists for artists. Not for profit visual arts
rights management organisation
33 Great Sutton Street London EC1V 0DX
Tel: 020 7336 8811
info@dacs.org.uk
www.dacs.org.uk

Design and Technology Association DATA
Professional association - inspires, develops
and supports excellence in design and
technology education for all
16 Wellesbourne House Walton Road
Wellesbourne Warwickshire CV35 9JB
Tel: 01789 470007
info@data.org.uk
www.data.org.uk

Design Council
Incorporating CABE. Provides a one stop
shop for design support and advice to
industry, communities, central and local
government
Angel Building 407 St John Street London
EC1V 4AB
Tel: 020 7420 5200
info@designcouncil.org.uk
www.designcouncil.org.uk

Design Museum
Shad Thames London SE1 2YD
Tel: 020 7403 6933
info@designmuseum.org
www.designmuseum.org

Development Education Association now
see Think Global

Development Education Project
Support and training to teachers
St Margarets Centre Brantingham Road
Chortlon-Cum-Hardy Manchester M21 0TT
Tel: 0161 881 8332
info@dep.org.uk
www.dep.org.uk

**Development in Special Needs Education
(European Agency for)** see Special Needs
Education (European Agency for Development
in)

Diabetes UK
Caring for those living with diabetes
Macleod House 10 Parkway
London NW1 7AA
Careline: 0845 120 2960
Tel: 020 7424 1000
info@diabetes.org.uk
www.diabetes.org.uk

& Scotland
The Venlaw 349 Bath Street
Glasgow G2 4AA
Careline: 0845 120 2960
Tel: 0141 245 6380
scotland@diabetes.org.uk
www.diabetes.org.uk

& Northern Ireland
Bridgewood House Newforge Business Park
Newforge Lane Belfast BT9 5NW
Tel: 028 9066 6646
n.ireland@diabetes.org.uk
www.diabetes.org.uk

& Cymru
Argyle House Castlebridge Cowbridge Road
East Cardiff CF11 9AB
Tel: 029 2066 8276
wales@diabetes.org.uk
www.diabetes.org.uk

Diabetes.co.uk The global diabetes community
www.diabetes.co.uk

Dial UK Disability Information and Advice Lines
Provides services and support to over 150
disability advice centres
St Catherine's Tickhill Rd
Doncaster DN4 8QN
Tel/Textphone: 01302 310123
informationenquiries@dialuk.org.uk
www.dialuk.info

Dietetic Association (British)
Professional association and trade union for
state registered dieticians
5th Floor Charles House
148-9 Great Charles Street Queensway
Birmingham B3 3HT
Tel: 0121 200 8080
info@bda.uk.com
www.bda.uk.com

Different Strokes
Charity helping stroke survivors of working
age to optimise their recovery, take control
of their own lives and regain as much
independence as possible by offering
rehabilitative services, information and
advice
9 Canon Harnett Court Wolverton Mill
Milton Keynes MK12 5NF
Tel: 0845 130 7172
Email via website
www.differentstrokes.co.uk

Digestive Disorders Foundation see CORE

Dignity in Dying
Membership organisation campaigning
nationally for greater choice and control to
alleviate suffering at the end of life
181 Oxford Street London W1D 2JT
Tel: 020 7479 7730
info@dignityindying.org.uk
www.dignityindying.org.uk/

DIPEx see Healthtalkonline and
Youthhealthtalk

**Direct Labour Organisations (Association
of)** see Public Service Excellence (Association for)

Direct Marketing Association
Trade association
DMA House 70 Margaret Street London
W1W 8SS
Tel: 020 7291 3300
dma@dma.org.uk
www.dma.org.uk

DirectGov
Links to all government websites
www.direct.gov.uk

Directors (Institute of)
Tel: 020 7766 8866
via website
www.iod.com

Directory of Social Change
Information and training for the voluntary
sector
24 Stephenson Way London NW1 2DP
Tel: 020 7391 4800
Tel: 08450 77 77 07 (Customer services team)
Email via website
www.dsc.org.uk

Disability Action
Northern Ireland organisation which works
to ensure that people with disabilities attain
their full rights as citizens
Portside Business Park 189 Airport Road
West Belfast BT3 9ED
Tel: 028 9029 7880
Textphone: 028 9029 7882
hq@disabilityaction.org
www.disabilityaction.org

Disability Arts Cymru
Work with individuals and organisations
to celebrate the diversity of Disabled &
Deaf People's arts and culture, and develop
equality across all art forms
Sbectrwm Bwlch Rd Fairwater
Cardiff CF5 3EF
Tel & textphone: 029 2055 1040
post@dacymru.com
www.dacymru.com

Disability Law Service
Free and confidential legal advice to disabled
people and their carers
39-45 Cavell Street London E1 2BP
Tel: 020 7791 9800
Minicom: 020 7791 9801
advice@dls.org.uk
www.dls.org.uk

**Disability Pregnancy & Parenthood
International**
National information charity on disability
and parenthood
336 Brixton Road London SW9 7AA
Tel: 0800 018 4730
Textphone: 0800 018 9949
info@dppi.org.uk
www.dppi.org.uk

Disability Rights Commission now see
Equality and Human Rights Commission

Disability Rights UK formerly Disability
Alliance, Radar and National Centre for
Independent Living
>Provides information on benefits through
publications, training and website
12 City Forum 250 City Road London EC1V 8AF
See website for choice of telephone numbers
Tel: 020 7250 3222
enquiries@disabilityrightsuk.org
www.disabilityrightsuk.org

Disability Snowsport UK
>Providing snowsports for all disabilities.
Qualified instructors and helpers attend on
lessons/activity weeks
Glenmore Grounds Aviemore PH22 1QU
Tel: 01479 861272
email via website
www.disabilitysnowsport.org.uk

Disability Sport (English Federation of)
>National body for disabled people in sport
and physical activity throughout England.
SportPark- Loughborough University
3 Oakwood Drive Loughborough
Leicestershire LE11 3QF
Tel: 01509 227750
email via website
www.efds.co.uk

Disabled Children (Council for) now see NCB

Disabled Living Foundation DLV
>Offers advice and information on equipment
and daily living for people with disabilities,
older people and carers
380-384 Harrow Rd London W9 2HU
Helpline: 0845 130 9177 (Textphone) 020
Tel: 020 7289 6111
info@dlf.org.uk
www.dlf.org.uk

Disabled Motoring UK
>To improve independence of disabled
people through better mobility
Nat. HQ Ashwellthorpe Norwich NR16 1EX
Tel: 01508 489449
info@disabledmotoring.org
www.disabledmotoring.org

Disabled Parents Network
>National organisation of and for disabled
people who are parents or who hope to
become parents, and their families, friends
and supporters
Poynters House Poynters Road Dunstable
Bedfordshire LU5 4TP
Helpline & General Enquiries: 0300 3300 639
email via website
www.disabledparentsnetwork.org.uk

Disabled People's Council (UK)
>National umbrella organisation
Stratford Advice Arcade 107-109 The Grove
Stratford London E15 1HP
Tel: 020 8522 7433
ceo@ukdpc.net
www.ukdpc.net

Disablement Information see Dial UK

Disasters Emergency Committee DEC
>Co-ordinates national appeals for response
to major overseas disasters
1st Floor 43 Chalton Street London NW1 1DU
Tel: 0207 387 0200
info@dec.org.uk
www.dec.org.uk

Disfigurement Guidance Centre
>A range of services to provide support for
disfigured people and their families. Also
publishes directory of skin laser clinics
PO Box 7 Cupar Fife KY15 4PF
Tel: 01337 870 281
Tel: 01334 839084
www.timewarp.demon.co.uk/dgc.html

Dispute Resolution see Effective Dispute
Resolution (Centre for)

Divers Marine Life Rescue (British)
>Dedicated to the rescue and well being of all
marine animals in distress around the UK
Lime House Regency Close Uckfield East
Sussex TN22 1DS
Tel: 01825 765546
info@bdmlr.org.uk
www.bdmlr.org.uk

Divorce see also Families Need Fathers,
Fathers4Justice, Relate

**Divorced & Separated (National Council
for the)**
>Helps divorced, separated and widowed
people
68 Parkes Hall Road Woodsetton Dudley
DY1 3SR
Tel: 07041 478120
email via website
www.ncds.org.uk

Do-it Volunteering made easy
>A searchable central database about all
aspects of volunteering
www.do-it.org.uk

Doglost
>The National Database for Lost and Found Dogs
Tel: 0844 800 3220
email via website
www.doglost.co.uk

Dogs see also Battersea Dogs' Home, Canine
Partners, Crufts Dog Show, Guide Dogs for
the Blind Association, Hearing Dogs for Deaf
People, Kennel Club, Pets as Therapy, Support
Dogs

Dogs for the Disabled
Provides trained assistance dogs to help disabled people
The Frances Hay Centre Blacklocks Hill Banbury OX17 2BS
Tel: 01295 252600
info@dogsforthedisabled.org
www.dogsforthedisabled.org

Dogs Trust
Largest dog welfare charity in the UK. Cares for dogs at a nationwide network of rehoming centres and gives educational presentations
17 Wakley St London EC1V 7RQ
Tel: 020 7837 0006
Email via website
www.dogstrust.org.uk

Domain names see Nominet UK

Domestic Violence see also Advocacy
After Fatal Domestic Abuse, Ahimsa, Broken Rainbow, Concord Media, Eaves Housing for Women, Family Action, Hideout, Men's Advice Line, Refuge, Women's Aid, Women's Aid Federation

Domestic Violence (Campaign Against)
CADV
Campaigns to increase awareness and to improve facilities and services for women. Campaign for legal change and the recognition of domestic violence as a workplace issue
PO Box 2371 London E1 5NQ
Freephone 24 Hour 0808 2000 247
Tel: 020 8520 5881
enquiries@cadv.org.uk
www.cadv.org.uk

Donkey Breed Society
The Hermitage Pootings Edenbridge Kent TN8 6SD
Tel: 01732 864414
societysecretary@donkeybreed society.co.uk
www.donkeybreedsociety.co.uk

Donkey Sanctuary
Registered charity working worldwide for donkeys
Sidmouth Devon EX10 0NU
Tel: 01395 578222
email via website
www.thedonkeysanctuary.org.uk

Donor Conception Network
Self-help network of over 1,300 families created with the help of donated eggs, sperm or embryos; couples and individuals seeking to found a family this way; and adults conceived using a donor
154 Caledonian Road London N1 9RD
Tel: 020 7278 2608
email via website
www.donor-conception-network.org

Donor Family Network
Supports donor families and promotes awareness of organ donation
PO Box 13825 Birmingham B42 9DJ
Tel: 0845 680 1954
info@donorfamilynetwork.co.uk
www.donorfamilynetwork.co.uk

Douglas Bader Foundation
Exists to advance and promote the physical, mental and spiritual welfare of persons who are without one or more limbs, or otherwise physically disabled
45 Dundale Road Tring Herts HP23 5BU
Tel: 01442 826662
douglasbaderfdn@btinternet.com
www.douglasbaderfoundation.co.uk

Down Syndrome Education International
Applied research and practical support improves education and transforms the lives of thousands of children worldwide
6 Underley Business Centre Kirkby Lonsdale Cumbria LA6 2DY
Tel:0300 330 0750
info@dseinternational.org
www.dseinternational.org

Down to Earth International Campaign for Ecological Justice in Indonesia
Works with partners in Indonesia and internationally to promote climate justice and sustainable livelihoods in Indonesia
Greenside Farmhouse Hallbankgate Cumbria CA8 2PX
Tel: 016977 46266
dte@gn.apc.org
www.downtoearth-indonesia.org/

Down's Heart Group
Support and information for families who have a member with Down's Syndrome and congenital heart defects
PO Box 4260 Dunstable Beds LU6 2ZT
Tel: 0844 288 4800
info@dhg.org.uk
www.dhg.org.uk

Down's Syndrome Association
Langdon Down Centre 2a Langdon Park Teddington TW11 9PS
tel:020 8614 5100
info@downs-syndrome.org.uk
www.downs-syndrome.org.uk

Down's Syndrome Medical Interest Group
Essential information for healthcare professionals on 'best practice' medical care for people with Down's syndrome in the UK and Ireland. Produced by a network of doctors from the UK and Republic of Ireland
www.dsmig.org.uk

Down's Syndrome Scotland
158/160 Balgreen Road
Edinburgh EH11 3AU
Tel: 0131 313 4225
info@dsscotland.org.uk
www.dsscotland.org.uk

Downing Street see 10 Downing Street
Website

Dr Edward Bach see Bach Centre

Dr Hadwen Trust for Humane Research
DHT
UK's leading non-animal medical research
charity
Suite 8 Portmill House Portmill Lane
Hitchin Hertfordshire SG5 1DJ
01462 436819
info@drhadwentrust.org
http://www.drhadwentrust.org

Dragonfly Society (British)
23 Bowker Way Whittlesey
Peterborough PE7 1PY
Tel: 01733 204286
secretary@british-dragonflies.org.uk
www.british-dragonflies.org.uk

Drama see also National Drama, NODA, RADA,
Student Drama Festival (National), Teaching of
Drama (National Association for the), Theatre
Council (Independent), Theatre for Children and
Young People (International Association), Youth
Theatres (National Association of)

Drama Association of Wales Cymdeithas
Ddrama Cymru
Increasing opportunities for people in the
community to be creatively involved in
drama. Houses the largest specialist Drama
lending library in the world
Unit 2, The Maltings East Tyndall Street
Cardiff CF24 5EA
Tel: 029 2045 2200
info@dramawales.org.uk
www.dramawales.org.uk

Drama Schools (The Conference of) now
see Drama UK

Drama Training (National Council for) now
see Drama UK

Drama UK formerly Drama Training (National
Council for) and Drama Schools (The
Conference of)
Provides a list of accredited drama courses
& can offer advice on obtaining grants &
careers advice
2nd Floor 23 Tavistock Street
London WC2E 7NX
Tel: 020 7420 7740
info@dramauk.co.uk
www.drama.ac.uk

Dramatic Need
Sends international volunteers from
the creative arts to South Africa to host
workshops with children living in rural
communities
37 Wakeman Road London NW10 5BJ
info@dramaticneed.org
www.dramaticneed.org

Drawing (The Campaign for)
Organises events to promote drawing,
including 'The Big Draw' in October UK-wide
7 Gentlemen's Row Enfield EN2 6PT
Tel: 020 8351 1719
admin@campaignfordrawing.org
www.campaignfordrawing.org

Drink Helpline (National)
Free confidential advice about alcohol
related problems
Drinkline: 0800 917 8282

Drinkaware
Useful information about alcohol and
drinking
Samuel House 6 St Albans St
London SW1Y 4SQ
Tel: 020 7766 9900
Email via website
www.drinkaware.co.uk

Drinking & Driving see CADD

**Drinking Water Inspector - Northern
Ireland** DWINI
Tel: 028 9056 9282
dwi@doeni.gov.uk
www.doeni.gov.uk/niea/water-home/
drinking_water.htm

Drinking Water Inspectorate
Checks that the water companies in England
and Wales supply safe drinking water that
is acceptable to consumers and meets the
standards set down in law
Area 4a Ergon House Horseferry Road
London SW1P 2AL
Tel: 030 0068 6400
dwi.enquiries@defra.gsi.gov.uk
dwi.defra.gov.uk

**Drinking Water Quality Regulator For
Scotland** DWQR
PO Box 23598 EDINBURGH EH6 6WW
Tel: 0131 244 0190
via website
www.dwqr.org.uk

Driver and Vehicle Licensing Agency see
DVLA

Drug Education Forum

Online forums for those involved in drug education. In particular to those interested in the development of policy and practice
c/o Mentor UK 4th Floor 74 Great Eastern Street London EC2A 3JG
Tel: 0207 739 8494
email via website
www.drugeducationforum.com

Drugs and Crime (UN Office on) UNODC

www.unodc.org

Drugs Forum (Scottish)

National non government agency for policy and information work
91 Mitchell Street Glasgow G1 3LN
Tel: 0141 221 1175
enquiries@sdf.org.uk
www.sdf.org.uk

Drugs Helpline (National) now see Frank

DrugScope

Centre of expertise on drugs which works to inform policy development and reduce drug related risk
Prince Consort House Suite 204 (2nd Floor) 109/111 Farringdon Road London EC1R 3BW
Tel: 020 7520 7550
info@drugscope.org.uk
www.drugscope.org.uk

Duke of Edinburgh's Award

Leading youth Charity. Gives all young people aged 14 to 24 the chance to develop skills for work and life, fulfil their potential and have a brighter future
Head Office Gulliver House Madeira Walk Windsor SL4 1EU
Tel: 01753 727400
info@DofE.org
www.dofe.org

& Scotland
Rosebery House 9 Haymarket Terrace Edinburgh EH12 5EZ
Tel: 0131 343 0920
scotland@DofE.org

& Northern Ireland
Unit 4 Lower Ground Floor Forestgrove Business Park Newtownbreda Road Belfast BT8 6AW
Tel: 028 9069 9100
nireland@DofE.org

& Wales
Market House Market Approach Brecon Powys LD3 7DA
Tel: 01874 623086
wales@DofE.org

Dulwich Picture Gallery

England's first public art gallery
Gallery Rd London SE21 7AD
Tel: 020 8693 5254
email via website
www.dulwichpicturegallery.org.uk

DVLA Driver and Vehicle Licensing Agency

Swansea SA6 7JL
Tel: 0300 790 6801 (Drivers enquiries)
Textphone: 0300 123 1278
email via website
www.dft.gov.uk/dvla/

Dying Matters

Raising awareness of dying, death and bereavement, encouraging people to talk about their wishes towards the end of their lives, including where they want to die and their funeral plans with friends, family and loved ones.
Email via website
www.dyingmatters.org

Dyslexia Action

Park House Wick Rd Egham Surrey TW20 0HH
Tel: 01784 222300
email via website
www.dyslexiaaction.org.uk

Dyslexia Association (British) BDA

Unit 8, Bracknell Beeches Old Bracknell Lane Bracknell RG12 7BW
Helpline: 0845 251 9002
Tel: 0845 251 9003
admin@bdadyslexia.org.uk
helpline@bdadyslexia.org.uk
www.bdadyslexia.org.uk

Dyspraxia Foundation

8 West Alley Hitchin Herts SG5 1EG
Tel: 01462 454 986
Tel: 01462 455 016
dyspraxia@dyspraxiafoundation.org.uk
www.dyspraxiafoundation.org.uk

E

e-Learning Foundation
Helps schools give access to IT to their most deprived students and their families
3000 Hillswood Drive Hillswood Business Park Chertsey Surrey KT16 0RS
Tel: 01932 796 036
info@e-learningfoundation.com
www.e-learningfoundation.com

E-MINE Electronic Mine Information Network
Supports planning & co-ordination of global mine action programmes, issues, best practice & technologies
www.mineaction.org

Early Childhood Education (British Association for) now see Early Education

Early Education
Works to improve educational provision for children from birth to 8 years
British Association for Early 136 Cavell St London E1 2JA
Tel: 020 7539 5400
office@early-education.org.uk
www.early-education.org.uk

Early Years The organisation for young children
Provides information and training for parents, childcare providers, employers and local authorities
6c Wildflower Way
Apollo Road Boucher Road Belfast BT12 6TA
Tel: 028 9066 2825
email via website
www.early-years.org

Earth First! Worldwide
Direct action movement
www.earthfirst.org

EarthAction
A global action alert network
www.earthaction.org

Earthquake Locator (World Wide)
Website giving locations and other details of recent earthquakes
tsunami.geo.ed.ac.uk/local-bin/quakes/mapscript/home.pl

Earthwatch Institute
An environmental charity supporting scientific field research
Mayfield House 256 Banbury Rd Oxford OX2 7DE
Tel: 01865 318 838
info@earthwatch.org.uk
www.earthwatch.org

Eating Disorders see BEAT

Eating Problems Service
Tel: 020 7602 0862
post@eatingproblems.org
www.eatingproblems.org

Eaves
Support housing and refuge accommodation for homeless women and women escaping domestic violence plus other violence against women projects
Unit 2.03, Canterbury Court 1-3 Brixton Rd London SW9 6DE
Tel: 020 7735 2062
post@eaveshousing.co.uk
www.eaves4women.co.uk

ECB see Cricket Board (England & Wales)

ECHO
European Union's humanitarian arm, providing emergency assistance and relief to the victims of natural disaster or armed conflict worldwide
ec.europa.eu/echo/index_en.htm

Eco-Schools
Promotes environmental awareness & has a scheme of awards
Keep Britain Tidy Elizabeth House The Pier Wigan WN3 4EX
Tel: 01942 612621
eco-schools@keepbritaintidy.org
www.keepbritaintidy.org/ecoschools/

Ecological Society (British)
Publishes a range of scientific literature, organises and sponsors a wide variety of meetings, funds numerous grant schemes, education work and policy work
Charles Darwin House
12 Roger Street London WC1N 2JU
Tel: 0207 685 2500
info@BritishEcologicalSociety.org
www.britishecologicalsociety.org

Ecology & Hydrology (Centre for) see CEH

Ecology Building Society
Ethical savings and green mortgages for properties in need of renovation and ecological new builds
7 Belton Road Silsden Keighley West Yorkshire BD20 0EE
Tel: 0845 674 5566
Tel: 01535 650 770
info@ecology.co.uk
www.ecology.co.uk

Economic & Social Research (National Institute of)
2 Dean Trench Street Smith Square London SW1P 3HE
Tel: 0207 222 7665
enquiries@niesr.ac.uk
www.niesr.ac.uk

Economics, Business and Enterprise Association EBEA
Subject association for teachers
www.ebea.org.uk

Ecotourism Society (The International)
Seeks to be the global source of knowledge and advocacy uniting communities, conservation, and sustainable travel
www.ecotourism.org

ECRA see Ethical Consumer Research Association

Eczema Society (National)
Hill House Highgate Hill London N19 5NA
Helpline: 0800 089 1122
Tel: 020 7281 3553
helpline@eczema.org
info@eczema.org
www.eczema.org

Eden Project
Centre for plants & a new scientific institute
Bodelva Cornwall PL24 2SG
Tel: 01726 811911
email via website
www.edenproject.com

Edexcel
Examining & awarding body
190 High Holborn London WC1V 7BH
emai via website
www.edexcel.org.uk

Edinburgh International Book Festival
Organises the world's largest book festival in Charlotte Square Gardens every August
5a Charlotte Square Edinburgh EH2 4DR
Tel: 0131 718 5666
admin@edbookfest.co.uk
www.edbookfest.co.uk

Edinburgh International Festival
A festival of the arts taking place every August
The Hub Castlehill Edinburgh EH1 2NE
Tel: 0131 473 2099
Email via website
www.eif.co.uk

Editors and Proofreaders (Society for)
Apsley House 176 Upper Richmond Road Putney London SW15 2SH
Tel: 020 8785 6155
administrator@sfep.org.uk
www.sfep.org.uk

Education (Department for)
Responsible for education and children's services
Tel: 0370 000 2288
Typetalk: 18001 0370 000 2288
email via website
www.education.gov.uk

Education (Global Campaign for)
www.campaignforeducation.org

Education & Industry (Centre for)
Centre of expertise in education, especially work related learning
University of Warwick Coventry CV4 7AL
Tel: 024 7652 3909
cei@warwick.ac.uk
www2.warwick.ac.uk/fac/soc/cei

Education & Research Networking Association (UK) see JANET

Education and Culture (Directorate General for) European Commission
ec.europa.eu/dgs/education_culture/index_en.htm

Education and Training (Centre for the Study of) CSET
Researches education, training & careers
Department of Educational Research County South Lancaster University Lancaster LA1 4YD
Tel: 01524 592679
d.daglish@lancaster.ac.uk
www.lancs.ac.uk/fss/centres/cset

Education Business Excellence (Institute for) IEBE
Provides links between the worlds of business and education to offer young people a rewarding and realistic introduction to the world of work
Tel: 020 8481 3367
email via website
www.iebe.org.uk

Education Consultants (Society of)
Network of individual consultants working under a code of practice
309 Scott House The Custard Factory Gibb Street Birmingham B9 4AA
Tel: 0845 345 7932
administration@sec.org.uk
www.sec.org.uk

Education for Choice
Provides educational materials about abortion
421 Highgate Studios 53 - 79 Highgate Road London NW5 1TL
Tel: 020 7284 6040
efc@efc.org.uk
www.efc.org.uk

Education in Art and Design (National Society for) see Art and Design (National Society for Education in)

Education Index (British)
An index to the contents of 300 education and training journals
Brotherton Library University of Leeds Leeds LS2 9JT
Tel: 0113 343 5525
bei@leeds.ac.uk
www.leeds.ac.uk/bei

Education of Adults (European Association for the) EAEA
www.eaea.org

Education Otherwise
For families who want to educate children outside the school system
PO Box 3761 Swindon SN2 9GT
Helpline: 0845 478 6345
email via website
www.education-otherwise.net

Education Scotland
Advice, guidance, products and services relating to the pre-school and school curriculum
Denholm House Almondvale Business Park Almondvale Way Livingstone EH54 6GA
Tel: 0141 282 5000
Textphone: 01506 600 236
enquiries@educationscotland.gov.uk
www.ltscotland.org.uk

Education Statistics (National Center for)
Collects & analyses data about the USA & other nations. Part of the US Dept of Education
nces.ed.gov

Educational Psychologists (Association of)
Trade union and professional association
4 The Riverside Centre Frankland Lane Durham DH1 5TA
Tel: 0191 384 9512
email via website
www.aep.org.uk

Educational Recording Agency
Licenses UK educational establishments to record TV & radio programmes for non commercial educational use
Verulam House 60 Gray's Inn Road London WC1X 8LU
Tel: 020 7837 3222
era@era.org.uk
www.era.org.uk

Educational Visits & Exchanges see British Council, Commonwealth Youth Exchange Council, Daneford Trust, Fulbright Commission, Youth in Action

Effective Dispute Resolution (Centre for)
Aims to encourage cost-effective resolution and prevention techniques
70 Fleet Street London EC4Y 1EU
Tel: 020 7536 6000
info@cedr.com
www.cedr.com

Egg Information Service (British)
Represents 'Lion' egg producers. Provides leaflets and information about eggs
52A Cromwell Road London SW7 5BE
Tel: 0207 052 8899
www.britegg.co.uk

EIRIS Experts in Responsible Investment Solutions
Researches the social and environmental aspects of companies. Provides general ethical investment information (non financial) to the public
80-84 Bondway London SW8 1SF
Tel: 020 7840 5700
info@eiris.org
www.eiris.org

Elastic Rope Sports Association (British) BERSA
Certification body for bungee jumping
33a Canal Street Oxford OX2 6BQ
Tel: 01865 311179
info@bersa.org
www.bungeezone.com/orgs/bersa.shtml

Elder Abuse (Action on)
For anyone concerned about abuse of an older person
PO Box 60001 Streatham SW16 9BY
Helpline: 0808 808 8141
Tel: 020 8835 9280
enquiries@elderabuse.org.uk
www.elderabuse.org.uk

Elderly Accommodation Counsel
Promoting choice for older people
Aims to help older people make informed choices about meeting their housing and care needs
3rd Floor 89 Albert Embankment London SE1 7TP
Tel: 0800 377 7070
email via website
www.eac.org.uk

Elders (The)
The Elders are an independent group of eminent global leaders, brought together by Nelson Mandela, who offer their collective influence and experience to support peace building, help address major causes of human suffering and promote the shared interests of humanity
www.theelders.org

Electoral Reform Services
The Election Centre 33 Clarendon Rd London N8 0NW
Tel: 020 8365 8909
enquiries@electoralreform.co.uk
www.electoralreform.co.uk

Electoral Reform Society
Campaigns to strengthen democracy through changes to the voting system
Thomas Hare House
6 Chancel St London SE1 0UU
Tel: 020 7928 1622
ers@electoral-reform.org.uk
www.electoral-reform.org.uk

& Scotland
12 South Charlotte Street Edinburgh EH2
4AX
Tel: 0131 624 9853
scotland@electoral-reform.org.uk
www.electoral-reform.org.uk

& Wales
Temple Court Cathedral Road Cardiff CF11
9HA
Tel: 029 2078 6522/3
wales@electoral-reform.org.uk
www.electoral-reform.org.uk

Electricity Regulation see Ofgem

Ellen MacArthur Cancer Trust
Takes young people aged between 8-24
sailing to help them regain their confidence,
on their way to recovery from cancer,
leukaemia and other serious illness.
Units 53-57, East Cowes Marina Off Britannia
Way East Cowes Isle of Wight PO32 6UB
Tel: 01983 297750
info@emcancertrust.org
www.ellenmacarthurtrust.org

Embarrassing Problems
A doctor's website that deals with health
problems that can be difficult to discuss
www.embarrassingproblems.com

EMDP Exercise, Movement and Dance Partnership
Governing body
1 Grove House Foundry Lane Horsham
West Sussex RH13 5PL
Tel: 01403 266000
info@emdp.org
www.emdp.info

EMI Music Sound Foundation
Independent charity providing funds for
music education
27 Wrights Lane London W8 5SW
Tel: 020 7795 7000
enquiries@emimusicsoundfoundation.com
www.emimusicsoundfoundation.com

Emily's List UK now see Labour Women's
Network

Emmaus
Emmaus Communities offer homeless
people a home, work and the chance to
rebuild their self-respect.
76 - 78 Newmarket Road Cambridge CB5 8DZ
Tel: 01223 576103
contact@emmaus.org.uk
www.emmaus.org.uk

Employment & Learning (Department for)
Northern Ireland
Adelaide House 39-49 Adelaide Street
Belfast BT2 8FD
Tel: 028 9025 7777
info@delni.gov.uk
www.delni.gov.uk

Employment Appeals Tribunal now see
Justice

**Employment Research (Warwick Institute
for)**
A leading research centre in the field of
labour market analysis
Social Sciences Building University of
Warwick Coventry CV4 7AL
Tel: 02476 523283
ier@warwick.ac.uk
www2.warwick.ac.uk/fac/soc/ier

Employment Rights (Institute of)
Independent think tank specialising in
employment and trade union law
4th Floor Jack Jones House 1 Islington
Liverpool L3 8EG
Tel: 0151 207 5265
office@ier.org.uk
www.ier.org.uk

Employment Solicitors
www.employment-solicitors.co.uk

Employment Studies (Institute for)
Independent research and consultancy,
employment and human resources issues
Sovereign House Church Street Brighton
BN1 1UJ
Tel: 01273 763400
email via website
www.employment-studies.co.uk

Empty Homes Agency
Campaigns to bring empty buildings in the
UK back into use
75 Westminster Bridge Road London SE1
7HS
Tel: 020 7921 4450
info@emptyhomes.co.uk
www.emptyhomes.com

ENABLE Scotland
Charity for people with learning disabilities &
their families in Scotland
Enable Direct: 0300 0200 101
Tel: 0141 226 4541
enabledirect@enable.org.uk
www.enable.org.uk

ENCAMS now see Keep Britain Tidy

End violence against women
UK-wide coalition calling for urgent action
to end all forms of violence against women
and girls
17-25 New Inn Yard London EC2A 3EA
Tel: 020 70331559
admin@evaw.org.uk
www.endviolenceagainstwomen.org.uk

Endeavour Training Limited

Providing personal development training for young people
Units 5 & 6 Sheepbridge Centre Sheepbridge Lane Chesterfield S41 9RX
Tel: 01246 454 957
info@endeavour.org.uk
www.endeavour.org.uk

Endometriosis UK

Information and support
Suites 1 & 2 Manchester Street
London W1U 7LS
Helpline: 0808 808 2227
Tel: 020 7222 2781
admin@endometriosis-uk.org
www.endometriosis-uk.org

Energy Association (International)

Intergovernmental body committed to advancing security of energy supply, economic growth and environmental sustainability
www.iea.org

Energy Charity see National Energy Action

Energy Foundation (National)

Charity providing advice and information on energy efficiency and renewable energy
Davy Avenue Knowlhill Milton Keynes MK5 8NG
Tel: 01908 665555
info@nef.org.uk
www.nef.org.uk

Energy Saving Trust

UK's leading impartial organisation helping people to save energy and reduce carbon emissions
21 Dartmouth Street London SW1H 9BP
Advice line: 0800 512 012
Tel: 020 7222 0101
Email via website
www.energysavingtrust.org.uk

& Scotland
2nd Floor Ocean Point 1 94 Ocean Drive
Edinburgh EH6 6JH
Advice line: 0800 512 012
Tel: 0131 555 7900
Email via website
www.energysavingtrust.org.uk

& Wales
1 Caspian Point Caspian Way Cardiff Bay
Cardiff CF10 4DQ
Advice line: 0800 512 012
Tel: 029 2046 8340
Email via website
www.energysavingtrust.org.uk

& Northern Ireland
Enterprise House 55/59 Adelaide Street
Belfast BT2 8FE
Advice line: 0800 512 012
Tel: 028 9072 6006
Email via website
www.energysavingtrust.org.uk

Energywatch now see Consumer Focus

Engage

The National Association for Gallery Education – Promotes understanding and enjoyment of the visual arts
35-47 Bethnal Green Road London E1 6LA
Tel: 020 7729 5858
info@engage.org
www.engage.org

& Scotland
Tel: 01738 787137
scotland@engage.org
www.engagescotland.org.uk

& Cymru
Tel: 01834 870121
cymru@engage.org
www.engagecymru.org.uk

Engineering Council

Regulates the engineering profession in the UK and runs the register of Chartered Engineers, Incorporated Engineers & Engineering Technicians
246 High Holborn London WC1V 7EX
Tel: 020 3206 0500
email via website
www.engc.org.uk

England & Wales Cricket Board see Cricket Board (England & Wales)

England Athletics

National Governing Body for the sport, developing and promoting Athletics across the whole of the country
Athletics House Alexander Stadium Walsall Road, Perry Barr Birmingham B42 2BE
Tel: 0121 347 6543
enquiries@englandathletics.org
www.englandathletics.org

England Golf

Governing body for all amateur golf in England
The National Golf Centre, Woodhall Spa Lincolnshire LN10 6PU
01526 354500
info@englandgolf.org
www.englandgolf.org

England Hockey

National governing body for hockey in England
Bisham Abbey NSC Bisham Marlow Buckinghamshire SL7 1RR
Tel: 01628 897500
info@englandhockey.org
www.englandhockey.co.uk

England Netball

Netball House 9 Paynes Park Hitchin SG5 1EH
Tel: 01462 442344
info@englandnetball.co.uk
www.englandnetball.co.uk

England Squash & Racketball
The governing body for squash in England
National Squash Centre Sportcity
Manchester M11 3FF
Tel: 0161 231 4499
enquiries@englandsquashandracketball.com
www.englandsquashandracketball.com

English and Media Centre
Good practice in teaching English and media
via INSET and publications and website
resources.
18 Compton Terrace London N1 2UN
Tel: 020 7359 8080
info@englishandmedia.co.uk
www.englishandmedia.co.uk

English Association
Aims to further knowledge, understanding
and enjoyment of the English language and
its literatures and to foster good practice in
its teaching and learning at all levels
University of Leicester University Rd
Leicester LE1 7RH
Tel: 0116 229 7622
engassoc@le.ac.uk
www.le.ac.uk/engassoc

English Heritage
Official government agency which manages
historic buildings & ancient monuments.
Education section provides resource material
and free educational visits to English
Heritage sites
1 Waterhouse Square 138-142 Holborn
London EC1N 2ST
Customer Service: 0870 333 1181
Tel: 020 7973 3000 (Head Office)
Minicom: 0800 015 0516
customers@english-heritage.org.uk
www.english-heritage.org.uk
www.english-heritage.org.uk/education

English Language
see Bilingualism
& Literacies Education Network, IATEFL
(International Association of Teachers of
English as a Foreign Language), Plain English
Campaign, Teaching of English (National
Association for the)

English National Ballet
Markova House 39 Jay Mews
London SW7 2ES
Tel: 020 7581 1245
comments@ballet.org.uk
www.ballet.org.uk

English National Opera
Performs all opera in English
London Coliseum St Martin's Lane London
WC2N 4ES
Tel: 020 7836 0111
feedback@eno.org
www.eno.org

English PEN
Promotes literature, upholds writers'
freedoms and campaigns against the
persecution of writers for stating their views
Free Word Centre 60 Farringdon Road
London EC1R 3GA
Tel: 020 7324 2535
email via website
www.englishpen.org

English Schools' Athletic Association
(ESSA) see Athletic Association (English
Schools')

English Speaking Union
Creates international understanding and
promotes human achievement through the
widening use of the English language
Dartmouth House 37 Charles St London
W1J 5ED
Tel: 020 7529 1550
speech.debate@esu.org
www.esu.org

English Touring Theatre
Touring productions of clarity and style
throughout the UK
25 Short St London SE1 8LJ
Tel: 020 7450 1990
admin@ett.org.uk
www.ett.org.uk

ENO see English National Opera

Enterprise Education Trust
Brings business to life for students, aged 14
to 19
Enterprise House 1-2 Hatfields London SE1
9PG
Tel: 020 7620 0735
info@enterprise-education.org.uk
www.enterprise-education.org.uk

Entomologists' Society (Amateur)
For people interested in insects
PO Box 8774 London SW7 5ZG
email via website
www.amentsoc.org

Entrepreneurs see Social Entrepreneurs
(School for)

Enuresis Resource & Information Centre
see ERIC – Education and Resources for
Improving Childhood Continence

Environment (Young People's Trust for
the)
Charity that aims to encourage young
people's understanding of the environment
and the need for sustainability
3A Market Square Crewkerne Somerset
TA18 7LE
Tel: 01460 271717
info@ypte.org.uk
www.ypte.org.uk

Environment Agency
Protects and improves environment, and promotes sustainable development
National Customer Contact Centre PO Box 544 Rotherham S60 1BY
24hr Floodline: 0845 988 1188
Tel: 03708 506 506
Minicom: 08702 422 549
enquiries@environment-agency.gov.uk
www.environment-agency.gov.uk

Environment and Development (International Institute for)
80-86 Gray's Inn Road London WC1X 8NH
Tel: 020 3463 7399
info@iied.org
www.iied.org

Environment Council
Helps stakeholders to find sustainable solutions to environmental issues
www.the-environment-council.org.uk

Environment Protection Agency (Scottish)
SEPA
Erskine Court Castle Business Park Stirling FK9 4TR
Pollution Hotline - 0800 80 70 60
Floodline service - 0845 988 1188
Tel: 01786 457700
Email via website
www.sepa.org.uk

Environment, Food & Rural Affairs (Department for) see Defra

Environmental Investigation Agency
Non-governmental organisation investigating and exposing the illegal trade in endangered species
62/63 Upper St London N1 0NY
Tel: 020 7354 7960
ukinfo@eia-international.org
www.eia-international.org

Environmental Law & Development (Foundation for International) see FIELD

Environmental Law Foundation
National UK charity linking communities and individuals to legal and technical expertise to prevent damage to the environment
2-10 Princeton Street London WC1R 4BH
Tel: 020 7404 1030
info@elflaw.org
www.elflaw.org

Environmental Noise Maps
Maps of noise from roads, rail and industry in England
services.defra.gov.uk/wps/portal/noise

Environmental Protection UK
Membership based charity. Aims to promote policies and practices to reduce the negative effects on health and the environment of air pollution and greenhouses gases, manage and control noise and encourage the use and reuse of land
c/o Land and Environmental Services Glasgow City Council 231 George Street Glasgow G1 1RX
admin@environmental-protection.org.uk
www.environmental-protection.org.uk

Environmental Transport Association
Environmental breakdown company and lobby for a sustainable transport system
68 High St Weybridge KT13 8RS
Freephone: 0800 212 810
eta@eta.co.uk
www.eta.co.uk

ENYAN English National Youth Arts Network
Aims to raise the profile and support for youth arts within England, creating more opportunities for the creative and personal development of young people, especially young people at risk.
c/o Artswork Ltd, Unit 26, The Bargate Shopping Centre Southampton, SO14 1HF
Tel: 023 80332491
info@artswork.org.uk
www.enyan.co.uk

Epidermolysis Bullosa see DEBRA

Epilepsy (National Centre for Young People with) NCYPE
Runs courses for teachers and other education professionals.
St Piers Lane Lingfield Surrey RH7 6PW
Confidential enquiry line: 01342 831342
Tel: 01342 832243
info@youngepilepsy.org.uk
www.ncype.org.uk

Epilepsy Action
Acting as the voice for the UK's estimated 456,000 people with epilepsy, as well as their friends, families, carers, health professionals
New Anstey House Gate Way Drive Yeadon Leeds LS19 7XY
Freephone Helpline: 0808 800 5050
Tel: 0113 210 8800
helpline@epilepsy.org.uk
epilepsy@epilepsy.org.uk
www.epilepsy.org.uk

Epilepsy Scotland
48 Govan Rd Glasgow G51 1JL
Helpline: 0808 800 2200
Tel: 0141 427 4911
enquiries@epilepsyscotland.org.uk
www.epilepsyscotland.org.uk

Epilepsy Society
Charity providing epilepsy research, treatment, assessment, care, info and training
Chesham Lane Chalfont St Peter Bucks SL9 0RJ
Helpline: 01494 601400
Tel: 01494 601 300
Email via website
www.epilepsysociety.org.uk

Equal Opportunities Commission now see
Equality and Human Rights Commission

Equality and Human Rights Commission
Creating a fairer Britain
Independent statutory body established to help promote and monitor human rights and to protect, enforce and promote equality across the nine "protected" grounds - age, disability, gender, race, religion and belief, pregnancy and maternity, marriage and civil partnership, sexual orientation and gende
Offices in Manchester, London, Glasgow and Cardiff.
email via website
www.equalityhumanrights.com

Equality Britain
Promotes opportunities for everyone regardless of race, age, disability, religion or belief, sexual orientation, gender or transgender status
Tel:0151 920 0074
Email via website
www.equalitybritain.co.uk

Erasmus
European exchange programme for higher education
Bridgewater House Manchester M1 6BB
Tel: 0161 957 7755
erasmus.enquiries@britishcouncil.org
www.britishcouncil.org/erasmus

Ergonomics & Human Factors (Institute of)
Promoting ergonomics and supporting professionals using information about people to design for comfort, efficiency & safety. Ergonomics 4 Schools website is suitable for anyone but is aimed primarily at secondary schools
Elms Court Elms Grove Loughborough LE11 1RG
Tel: 01509 234904
iehf@ergonomics.org.uk
www.ergonomics.org.uk
www.ergonomics4schools.com

ERIC - Education and Resources for Improving Childhood Continence
Information, support and resources on childhood bedwetting and daytime wetting
36 Old School House Britannia Rd Kingswood Bristol BS15 8DB
Helpline: 0845 370 8008
Tel: 0117 960 3060
info@eric.org.uk
www.eric.org.uk

ERYICA see European Youth Info. and Counselling Agency

ESAA see Athletic Association (English Schools')

Esperanto Association of Britain
Promotes the international language of Esperanto
Esperanto House Station Rd Barlaston Stoke-on-Trent ST12 9DE
Tel: 0845 230 1887
eab@esperanto-gb.org
www.esperanto.org.uk

ESU European Students' Union
Represents the 10 million students across Europe to European Institutions such as the Parliament
Tel: 00 32 2502 23 62
Email via website
www.esu-online.org

ETCO European Transplant Coordinators Organisation
Promotes organ and tissue donation in all member countries
Email via website
www.europeantransplantcoordinators.org/clinical-resources/irodat/

Ethical Consumer Research Association (ECRA)
Publishers of ethical consumer magazine
Unit 21 41 Old Birley St Manchester M15 5RF
Tel: 0161 226 2929
Email via website
www.ethicalconsumer.org

Ethical Investment Research Service now see EIRIS

Ethical Treatment of Animals (People for the) see PETA Foundation

Ethiopiaid
Aims to create lasting and positive change in Ethiopia by tackling the problems of poverty, ill health and poor education
PO Box 31052 London SW1X 9WB
Tel: 020 7201 9981
Via website
www.ethlopiaid.org.uk

EU in the United Kingdom European Commission Representation in the UK
Speaking for the Commission as its voice in the UK
Europe House 32 Smith Square London SW1P 3EU
Tel: 020 7973 1992
jonathan.scheele@ec.europa.eu
ec.europa.eu/unitedkingdom

& 74 - 76 Dublin Road Belfast BT2 7HP
London SW1P 3EU
Tel: 028 9024 0708
karen.morrison@ec.europa.eu
http://ec.europa.eu/unitedkingdom/about_us/office_in_northern_ireland/index_en.htm

& 9 Alva Street Edinburgh EH2 4PH
Tel: 0131 225 2058
graham.blythe@ec.europa.eu
ec.europa.eu/unitedkingdom/about_us/office_in_scotland/index_en.htm

& 2 Caspian Point Caspian Way
Cardiff CF10 4QQ
Tel: 029 20895020
david.hughes@ec.europa.eu
ec.europa.eu/unitedkingdom/about_us/office_in_wales/index_en.htm

Eureka! The National Children's Museum
Hands on museum for children aged birth to twelve
Discovery Road Halifax HX1 2NE
Tel: 01422 330069
Education Bookings: 01422 330012
email via website
www.eureka.org.uk

Eurodesk
Europe-wide information service on European opportunities for young people
National Youth Agency 19-23 Humberstone Road Leicester LE5 3GJ
Tel: 0116 2427400
yia@nya.org.uk
www.eurodesk.org.uk

Eurogroup for Animals
Represents a united voice for animal welfare organisations in Europe
6 rue des Patriotes 1000 Brussels Belgium
Tel: 00 32 2 740 08 20
info@eurogroupforanimals.org
www.eurogroupforanimals.org

Europa
Gateway to the European Union
www.europa.eu

Europe (Council of) see Council of Europe

Europe in the UK
EU information with sections on news, culture, youth and education
www.europe.org.uk

European Central Bank
Central bank for Europe's single currency, the euro. The ECB's main task is to maintain the euro's purchasing power and thus price stability in the euro area
www.ecb.int

European Commission Agriculture and Rural Development
ec.europa.eu/agriculture/index_en.htm

European Investment Bank
98-100, boulevard Konrad Adena L-2950 Luxembourg
Tel: 00 352 43 79 22000 (General Information)
Email via website
www.eib.org

European Movement UK
Pro-European campaigning
Ms Cherry Clarke, Administrative Officer
The Lodge, Deaks Lane, Cuckfield, West Sussex, RH17 5JB
Tel: 07753 423 225
emoffice@euromove.org.uk
www.euromove.org.uk

European Parliament Information Office in Edinburgh
The Tun 4 Jackson's Entry Holyrood Rd
Edinburgh EH8 8PJ
Tel: 0131 557 7866
epedinburgh@europarl.europa.eu
www.europarl.org.uk

European Parliament Information Office in the United Kingdom
32 Smith Square London SW1P 3EU
Tel: 020 7227 4300
eplondon@europarl.europa.eu
www.europarl.org.uk

European Parliamentary Labour Party
EPLP
Europe House 32 Smith Square London SW1P 3EU
Tel: 0207 222 1719
info@eurolabour.org.uk
www.eurolabour.org.uk

European Students' Union see ESU

European Trade Union Confederation
International Trade Union Hous Boulevard Roi Albert II, 5
B-1210 Brussels Belgium
Tel: 00 32 02 224 0411
email via website
www.etuc.org

European Transplant Coordinators Organisation see ETCO

European Union (Court of Justice of the)
CURIA
curia.europa.eu

European Union Committee of the Regions
The EU's assembly of regional and local representatives
Bâtiment Jacques Delors Rue Belliard 99-101
B - 1040 Brussels - Belgium
Tel: 00 32 2282 2211
email via website
www.cor.europa.eu

European Youth Card Association
Non-profit organisation that represents 40 youth card organisations in 38 countries issuing the European Youth Card which provides young people with benefits in the fields of culture, mobility, accommodation, services and products
www.euro26.org

European Youth Forum
Brings together tens of millions of young people from all over Europe, organised in order to represent their common interests
www.youthforum.org

European Youth Information and Counselling Agency ERYICA
European umbrella organisation for national youth info & counselling networks
26 Place de la Gare L-1616 Luxembourg
Tel: 00 352 248 73992
email via website
www.eryica.org

European Youth Music Week
Summer course for advanced young instrumentalists aged 16-26, offering the chance to play a great repertoire and meet like-minded people from across the continent
www.eymw.org

Euthanasia see Care Not Killing, Dignity in Dying

Evangelical Alliance Uniting to change society
Whitefield House 186 Kennington Park Rd
London SE11 4BT
Tel: 020 7207 2100
info@eauk.org
www.eauk.org

& Northern Ireland
Downview House 440 Shore Road
Newtownabbey BT37 9RU
Tel: 028 9029 2266
nireland@eauk.org
www.eauk.org/northern-ireland/index.cfm

& Wales
20 High Street Cardiff CF10 1PT
Tel: 02920 229822
cymru@eauk.org
www.eauk.org/wales/index.cfm

& Scotland
International Christian College 110 St James Road Glasgow G4 0PS
Tel: 0141 548 1555
scotland@eauk.org
www.eauk.org/scotland/index.cfm

Every Child a Chance Trust
Aims to unlock the educational potential of socially disadvantaged children through the development and promotion of evidence-based, early intervention programmes.
The KPMG Foundation 15 Canada Square
London E14 5GL
Tel: 020 7311 8039
email via website
www.everychildachancetrust.org

Every child matters see Department for Education

EveryChild
international development charity working to stop children growing up vulnerable and alone
4 Bath Place Rivington St London EC2A 3DR
Tel: 020 7749 2468
email via website
www.everychild.org.uk

Everyman Project
Counselling programme for men who wish to change violent behaviour, and helpline for anyone affected by abuse or violence from men
1a Waterlow Road London N19 5NJ
Adviceline: 0207 263 8884
everymanproject@btopenworld.com
www.everymanproject.co.uk

Exchanges see British Council, Commonwealth Youth Exchange Council, Daneford Trust, Fulbright Commission, Youth in Action

Exclusion see also Communities Empowerment Network, Include

Exercise, Movement and Dance Partnership see EMDP

Expeditions see Brathay Exploration Group, BSES Expeditions, Raleigh, Scientific Exploration Society, Wind Sand & Stars

Exploratorium
Museum of science, art and human perception
www.exploratorium.edu

Extension College see National Extension College

Extreme Inequality
Network of journalists trying to look beyond conventional economics
extremeinequality.org

Eyecare Trust
PO Box 804 Aylesbury Bucks HP20 9DF
Tel: 0845 129 5001
info@eyecaretrust.org.uk
www.eyecaretrust.org.uk

F

Fabian Society
Left of centre think tank
11 Dartmouth St London SW1H 9BN
Tel: 020 7227 4900
info@fabians.org.uk
www.fabians.org.uk

Facial Disfigurement see Changing Faces, Disfigurement Guidance Centre, Let's Face It, Operation Smile UK, Saving Faces

Facsimile Preference Service
Set up to help people being bothered by unwanted and commercial sales faxes
DMA House, 70 Margaret Street
London W1W 8SS
FPS Registration line: 0845 070 0702
Tel: 020 7291 3330 Complaints Department
fps@dma.org.uk
www.fpsonline.org.uk

Fair Access (Office for)
Helps people from poor backgrounds go to university. October 2010: Future under consideration
Northavon House Coldharbour Lane Bristol BS16 1QD
Tel: 0117 931 7171
enquiries@offa.org.uk
www.offa.org.uk

Fair Play for Children Association
Advice & information on play issues & protecting children at play
32 Longford Road Bognor Regis PO21 1AG
Tel: 0843 289 2578
fpfc@fairplayforchildren.net
www.fairplayforchildren.org

Fair Trade Shops (British Association for)
BAFTS
Campaigns for fair trade. List of shops and info leaflet on receipt of sae
66 Longstomps Avenue Chelmsford CM2 9LA
Tel: 07866 759201
info@bafts.org.uk
www.bafts.org.uk

Fair Trading (Office of)
UK's consumer and competition authority - aims to make markets work well for consumers
Fleetbank House 2-6 Salisbury Square
London EC4Y 8JX
Tel: 020 7211 8000
Public enquiries: 08457 22 44 99
enquiries@oft.gsi.gov.uk
www.oft.gov.uk

Fair Trials International

Working for a world where every person's right to a fair trial is respected, whatever their nationality, wherever they are accused
3/7 Temple Chambers Temple Avenue London EC4Y 0HP
Tel: 0207 822 2370
email via website
www.fairtrials.net

Fairbridge now see Prince's Trust

Fairtrade Foundation

Awards Fairtrade Mark
3rd Floor Ibex House 42-47 Minories London EC3N 1DY
Tel: 020 7405 5942
email via website
www.fairtrade.org.uk

Families Anonymous

Support for the families and friends of drug users
Doddington & Rollo Community Association Charlotte Despard Avenue Battersea London SW11 5HD
Helpline: 0845 1200 660
office@famanon.org.uk
www.famanon.org.uk

Families Need Fathers

Maintaining a child's contact with both parents after family break-up
134 Curtain Rd London EC2A 3AR
National helpline: 0300 0300 363
Tel: 020 7613 5060
fnf@fnf.org.uk
www.fnf.org.uk

Family Action

UK's leading family charity, supporting over 45,000 families every year. Tackle some of the most complex and difficult issues facing families today - including domestic abuse, mental health problems, learning disabilities and severe financial hardship
501-505 Kingsland Road London E8 4AU
Tel: 020 7254 6251
email via website
www.family-action.org.uk

Family and Parenting Institute

Independent charity working to support parents in bringing up their children, to promote the well-being of families and to make society more family friendly
430 Highgate Studios 53-79 Highgate Rd London NW5 1TL
Tel: 020 7424 3460
info@familyandparenting.org
www.familyandparenting.org

Family Holiday Association

Addresses issues of poverty and disadvantage through increasing access to holidays and other recreational activities
3 Gainsford Street London SE1 2NE
Tel: 020 3117 0650
info@fhaonline.org.uk
www.fhaonline.org.uk

Family Lives

Providing help and support in all aspects of family life
CAN Mezzanine 49-51 East Road London N1 6AH
Parentline : 0808 800 2222
Tel: 020 7553 3080
parentsupport@familylives.org.uk
www.familylives.org.uk

Family Mediation Scotland now see Relationships Scotland

Family Names Profiling (GB)

Maps the distribution of surnames in Great Britain, both current and historic, showing patterns of population movement, social mobility, regional economic development and cultural identity. Link to world family name maps via website
gbnames.publicprofiler.org

Family Planning Association

The UK's leading sexual health charity working to improve the sexual health and reproductive rights and choices of people throughout the UK
50 Featherstone Street London EC1Y 8QU
Helpline England: 0845 122 8690
Helpline Northern Ireland: 0845 122 8687
general@fpa.org.uk
www.fpa.org.uk

Family Records Centre now see National Archives

Family Rights Group

Advice by letter or telephone to families whose children are involved with social services
The Print House 18 Ashwin St London E8 3DL
advice service: 0808 801 0366
Tel: 020 7923 2628
via website
www.frg.org.uk

Family Search

Internet genealogy service run by The Church of Jesus Christ of Latter Day Saints
www.familysearch.org

Family Therapy (Institute of)

Training in family & couple therapy and clinical services
24-32 Stephenson Way London NW1 2HX
Tel: 020 7391 9150
email via website
www.ift.org.uk

Family Welfare Association now see Family Action

Faramir Sailing Trust see Cirdan Sailing Trust

FareShare Fighting hunger, tackling food waste
National food charity that fights hunger in the UK by redistributing quality surplus food from the food industry to support homeless and other vulnerable people
Unit H04 Tower Bridge Business Complex
100 Clements Road Bermondsey London
SE16 4DG
Tel: 020 7394 2468
enquiries@fareshare.org.uk
www.fareshare.org.uk

Farm Animal Welfare Committee FAWC
Provides independent advice to Defra on the welfare of farmed animals and necessary improvements
FAWC Secretariat Area 8B, 9 Millbank c/o 17 Smith Square London SW1P 3JR
08459 33 55 77
Tel: 0207 238 6340 / 4926 / 5016
fawcsecretariat@defra.gsi.gov.uk
www.defra.gov.uk/fawc/

Farmers' Markets (Scottish Association of)
Information on markets in Scotland
www.scottishfarmersmarkets.co.uk

Farmers' Retail & Markets Association (National) FARMA
Information on where and when markets are held
12 Southgate Street Winchester SO23 9EF
Tel: 0845 45 88 420
info@farma.org.uk
www.farma.org.uk

Farming & Countryside Education FACE
A one-stop shop for all information and educational materials about food, farming and the countryside
Arthur Rank Centre Stoneleigh Park
Warwickshire CV8 2LG
Tel: 0845 838 7192
enquiries@face-online.org.uk
www.face-online.org.uk

Farms for City Children
Aims to provide young children from urban areas with a week in which they work actively and purposefully on a farm
Bridge House 25 Fore Street Okehampton
Devon EX20 1DL
Tel: 01837 55876
email via website
www.farmsforcitychildren.co.uk

Fatherhood Institute
Seeks to promote positive relationships between men & their children
Unit 1 Warren Courtyard Savernake
Marlborough Wiltshire SN8 3UU
Tel: 0845 634 1328
mail@fatherhoodinstitute.org
www.fatherhoodinstitute.org

Fathers see also Dad, Dad Talk, Dads House, Families Need Fathers

Fathers Direct now see Fatherhood Institute

Fathers4justice Ltd
office@fathers-4-justice.org
www.fathers-4-justice.org

Fauna & Flora International
Conservation worldwide of threatened species
4th Floor Jupiter House Station Road
Cambridge CB1 2JD
Tel: 01223 571000
info@fauna-flora.org
www.fauna-flora.org

FAWC see Farm Animal Welfare Committee

Fawcett Library see Women's Library

Fawcett Society
Campaigning for equality between women and men at work, in the home and in public life
1-3 Berry Street London EC1V 0AA
Tel: 020 7253 2598
Email via website
www.fawcettsociety.org.uk

FBI Federal Bureau of Investigation
US government agency
www.fbi.gov

Feline Advisory Bureau
Taeselbury High St Tisbury Wilts SP3 6LD
Tel: 01747 871 872
information@fabcats.org
www.fabcats.org

Fell Runners Association
www.fellrunner.org.uk

Female Education see CAMFED International

Feminist Archive
Holds a wide variety of material relating to the Women's Liberation Movement (WLM) from 1969 to the present. The Archive has gone into storage, care of the University of Bristol, who will eventually rehouse it
www.feministarchivenorth.org.uk/
feministarchivesouth/index.htm

Fencing (British Academy of)
www.baf-fencing.org

Fencing Association (British)
1 Baron's Gate 33-35 Rothschild Road
London W4 5HT
Tel: 020 8742 3032
headoffice@britishfencing.com
www.britishfencing.com

Fertility see also Fertility Friends, Human
Fertilisation & Embryology Authority, Infertility
Network UK

Fertility Friends
A self help community for those
experiencing infertility
Email via website
www.fertilityfriends.co.uk

Fertility UK
The National Fertility Awareness & Natural
Family Planning Service
Bury Knowle Health Centre 207 London Rd
Headington Oxford OX3 9JA
admin@fertilityuk.org
www.fertilityuk.org

Festivals (British & International Federation of)
Umbrella body for festivals of the performing
arts in the UK and beyond
Festivals House 198 Park Lane Macclesfield
SK11 6UD
Tel: 01625 428297 / 611578
info@federationoffestivals.org.uk
www.federationoffestivals.org.uk

FFLAG see Lesbians & Gays (Families & Friends
of)

FIELD Environmental Law & Development
(Foundation for International)
Legal assistance in environmental and
sustainable development
Suite D, 1st Floor The Merchant Centre
1 New Street Square London EC4A 3BF
Tel: 20 7842 8521
field@field.org.uk
www.field.org.uk

Field Sports Society (British) now see
Countryside Alliance

Field Studies Council
Charity works with schools and individuals
through network of centres to bring
environmental understanding to all
Preston Montford Montford Bridge
Shrewsbury SY4 1HW
Tel: 01743 852100
Tel: 0845 3454071 (Local rate phone call
enquiries@field-studies-council.org
www.field-studies-council.org

Fields in Trust - FIT
Responsible for acquiring, protecting and
improving playing fields and play space,
especially for children and those with
disabilities
15 Crinan Street London N1 9SQ
Tel: 0207 427 2110
info@fieldsintrust.org
www.fieldsintrust.org

& Cymru
Sport Wales National Centre Sophia Gardens
Cardiff CF11 9SW
Tel: 029 20334 935
cymru@fieldsintrust.org

& Scotland
Dewar House Claverhouse Staffa Place
Dundee DD2 3SX
Tel: 01382 817 427
scotland@fieldsintrust.org

FIFA
International governing body for football
FIFA-Strasse 20 P.O. Box 8044 Zurich
Switzerland
Tel: 0041 43 2227777
Email via website
www.fifa.com

Film see also British Film Institute, Creative
Scotland, History of Cinema & Popular Culture
(The Bill Douglas Centre for the)

Film & Television Archive (Northern Region)
Collect, preserve and provide access to film,
television and other moving image material
related to the history & heritage of the North
East of England
School of Arts and Media Teesside University
Middlesbrough TS1 3BA
Tel: 01642 384022
enquiries@nrfta.org.uk
www.nrfta.org.uk

Film & Video Development Agency now
see Film London

Film and Television School (National) NFTS
MA/Diploma courses in professional
disciplines for film and television. Short
courses for freelancers
Beaconsfield Studios Station Rd
Beaconsfield Bucks HP9 1LG
Tel: 01494 671234
info@nfts.co.uk
www.nfts.co.uk

Film Classification (British Board of)
Independent, non-governmental body
which classifies cinema films and videos/
DVDs
3 Soho Square London W1D 3HD
Tel: 020 7440 1570
feedback@bbfc.co.uk
www.bbfc.co.uk

Film Council (UK) now see British Film Institute or Film London

Film Education
Provides award-winning teaching resources, teacher training and cinema based events which support the use of film within the curriculum
91 Berwick Street London W1F 0BP
Tel: 020 7292 7330
email via website
www.filmeducation.org

Film Institute (British) see British Film Institute

Film London
Regional media development agency
Suite 6.10 The Tea Building 56 Shoreditch High Street London E1 6JJ
Tel: 020 7613 7676
info@filmlondon.org.uk
www.filmlondon.org.uk

Financial Ombudsman Service
Power to settle financial complaints
South Quay Plaza 183 Marsh Wall London E14 9SR
Helpline: 0800 0 234 567 Tel: 020 7964 1000
complaint.info@financial-ombudsman.org.uk
www.financial-ombudsman.org.uk

Financial Services Authority
Regulatory body
25 The North Colonnade Canary Wharf London E14 5HS
Consumer Helpline: 0845 606 1234
Tel: 020 7066 1000
email via website
www.fsa.gov.uk

Find a Parent or Child
Reuniting parents and children
www.findaparentorchild.co.uk

Findhorn Foundation
Spiritual community, educational centre and thriving ecovillage
The Park Findhorn IV36 3TZ
Tel: 01309 690311
email via website
www.findhorn.org

Finnish Institute
Work with artists, researchers, experts and policy makers in the United Kingdom, Finland and the Republic of Ireland to promote strong networks in the fields of culture and society
35-36 Eagle St London WC1R 4AQ
Tel: 020 7404 3309
info@finnish-institute.org.uk
www.finnish-institute.org.uk

Fire Brigade (London)
Full listings and links to all the fire brigades in the UK
169 Union Street London SE1 0LL
tel: 020 8555 1200
info@london-fire.gov.uk
www.london-fire.gov.uk

Fire Protection Association
Organises fire protection seminars. Fire Prevention' often covers school fire issues
London Road Moreton in Marsh
Glos GL56 0RH
Tel: 01608 812500
fpa@thefpa.co.uk
www.thefpa.co.uk

First Light
Helps young people from all backgrounds to develop their skills, talent, creativity, confidence and entrepreneurial capabilities. Provide opportunities for young people to work with industry professionals on high quality, youth led digital media projects
Studio 28 Fazeley Studios 191 Fazeley Street Birmingham B5 5SE
Tel: 0121 224 7511
info@firstlightonline.co.uk
www.firstlightonline.co.uk

FirstSigns (Self-Injury Guidance & Network Support)
Online, user-led voluntary organisation founded to raise awareness about self-injury and provide information and support to people of all ages affected by self-injury
info@firstsigns.org.uk
www.firstsigns.org.uk

Fiscal Studies (Institute for)
Independent research into UK public policy
7 Ridgmount St London WC1E 7AE
Tel: 020 7291 4800
email via website
www.ifs.org.uk

Fishing see Marine Stewardship Council, Peta Foundation, Seafish

Fit for Travel
Travel health information for people travelling abroad from the UK
www.fitfortravel.scot.nhs.uk

Fitness Industry Association
Non-profit making trade association for the entire health and fitness industry
Castlewood House 77-91 New Oxford Street London WC1A 1PX
Tel: 020 7420 8560
email via website
www.fia.org.uk

Fitness League
Teaches rhythmic exercise to music
1 Grove House Foundry Lane Horsham
West Sussex RH13 5PL
Tel: 01403 266000
info@thefitnessleague.com
www.thefitnessleague.com

Fitness Northern Ireland
Governing body for fitness instructors
The Robinson Centre Montgomery Rd
Belfast BT6 9HS
Tel 028 9070 4080
fitnessni@aol.com
www.fitnessni.org

Fitzwilliam Museum
Trumpington St Cambridge CB2 1RB
Tel: 01223 332900
Education: 01223 332993
Group Bookings: 01223 332904
fitzmuseum-enquiries@lists.cam.ac.uk
www.fitzmuseum.cam.ac.uk

Five
Customer Services Channel 5 Television
10 Lower Thames Street London EC3R 6EN
Tel: 020 8612 7700
Tel: 0845 705 0505
customerservices@channel5.com
www.channel5.com

Floodline
24 hr advice & info
Floodline: 0845 988 1188
Type talk: 0845 602 6340

Flower Arrangement Societies (National Association of)
Osborne House 12 Devonshire Sq London
EC2M 4TE
Tel: 020 7247 5567
flowers@nafas.org.uk
www.nafas.org.uk

Folger Shakespeare Library Advancing
knowledge & the arts
Independent research library located on
Capitol Hill in Washington, DC
www.folger.edu

Food & Agricultural Organisation (United Nations)
Leads international efforts to defeat hunger.
Helps developing countries and countries
in transition modernise and improve
agriculture, forestry and fisheries practices
and ensure good nutrition for all
Viale delle Terme di Caracalla 00153
Rome Italy
Tel: 00 39 06 57051
FAO-HQ@fao.org
www.fao.org

Food & Drink Federation
Trade organisation for the food
manufacturing industry
6 Catherine St London WC2B 5JJ
Tel: 020 7836 2460
Email via website
www.fdf.org.uk

Food & Drug Administration (US)
www.fda.gov

Food Alliance (National) see Sustain

Food Commission (UK) Watchdog on food
issues
Independent watchdog on food issues. In
2011, it will be a virtual organisation with a
website and email maintained by volunteers
and supported by donations and by the
Food Commission Research Charity
94 White Lion Street London N1 9PF
info@foodmagazine.org.uk
www.foodmagazine.org.uk

Food Science & Technology (Institute of)
see IFST

Food Standards Agency
Provision of advice/information on food
safety issues to consumers
Aviation House 125 Kingsway
London WC2B 6NH
Helpline: 020 7276 8829
Tel: 020 7276 8000 (switchboard)
helpline@foodstandards.gsi.gov.uk
www.food.gov.uk

Food Standards Agency (Northern Ireland)
10 A-C Clarendon Road Belfast BT1 3BG
Tel: 028 9041 7700
infofsani@foodstandards.gsi.gov.uk
www.food.gov.uk

Food Standards Agency (Scotland)
St Magnus House 6th Floor 25 Guild St
Aberdeen AB11 6NJ
Tel: 01224 285100
scotland@foodstandards.gsi.gov.uk
www.food.gov.uk

Food Standards Agency (Wales)
11th Floor Southgate House Wood Street
Cardiff CF10 1EW
Tel: 02920 678999
wales@foodstandards.gsi.gov.uk
www.food.gov.uk

Football see also FIFA, Footy4kids, Kick It Out, Professional Footballers Association, Show Racism the Red Card, World Cup

Football Association
Governing body of football in England
Wembley Stadium PO Box 1966 London
SW1P 9EQ
Customer relations: 0844 980 8200
www.thefa.com

Football Association (English Schools)
4 Parker Court Staffordshire Technology Park
Stafford ST18 0WP
Tel: 01785 785970
office@esfa.co.uk
www.esfa.co.uk

Football Association (Irish)
20 Windsor Avenue Belfast BT9 6EG
Tel: 028 90 669 458
info@irishfa.com
www.irishfa.com

Football Association (Scottish) SFA
Hampden Park Glasgow G42 9AY
Tel: 0141 616 6000
info@scottishfa.co.uk
www.scottishfa.co.uk

Football Foundation
Funds football and other sporting facilities
Whittington House 19-30 Alfred Place
London WC1E 7EA
Tel: 0845 345 4555
enquiries@footballfoundation.org.uk
www.footballfoundation.org.uk

Football Industry Group
Conducts academic research into the social,
economic, historical, business, cultural and
political aspects of football in the UK and
abroad
www.liv.ac.uk/footballindustry

Football League
The central administrative office of the clubs
in The Championship, League One, League
Two and the Coca Cola Football League
Edward VII Quay Navigation Way
Preston PR2 2YF
Tel: 0844 463 1888
enquiries@football-league.co.uk
www.football-league.co.uk

Football League (Scottish) SFL
The National Stadium Hampden Park
Glasgow G42 9EB
Tel: 0141 620 4160
info@scottishfootballleague.com
www.scottishfootballleague.com

Football Museum (National)
Opening in early 2012
Urbis Building Cathedral Gardens
Manchester M4 3BG
Tel: 0161 605 8200
info@nationalfootballmuseum.com
www.nationalfootballmuseum.com/

Football Museum (Scottish)
Hampden Park Glasgow G42 9BA
Tel: 0141 616 6139
email via website
www.scottishfootballmuseum.org.uk

Football Supporters' Federation
Kingsmeadow Jack Goodchild Way 422A
Kingston Road Kingston upon Thames KT1
3PB
Tel: 0330 44 000 44
info@fsf.org.uk.
www.fsf.org.uk
www.fsf.org.uk/campaigns/safestanding.php

Football Unites, Racism Divides
The U-Mix Centre Asline Road ,Lowfield,
Sheffield S2 4UJ.
Tel: 0114 2553156
enquiries@furd.org
www.furd.org

Footy4kids
Website dedicated to drills, articles, practice
plans and forums where advice from
experienced youth soccer coaches is offered
www.footy4kids.co.uk

Foreign and Commonwealth Office
Provides services to British nationals and
British businesses overseas through a global
network of Embassies. Provides practical
advice, assistance and support to travellers in
emergencies
King Charles St London SW1A 2AH
Tel: 020 7008 1500
Email via website
www.fco.gov.uk

Foreign and Commonwealth Office Travel Advice
Advice to British Nationals on whether it is
safe to travel abroad
King Charles Street London SW1A 2AH
Tel: 0845 850 2829
TravelAdvicePublicEnquiries@fco.gov.uk
www.fco.gov.uk/en/travel-and-living-
abroad/travel-advice-by-country/

Foreign Policy Centre
Research into business ethics, foreign policy,
human rights and international economics
Suite 11, 2nd Floor 23-28 Penn Street
London N1 5DL
Tel: 020 7729 7566
events@fpc.org.uk
www.fpc.org.uk

Forest Peoples Programme
Works to assist tribal tropical forest peoples
to protect their rights and livelihood
1c Fosseway Business Centre Stratford Road
Moreton-in-Marsh GL56 9NQ
Tel: 01608 652893
email via website
www.forestpeoples.org

Forest School Camps
Educational charity and voluntary
organisation
www.fsc.org.uk

Forestry Commission Great Britain England
National Office
Government department responsible for the
protection and expansion of Britain's forests
and woodlands
620 Bristol Business Park Coldharbour Lane
Bristol BS16 1EJ
Tel: 0117 906 6000
fe.england@forestry.gsi.gov.uk
www.forestry.gov.uk

& Scotland National Office
Silvan House 231 Corstorphine Road
Edinburgh EH12 7AT
Tel: 0131 334 0303
www.forestry.gov.uk

& Wales National Office
Welsh Assembly Government Rhodfa Padarn
Llanbadarn Fawr Aberystwyth Ceredigion
SY23 3UR
Tel: 0300 068 0300
www.forestry.gov.uk

Forestry Society (Royal)
Educational charity dedicated to promoting
the wise management of trees and woods
102 High St Tring Herts HP23 4AF
Tel: 01442 822028
rfshq@rfs.org.uk
www.rfs.org.uk

Forgiveness Project
An organisation working with grassroots
projects in the fields of conflict resolution,
reconciliation and victim support
42a Buckingham Palace Road
London SW1W 0RE
Tel: 0207 821 0035
info@theforgivenessproject.com
www.theforgivenessproject.com

Forum for the Future
Charity with mission to achieve sustainability
taking a positive solutions orientated
approach
Overseas House 19-23 Ironmonger Row
London EC1V 3QN
Tel: 020 7324 3630
info@forumforthefuture.org
www.forumforthefuture.org/

Forward Foundation for Women's Health
Research & Development
International charity acting for the health,
wellbeing and rights of African women &
girls, tackling female genital mutilation, child
marriage and related rights
Suite 2.1 Chandelier Building 2nd Floor 8
Scrubs Lane London NW10 6RB
Tel: 0208 960 4000
Email via website
www.forwarduk.org.uk

Fostering see also thematic guide Adoption
and Fostering

Fostering Network London Office
Charity for everyone involved in fostering
87 Blackfriars Road London SE1 8HA
Tel: 020 7620 6400
info@fostering.net
www.fostering.net

& Belfast Office
Unit 10 40 Montgomery Road
Belfast BT6 9HL
Tel: 028 9070 5056
ni@fostering.net
www.fostering.net/northern-ireland

& Cardiff Office
1 Caspian Point Pierhead Street Cardiff Bay
CF10 4DQ
Tel: 029 2044 0940
wales@fostering.net
www.fostering.net/wales/

& Glasgow Office
Ingram House, 2nd Floor 227 Ingram Street
Glasgow G1 1DA
Tel: 0141 204 1400
scotland@fostering.net
www.fostering.net/scotland/

**Foundation For Peace (Tim Parry
Johnathan Ball)**
Works nationally and internationally with:
victims and survivors of acts of terrorism and
other politically motivated conflict; former
combatants who are no longer involved
in violence and young people whose
communities are divided by faith or racial
prejudice
Peace Centre Peace Drive Great Sankey
Warrington WA5 1HQ
Tel: 01925 581231
info@foundation4peace.org
www.foundation4peace.org

Foyer Federation
National umbrella organisation for Foyers:
affordable accommodation, training &
support for disadvantaged young people
3rd Foor 5-9 Hatton Wall London EC1N 8HX
Tel: 020 7430 2212
inbox@foyer.net
www.foyer.net

Fragile X Society
Supports those affected by the most
common cause of inherited learning
disability
Rood End House 6 Stortford Road Great
Dunmow Essex CM6 1DA
Tel: 01371 875100
info@fragilex.org.uk
www.fragilex.org.uk

FRAME Fund for the Replacement of Animals
in Medical Experiments
Researches alternatives to animal testing
Russell & Burch House 96-98 North
Sherwood St Nottingham NG1 4EE
Tel: 0115 958 4740
frame@frame.org.uk
www.frame.org.uk

**France: culture and communications
website**
www.culture.fr

Franco British Council
To promote better understanding between
Britain and France. A short story prize exists
to promote France and French to a younger
age group
British Section 10-11 Dacre Street London
SW1H 0DJ
Tel: 020 7976 8380
info@francobritishcouncil.org.uk
www.francobritishcouncil.org.uk

Franco-Scottish Society of Scotland
Association Franco-Ecossaise
To foster educational, cultural and social
activities between France & Scotland
21 Lindsay Drive Glasgow G12 0HD
email via website
www.franco-scottish.org.uk

Frank National Drugs Helpline
Advice, information and support to anyone
affected by drugs
Tel: 0800 77 66 00 (24hr freefone)
Email via website
www.talktofrank.com

Frankfurt Book Fair
info@book-fair.com
www.buchmesse.de/en

Fredericks Foundation
Helps disadvantaged people of any age to
realise their potential, often by helping them
to start their own business
Tel: 01276 472 722
mail@fredericksfoundation.net
www.fredericksfoundation.org

Free the Children
Children under 18 years old helping children
to end abuse and exploitation
www.freethechildren.com

Free Tibet
Campaigning for an end to the Chinese
occupation of Tibet
28 Charles Square London N1 6HT
Tel: 020 7324 4605
mail@freetibet.org
www.freetibet.org

FreeBMD
Free online access to transcribed records of
births, marriages and deaths in England and
Wales
www.freebmd.org.uk

Freecycle
A grassroots movement of people who are
giving (& getting) stuff for free in their own
towns
www.freecycle.org

Freedom Association
A pressure group campaigning for limited
government & for individual freedom
Richwood House 1 Trinity School Lane
Cheltenham Gloucestershire GL52 2JL
Tel: 0845 833 9626
email via website
www.tfa.net

Freedom from Torture Medical Foundation
for the Care of Victims of Torture
Charity dedicated solely to the treatment of
torture survivors. Provides help for victims,
documentary evidence of torture, training
for professionals and education for the
public
111 Isledon Road London N7 7JW
Tel: 020 7697 7777
email via website
www.freedomfromtorture.org

Freedom of Information (Campaign for)
Suite 102 16 Baldwins Gardens London
EC1N 7RJ
Tel: 020 7831 7477
admin@cfoi.demon.co.uk
www.cfoi.org.uk

Freegle
National grassroots organisation of people
who are giving and receiving free unwanted
items in their immediate communities
www.ilovefreegle.org

Freshfield Service
Confidential counselling & advice for drug
users & their families in Cornwall & Isles of
Scilly
Drugs advice: 0500 241952
www.freshfieldservice.co.uk

Freshfields Donkey Village
Provide a sanctuary for donkeys rescued
from abandonment, abuse or neglect and
provides a safe place where special needs
children can adopt a donkey and help feed,
groom and care for it during their visit
The Michael Elliott Trust Freshfields Farm
Peak Forest Derbyshire SK17 8EE
Tel: 01298 79775
www.donkey-village.org.uk

Friedreich's Ataxia Group now see Ataxia UK

Friedrich Ebert Foundation
Promotes better understanding of British-German relations
London Office 66 Great Russell Street
London WC1B 3BN
Tel: 020 70250990
info@feslondon.net
www.feslondon.org.uk

Friends at the end
Friends at the End is a members' democratic society, dedicated to promoting knowledge about end-of-life choices and dignified death
11 Westbourne Gardens Glasgow G12 9XD
Tel: 0141 334 3287
info@friends-at-the-end.org.uk
www.friends-at-the-end.org.uk

Friends of Friendless Churches
Campaigns for the preservation of ancient and beautiful but redundant churches
St Ann's Vestry Hall 2 Church Entry London
EC4V 5HB
Tel: 020 7236 3934
office@friendsoffriendlesschurches.org.uk
www.friendsoffriendlesschurches.org.uk

Friends of the Earth
Environmental pressure group and charity
26-28 Underwood St London N1 7JQ
Tel: 020 7490 1555
Email via website
www.foe.co.uk/

& Cymru
33 Castle Arcade Balcony Cardiff CF10 1BY
Tel: 029 20229577
cymru@foe.co.uk
www.foe.co.uk/cymru_english.html

& Northern Ireland
7 Donegall Street Place BELFAST BT1 2FN
Tel: 028 9023 3488
foe-ni@foe.co.uk
www.foe.co.uk/northern_ireland_index.html

Friends of the Earth International
Environmental pressure group and charity
www.foei.org

Friends of the Earth Scotland
Campaigning for environmental justice, a decent environment for all and a fair share of the earth's resources
Thorn House 5 Rose Street Edinburgh EH2 2PR
Tel: 0131 243 2700
email via website
www.foe-scotland.org.uk

Friends United Network now see Friendship Works

Friends, Families and Travellers
Charity working on behalf of all Gypsies and Travellers regardless of ethnicity, culture or background. Offers advice and information
Community Base 113 Queens Rd Brighton
BN1 3XG
Tel: 01273 234 777
fft@gypsy-traveller.org
www.gypsy-traveller.org

Friendship Works
Children's mentoring charity providing support for children across London
Studio 442 Highgate Studios 53-79
Highgate Rd London NW5 1TL
Tel: 020 7485 0900
info@friendshipworks.org.uk
www.friendshipworks.org.uk

Froglife
Conservation and promotion of native reptiles & amphibians to benefit biodiversity and people
2A Flag Business Exchange
Vicarage Farm Road Fengate Peterborough
PE1 5TX
Tel: 01733 558844
Tel: 01733 558960 (Wildlife Information)
info@froglife.org
www.froglife.org

Fulbright Commission (The US-UK)
Awards and advice for US-UK exchange. Promotes peace and cultural understanding through educational exchange
Battersea Power Station   188 Kirtling Street
London SW8 5BN
Tel: 020 7498 4010
programmes@fulbright.co.uk
www.fulbright.co.uk

Full Time Mothers now see Mothers at home Matter

Fund for Animal Welfare (International)
see IFAW

Fur Trade see PETA Foundation, Respect for Animals

Furniture Re-use Network
Co-ordinating body for furniture recycling projects in UK
48-54 West Street St Philips Bristol BS2 0BL
donations: 0845 602 8003
Tel: 0117 954 3571
info@frn.org.uk
www.frn.org.uk

Further Education National Training Organisation see Lifelong Learning

G

Gaelic Books Council
Supports Gaelic publishing with grants and
services and has its own bookshop
32 Mansfield St Glasgow G11 5QP
Tel: 0141 337 6211
Email via website
www.gaelicbooks.org

Gaia Foundation
The Gaia Foundation works towards cultural
and biological diversity, ecological justice
and Earth democracy
6 Heathgate Place Agincourt Road London
NW3 2NU
Tel: 020 7428 0055
info@gaianet.org
www.gaiafoundation.org

Galapagos Conservation Trust
UK charity set up to raise funds for, and
awareness of, the conservation needs of the
Galapagos Islands
Charles Darwin Suite 28 Portland Place
London W1B 1LY
Tel: 020 7399 7440
gct@gct.org
www.savegalapagos.org

Gallery of Modern Art GoMA
Royal Exchange Square Glasgow G1 3AH
Tel: 0141 287 3050
Text Phone: 0141 287 3005
museums@glasgowlife.org.uk
www.glasgowlife.org.uk/museums/our-
museums/goma/Pages/home.aspx

Gam-Anon UK & Ireland
UK fellowship for those affected by
compulsive gambling
National Helpline: 08700 50 88 80
www.gamanon.org.uk

Gambia Horse and Donkey Trust
Ensuring that the horses and donkeys on
which farmers depend are well cared for
Brewery Arms Cottage Stane Street Ockley
Surrey RH5 5TH
Tel: 01306 627568
email via website
www.gambiahorseanddonkey.org.uk

Gamblers Anonymous
Fellowship of men and women who have
joined together to do something about
their own gambling problem and to help
other compulsive gamblers do the same.
Some meetings also have a meeting called
GAMANON. This is for family and friends
email via website
www.gamblersanonymous.org.uk

Gamblers Anonymous Scotland
St Columbkilles Halls 2 Kirkwood St
Rutherglen Glasgow G73 2SL
Helpline: 0370 050 8881
email via website
www.gascotland.org

GAMCARE
Information, advice, support and free
counselling for the prevention and treatment
of problem gambling
2nd Floor 7-11 St John's Hill
London SW11 1TR
Helpline: 0808 8020 133
Tel: 020 7801 7000
info@gamcare.org.uk
www.gamcare.org.uk

Gamete Donation Trust (National)
Information mainly for those considering
becoming an egg or sperm donor but also
for health professionals and those requiring
treatment with donor eggs or sperm
PO Box 2121 Gloucester GL19 4WT
Confidential helpline: 0845 226 9193
info@ngdt.co.uk
www.ngdt.co.uk

Gap Activity Projects now see Lattitude
Global Volunteering

Garden History Society
Promotes the study of the history of
gardening, landscape gardening and
horticulture. Encourages conservation,
advises on restoration and supports the
development of parks, gardens and designed
landscapes
70 Cowcross St London EC1M 6EJ
Tel: 020 7608 2409
enquiries@gardenhistorysociety.org
www.gardenhistorysociety.org

Garden Organic
Researching and promoting organic
gardening, farming and food
Coventry Warwickshire CV8 3LG
Tel: 02476 303517
enquiry@gardenorganic.org.uk
www.gardenorganic.org.uk

Gardens see also Allotment and Leisure
Gardeners Ltd. (National Society of),
Botanic Garden of Wales (National), City
Farms & Community Gardens (Federation
of), Community Composting Network,
Conservation of Plants & Gardens (National
Council for the), Historic Houses Association,
Landscape Institute, Royal Botanic Gardens,
Thrive

Gardens Scheme (National)
Opening gardens of quality, character and interest to the public for charity
Hatchlands Park East Clandon Guildford GU4 7RT
Tel: 01483 211535
email via website
www.ngs.org.uk

Gas & Electricity Markets (Office of) see Ofgem

GASP One Stop Shop for Smokefree Solutions
Educational resources and consultancy
Unit 9, Parkway Trading Estate St Werburghs Bristol BS2 9PG
Tel 0117 955 0101
gasp@gasp.org.uk
www.gasp.org.uk

Gateway Award
Recreation, education resources for people with learning disabilities
Mencap 3rd Floor Delta View 2309 - 2311Coventry Road Birmingham B26 3PG
Tel: 0808 808 1111
Gateway.award@mencap.org.uk
www.mencap.org.uk

Gateway Award see Mencap

Gay Issues see thematic guide - Sexual Issues

GCSE Revision
www.gcse.com

Genealogists (Society of)
National library and education centre for family history
14 Charterhouse Buildings Goswell Rd London EC1M 7BA
Tel: 020 7251 8799
email via website
www.sog.org.uk

General Medical Council GMC
Governing body for doctors in UK
Regent's Place, 350 Euston Rd London NW1 3JN
Tel: 0161 923 6602 (general enquiries)
gmc@gmc-uk.org
www.gmc-uk.org

General Register Office see Registering life events

Genetic Alliance UK
Umbrella group for charities concerned with human genetic disorders
Unit 4D, Leroy House, 436 Essex Rd London N1 3QP
Tel: 0207 704 3141
contactus@geneticalliance.org.uk
www.geneticalliance.org.uk

Genetics see also Jeans for Genes

Genocide see Aegis Trust

Geographic Society (National)
American non-profit scientific and educational organisation
www.nationalgeographic.com

Geographical Association
National subject teaching association for geography teachers in the UK
160 Solly St Sheffield S1 4BF
Tel: 0114 296 0088
email via website
www.geography.org.uk

Geographical Society (Royal) see Royal Geographical Society

Geological Society
Professional & learned society for working geologists
Burlington House Piccadilly London W1J 0BG
Tel: 020 7434 9944
Email via website
www.geolsoc.org.uk

Geological Survey (British)
Natural environment research council
Kingsley Dunham Centre Keyworth Nottingham NG12 5GG
Tel: 0115 936 3100 (switchboard)
Tel: 0115 936 3143 (enquiries)
enquiries@bgs.ac.uk
www.bgs.ac.uk

Geological Survey (US)
Provides impartial information on the health of our ecosystems and environment, the natural hazards that threaten us, the natural resources we rely on, the impacts of climate and land-use change
www.usgs.gov

Geologists Association
Charitable organisation that exists for all geologists and earth scientists, both professional and amateur, bringing together enthusiasts of all ages and backgrounds to meet people with similar interests
Burlington House Piccadilly London W1J 0DU
Tel: 020 7434 9298
email via website
www.geologistsassociation.org.uk

Georgian Group
Architectural group
6 Fitzroy Sq London W1T 5DX
Tel: 087 1750 2936
info@georgiangroup.org.uk
www.georgiangroup.org.uk

Get connected
Runaway children can call free to talk to trained volunteers
Helpline: 0808 808 4994
Email via website
www.getconnected.org.uk

Get Global!
Support and training for teachers involved in global citizenship
www.getglobal.org.uk

Get Safe Online
Protect yourself against internet threats. The site is sponsored by government and leading businesses working together to provide a free, public service
www.getsafeonline.org/

GFS Platform for Young Women
Support for young women in community projects
Unit 2, Angel Gate 326 City Road London EC1V 2PT
Tel: 020 7837 9669
info@gfsplatform.org.uk
www.gfsplatform.org.uk

Gifted Children (National Association for)
Works with the whole family to support the child who is gifted and talented
Suite 1.2 Challenge House Sherwood Drive Bletchley Bucks MK3 6DP
Tel: 01908 646433
amazingchildren@nagcbritain.org.uk
www.nagcbritain.org.uk

Gifted Children's Information Centre
Assessment, guidance and legal help for children with special needs eg gifted dyslexics, ADHD, Aspberger's Syndrome
Hampton Grange 21 Hampton Lane Solihull B91 2QJ
Tel: 0121 705 4547
petercongdon@blueyonder.co.uk
www.dyslexiabooks.biz/
www.syntheticphonics.uk.com

Gingerbread National Council for One Parent Families
Offer advice, practical support and campaign for single parents
255 Kentish Town Road London NW5 2LX
Single parent helpline: 0808 802 0925
Tel: 020 7428 5400
email via website
www.gingerbread.org.uk

Girlguiding UK
UK's largest voluntary organisation for girls and young women with around 600,000 members
17-19 Buckingham Palace Rd London SW1W 0PT
Freephone: 0800 1 69 59 01 (info about joining)
Tel: 0207 834 6242
chq@girlguiding.org.uk
www.girlguiding.org.uk

Girls Venture Corps Air Cadets
A uniformed organisation for girls aged 11-20 years. With interests in aviation, adventure and travel.
1 Bawtry Gate Sheffield S9 1UD
Tel: 0114 2448405
gvcac@toucansurf.com
www.gvcac.org.uk

Girls' Brigade England & Wales
PO Box 196 129 Broadway Didcot Oxfordshire OX11 8XN
Tel: 01235 510425
gbco@girlsbrigadeew.org.uk
www.girlsb.org.uk

Giving Nation
Works with young people throughout the UK to show them how they can change the world by giving
Citizenship Foundation First Floor 50 Featherstone Street London EC1Y 8RT
Tel: 020 7566 4141
info@g-nation.org.uk
www.g-nation.co.uk

Glasgow Life
Encourage participation, involvement and engagement in culture and sport for all. Links to Sport, Museums, Libraries, Events, Arts, Music etc
www.glasgowlife.org.uk

Glasgow Museums Resource Centre
Store for the museums' collections when they're not on display - accessible to the public
200 Woodhead Road South Nitshill Industrial Esta Glasgow G53 7NN
Tel: 0141 276 9300
Text Phone: 0141 276 9428
GMRCbookings@glasgowlife.org.uk

Glass Centre (National)
Exploring ideas through glass and providing opportunities for people to be creative, enjoy themselves and feel inspired
Liberty Way Sunderland SR6 0GL
Tel: 0191 515 5555
reception@nationalglasscentre.com
www.nationalglasscentre.com

GLE Greater London Enterprise
Training & support for young people who are thinking of starting their own business
10-12 Queen Elizabeth Street London SE1 2JN
Tel: 020 7403 0300
info@gle.co.uk
www.gle.co.uk

Gliding Association (British)
National governing body
8 Merus Court Meridian Business Park Leicester LE19 1RJ
Tel: 0116 289 2956
office@gliding.co.uk
www.gliding.co.uk

Global Action Plan Creating the climate for change
Aims to engage people in practical solutions to environmental & social problems
9-13 Kean Street London WC2B 4AY
Tel: 020 7420 4444
Email via website
www.globalactionplan.org.uk

Global Crop Diversity Trust A foundation for food security
Organisation set up to ensure the conservation and availability of crop diversity for food security worldwide
www.croptrust.org

Global Dimension
Explores our connections with the rest of the world. With a global dimension to their education, learners can engage with complex global issues and explore the links between their own lives and people, places and issues throughout the world
www.globaldimension.org.uk

Global Eye
Aims to increase awareness of development issues
www.globaleye.org.uk

Global Witness
Focuses on areas where profits from environmental exploitation fund human rights abuses
6th Floor, Buchanan House 30 Holborn
London EC1N 2HS
Tel: 0207 4925820
mail@globalwitness.org
www.globalwitness.org

Globe Theatre see Shakespeare's Globe Theatre

GM see GM Freeze

GM Freeze
Campaign on GM food, crops and patenting of genetic resources
50 South Yorkshire Buildings Silkstone Common Barnsley S75 4RJ
Tel: 0845 217 8992
info@gmfreeze.org
www.gmfreeze.org

GMC see General Medical Council

Go4awalk
Website for walkers and hikers
www.go4awalk.com

Goethe-Institut London
Promotes German language & culture abroad
50 Princes Gate Exhibition Rd
London SW7 2PH
Tel: 020 7596 4000
info@london.goethe.org
www.goethe.de/london

Goethe-Institut Glasgow
3 Park Circus Glasgow G3 6AX
London SW7 2PH
Tel: 0141 3322555
info@glasgow.goethe.org
www.goethe.de/glasgow

Golf see also Blind Golf Association (English), Ladies' Golf Union, Professional Golfers' Association,

Golf Association (European)
Place de la Croix-Blanche 19 CH-1066
Epalinges Switzerland
Tel: 00 41 21785 70 60
info@ega-golf.ch
www.ega-golf.ch

Gorilla Organization
International charity led by African conservationists dedicated to saving the world's last remaining gorillas from extinction
110 Gloucester Av London NW1 8HX
Tel: 020 7483 2681
info@gorillas.org
www.gorillas.org

Government Actuary's Department
Finlaison House 15-17 Furnival Street
London EC4A 1AB
Tel: 020 7211 2601
enquiries@gad.gov.uk
www.gad.gov.uk

Government Websites see DirectGov

Governors' Association (National) NGA
Independent organisation that represents school governors in England. Aims to improve the well-being of children and young people by promoting high standards in schools
Ground Floor
36 Great Charles Street Birmingham B3 3JY
Tel: 0121 237 3780
governorhq@nga.org.uk
www.nga.org.uk

Grandparents Plus
Promotes the vital role of grandparents and the extended family in children's lives, particularly when parents are no longer able to care for their children.
18 Victoria Park Square Bethnal Green
London E2 9PF
Advice & information: 0300 123 7015
Tel: 020 8981 8001
advice@grandparentsplus.org.uk
www.grandparentsplus.org.uk

Grandparents' Association
Moot House The Stow Harlow CM20 3AG
Helpline: 0845 434 9585
Tel: 01279 428040
info@grandparents-association.org.uk
www.grandparents-association.org.uk

GreatBuildings
Data and illustrations of many significant buildings worldwide
www.greatbuildings.com

Greater London Authority
Home to the Mayor of London and the London Assembly
City Hall The Queen's Walk More London
London SE1 2AA
Tel: 020 7983 4000
email via website
www.london.gov.uk

Greater London Enterprise see GLE

Green Alliance
Promotes sustainable development by ensuring that the environment is at the heart of decision making
36 Buckingham Palace Rd
London SW1W 0RE
Tel: 020 7233 7433
ga@green-alliance.org.uk
www.green-alliance.org.uk

Green Mark
Environmental management and sustainable development. Environmental training & consultancy for the public & private sectors
GLE Consulting 10-12 Queen Elizabeth St
London SE1 2JN
Tel: 020 7940 1562
green.mark@gle.co.uk
www.greenmark.co.uk

Green Party
Political party committed to social justice and ecological sustainability
56-64 Development House Leonard Street
London EC2A 4LT
Tel: 020 7549 0310
office@greenparty.org.uk
www.greenparty.org.uk

GreenMoves
Dedicated to advertising homes for sale that are more energy efficient than conventional home
Orchard Cottage
  Charlynch
  Somerset TA5 1BL
Tel: 0845 0944663
enquiries@greenmoves.com
www.greenmoves.com

Greenpeace
Defends the natural world and promotes peace by investigating, exposing and confronting environmental abuse, and championing environmentally responsible solutions
Canonbury Villas London N1 2PN
Tel: 020 7865 8100
info@uk.greenpeace.org
www.greenpeace.org.uk

Groundwork UK
Working in partnership to improve local environments & contribute to economic & social regeneration
Lockside 5 Scotland Street Birmingham B1 2RR
Tel: 0121 236 8565
info@groundwork.org.uk
www.groundwork.org.uk

Guide Dogs for the Blind Association
Burghfield Common Reading RG7 3YG
Tel: 0118 983 5555
guidedogs@guidedogs.org.uk
www.gdba.org.uk

Guitar Foundation (International) IGF
Arts agency dedicated to the promotion, understanding and enjoyment of the guitar, its music and artist. Stages festivals and large-scale summer schools
www.igf.org.uk

Gulf Veterans & Families Association (National)
Building E, Office 8
Chamberlain Business Centre
Chamberlain Road Hull HU8 8HL
Tel: 0845 257 4853
info@ngvfa.org.uk
www.ngvfa.com/

Gun Control Network
Working towards a tighter control of firearms and a gun-free environment
PO Box 11495 London N3 2FE
Crimestoppers: 0800 555 111
contact@gun-control-network.org
www.gun-control-network.org

Gutenberg see Project Gutenberg

Gymnastics (British)
Governing body
Ford Hall Lilleshall National Sports Cen
Newport Shrops TF10 9NB
Tel: 0845 129 7129
information@british-gymnastics.org
www.british-gymnastics.org

Gypsy Association
Information, advice, liaison & support.
Address on request
Tel: 07963 56 59 52
info@gypsy-association.com
www.gypsy-association.co.uk

H

Habitat for Humanity Great Britain
International development organisation that builds homes with volunteers and people in need
46 West Bar Street Banbury OX16 9RZ
Tel: 01295 264240
SupporterServices@habitatforhumanity.org.uk
www.habitatforhumanity.org.uk

Hadley Centre for Climate Prediction and Research see Met Office

Haemochromatosis Society
Support for sufferers from this common genetic iron overload disorder
Hollybush House Hadley Green Road Barnet EN5 5PR
Tel: 0208 449 1363
info@haemochromatosis.org.uk
www.haemochromatosis.org.uk

Haemophilia Society
National and independent organisation for all people affected by bleeding disorders
First Floor Petersham House 57a Hatton Garden London EC1N 8JG
Support Line: 0800 018 6068
Tel: 020 7831 1020
info@haemophilia.org.uk
www.haemophilia.org.uk

Hairline International
The Alopecia Patients Society
Lyons Court 1668 High Street Knowle West Midlands B93 0LY
www.hairlineinternational.com/

Half the Sky Foundation
Aims to ensure that every one of China's orphans has a caring adult in their life
PO Box 332 Telford TF1 9DG
Tel: 01952.812244
Email via website
www.halfthesky.org

HALO Trust
Mine clearance and bomb disposal in the developing world
Carronfoot Thornhill Dumfies DG3 5BF
Tel: 01848 331100
mail@halotrust.org
www.halotrust.org

Hamster Council (National)
www.hamsters-uk.org

Handball Association (England)
National governing body for Handball and Beach Handball in England
The Halliwell Jones Stadium Winwick Road Warrington WA2 7NE
Tel: 01925 246482/3
handball@englandhandball.com
www.englandhandball.com

Handball Association (Scottish)
National Sports Centre Invercl Burnside Road Largs Scotland KA30 8RW
Tel: 01475 687820
Anne.Mclaughlin@scottishhandball.com
www.scottishhandball.com

Handsel Trust
Promotes effective support in the UK for all children with disabilities and special needs and their families
43 Newman Road Birmigham B24 9AG
Tel: 0121 373 2747
enquiries@handseltrust.org
www.handseltrust.org

Hang Gliding and Paragliding Association (British)
8 Merus Court Meridian Business Park Leicester LE19 1RJ
Tel: 0116 289 4316
office@bhpa.co.uk
www.bhpa.co.uk

Hansard Society
Educational charity to promote effective parliamentary democracy
5th Floor 9 King St London EC2V 8EA
Tel: 020 7710 6070
contact@hansardsociety.org.uk
www.hansardsociety.org.uk

HAPPA Horses and Ponies Protection Association
Equine welfare
Taylor Building, Shores Hey Farm Black House Lane Halifax Road Briercliffe
Nr Burnley BB10 3QU
Tel: 01282 455992
www.happa.org.uk

Hawk and Owl Trust
Protect & conserve wild birds of prey & their habitats
PO Box 400 Bishops Lydeard Taunton TA4 3WH
Tel: 0844 984 2824
Email: Via Website
www.hawkandowl.org

Hay Festival
Book festival
The Drill Hall 25 Lion Street
Hay-on-Wye HR3 5AD
Tel: 01497 822 620 (admin)
admin@hayfestival.com
www.hayfestival.com

Hayward Gallery
Southbank Centre
Belvedere Rd Belvedere Road
London SE1 8XX
Tel: 020 7960 4200 (switchboard)
Ticket Office: 0844 875 0073
customer@southbankcentre.co.uk
www.southbankcentre.co.uk/venues/hayward-gallery

Headliners

Charity that inspires and encourages the personal development of young people through journalism. Young people are trained to research and produce stories on issues important to them for publication and broadcast in national and local newspapers, magazines, television, radio and online
Rich Mix 35-47 Bethnal Green Road
London E1 6LA
Tel: 020 7749 9360
enquiries@headliners.org
www.headliners.org

Headlong Theatre

34-35 Berwick Street London W1F 8RP
Tel: 020 74780270
info@headlongtheatre.co.uk
www.headlongtheatre.co.uk

HEADWAY The Brain Injury Association

Support for brain injury survivors and their families
Bradbury House 190 Bagnall Road
Old Basford Nottingham NG6 8SF
Free helpline: 0808 800 2244
Tel: 0115 924 0800
enquiries@headway.org.uk
helpline@headway.org.uk
www.headway.org.uk

Healing Organisations (Confederation of)

To make contact & distant healing available on NHS & in private medicine
www.the-cho.org.uk

Health (Department of)

Richmond House 79 Whitehall London SW1A 2NS
Tel: 020 7210 4850
Textphone: 020 7210 5025
Email via website
www.dh.gov.uk

Health & Safety Executive

The purpose of HSE is to prevent people being killed, injured or made ill by work. From September 2011 it operated mainly as an online service
Redgrave Court Merton Road Bootle Merseyside L20 7HS
www.hse.gov.uk

Health Information Resources

www.evidence.nhs.uk

Health Professions Council

Training, performance and conduct for 13 health professions (excluding doctors and nurses). Check online if a health professional is registered
Park House 184 Kennington Park Road London SE11 4BU
Tel: 0845 300 6184
See website for email
www.hpc-uk.org

Health Protection Agency

From April 2012 the HPA will become part of Public Health England
email via website
www.hpa.org.uk

Health Service Ombudsman now see
Parliamentary and Health Service Ombudsman

Health, Social Services and Public Safety (N. Ireland Department of)

Castle Buildings Stormont Belfast BT4 3SJ
Tel: 028 9052 0500
webmaster@dhsspsni.gov.uk
www.dhsspsni.gov.uk

Healthtalkonline

Unique database of personal and patient experiences
DIPEx PO Box 428 Witney Oxon OX28 9EU
Tel: 01865 201330
info@healthtalkonline.org
www.healthtalkonline.org

Healthy Schools

Offers support for schools to equip young people with the knowledge to make informed health choices
www.education.gov.uk/schools/pupilsupport/pastoralcare/a0075278/healthy-schools

Hear From Your MP

Allows constituents to sign up to get emails from their local MP about local issues
www.hearfromyourmp.com

Hearing Dogs for Deaf People

National charity and centre for training dogs to alert their deaf owners to important sounds and danger signals in the home, work place and public buildings
The Grange Wycombe Rd Saunderton Princes Risborough Bucks HP27 9NS
Tel: 01844 348 100
info@hearingdogs.org.uk
www.hearingdogs.org.uk

Heart Foundation (British) see British Heart Foundation

Heart Programme

Run by Childline. Designed to improve the life chances of young people in London by giving advice on healthy relationships and problems relating to gang violence and youth crime
Childline: 0800 1111
www.heartprogramme.org

Heart Research UK

Suite 12D Joseph's Well Leeds LS3 1AB
Tel: 0113 234 7474
info@heartresearch.org.uk
www.heartresearch.org.uk

Heartstone
Uses story, fiction and photojournalism to challenge racism and intolerance
Mayfield High Street Dingwall Ross-shire IV15 9SS
Tel: 01349 865400
info@heartstone.co.uk
www.heartstone.co.uk

Heat is Online
Extreme weather worldwide
www.heatisonline.org

Hedgehog Preservation Society (British)
Hedgehog House Dhustone Ludlow Shropshire SY8 3PL
Helpline:01584 890 801
Tel: 01584 890801
info@britishhedgehogs.org.uk
www.britishhedgehogs.org.uk

HELP Holiday Endeavour for Lone Parents
Offers reduced cost holidays to lone parent families
25 Brook Street Hemswell Gainsborough DN21 5UJ
Tel: 01427 668717
janice@help.fslife.co.uk
www.helphols.co.uk

Help - For a life without tobacco
www.help-eu.com

Help for Heroes
Raises money to support members of the armed forces who have been wounded in the service of their country
Unit 6 Aspire Business Centre Ordnance Road Tidworth SP9 7QD
Tel: 0845 673 1760
email via website
www.helpforheroes.org.uk

Help the aged now see Age Cymru, Age UK, Age NI, Age Scotland

Help the Hospices
Worldwide link for information about hospice/palliative care
Hospice House 34-44 Britannia St London WC1X 9JG
Tel: 020 7520 8200
info@helpthehospices.org.uk
www.helpthehospices.org.uk

Henry Doubleday Research Association
see Garden Organic

Henry Moore Foundation
Registered charity. Founded by the artist in 1977 to encourage public appreciation of the visual arts, especially sculpture
Dane Tree House Perry Green Herts SG10 6EE
Tel: 01279 843 333
Email via website
www.henry-moore.org

Heraldry Society
Exists to increase and extend interest in and knowledge of heraldry, armory, chivalry, genealogy and allied subjects.
PO Box 772 Guildford Surrey GU3 3ZX
Tel: 01483 237373
email via website
www.theheraldrysociety.com

Heraldry Society of Scotland
25 Craigentinny Crescent Edinburgh EH7 6QA
info@heraldry-scotland.co.uk
www.heraldry-scotland.co.uk

Herb Society
Sulgrave Manor PO Box 946 Northampton NN3 0BN
Tel: 0845 491 8699
info@herbsociety.org.uk
www.herbsociety.org.uk

Herbalists see Medical Herbalists (National Institute of)

Hereditary Breast Cancer Helpline (National)
Aims to ensure that those worried about their family history have full access to information on the options available to enable them to make informed choices
Helpline: 01629 813000
canhelp@btopenworld.com
www.breastcancergenetics.co.uk/

Heritage Lottery Fund
Gives grants to support heritage: museums, parks and historic places, archaeology, natural environment and cultural traditions
7 Holbein Place London SW1W 8NR
020 7591 6000
enquire@hlf.org.uk
www.hlf.org.uk

Heritage Railway Association
A trade organisation for heritage railways
email via website
www.heritagerailways.com

Herpes Viruses Association
Gives help and advice to people with herpes viruses. Enclose sae for information
41 North Road London N7 9DP
Tel: 0845 123 2305
info@herpes.org.uk
www.herpes.org.uk

Hi8us First Light Now see First Light

Hibiscus Female Prisoners Welfare Project
Addresses the special needs of foreign national women imprisoned in the UK.
Holloway Resource Centre 356 Holloway Road London N7 6PA
Tel: 020 7697 4120
fpwphibiscus@aol.com
fpwphibiscus.org.uk

Hideout
National website supporting children and young people living with domestic violence
www.thehideout.org.uk

Higher Education Funding Council for England
Distributes public funding for teaching and research and related activities in universities and colleges.
Northavon House Coldharbour Lane Bristol BS16 1QD
Tel: 0117 931 7317
hefce@hefce.ac.uk
www.hefce.ac.uk

Hindu Universe - Hindu Resource Center
www.hindunet.org

Hispanic & Luso Brazilian Council
A focal point for the Spanish & Portuguese speaking worlds: commercial, cultural, educational and diplomatic.
Canning House 2 Belgrave Sq London SW1X 8PJ
Tel: 020 7235 2303
enquiries@canninghouse.org
www.canninghouse.org

Historic Houses Association
Representative body for private owners of historic houses, parks and gardens
2 Chester St London SW1X 7BB
Tel: 020 7259 5688
info@hha.org.uk
www.hha.org.uk

Historic Monuments (Welsh) see Cadw

Historic Scotland
Longmore House Salisbury Place Edinburgh EH9 1SH
Tel: 0131 668 8600
hs.website@scotland.gsi.gov.uk
www.historic-scotland.gov.uk

Historical Association
59a Kennington Park Rd London SE11 4JH
Tel: 0300 100 0223
emaiil via website
www.history.org.uk

Historical Manuscripts Commission see National Archives

Historical Maritime Society
UK based historical research and re-enactment group recreating the Royal Navy
2 Mount Zion Brownbirks Street Cornholme Todmorden OL14 8PG
Tel: 01706 819248
grog@tesco.net
www.hms.org.uk

History Museum (National): St Fagans see St Fagans: National History Museum

History of Cinema & Popular Culture (The Bill Douglas Centre for the)
Museum & academic research centre
University of Exeter The Old Library Prince of Wales Rd Exeter EX4 4SB
Tel: 01392 724321
bdc@exeter.ac.uk
www.billdouglas.org

History World
Site run by Bamber Gascoigne covering in 1 million words 400 separate histories and 4000 key events
www.historyworld.net

HIV InSite
Up-to-date information on HIV/AIDS treatment and prevention
hivinsite.ucsf.edu/

HIV/AIDS see also AVERT, Body Positive North West, HIV/Aids Alliance (International), HIV InSite, ONE International, PACE, Positively UK, Terrence Higgins Trust

HIV/Aids Alliance (International)
Supporting community action on AIDS in developing countries
1st and 2nd Floor Preece House 91-101 Davigdor Road Hove BN3 1RE
Tel: 01273 718900
mail@aidsalliance.org
www.aidsalliance.org

HM Prison Service now see Sentencing, prison and probation

HM Revenue and Customs
Advice on VAT, excise & customs
www.hmrc.gov.uk

HM Treasury
Correspondence and Enquiries Unit 1 Horse Guards Rd London SW1A 2HQ
Tel: 020 7270 4558
public.enquiries@hm-treasury.gov.uk
www.hm-treasury.gov.uk

HMRC Education Zone
www.hmrc.gov.uk/education-zone/index.htm

HMS Belfast part of the Imperial War Museum
The Queen's Walk London SE1 2JH
Tel: 020 7940 6300
hmsbelfast@iwm.org.uk
hmsbelfast.iwm.org.uk
www.iwm.org.uk

Holiday Care see Tourism for All

Holiday Endeavour for Lone Parents see HELP

Holidays see also BAPA, Calvert Trust, Family Holiday Association, Jubilee Sailing Trust, Landmark Trust, National Trust Holiday Cottages, National Trust Working Holidays

Holistic Therapists (Federation of)
Professional body representing over 20,000 professional therapists offering massage, aromatherapy, reflexology, beauty and fitness therapies.
18 Shakespeare Business Centre Hathaway Close Eastleigh Hampshire SO50 4SR
Tel: 023 8062 4350
email via website
www.fht.org.uk

Holocaust Educational Trust
BCM Box 7892 London WC1N 3XX
Tel: 020 7222 6822
email via website
www.het.org.uk

Holy See see Vatican

Home Business Alliance
Werrington Business Centre 86 Papyrus Road Peterborough PE4 5BH
Tel: 0871 284 5100
info@homebusiness.org.uk
www.homebusiness.org.uk

Home Office Public Enquiries Unit
Direct Communications Unit 2 Marsham Street London SW1P 4DF
Tel: 020 7035 4848
public.enquiries@homeoffice.gsi.gov.uk
www.homeoffice.gov.uk

Home-Start
Offers support to parents with at least one child under 5, who are finding it difficult to cope
8-10 West Walk Leicester LE1 7NA
Free info line: 0800 068 63 68
Tel: 0116 258 7900
info@home-start.org.uk
www.home-start.org.uk

Homeless International
Supports community-led housing and infrastructure related developments in Asia, Africa and Latin America
Queens House 16 Queens Rd Coventry CV1 3EG
Tel: 024 7663 2802
info@homeless-international.org
www.homeless-international.org

Homeless Link
Umbrella organisation for organisations working with homeless people
Gateway House Milverton Street, London SE11 4AP
Tel: 020 7840 4430
Email via website
www.homeless.org.uk

Homeopathic Association (British)
29 Park St West Luton LU1 3BE
Tel: 01582 408675
info@britishhomeopathic.org
www.britishhomeopathic.org

Homeopaths (Society of)
Professional association
11 Brookfield Duncan Close Moulton Park Northampton NN3 6WL
Tel: 0845 450 6611
Info@homeopathy-soh.org
www.homeopathy-soh.org

Homework High
Channel 4's website where teachers answer questions. Also contains a searchable bank of questions already asked & their answers
www.channel4learning.com/apps/homeworkhigh/

Homeworking
Free information for those wishing to work from home
www.homeworking.co.uk

Honour abuse see Karma Nirvana

Hope UK
Drug education charity specialising in work with children & young people
25f Copperfield St London SE1 0EN
Tel: 020 7928 0848
enquiries@hopeuk.org
www.hopeuk.org

Horse Society (British)
Abbey Park Stareton Kenilworth Warwickshire CV8 2XZ
Tel: 0844 848 1666
Tel: 02476 840500
email via website
www.bhs.org.uk

Horses (International League for the Protection of) now see World Horse Welfare

Horses and Ponies Protection Association see HAPPA

Horticultural Society (Royal) see Royal Horticultural Society

Hospices see Help the Hospices

Hospital and Community Friends now see Attend

Hospital Broadcasting Association HBA
www.hbauk.co.uk

Hostelling International
Has 90 Youth Hostel Associations in 90 countries, operating 4,000 hostels
2nd Floor, Gate House Fretherne Road Welwyn Garden City AL8 6RD
Tel: 01707 324170
info@hihostels.com
www.hihostels.com

Hostelling International (N. Ireland)
22-32 Donegall Rd Belfast BT12 5JN
Tel: 028 9032 4733
info@hini.org.uk
www.hini.org.uk

Hostels.com
List of youth hostels worldwide in a continually updated database
www.hostels.com

House of Commons Information Office
London SW1A 2TT
Tel: 020 7219 4272
Text phone: dial 18001 followed by 020 7219 4272
hcinfo@parliament.uk
www.parliament.uk/mps-lords-and-offices/offices/commons/hcio/

House of Lords
London SW1A 0PW
Tel: 020 7219 3107
hlinfo@parliament.uk
www.parliament.uk/business/lords/

Housing (Chartered Institute of) see CIH

Housing (Confederation of Co-operative)
The UK organisation for housing co-operatives, tenant-controlled housing organisations and regional federations of housing co-ops
19 Devonshire Road Liverpool L8 3TX
Tel: 0151 726 2228
info@cch.coop
www.cch.coop

Housing Advice Northern Ireland
Independent housing advice
10-12 High Street Belfast BT1 2BA
Tel: 028 9024 5640
email via website
www.housingadviceni.org

Housing Federation (National)
Representative organisation for registered social landlords (mainly housing associations)
Lion Court 25 Procter Street
London WC1V 6NY
Tel: 020 7067 1010
email via website
www.housing.org.uk

Housing Justice
Takes practical action to prevent, and campaigns against homelessness
256 Bermondsey Street London SE1 3UJ
TEL: 020 3544 8094
email via wesite
www.housingjustice.org.uk

Housing Ombudsman Service
The Ombudsman Service is free for users. People with speech or hearing problems can contact the service via typetalk
81 Aldwych London WC2B 4HN
Tel: 0300 111 3000
info@housing-ombudsman.org.uk
www.housing-ombudsman.org.uk

Housing Policy (Centre for)
Research institute
University of York Heslington
York YO10 5DD
Tel: 01904 321480
chp@york.ac.uk
www.york.ac.uk/inst/chp/

HousingCare.org Information for older people
Aims to help older people make decisions about where to live, and any support or care they need
EAC FirstStop Advice 3rd Floor 89 Albert Embankment London SE1 7TP
Tel: 0800 377 7070
email via website
www.housingcare.org

Howard League for Penal Reform
Works for humane, effective and efficient reform of the penal system
1 Ardleigh Rd London N1 4HS
Tel: 020 7249 7373
info@howardleague.org
www.howardleague.org

Howtocomplain.com Your right to be heard
Independent British website aimed at making complaints work for everyone
PO Box 1290 Salisbury SP1 1YN
complaints@howtocomplain.com
www.howtocomplain.com

Hull Truck Theatre
50 Ferensway Hull HU2 8LB
Box Office: 01482 323638
Information: 01482 224800
boxoffice@hulltruck.co.uk
admin@hulltruck.co.uk
www.hulltruck.co.uk

Human Dignity Trust
Helps local groups and individuals challenge the legality of laws which criminalise private consensual sexual activity between adults of the same sex, wherever those laws exist in the world
PO Box 63583 London N6 9BL
info@humandignitytrust.org
www.humandignitytrust.org

Human Fertilisation & Embryology Authority
A statutory body that regulates infertility treatments including IVF, the use of donated sperm or eggs, and human embryo research
Finsbury Tower 103-105 Bunhill Row
London, EC1Y 8HF
Tel: 020 7291 8200
email via website
www.hfea.gov.uk

Human Power Club (British) BHPC
Non-conformist wheeled vehicles (recumbents). Organise races and provide information and support for those interested in all kinds of human powered vehicles (HPVs)
www.bhpc.org.uk

Human Rights (European Court of)
Council of Europe 67075 Strasbourg-Cedex France
Tel: 0033 3 88 41 20 18
www.echr.coe.int

Human Rights Commission (N. Ireland)
Aims to protect and promote the human rights in law, policy and practice
Temple Court 39 North St Belfast BT1 1NA
Tel: 028 9024 3987
Textphone: 028 9024 9066
email via website
www.nihrc.org

Human Rights Education Association
International non-governmental organisation that supports human rights learning
www.hrea.org

Human Rights Policy (International Council on)
The Council itself ceased to function in February 2012 but this website cotains an archive of its work.
www.ichrp.org

Human Rights Watch
1st Floor Audrey House 16-20 Ely Place London EC1N 6SN
Tel: 020 7713 1995
Email via website
www.hrw.org

Human Rights(British Institute of) see BIHR

Human Scale Education Movement
Helps large schools find ways to work in smaller units and support parents and teachers wishing to set up their own schools
Unit 8, Fairseat Farm Chew Stoke Bristol BS40 8XF & CAN Mezzanine 49-51 East Road London N1 6AH
Tel: 01275 332516
info@hse.org.uk
www.hse.org.uk

Human Writes
Support through letter writing to those on death row
4 Lacey Grove Wetherby West Yorkshire LS22 6RL
email via website
www.humanwrites.org

Humane Research Trust
Charity working to fund and promote medical research which does not involve animals or animal tissue. Aims to eliminate the need for animals in human medical research
29 Bramhall Lane South Bramhall Stockport SK7 2DN
Tel: 0161 439 8041
info@humaneresearch.org.uk
www.humaneresearch.org.uk

Humane Slaughter Association
Charity exclusively concerned with the welfare of animals during marketing, transport and slaughter
The Old School Brewhouse Hill Wheathampstead Herts AL4 8AN
Tel: 01582 831 919
info@hsa.org.uk
www.hsa.org.uk

Humanist Association (British)
A non-religious approach to life based on reason & common humanity
1 Gower St London WC1E 6HD
Tel: 020 7079 3580
info@humanism.org.uk
www.humanism.org.uk

Hunger Education Service (World) & Hunger Notes
Educate the general public and target groups about the extent and causes of hunger and malnutrition in the United States and the world
www.worldhunger.org

Hunt Saboteurs Association
BM HSA London WC1N 3XX
Tel: 0845 4500727
info@huntsabs.org.uk
www.huntsabs.org.uk

Huntington's Disease Association
Suite 24 Liverpool Science Park Innovation Centre 1 131 Mount Pleasant Liverpool L3 5TF
Tel: 0151 331 5444
info@hda.org.uk
www.hda.org.uk

Hurricane Center (National)
US website
www.nhc.noaa.gov

Hydrology see CEH

Hyperactive Children's Support Group
Provides information, ideas & literature for parents, carers & professionals. Focuses on non medication
71 Whyke Lane Chichester W Sussex PO19 7PD
Tel: 01243 539966
hacsg@hacsg.org.uk
www.hacsg.org.uk

Hypermobility Syndrome Association
49 Orchard Crescent Oreston Plymouth PL9
7NF
Tel: 0845 345 4465
email via website
www.hypermobility.org

I

IAAF see Athletics Federations (International
Association of)

IASO see Obesity (International Association for
the Study of)

IATEFL International Association of Teachers of
English as a Foreign Language)
Educational charity supporting EFL teachers
worldwide
Darwin College University of Kent
Canterbury CT2 7NY
Tel: 01227 824430
generalenquiries@iatefl.org
www.iatefl.org

IBS Network
For help with problems related to
Inflammatory Bowel Disease (IBD) and
Irritable Bowel Syndrome
Unit 1.12 SOAR Works 14 Knutton Road
Sheffield, S5 9NU
Tel: 0114 272 3253
info@theibsnetwork.org
www.theibsnetwork.org

Ice Hockey UK
National governing body for ice hockey
Email: Via Website
www.icehockeyuk.co.uk

**Ice Skating Association of Great Britain
and N.I. (National)**
Body overseeing amateur ice skating in UK
Grains Building High Cross Street Hockley
Nottingham NG1 3AX
Tel: 0115 988 8060
email via website
www.iceskating.org.uk

ICON Institute of Conservation
Lead voice for the conservation of cultural
heritage in the UK. As a charity, Icon is
committed to public benefit through
promoting public understanding of and
access to all the diverse elements of cultural
heritage
1.5 Lafone House The Leathermarket
Weston Street London SE1 3ER
Tel: 0203 142 6799
Email: Via Website
www.icon.org.uk

ICSTIS now see Phonepay Plus

ICVA see Voluntary Agencies (International
Council of)

IDeA now see Local Government Improvement
and Development

Identity & Passport Service London
You will need to visit a Regional Passport Office if you need a passport urgently and want to apply in person using the Fast Track one-week or Premium one-day service. You must make an appointment by calling the passport advice line
Globe House 89 Eccleston Square London SW1V 1PN
Passport Adviceline: 0300 222 0000
Text Relay: 18001 0300 222 0000
Text Phone: 0300 222 0222
www.ips.gov.uk/passport/contact.asp
www.direct.gov.uk/en/TravelAndTransport/Passports/index.htm

& Belfast
Law Society House 90-106 Victoria Street Belfast BT1 3GN

& Glasgow regional passport office
3 Northgate 96 Milton Street Cowcaddens Glasgow G4 0BT

& Liverpool
101 Old Hall Street Liverpool L3 9BD

& Newport
Olympia House Upper Dock Street Newport Gwent NP20 1XA

& Peterborough
Aragon Court Northminster Road Peterborough PE1 1QG

& Durham
Millburngate House Durham DH1 5ZL

IDTA International Dance Teachers Association
An awarding body delivering qualifications in dance
76 Bennett Rd Brighton BN2 5JL
Tel: 01273 685 652
email via website
www.idta.co.uk

IFAW International Fund for Animal Welfare
Saving animals in crisis around the world
87-90 Albert Embankment London SE1 7UD
Tel: 020 7587 6700
info-uk@ifaw.org
www.ifaw.org

IFST Institute of Food Science & Technology
Professional qualifying body for food scientists and technologists and educational charity
5 Cambridge Court 210 Shepherds Bush Rd London W6 7NJ
Tel: 020 7603 6316
info@ifst.org
www.ifst.org

IKWRO Iranian & Kurdish Women's Rights Organisation
Helps Middle Eastern women living in the UK to escape violence
PO Box 65840 London EC2P 2FS
Tel: 0207 920 6460
Tel: 07846 275246 (Kurdish / Arabic 24 hrs)
Tel: 07846 310157 (Farsi / Dari / Turkish 24 hrs)
info@ikwro.org.uk
ikwro.handsupdigital.com

ILO see International Labour Organization

Imaginate
Promoting and developing performing arts for children and young people in Scotland
45a George Street Edinburgh EH2 2HT
Tel: 0131 225 8050
info@imaginate.org.uk
www.imaginate.org.uk

IMF see International Monetary Fund

Immigrants (Joint Council for the Welfare of)
115 Old St London EC1V 9RT
Tel: 020 7251 8708
info@jcwi.org.uk
www.jcwi.org.uk

Immigration see also UK Border Agency

Immigration & Asylum Tribunals Service
Hears appeals against asylum and immigration decisions
PO Box 7866 Loughborough LE11 2XZ
Tel: 0300 123 1711
Minicom: 0300 123 1264
customer.service@tribunals.gsi.gov.uk
www.tribunals.gov.uk/ImmigrationAsylum

Immigration Advice Service
Specialist immigration lawyers with over 30 years combined experience of providing advice on immigration, asylum and citizenship cases at all levels.
Beetham House 61 Tithebarn Street Liverpool L2 2SB
Telephone advice service: 0844 887 0111
Tel: 07773399271 out of hours only
Tel: 07554813156
info@iasservices.org.uk
www.iasuk.org

& Manchester
Conavon Court Blackfriars Street Manchester M3 5BQ
Telephone advice service: 0844 887 0111
Tel: 07773399271 out of hours only
info@iasservices.org.uk

& Sheffield
Suite 2 Saville Street Sheffield S4 7UD
Telephone advice service: 0844 887 0111
Tel: 07773399271 out of hours only
info@iasservices.org.uk

Immigration Aid Unit (Greater Manchester)
1 Delaunays Road Crumpsall Green
Manchester M8 4QS
Tel: 0161 740 7722
email via website
www.gmiau.org

Immigration Law Practitioners' Association
Lindsey House 40-42 Charterhouse St.
London EC1M 6JN
Tel: 020 7251 8383
info@ilpa.org.uk
www.ilpa.org.uk

Immigration Services Commissioner (Office of the)
Independent body committed to the
elimination of unscrupulous administration
advisers and the fair investigation of
complaints.
5th Floor Counting House 53 Tooley St
London SE1 2QN
Tel: 0845 000 0046
Tel: 0207 211 1500
info@oisc.gov.uk
www.oisc.gov.uk

Imperial Society of Teachers of Dancing
see ISTD

Imperial War Museum Collections
Collection covering all aspects of twentieth
and twenty-first century conflict involving
Britain and the Commonwealth
collections.iwm.org.uk
www.iwm.org.uk

Imperial War Museum Duxford
Cambridgeshire CB22 4QR
Tel: 01223 835000
duxford@iwm.org.uk
duxford.iwm.org.uk

Imperial War Museum London
Lambeth Road London SE1 6HZ
Tel: 020 7416 5320
mail@iwm.org.uk
london.iwm.org.uk

Imperial War Museum North
The Quays Trafford Wharf Road Manchester
M17 1TZ
Tel: 0161 836 4000
iwmnorth@iwm.org.uk
north.iwm.org.uk

Impotence Association see Sexual Advice
Association

Include
Projects for children excluded from or not
attending school and post 16 'hard to help'.
60 Queens Rd Reading RG1 4BS
Tel: 0118 902 1000
enquiries@cfbt.com
www.cfbt.com/teach/excludedyoungpeople/
include.aspx

Inclusion see Centre for Economic & Social
Inclusion

Inclusion (National Development Team for) NDTi
A not-for-profit organisation concerned with
promoting inclusion and equality for people
who risk exclusion and who need support to
lead a full life
Montreux House 18a James Street West
Bath BA1 2BT
Tel: 01225 789135
office@ndti.org.uk
www.ndti.org.uk

Inclusive Education (Alliance for)
Campaigning to end segregation in
education
336 Brixton Road London SW9 7AA
Tel: 020 7737 6030
info@allfie.org.uk
www.allfie.org.uk

Inclusive Education (Centre for Studies on)
Working for inclusive education for all
children and a gradual end to all segregated
education, based on human rights
arguments.
The Park Centre Daventry Road Knowle
Bristol BS4 1DQ
Tel: 0117 353 3150
admin@csie.org.uk
www.csie.org.uk

Incontinence see Bladder and Bowel
Foundation, ERIC

Independent Advice Centres see AdviceUK

Independent Living Alternatives
Promotes independent living for people with
disabilities
Trafalgar House Grenville Place London
NW7 3SA
Tel: 020 8906 9265
PAServices@ILAnet.co.uk
www.ilanet.co.uk

Independent Midwives Association see
Midwives UK (Independent)

Independent News Collective see INK

Independent Police Complaints Commission
PO Box 473 Sale M33 0BW
Tel: 0300 020 0096
Text Relay: 18001 0207 166 3000
Minicom: 020 7404 0431
enquiries@ipcc.gsi.gov.uk
www.ipcc.gov.uk

Independent Safeguarding Authority
To help prevent unsuitable people from
working with children and vulnerable adults
PO Box 181 Darlington DL1 9FA
Vetting and Barring Scheme: 0300 123 111
Tel: 01325 953 795
isadispatchteam@homeoffice.gsi.gov.uk
www.isa-gov.org

Independent Schools Council
Umbrella body representing 1,280
independent schools educating more than
500,000 children in the UK and Ireland
St Vincent House 30 Orange Street
London WC2H 7HH
Tel: 020 7766 7070
email via website
www.isc.co.uk

Independent Television Commission now
see OFCOM

Independent Television News see ITN

Index on Censorship
Defends free expression
www.indexoncensorship.org

Indexers (Society of)
Woodbourn Business Centre 10 Jessell Street
Sheffield S9 3HY
Tel: 0114 244 9561or 0845 872 6807
admin@indexers.org.uk
www.indexers.org.uk

Indian Census
www.censusindia.net

Indian Volunteers for Community Service
now see Volunteers For Rural India

Indigenous Tribal Peoples of the Tropical Forests (International Alliance of)
www.international-alliance.org

Indonesia Human Rights Campaign see
TAPOL

Industrial Injuries Advisory Council
2nd Floor Caxton House Tothill Street
Lonon SW1H 9NA
Tel: 020 7449 5618
iiac@dwp.gsi.gov.uk
www.iiac.org.uk

Infant Deaths (Foundation for the Study of)
Funds research into sudden infant death,
supports bereaving parents & disseminates
baby safety information
11 Belgrave Road London SW1V 1RB
Helpline: 0808 802 6868
Tel: 020 7802 3200
Fundraising: 020 7802 3201
office@fsid.org.uk
www.fsid.org.uk

Infertility see also Fertility Friends, Human
Fertilisation & Embryology Authority

Infertility Counselling Association (British) BICA
Professional association for infertility
counsellors and counselling in the UK
www.bica.net

Infertility Network UK
For those experiencing problems of infertility
Charter House 43 St Leonards Rd
Bexhill on Sea TN40 1JA
Tel: 0800 008 7464
admin@infertilitynetworkuk.com
www.infertilitynetworkuk.com

Inform Information Network on Religious
Movements
Help and information on new religious
movements & cults
Houghton St London WC2A 2AE
Tel: 020 7955 7654
inform@lse.ac.uk
www.inform.ac

Information Commissioner's Office
Enforces the Data Protection Act 1998 and
The Freedom of Information Act 2000
Wycliffe House Water Lane
Wilmslow SK9 5AF
Helpline: 0303 123 1113
Tel: 01625 545745
email via website
www.ico.gov.uk

Information Management (Association for) Aslib
Actively promotes best practice in the
management of information resources
Howard House Wagon Lane
Bingley BD16 1WA
Tel: 01274 777700
email via website
www.aslib.com

Injuries see Safety/Accidents/Injury theme

INK Independent News Collective
Association of UK's alternative press - future
under review, see website for details
F24 Acton Business Centre School Road
London NW10 6TD
Tel: 020 8453 1144
inkgateway@pro-net.co.uk
www.ink.uk.com

Inland Revenue see HM Revenue and
Customs

Inland Revenue Education Service now see
HMRC Education Zone

Inland Waterways Association
National charity run by volunteers.
Campaigns to use, maintain and restore
Britain's inland waterways
Island House Moor Road Chesham HP5 1WA
Tel: 01494 783 453
iwa@waterways.org.uk
www.waterways.org.uk

**Innovation in Mathematics Teaching
(Centre for)**
Aims to enhance the teaching and learning
3rd Floor, Nancy Astor Building University of
Plymouth Drake Circus Plymouth PL4 8AA
Tel: 01752 585346
www.cimt.plymouth.ac.uk

INQUEST United Campaigns for Justice
Helps the families & friends of those who
die in custody, special hospitals etc or other
controversial circumstances. General advice
on coroners inquest system.
89-93 Fonthill Rd London N4 3JH
Tel: 020 7263 1111
email via website
www.inquest.org.uk

Institute for Optimum Nutrition see
Optimum Nutrition (Institute for)

Institute of Contemporary Arts
12 Carlton House Terrace London SW1Y 5AH
Box office: 020 7930 3647
Switchboard: 020 7930 0493
email via website
www.ica.org.uk

Institute of Directors see Directors (Institute
of)

Institute of Race Relations see Race
Relations (Institute of)

Instituto Cervantes see Spanish Institute

Insurance Ombudsman see Financial
Ombudsman Service

**Integrated Education (N. Ireland Council
for)**
25 College Gardens Belfast BT9 6BS
Tel: 02890 972910
info@nicie.org.uk
www.nicie.org.uk

Intellect
UK trade association for information
technology, telecommunications and
electronics companies
Russell Square House 10-12 Russell Square
London WC1B 5EE
Tel: 020 7331 2000
info@intellectuk.org
www.intellectuk.org

Intellectual Property Office
Stimulates innovation and competitiveness
via patents, trade marks, copyrights etc.
Concept House Cardiff Rd Newport S Wales
NP10 8QQ
Tel: 0300 300 2000
Minicom (text phone): 0300 0200 015
information@ipo.gov.uk
www.ipo.gov.uk

Inter Faith Network for the UK
Promotes mutual respect and understanding
between different faith communities
2 Grosvenor Gardens London SW1W 0DH
Tel: 020 7730 0410
ifnet@interfaith.org.uk
www.interfaith.org.uk

Interact Worldwide
Advancing the rights of all people to free and
informed reproductive health choice and to
confidential sexual and reproductive health
services including family planning
5-7 Cranwood Street London EC1V 9LH
Tel: 0300 777 8500
programmes@interactworldwide.org
www.interactworldwide.org

Intercountry Adoption Centre
22 Union Street Barnet Hertfordshire EN5
4HZ
Advice Line: 0208 447 4753
Tel: 020 8449 2562
Email via website
www.icacentre.org.uk

Interights
Expert advice and assistance to those
defending human rights through the law
Lancaster House 33 Islington High Street
London N1 9LH
Tel: 020 7278 3230
ir@interights.org
www.interights.org

Intermediate Technology see Practical
Action

Intermix
Organisation for the benefit of mixed-race families, individuals and anyone who feels they have a multiracial identity
9 Dunster Gardens London NW6 7NG
Tel: 07961 982 398
contact@intermix.org.uk
www.intermix.org.uk

International Affairs (Royal Institute of)
Brings together people of all nationalities from government, politics, business, the academic world and the media
Chatham House 10 St James's Sq London SW1Y 4LE
Tel: 020 7957 5700
contact@chathamhouse.org.uk
www.chathamhouse.org.uk

International Baccalaureate Organization
Offers three programmes for students aged 3 to 19 help develop the intellectual, personal, emotional and social skills to live, learn and work in a rapidly globalising world
Route des Morillons 15 Grand-Saconnex, Genève CH-1218 Switzerland
Tel: 00 41 22 791 7740
ibhq@ibo.org
www.ibo.org

International Criminal Court
An independent, permanent court that tries persons accused of the most serious crimes of international concern, namely genocide, crimes against humanity and war crimes. It will not act if a case is investigated or prosecuted by a national judicial system.
www.icc-cpi.int

International Dance Teachers Association
see IDTA

International Development (Department for)
UK Government department responsible for promoting development and the reduction of poverty
1 Palace St London SW1E 5HE
Tel: 0845 300 4100
Tel: 020 7023 0000 (Switchboard)
enquiry@dfid.gov.uk
www.dfid.gov.uk

International Labour Organization ILO
UN agency which promotes fundamental principles and rights at work
4 route des Morillons CH-1211 Geneva 22 Switzerland
Tel: 00 41 22 799 6111
ilo@ilo.org
www.ilo.org

International Monetary Fund
www.imf.org

International Olympic Committee IOC
Chateau De Vidy, P.O. Box 356 1007 Lausanne Switzerland
Tel: 00 41 21 621 6111
www.olympic.org

International Registry of Organ Donation and Transplantation see Organ Donation and Transplantation (International Registry of)

International Service
2 year placements for experienced professionals with development projects in Latin America, West Africa and Palestine
Second Floor Rougier House 5 Rougier Street York YO1 6HZ
Tel: 01904 64 77 99
email via website
www.internationalservice.org.uk

International Union for Conservation of Nature see IUCN

Internet see also ipl2, Nobel Prize Internet Archive, Nominet, People's Network, Topmarks, Wired Safety

Internet Watch Foundation
To hinder potentially illegal material on the internet
Suite 7310 First Floor Building 7300 Cambridge Research Park Waterbeach Cambridge CB25 9TN
Tel: 01223 20 30 30
email via website
www.iwf.org.uk

Interpol
General Secretariat 200 quai Charles de Gaulle 69006 Lyon France
Email via website
www.interpol.int

IntoUniversity
Provides local learning centres in London where young people are inspired to achieve
95 Sirdar Road London W11 4EQ
el: 020 7243 0242
info@ntouniversity.org
www.intouniversity.org

Investment Ombudsman see Financial Ombudsman Service

IOC see International Olympic Committee

IOSH see Occupational Safety & Health (Institution of)

IOTF see Obesity (International Association for the Study of) & Obesity TaskForce (International)

ipl2
US website. A searchable, annotated subject directory of more than 8,500 internet resources selected & evaluated by librarians for their usefulness to users of public libraries
www.ipl.org

IPPL (UK) International Primate Protection League
Dedicated to the rescue of monkeys and apes
Southbank House Black Prince Road London SE1 7SJ
Tel: 020 3176 0089
enquiries@ippl-uk.org
www.ippl.org.uk

IPPR Institute for Public Policy Research
Progressive research think-tank
4th Floor 14 Buckingham Street London WC2N 6DF
Tel: 020 7470 6100
info@ippr.org
www.ippr.org

IPSEA Independent Parental Special Education Advice
Charity advising parents of children with special educational needs of the obligations of LEAs
Hunters Court Debden Road Saffron Walden CB11 4AA
Advice Line: 0800 0184016
Tel: 01799 582030
www.ipsea.org.uk

Ironbridge Gorge Museum
Coach Road Coalbrookdale Telford TF8 7DQ
Education: 01952 433970
Visitor Information Centre: 01952 433424
Email via website
www.ironbridge.org.uk

ISCIS now see Independent Schools Council

Islamic Human Rights Commission
PO Box 598 Wembley HA9 7XH
Tel: 020 89044222
info@ihrc.org
www.ihrc.org

Islamic Relief Worldwide
Brings relief & development aid to the world's poorest people
19 Rea St South Digbeth Birmingham B5 6LB
Tel: 0121 622 0622
Email via website
www.islamic-relief.com

ISSUE now see Infertility Network UK

ISTD Imperial Society of Teachers of Dancing
Teaching and examining body
22/26 Paul St London EC2A 4QE
Tel: 020 7377 1577
email via website
www.istd.org

Italian Cultural Institute in London
39 Belgrave Sq London SW1X 8NX
Tel: 020 7235 1461
icilondon@esteri.it
www.icilondon.esteri.it/IIC_Londra

ITC see OFCOM

ITDG see Practical Action

ITN Independent Television News
200 Gray's Inn Rd London WC1X 8XZ
Tel: 020 7833 3000
www.itn.co.uk

IUCN
Conservation of Nature and Natural Resources (International Union for)
mail@iucn.org
www.iucn.org

IVS GB International Voluntary Service
Thorn House 5 Rose Street Edinburgh EH2 2PR
Tel: 0131 243 2745
info@ivsgb.org
www.ivsgb.org

IXIA
National organisation for public art development in England
Unit 114 Custard Factory Gibb Street Birmingham B9 4AA
Tel: 0121 753 5301
info@ixia-info.com
www.ixia-info.com

Iyengar Yoga Institute see Yoga (Iyengar Institute)

J

Jane Tomlinson Appeal
Jane Tomlinson undertook feats of sporting endurance to raise money for charity and to show that people with a terminal prognosis can still lead an active and fruitful life
PO BOX 314 Rothwell Leeds LS26 1BY
Tel: 0113 216 2064
info@janetomlinsonappeal.com
www.janetomlinsonappeal.com

JANET The UKs Education and Research Network
A company operating and developing JANET information networks for use in higher education institutions
Lumen House Library Ave Harwell Oxford Didcot Oxon OX11 0SG
Tel: 01235 822 200
Service Desk: 0300 300 2212
service@ja.net
www.ja.net

Japan Foundation, London
A support centre for teachers of Japanese
6th Floor Russell Square House 10-12 Russell Square London WC1B 5EH
Tel: 020 7436 6698
info.language@jpf.org.uk
www.jpf.org.uk

Jeans for Genes
Helps children with genetic disorders
1st Floor Macmillan House Paddington Station London W2 1FT
Freephone: 0800 980 4800
Tel: 020 7199 3300
Email via website
www.jeansforgenes.com

Jewish Israel Appeal (United) see UJIA

Jewish Lads' & Girls' Brigade (JLGB)
Camperdown 3 Beechcroft Rd South Woodford London E18 1LA
Tel: 020 8989 8990
getinvolved@JLGB.org
www3.jlgb.org

Jewish Museum London
Raymond Burton House 129-131 Albert St Camden Town London NW1 7NB
Tel: 020 7284 7384
admin@jewishmuseum.org.uk
www.jewishmuseum.org.uk

Jewish Women (League of)
Volunteers who provide welfare care for all people
6 Bloomsbury Sq London WC1A 2LP
Tel: 020 7242 8300
office@theljw.org
www.theljw.org

Jews (Board of Deputies of British) see British Jews (Board of Deputies of)

Jo's Cervical Cancer Trust
The only UK charity dedicated to women and their families affected by cervical cancer and cervical abnormalities
16 Lincoln's Inn Fields London WC2A 3ED
Helpline: 0808 802 8000
Tel: 020 7936 7498
info@jostrust.org.uk
www.jostrust.org.uk

Jobcentre Plus
Helps people without jobs to find work & employers to fill their vacancies
jobseekers.direct.gov.uk

Jodrell Bank Observatory and Discovery Centre
Astronomical research centre of the University of Manchester, housing the Lovell Telescope
Macclesfield Cheshire SK11 9DL
Tel: 01477 571321
www.jodrellbank.net
www.jb.man.ac.uk

Joint Nature Conservation Committee
Advises Government on UK and international nature conservation.
Monkstone House City Road Peterborough PE1 1JY
Tel: 01733 562626
comment@jncc.gov.uk
www.jncc.gov.uk

Joseph Rowntree Foundation
Researches underlying causes of poverty and supports research into housing, social care & social policy
The Homestead 40 Water End
York YO30 6WP
Tel: 01904 629241
info@jrf.org.uk
www.jrf.org.uk

Journeys Toward recovery from depression
Supporting people to find their route to recovery from depression
120-122 Broadway Roath Cardiff CF24 1NJ
Tel: 029 2069 2891
info@journeysonline.org.uk
www.journeysonline.org.uk/

Journeywoman.com
US site for women travellers
www.journeywoman.com

Ju Jitsu Association GB National Governing Body (British)
5 Avenue Parade Accrington
Lancashire BB5 6PN
Tel: 07850 317553
chairman@bjjagb.com
www.bjjagb.com

Ju-Jitsu see also World Ju-Jitsu Federation (Ireland)

Jubilee Debt Campaign
Aiming to stop poor countries paying money to the rich world and cancellation of unpayable poor country debts
The Grayston Centre 28 Charles Square London N1 6HT
Tel: 020 7324 4722
info@jubileedebtcampaign.org.uk
www.jubileedebtcampaign.org.uk

Jubilee Sailing Trust
Adventure tallship sailing holidays for able bodied & disabled
12 Hazel Road Woolston Southampton SO19 7GA
Tel: 023 8044 9108
info@jst.org.uk
www.jst.org.uk

Judo Association (British)
Suite B, Loughborough Technology Centre
Epinal Way Loughborough LE11 3GE
Tel: 01509 631670
Email Via Website
www.britishjudo.org.uk

Judo Scotland
EICA: Ratho, South Platt Hill Ratho
Newbridge EH28 8AA
Tel: 0131 333 2981
info@judoscotland.com
www.judoscotland.com

Junk Mail see Facsimile Preference Service, Mailing Preference Service

Just for Kids Law JfK Law
Runs a number of programmes aimed at providing support, advocacy and assistance to young people with a variety of needs
402 Harrow Road London W9 2HU
Tel: 020 7266 7159
info@justforkidslaw.org
www.justforkidslaw.org

Justgiving
Fundraising website
First Floor 30 Eastbourne Terrace London W2 6LA
Tel: 0845 078 2063
Email via website
www.justgiving.com

Justice
Encompasses online content from the YJB, Ministry of Justice, Her Majesty's Courts Service, the Prison Service, the Legal Services Commission and many other justice agencies, enabling information on the administration, regulation and scrutiny of justice to be provided by one single site
www.justice.gov.uk

JUSTICE
All-party law reform and human rights charity
59 Carter Lane London EC4V 5AQ
Tel: 020 7329 5100
admin@justice.org.uk
www.justice.org.uk

Justin Campaign
Justin Fashanu was the world's first openly gay professional footballer - he committed suicide in 1998. The Campaign was founded to demonstrate that homophobia still exists in both grassroots and professional football
info@thejustincampaign.com
www.thejustincampaign.com

K

Karate and Kickboxing Association (World)
www.wkaworld.com

Karate and Martial Art Schools (National Association of) now see NAKMAS

Karate Board (N. Ireland)
89 Brooke Drive Belfast BT11 9NJ
Tel: 028 9061 6453 (Chairman/President)
obrunton@aol.com
www.irishkarate.com

Karate England
PO Box 490 Northwich CW9 9AU
Tel: 07931 545924
admin@karateengland.org.uk
www.karateengland.org.uk

Karate Governing Body Ltd (Welsh)
105 Queens Drive Llantwit Fardre
Pontypridd CF38 2NY
Tel: 01443 203733
email via website
www.welshkarate.org.uk

Karma Nirvana
To support victims and survivors of forced marriage and honour based violence. Also seeks to increase the reporting of victims and also survivors many of which are disowned by their families
PO Box 148   Leeds LS13 9DB
Honour Network Helpline: 0800 5999 247
Tel: 0113 218 0114
Email via website
www.karmanirvana.org.uk/honour-network

Keep Britain Tidy
Environmental charity and the anti-litter campaign for England. Also runs programmes such as Eco-Schools, Blue Flag and Quality Coast Awards for beaches, and the Green Flag for parks to demonstrate practical action
Elizabeth House The Pier Wigan WN3 4EX
Tel: 01942 612621
email via website
www.keepbritaintidy.org

Keep Fit Association KFA
1 Grove House Foundry Lane Horsham
West Sussex RH13 5PL
Tel: 01403 266000
office@emdp.org
www.keepfit.org.uk

Kelvingrove Art Gallery and Museum
Argyle Street Glasgow G3 8AG
Tel: 0141 276 9599
Text Phone: 0141 276 9500
museums@glasgowlife.org.uk
www.glasgowlife.org.uk/museums/our-museums/kelvingrove/Pages/home.aspx

Kennel Club
To promote in every way the general improvement of all dogs
1-5 Clarges St Piccadilly London W1J 8AB
Tel: 0844 463 3980
Email via website
www.thekennelclub.org.uk

Kew Gardens see Royal Botanic Gardens, Kew

Kick It Out
Football's anti-racism campaign
4th Floor South 1-5 Clerkenwell Road
London EC1M 5PA
Freephone: 0800 169 9414 (Hotline for reporting discrimination]
Tel: 020 7253 0162
info@kickitout.org
www.kickitout.org

Kid Info
US homework and research site
www.kidinfo.com/school_subjects.html

Kidney Patient Association (British) BKPA
Financial help, advice & literature for kidney patients & their families
3 The Windmills St Mary's Close Turk Street
Alton GU34 1EF
Tel: 01420 541424
info@britishkidney-pa.co.uk
www.britishkidney-pa.co.uk

Kidney Research UK
Nene Hall
Lynch Wood Park Peterborough PE2 6FZ
Tel: 0845 070 7601
enquiries@kidneyresearchuk.org
www.kidneyresearchuk.org

Kids Company
Emotional and practical support directly accessible by children - and not dependent on a carer
1 Kenbury Street London SE5 9BS
Tel: 0845 644 6838
Tel: 0207 274 8378
info@kidsco.org.uk
www.kidsco.org.uk

Kids for Kids
Helps children struggling to survive in remote villages in Darfur, Sudan
PO Box 456 Dorking Surrey RH4 2WS
Tel: 07957 206440
contact@kidsforkids.org.uk
www.kidsforkids.org.uk

Kids in Museums
Guiding museums and galleries across the country to make family visits engaging and enjoyable.
CAN Mezzanine 49-51 East Road
London N1 6AH
Tel: 020 7250 8338
getintouch@kidsinmuseums.org.uk
www.kidsinmuseums.org.uk

Kids' Clubs Network now see 4Children

Kidscape
Offers support and advice to parents of
bullied children. Confidence building
sessions for children who are bullied.
Provides booklets, literature, posters, training
guides and educational videos
2 Grosvenor Gardens London SW1W 0DH
Parents' Anti-Bullying Helpline:
08451 205 204
General Enquiries: 020 7730 3300
email via website
www.kidscape.org.uk

Kilvert (Alice) see Tampon Alert (Alice Kilvert)

King's Fund
An independent charitable foundation
working for better health, especially in
London
11-13 Cavendish Square London W1G 0AN
Tel: 020 7307 2400
enquiry@kingsfund.org.uk
www.kingsfund.org.uk

Kite Society of Great Britain
PO Box 2274 Gt Horkesley
Colchester CO6 4AY
Tel: 01206 271489
info@thekitesociety.org.uk
www.thekitesociety.org.uk

Kiva Loans that change Lives
Helps people out of poverty by direct
lending from individuals to selected
entrepreneurs in the developing world. Once
the money is repaid it can be withdrawn or
lent again
www.kiva.org

Know Cannabis
Website which can help you assess your
cannabis use, its impact on your life and how
to make changes if you want to
www.knowcannabis.org.uk

Kodaly see BKA

Kurdish Human Rights Project
11 Guilford Street London WC1N 1DH
Tel: 020 7405 3835
khrp@khrp.org
www.khrp.org

L

La Leche League GB
Breastfeeding support & information
PO Box 29 West Bridgford
Nottingham NG2 7NP
Helpline: 0845 120 2918
Tel: 0845 456 1855 (General enquiries)
Email Via Website
www.laleche.org.uk

Labour Behind the Label
Campaigns for better conditions for garment
workers around the world and for fair trade
THE CLEAN CLOTHES CAMPAIGN 10-12
Picton Street Bristol BS6 5QA
Tel: 0117 944 1700
Email via website
www.labourbehindthelabel.org

Labour Party
Labour Central Kings Manor Newcastle
Upon Tyne NE1 6PA
Tel: 0845 092 2299
Email via website
www2.labour.org.uk

Labour Research Department
78 Blackfriars Rd London SE1 8HF
Tel: 020 7928 3649
info@lrd.org.uk
www.lrd.org.uk

Labour Women's Network
Dedicated to supporting Labour women to
play a full part in the Party, and to securing
the election of more Labour women to
public office at every level
11 Well House Road LEEDS LS8 4BS
email via website
www.lwn.org.uk

Lacrosse Association (English)
Manchester Velodrome Stuart St M11 4DQ
Tel: 0843 658 5006
info@englishlacrosse.co.uk
www.englishlacrosse.co.uk

Ladies' Golf Union
Governing body of ladies' golf
The Scores St Andrews Fife KY16 9AT
Tel: 01334 475811
Email via website
www.lgu.org

Lady Lever Art Gallery
Housing one of the UK's finest collections of
fine and decorative art
Port Sunlight Village Wirral CH62 5EQ
Tel: 0151 478 4136
email via website
www.liverpoolmuseums.org.uk/ladylever

Lake District (Friends of the)
A regional conservation charity dedicated to the protection and enhancement of the landscape and countryside of Cumbria and the Lake District
Murley Moss Oxenholme Rd Kendal LA9 7SS
Tel: 01539 720788
info@fld.org.uk
www.fld.org.uk

Lake District National Park Authority
Murley Moss Oxenholme Rd Kendal LA9 7RL
Tel: 01539 724555
hq@lakedistrict.gov.uk
www.lakedistrict.gov.uk

Lake District Weather Line
Provides a weather forecast for the day. The next day's forecast is available after 5.15pm
Tel: 0844 846 2444
www.lakedistrictweatherline.co.uk

Land Registry
Register of ownership of land in England and Wales
Tel: 0844 892 1111
Email via website
www.landregistry.gov.uk

Land Yachts see Sand & Land Yacht Clubs (British Federation of)

Landlife
Environmental charity growing and selling wildflower seeds and plants, promoting new wildflower landscapes
National Wildflower Centre Court Hey Park Liverpool L16 3NA
Tel: 0151 737 1819
info@landlife.org.uk
www.landlife.org.uk

Landmark Trust
Charity that restores buildings of historic & architectural importance, then secures their future by letting them for holidays
Shottesbrooke Maidenhead Berks SL6 3SW
Tel: 01628 825920
info@landmarktrust.org.uk
www.landmarktrust.org.uk

Landmine Action Now see Action on Armed Violence

Landmines see also Action on Armed Violence, HALO Trust, Mines Advisory Group

Landmines (International Campaign to Ban)
Key umbrella organisation for anti-landmine groups worldwide
www.icbl.org

Landscape Institute
Professional body in UK for landscape architects and designers, planners and managers
Charles Darwin House 12 Roger Street London WC1N 2JU
Tel: 020 7685 2640
www.landscapeinstitute.org.uk

Language Awareness (Association for)
www.languageawareness.org

Language Learning (Association for)
Association for teachers of modern foreign languages
University of Leicester University Road Leicester LE1 7RH or visit at 106 New Walk Leicester LE1 7EA
Tel: 0116 229 7600
info@all-languages.org.uk
www.all-languages.org.uk

Language Teaching & Research (Centre for Information on) now see CILT

Languages (Scotland's National Centre for) SCILT
LH-232 Lord Hope Building University of Strathclyde 141 St James Road Glasgow, G4 0LT
Tel: 0141 444 8163
scilt@strath.ac.uk
www.strath.ac.uk/scilt

Laogai Research Foundation
Washington DC based organisation exposing human rights abuses in China
www.laogai.org

Lattitude Global Volunteering
International youth development charity offering volunteering and gap year placements for under 25s
42 Queens Road Reading RG1 4BB
Tel: 0118 959 4914
email via website
www.lattitude.org.uk

Lavender Trust at Breast Cancer Care
Raises money specifically to fund Breast Cancer Care's support and information services for younger women
Breast Cancer Care Helpline: 0808 800 6000
www.breastcancercare.org.uk/about-us/lavender-trust

Law Centres Federation
Co-ordinating body for community Law Centres
PO Box 65836 London EC4P 4FX
Tel 020 7842 0720
info@lawcentres.org.uk
www.lawcentres.org.uk

Law Commission
Steel House 11 Tothill Street
London SW1H 9LJ
Tel: 020 3334 0200
email via website
www.lawcom.gov.uk

Law Society of England & Wales
Professional body for solicitors
113 Chancery Lane London WC2A 1PL
Tel: 020 7242 1222
Email via website
www.lawsociety.org.uk

Law Society of Scotland
26 Drumsheugh Gardens
Edinburgh EH3 7YR
Tel: 0131 226 7411
email via website
www.lawscot.org.uk

Lawn Tennis Association
Governing body
National Tennis Centre 100 Priory Lane
Roehampton London SW15 5JQ
Tel: 020 8487 7000
Info@LTA.org.uk
www.lta.org.uk

League Against Cruel Sports see Cruel
Sports Ltd (League Against)

Leap Confronting Conflict
Provides opportunities for young people
and adults to explore creative approaches to
conflicts in their lives
Wells House (Unit 7) 5-7 Wells Terrace
Finsbury Park London N4 3JU
Tel: 020 7561 3700
info@leapcc.org.uk
www.leaplinx.com

learndirect
Provides adults with free advice on learning
and career opportunities
FREEPOST learndirect
Tel: 0800 101 901
www.learndirect.co.uk

Learning (Campaign for)
Charity working to stimulate learning that
will sustain people for life
24 Greencoat Place Westminster London
SW1P 1RD
Tel: 020 7798 6067
info@cflearning.org.uk
www.campaign-for-learning.org.uk/cfl/index.
asp

Learning (Institute for)
Professional body for teachers, trainers,
tutors, student teachers and assessors in the
further education and skills sector
First Floor 49-51 East Road London N1 6AH
Tel: 0844 815 3202
enquiries@ifl.ac.uk
www.ifl.ac.uk

Learning and Skills Council now see Skills
Funding Agency, Young People's Learning
Agency

Learning and Skills Improvement Service
LSIS
Formed from CEL and QIA to develop FE
provision
Friars House Manor House Drive Coventry
West Midlands CV1 2TE
Tel: 024 7662 7900 (Switchboard)
enquiries@lsis.org.uk
www.lsis.org.uk

Learning and Teaching Scotland see
Education Scotland

Learning Disabilities (British Institute of)
Campion House Green St Kidderminster
DY10 1JL
Tel: 01562 723010
enquiries@bild.org.uk
www.bild.org.uk

Learning Disabilities (The Foundation for People with)
Aims to improve the quality of life for people
with learning disabilities. Part of the Mental
Health Foundation
1st Floor Colechurch House 1 London
Bridge Walk London SE1 2SX
Tel: 020 7803 1100
email via website
www.learningdisabilities.org.uk

Learning Outside the Classroom (Council for)
Preston Montford Montford Bridge
Shrewsbury SY4 1HW
Email via website
www.lotc.org.uk

Learning Zone
BBC education website
www.bbc.co.uk/learningzone

Left 'n' Write
Provides information and resources for left
handed people, courses for teachers on
needs of left handed children
5 Charles St Worcester WR1 2AQ
Tel: 01905 25798
info@leftshoponline.co.uk
www.leftshoponline.co.uk

Legal Action Group
Working with lawyers and advisers to
promote equal access to justice through
publications, training and policy work
242 Pentonville Rd London N1 9UN
Tel: 020 7833 2931
lag@lag.org.uk
www.lag.org.uk

Legal Services Commission
Guarantees that people under police investigation or facing criminal charges can get legal advice and representation
Legal Services Commission 102 Petty France London SW1H 9AJ
Helpline (Legal Aid): 0845 345 4345
Tel: 0207 783 7000
Tel: 0800 085 6643 (Customer Service)
www.legalservices.gov.uk/criminal.asp

legislation.gov.uk
Branch of the National Archive which publishes all UK legislation. Provides online access and regulates Crown Copyright
www.legislation.gov.uk

LEPRA Health in action
Medical charity aiming to eradicate leprosy and other diseases of poverty
28 Middleborough Colchester Essex CO1 1TG
Tel: 01206 216700
lepra@leprahealthinaction.org
www.leprahealthinaction.org

Lesbian and Gay Switchboard (London)
Switchboard aims to operate a 24 hour service offering support, information and referrals to callers on any issue relating to lesbian, gay or bisexual life
PO Box 7324 London N1 9QS
Helpline: 0300 330 0630
Tel: 020 7837 6768
Email via website
www.llgs.org.uk

Lesbian Information Service
Archive of this service which ceased in 1998. Research publications concerned with needs of lesbians and gays and can be downloaded from website
www.lesbianinformationservice.org

Lesbians & Gays (Families & Friends of)
FFLAG
A national voluntary organisation for parents of gay sons and lesbian daughters. It provides information and support through confidential helplines, groups and publications
PO Box 495 Little Stoke Bristol BS34 9AP
Helpline: 0845 652 0311
info@fflag.org.uk
www.fflag.org.uk

Let's Face It
For people with facial disfigurement ie cancer, accidents, congenital acne
72 Victoria Ave Westgate-on-Sea Kent CT8 8BH
Tel: 01843 833 724
chrisletsfaceit@aol.com
www.lets face it.org.uk

Letslink UK
Community development - local exchange of goods & services
12 Southcote Rd London N19 5BJ
Tel: 020 7607 7852
admin@letslinkuk.net
www.letslink.org

Leukaemia see also Children with Cancer, CLICSargent

Leukaemia and Lymphoma Research
UK charity solely dedicated to research into blood cancers, including leukaemia, lymphoma and myeloma.
39-40 Eagle Street London WC1R 4TH
Tel: 020 7504 2200
info@beatingbloodcancers.org.uk
www.beatbloodcancers.org

LGA see Local Government Association

Liberal Democrats
8-10 Great George Street London SW1P 3AE
Tel: 020 7222 7999
Email via website
www.libdems.org.uk

Liberty National Council for Civil Liberties
21 Tabard St London SE1 4LA
Advice line: 0845 123 2307
Tel: 020 7403 3888 (Switchboard)
email via website
www.liberty-human-rights.org.uk

Libraries for Life for Londoners
Campaigning for a comprehensive, high quality library service for all Londoners
email via website
www.librarylondon.btck.co.uk

Library Association see CILIP

Library Association (Scottish) see CILIPS

Library Campaign
Supporting friends and users of public libraries
22 Upper Woburn Place London WC1H 0TB
Tel: 0845 450 5946
librarycam@aol.com
www.librarycampaign.com

Library of France (National)
Web page giving information about the National Library of France in French and in English
www.bnf.fr/en/tools/lsp.site_map.html

Life
Supporting vulnerable pregnant mothers and young families
1 Mill Street Leamington Spa Warwickshire CV31 1ES
National Helpline: 0808 802 5433
Tel: 01926 421587
email via website
www.lifecharity.org.uk

Life Science Centre A centre for world-class science
Exhibitions, events, theatre shows and the biggest planetarium in the North
Times Square Newcastle Upon Tyne NE1 4EP
Tel: 0191 243 8210
info@life.org.uk
www.life.org.uk

Lifeguard Skills
Practical tips on water safety
www.lifeguardskills.co.uk

Lifelong Learning
Includes advice about financing study
www.lifelonglearning.co.uk

Lifesavers The Royal Life Saving Society UK
Dedicated to the prevention of unnecessary loss of life, transforming bystanders into lifesavers
River House High Street Broom Alcester Warwickshire B50 4HN
Tel: 01789 773994
email via website
www.lifesavers.org.uk

Liftshare.com Ltd
UK wide & web based car share scheme provider
www.liftshare.com

Light Rail Transit Association
c/o 138 Radnor Avenue Welling DA16 2BY
Tel: 01179 517785
office@lrta.org
www.lrta.org

likeitis.org
Gives young people access to information about all aspects of sex education and teenage life
www.likeitis.org

Lilith Research and Development
Research, campaigning and development project run by Eaves, that works on all issues of violence against women,
Unit 2.03 Canterbury Court 1-3 Brixton Road London SW9 6DE
Tel: 020 7735 2062
post@eavesforwomen.org.uk
www.eavesforwomen.org.uk

Lilleshall see Sports Centre (Lilleshall National)

Limbless Association
Providing information and support to UK amputees and the limb-loss community
Unit 16 Waterhouse Business Centre 2 Cromar Way Chelmsford CM1 2QE
Helpline: 0800 644 0185
Tel: 01245 216670, 01245 216671 or 01245 216672.
enquiries@limbless-association.org
www.limbless-association.org

Linguists (Chartered Institute of)
Professional association and examining board for linguists, interpreters, translators, educationists and other professionals for whom a foreign language is a requirement for their daily jobs
Saxon House 48 Southwark St London SE1 1UN
Tel: 020 7940 3100
info@iol.org.uk
www.iol.org.uk

Linnean Society of London
For the study of natural history
Burlington House Piccadilly London W1J 0BF
Tel: 020 7434 4479
info@linnean.org
www.linnean.org

Listening Books
Audio books postal library service for people who find it difficult or impossible to read due to illness or disability
12 Lant St London SE1 1QH
Tel: 020 7407 9417
info@listening-books.org.uk
www.listening-books.org.uk

Literacy Association (National)
Works with children and young people who are underachieving in literacy
87 Grange Road Ramsgate Kent CT11 9QB
Tel: 01843 239 952
wendy@nla.org.uk
www.nla.org.uk

Literacy Association (UK)
For teachers, advisers and researchers into literacy education
University of Leicester Leicester LE1 7RH
Tel: 0116 223 1664
admin@ukla.org
www.ukla.org

Literacy in Primary Education (Centre for)
CLPE
Webber St London SE1 8QW
Tel: 020 7401 3382/3
Tel: 0207 633 0840
info@clpe.co.uk
www.clpe.co.uk

Literacy Trust (National)
Works in partnership to enhance literacy standards in the UK
68 South Lambeth Road London SW8 1RL
Tel: 020 7587 1842
email via website
www.literacytrust.org.uk

Live Music Now LMN UK
Takes live music to those who don't have easy access & offers performance opportunities to young professional musicians. See website to find out more about LMN in your area
Music Base Kings Place 90 York Way
London N1 9AG
Tel: 01653 668551
email via website
www.livemusicnow.org

Live Theatre
Broad Chare Quayside Newcastle upon Tyne
NE1 3DQ
Box Office: 0191 232 1232
Tel: 0191 261 2694 (Admin)
tickets@live.org.uk
www.live.org.uk

Liver Trust (British) Fighting liver disease
National charity working to reduce the impact of liver disease in the UK through support, information and research
2 Southampton Road Ringwood Hampshire
BH24 1HY
Helpline: 0800 652 7330
Tel: 01425 481 320
info@britishlivertrust.org.uk
www.britishlivertrust.org.uk

Liverpool (Museum of)
Tells the story of Liverpool
Pier Head Liverpool L3 1DG
Tel: 0151 478 4545
email via website
www.liverpoolmuseums.org.uk/mol/

Liverpool (National Museums)
Collections from living bugs to The Beatles, fine art to photography, the Titanic to ancient Egypt - holds over 4 million objects across the collections in all their museums and galleries
Collections Management Divisio
Midland Railway Building 1 Peter Street
Liverpool L1 6BL
Tel: 0151 478 4812
email via website
www.liverpoolmuseums.org.uk/conservation

Living Earth Foundation Ideas into action
Non-membership organisation. International, national and local environmental and community education programmes
5 Great James Steet London WC1N 3DB
Tel: 020 7440 9750
info@livingearth.org.uk
www.livingearth.org.uk

Living Museum of the North see Beamish

Living Streets
National charity that stands up for pedestrians. Campaigns to achieve safe, pleasant, vibrant & healthy streets for all. Organises Walk to School campaign
4th Floor Universal House
88-94 Wentworth Street
London E1 7SA
Tel: 020 7377 4900
info@ livingstreets.org.uk
www.livingstreets.org.uk

Living Wills see Dignity in Dying

Llamau
Helping vulnerable young people realise their potential
23 Cathedral Road Cardiff CF11 9HA
Tel: 029 2023 9585
email via website
www.llamau.org.uk

Local Authorities (Convention of Scottish)
now see COSLA

Local Economic Strategies (Centre for)
now see CLES

Local Economy Policy Unit
Centre for action on local economic development and urban regeneration
London South Bank University 103 Borough Rd London SE1 0AA
Tel: 020 20 7815 7798
localeconomy@lsbu.ac.uk
www.lsbu.ac.uk/lepu

Local Government Association LGA
Lobby and campaign for changes in policy, legislation and funding on behalf of their member councils and the people and communities they serve
Local Government House Smith Square
London SW1P 3HZ
Tel: 020 7664 3000
info@local.gov.uk
www.lga.gov.uk

Local Government Information Unit LGiU
22 Upper Woburn Place London WC1H 0TB
Tel: 020 7554 2800
info@lgiu.org.uk
www.lgiu.org.uk

Local Government Ombudsman (England)
Investigates complaints made about maladministration by local authorities in England
PO Box 4771 Coventry CV4 0EH
Tel: 0300 061 0614
Tel: 0845 602 1983
email via website
www.lgo.org.uk

Local History (British Association for)
BALH
PO Box 6549 Somersal Herbert Ashbourne
DE6 5WH
Tel: 01283 585947
info@balh.co.uk
www.balh.co.uk

**Logistics and Transport in the UK
(Chartered Institute of)**
Logistics & Transport Centre Earlstrees Court
Earlstrees Rd Corby Northants NN17 4AX
Tel: 01536 740104
membership@ciltuk.org.uk
www.ciltuk.org.uk

London (Museum of)
150 London Wall London EC2Y 5HN
Tel: 020 7001 9844
info@museumoflondon.org.uk
www.museumoflondon.org.uk

London Charity Orchestra
Professional musicians, music students and
experienced amateurs who help charitable
causes
info@lco.org.uk
www.londoncharityorchestra.co.uk

London Children's Ballet
73 St Charles Square London W10 6EJ
Tel: 020 8969 1555
info@londonchildrensballet.com
www.londonchildrensballet.com

London Citizens now see Citizens UK

London Drug & Alcohol Network
c/o DrugScope Prince Consort House Suite
204 109/111 Farringdon Road London EC1R
3BW
Tel: 020 7520 7566
info@drugscope.org.uk
www.ldan.org.uk

London Environment Centre now see Green
Mark

London Green Belt Council
Tel: 07794 592 924
info@londongreenbeltcouncil.org.uk
londongreenbeltcouncil.org.uk

London Hazards Centre
Resource centre for Londoners fighting
health & safety hazards in the workplace &
community
Hampstead Town Hall Centre
213 Haverstock Hill London NW3 4QP
Tel: 020 7794 5999
mail@lhc.org.uk
www.lhc.org.uk

London Library
Subscription library
14 St James's Square London SW1Y 4LG
Tel: 020 7930 7705
enquiries@londonlibrary.co.uk
www.londonlibrary.co.uk

London Marathon
Tel: 020 7902 0200
www.virginlondonmarathon.com

London Symphony Orchestra LSO
6th Floor, Barbican Centre Silk Street
London EC2Y 8DS
Box office: 020 7638 8891
Tel: 020 7588 1116
email via website
www.lso.co.uk

London Theatre (Official)
Guide to West End Theatres
www.officiallondontheatre.co.uk/access

London theatres: online
www.officiallondontheatre.co.uk

London Tourist Board see Visit London

London Transport Museum
Covent Garden Piazza London WC2E 7BB
Main switchboard: 020 7379 6344
Tel: 020 7565 7298 (School visits servic
24 hour information: 020 7565 7299
Minicom: 020 7565 7310
Email via website
www.ltmuseum.co.uk

London Travel Information now see
Transport for London

London Youth Federation of London Youth
Clubs
47-49 Pitfield Street London N1 6DA
Tel: 020 7549 8800
hello@londonyouth.org.uk
www.londonyouth.org.uk

Lone Parents see also Families Need Fathers,
Friendship Works, Gingerbread, HELP, One Plus
One

Lone Twin Network
Offers a network of contacts and support to
anyone whose twin has died
54 Ventnor Avenue Hodge Hill Birmingham
B36 8EF
info@lonetwinnetwork.org.uk
www.lonetwinnetwork.org.uk

Long Distance Walkers Association
www.ldwa.org.uk

Lord Dowding Fund
Funds and sponsors non-animal research
Millbank Tower Millbank London SW1P 4QP
Tel: 020 7630 3340
email via website
www.ldf.org.uk

Lord's Day Observance Society now see
Day One Christian Ministries

Lorna Young Foundation
Internationally, the LYF supports smallholder
producers in developing countries to build
their commercial capacity, shorten supply
chains; and create local brands and markets
47 Lea Lane Netherton
Huddersfield HD4 7DP
Tel: 07944 979 721
projectmanager@lyf.org.uk
www.lyf.org.uk

Lottery see Big Lottery Fund

Low Pay Commission
Independent statutory public body advising
the Government on all aspects of the
minimum wage
6th Floor Victoria House Southampton Row
London WC1B 4AD
Tel: 020 7271 0450
lpc@lowpay.gov.uk
www.lowpay.gov.uk

Lowry Theatre and art gallery
Pier 8, Salford Quays Manchester M50 3AZ
Tel: 0843 208 6000
Groups: 0843 208 6003
email via website
www.thelowry.com

LSO see London Symphony Orchestra

Lucy Faithfull Foundation Working to
protect children
Bordesley Hall The Holloway, Alvechurch
Birmingham B48 7QA or Nightingale House
46-48 East Street
Freephone Helpline 0808 1000 900
Tel: 01527 591922
Tel: 01372 847160
email via website
www.lucyfaithfull.org
www.stopitnow.org.uk

Lung Foundation (British)
Funds research into lung diseases, produces
information literature & has support groups
73-75 Goswell Road London EC1V 7ER
Helpline: 03000 030 555
Head office: 020 7688 5555.
Email via website
www.lunguk.org

Lupus UK
St James House Eastern Road Romford
Essex RM1 3NH
Tel: 01708 731251
headoffice@lupusuk.org.uk
www.lupusuk.org.uk

M

Macmillan Cancer Support
Aims to improve the lives of people affected
by cancer. Provides practical, medical and
financial support and pushes for better
cancer care
89 Albert Embankment London SE1 7UQ
Macmillan Support Line: 0808 808 0000
Tel: 020 7840 7840
email via website
www.macmillan.org.uk

Magic Breakfast
Dedicated to ensuring every child starts their
school day with the right breakfast as fuel for
learning
One90 High Holborn London WC1V 0RL
Tel: 020 7836 5434
info@magicbreakfast.com
www.magicbreakfast.com

Magistrates' Association
Membership organisation representing
over 80% of serving volunteer magistrates.
Promotes the sound administration of the
law
28 Fitzroy Square London W1T 6DD
Tel: 020 7387 2353
information@magistrates-association.org.uk
www.magistrates-association.org.uk

Magna: science adventure centre
Sheffield Rd Rotherham S60 1DX
Tel: 01709 720002
www.visitmagna.co.uk

Mailing Preference Service
Allows consumers to remove their names
from mailing lists
DMA House 70 Margaret St
London W1W 8SS
Registration line: 0845 703 4599
Tel: 020 7291 3310
mps@dma.org.uk
www.mpsonline.org.uk

Makaton Charity
Language programme for children and
adults with communication and learning
disabilities
Manor House 46 London Road Blackwater
Camberley Surrey GU17 0AA
Tel: 01276 606760
email via website
www.makaton.org

Make Roads Safe Campaign for Global Road
Safety
Campaigns to stop the daily tragedy of
thousands of preventable deaths and injuries
on the world's roads
www.makeroadssafe.org/Pages/home.aspx

Making Music National Federation of Music Societies
Supports and champions voluntary and amateur music groups and amateur musicians
2-4 Great Eastern Street London EC2A 3NW
Tel: 020 7422 8280
email via website
www.makingmusic.org.uk

Malaria No More UK
Part of a global effort to put an end to the suffering and death caused by malaria
33 Ransomes Dock 35-37 Parkgate Road London SW11 4NP
Tel: 020 7801 3840
info@malarianomore.org.uk
www.malarianomore.org.uk

Management (Institute of) see Chartered Management Institute

Manchester Museum
University of Manchester Oxford Rd Manchester M13 9PL
Tel: 0161 275 2634
museum@manchester.ac.uk
www.museum.manchester.ac.uk

Manic Depression Fellowship see MDF The Bipolar Organisation

ManKind Initiative
Provides help and support for male victims of domestic abuse and domestic violence
Flook House Belvedere Road Taunton Somerset TA1 1BT
Helpline: 01823 334 244
admin@mankind.org.uk
www.mankind.org.uk

Mankind UK
Support and resource service for men who have been sexually abused, sexually assaulted and/or raped.
P.O.Box 124 Newhaven East Sussex BN9 9TQ
Tel: 01273 510447
admin@mankindcounselling.org.uk
www.mankindcounselling.org.uk

Mapping see Ordnance Survey

Marathon (London) see London Marathon

Marfan Association UK
Supports sufferers from disorders of the connective tissue
Rochester House 5 Aldershot Road Fleet Hampshire GU51 3NG
Tel: 01252 810472
contactus@marfan-association.org.uk
www.marfan-association.org.uk

Margaret Pyke Centre
Provides advice and treatment on contraception, family planning, HRT, plus pregnancy testing
73 Charlotte St London W1T 4PL
Tel: 020 33173737 (switchboard)
www.margaretpyke.org

Marie Curie Cancer Care
Free practical nursing care at home and specialist care at 10 centres. Conducts research into the causes and treatment of cancer
89 Albert Embankment London SE1 7TP
Free phone: 0800 716 146
supporter.services@mariecurie.org.uk
www.mariecurie.org.uk

Marie Stopes International
Counselling and help with women's sexual health, termination of pregnancy, contraception, sterilisation, vasectomy
Helpline: 0845 300 8090 (24 hours)
Tel: 020 7636 6200
services@mariestopes.org.uk
www.mariestopes.org.uk

Marine Conservation Society
The UK charity dedicated to the protection of the marine environment and its wildlife
Unit 3, Wolf Business Park Alton Road Ross-on-Wye HR9 5NB
Tel: 01989 566017
email via website
www.mcsuk.org

& Scotland
11A Chester Street Edinburgh EH3 7RF
Tel: 0131 226 6360/2391
www.mcsuk.org/scotland

& Wales
www.mcsuk.org/wales

Marine Leisure Association (MLA)
Trade association for training, charter & holidays
Marine House Thorpe Lea Road Egham Surrey TW20 8BF
Tel: 01784 223640
info@marineleisure.co.uk
www.marineleisure.co.uk

Marine Life Rescue see Divers Marine Life Rescue (British)

Marine Life Study Society (British)
Glaucus House 14 Corbyn Cres Shoreham-by-Sea BN43 6PQ
Tel: 01273 465433
glaucus@hotmail.com
www.glaucus.org.uk

Marine Society and Sea Cadets
202 Lambeth Rd London SE1 7JW
Tel: 020 7654 7000
info@ms-sc.org
www.ms-sc.org

Marine Stewardship Council
Promotes responsible fishing practices
Marine House 1 Snow Hill
London EC1A 2DH
Tel: 020 7246 8900
Email via website
www.msc.org

Maritime & Coastguard Agency
Spring Place 105 Commercial Rd
Southampton SO15 1EG
Tel: 02380 329100
Email via website
www.dft.gov.uk/mca

Maritime Museum (Merseyside)
Uncover objects from the Titanic, find out
about life at sea and learn about the port of
Liverpool
Albert Dock Liverpool L3 4AQ
Tel: 0151 478 4499
email via website
www.liverpoolmuseums.org.uk/maritime

Maritime Museum (National)
Maritime Galleries Park Row Greenwich
London SE10 9NF
Museum switchboard: 020 8858 4422
Recorded information line: 020 8312 6565
Bookings;: 020 8312 6608
bookings@rmg.co.uk
www.rmg.co.uk/national-maritime-museum

Maritime Trust see Cutty Sark Trust

Martial Arts see thematic guide - Sport &
Leisure

Martial Association (Amateur)
National association of martial arts and
kickboxing
169 Cotswold Crescent Walshaw Park Bury
BL8 1QL
Tel: 0161 763 5599
www.amauk.co.uk

Martin Luther King Jr. Center for nonviolent
social change
Set up in 1968 as a memorial to Dr Martin
Luther King Jnr to further his philosophy of
non-violence in human relations
www.thekingcenter.org

Marx Memorial Library
Collection of books about politics,
economics and social sciences with a left-
wing emphasis
37a Clerkenwell Green London EC1R 0DU
Tel: 0207 253 1485
info@marx-memorial-library.org
www.marx-memorial-library.org

Mary's Meals
An international movement to set up school
feeding projects in communities where
poverty and hunger prevent children from
gaining an education.
Craig Lodge Dalmally Argyll PA33 1AR
Tel: 01838 200605
info@marysmeals.org
www.marysmeals.org

Marylebone Cricket Club see MCC

MASTA Medical Advisory Services for Travellers
Abroad
Provider of travel vaccines and travel health
advice to the NHS and many companies and
organisations
Moorfield Rd Yeadon Leeds LS19 7BN
www.masta-travel-health.com

MATCH Mothers Apart from Their Children
For mothers living apart from their children,
and those mothers who have little or no
contact with their children
BM Box No. 6334 London WC1N 3XX
enquries@matchmothers.org
www.matchmothers.org

**Maternal & Childhealth Advocacy
International** MCAI
Charity dedicated to saving the lives of
seriously ill pregnant women, children and
babies in countries where there is extreme
poverty.
83 Derby Road Nottingham NG1 5BB
Tel: 0115 950 6662
office@mcai.org.uk
www.mcai.org.uk

**Maternity Services (Association for
Improvements in the)** see AIMS

Mathematical Association
Long established professional subject
association devoted to the needs of
classroom mathematics teachers & lecturers
259 London Rd Leicester LE2 3BE
Tel: 0116 221 0013
office@m-a.org.uk
www.m-a.org.uk

Mathematics see also Innovation in
Mathematics Teaching (Centre for), Teachers of
Mathematics (Association of)

MCC Marylebone Cricket Club
Guardian of the laws of cricket
Lord's Cricket Ground St John's Wood
London NW8 8QN
Tel: 020 7616 8500
email via web
www.lords.org

MDF The Bipolar Organisation
Provides support for all affected by manic depression
11 Belgrave Road London SW1V 1RB
Tel: 020 7931 6480
email via website
www.bipolaruk.org.uk

ME see also Young People with ME (Association of)

ME (Action for)
Information and campaigning to support people with ME
PO Box 2778 Bristol BS1 9DJ
Tel: 0845 123 2380
Tel: 0117 927 9551
admin@actionforme.org.uk
www.afme.org.uk

ME Association
Funds and supports research and provides information and support, education and training
7 Apollo Office Court Radclive Road
Gawcott Bucks MK18 4DF
Helpline: 0844 576 5326
Tel: 01280 827070
meconnect@meassociation.org.uk
www.meassociation.org.uk

Meat & Livestock Commission now see Agriculture and Horticulture Development Board

Mechanics' Institute
Conference/function centre
The Mechanics Centre 103 Princess St
Manchester M1 6DD
Tel: 0161 236 9336
mailhost@mechanicsinstitue.co.uk

Medau Movement for life
Dance based workout
1 Grove House Foundry Lane Horsham
West Sussex RH13 5PL
Tel: 01403 266000
office@emdp.org
www.medau.org.uk

Médecins Sans Frontières (UK)
International medical aid organisation
67-74 Saffron Hill London EC1N 8QX
Tel: 020 7404 6600
office-ldn@london.msf.org
www.msf.org.uk

Media Center (Independent)
Grassroots, non-corporate coverage of world news
www.indymedia.org

Media for Development
A media consultancy specialising in the design & implementation of public education campaigns in the developing world and the UK
16 Hoxton Square London N1 6NT
Tel: 020 7033 2170
jonathanw@mediafordevelopment.org.uk
www.mediafordevelopment.org.uk

Media Trust
Charity building partnerships between the media & the voluntary sector
4th Floor Block A, Centre House Wood Lane
London W12 7SB
Tel: 020 7871 5600
info@mediatrust.org
www.mediatrust.org

MediaWise Trust
Registered charity providing advice, information and training on media matters
University of the West of Engl Canon Kitson
Oldbury Court Road Bristol BS16 2JP
Tel: 0117 93 99 333
info@mediawise.org.uk
www.mediawise.org.uk

Medical Accidents (Action Against) AvMA
National charity that provides independent advice and support to anyone who has suffered a medical accident
44 High Street Croydon Surrey CR0 1YB
Helpline: 0845 123 2352
www.avma.org.uk

Medical Advisory Service
Various helplines on different medical matters
www.medicaladvisoryservice.org.uk

Medical Advisory Services for Travellers Abroad see MASTA

Medical Aid for Palestinians
33a Islington Park St London N1 1QB
Tel: 020 7226 4114
info@map-uk.org
www.map-uk.org

Medical Conditions at School
Information to help schools and school healthcare professionals support all pupils with medical conditions
c/o Asthma UK Summit House 70 Wilson Street London EC2A 2DB
www.medicalconditionsatschool.org.uk

Medical Emergency Relief International see MERLIN

Medical Foundation for the Care of Victims of Torture Now see Freedom from Torture

Medical Helpline (General)
Covers all general medical queries
Helpline: 020 8994 9874

Medical Herbalists (National Institute of)
Clover House James Court, South Street
Exeter EX1 1EE
Tel: 01392 426022
info@nimh.org.uk
www.nimh.org.uk

Medical Progress (Europeans for) now see
Safer Medicines Campaign

Medical Research Charities (Association of)
Membership organisation that works to
advance medical research in the UK and, in
particular, aims to improve the effectiveness
of the charitable sector in medical research
Charles Darwin House 12 Roger Street
London WC1N 2JU
Tel:020 7685 2620
www.amrc.org.uk

Medical Research Council MRC
14th Floor One Kemble Street London
WC2B 4AN
Tel: 01793 416200
corporate@headoffice.mrc.ac.uk
www.mrc.ac.uk

Medical Trust (Britain-Nepal)
Works on projects within Nepal's own
developing health programme
130 Vale Rd Tonbridge Kent TN9 1SP
Tel: 01732 360 284
info@britainnepalmedicaltrust.org.uk
www.britainnepalmedicaltrust.org.uk

MedicAlert Foundation
Emergency identification system for people
with hidden medical conditions and allergies
MedicAlert House 327-329 Witan Court
Upper 4th Street Milton Keynes MK9 1EH
Tel: 0800 581 420
info@medicalert.org.uk
www.medicalert.org.uk

**Medicines & Healthcare products
Regulatory Agency**
Ensures that all medicines & healthcare
products on the UK market meet appropriate
standards of safety, quality and efficacy
151 Buckingham Palace Road, Victoria
London, SW1W 9SZ
Tel: 020 3080 6000.
info@mhra.gsi.gov.uk
www.mhra.gov.uk

Men's Advice Line
Advice and support for men experiencing
domestic violence by a current or ex-partner.
This includes all men - in heterosexual or
same-sex relationships
Confidential Helpline: 0808 801 0327
info@mensadviceline.org.uk
www.mensadviceline.org.uk

Men's Health Helpline
Helpline: 020 8995 4448

**Men's Morris & Sword Dance Clubs
(National Association of)**
www.themorrisring.org.uk/

Mencap
123 Golden Lane London EC1Y 0RT
Learning Disability Helpline: 0808 808 1111
Tel: 020 7454 0454
Mencap Direct:
0300 333 1111
help@mencap.org.uk
www.mencap.org.uk

Mencap Cymru
31 Lambourne Crescent Cardiff Business
Park Llanishen Cardiff CF14 5GF
Wales Learning Disability Helpline: 0808
Tel: 02920 747588
Mencap Direct:
0300 333 1111
helpline.wales@mencap.org.uk
www.mencap.org.uk/wales

Mencap Northern Ireland
Segal House 4 Annadale Avenue Belfast
BT7 3JH
Learning Disability Helpline:
0808 808 1111
Tel: 02890 691351
Mencap Direct:
0300 333 1111
helpline.ni@mencap.org.uk
www.mencap.org.uk/northern-ireland

Meningitis Research Foundation
England & Wales
Funds scientific research into meningitis &
septicaemia, raises awareness of the diseases
and supports those affected
Midland Way Thornbury Bristol BS35 2BS
Helpline: 080 8800 33 44
Tel: 01454 281 811
info@meningitis.org
www.meningitis.org

& Scotland
28 Alva Street Edinburgh EH2 4PY
Helpline: 080 8800 33 44
Tel: 0131 510 2345
info@scotland-meningitis.org.uk

& Northern Ireland
71 Botanic Avenue Belfast BT7 1JL
Helpline: 080 8800 33 44
Tel: 028 9032 1283
info@meningitis-ni.org

& Republic of Ireland
63 Lower Gardiner Street Dublin 1
Helpline: 080 8800 33 44
Tel: 01 819 6931
info@meningitis-ireland.org

Meningitis Trust
Working towards a world that is free from meningitis where those affected by the disease receive quality care and support
Fern House Bath Rd Stroud GL5 3TJ
UK Freephone: 0808 80 10 388
Children's Helpline (UK only): Freephone
Tel: 01453 768000
info@meningitis-trust.org
www.meningitis-trust.org

Menopause see Daisy Network

Mental Health (Scottish Association for)
SAMH
Brunswick House 51 Wlilson Street Glasgow G1 1UZ
Tel: 0141 530 1000
enquire@samh.org.uk
www.samh.org.uk

Mental Health Act Commission now see
Care Quality Commission

Mental Health Foundation
Covers all aspects of mental illness & learning disabilities
Colechurch House 1 London Bridge Walk
London SE1 2SX
Tel: 020 7803 1100
email via web
www.mentalhealth.org.uk

& Scotland
Merchants House 30 George Square
Glasgow G2 1EG
Tel: 0141 572 0125
Email via website
www.mentalhealth.org.uk

& Scotland
18 Walker Street Edinburgh EH3 7LP
Tel: 0131 243 3800
Email via website
www.mentalhealth.org.uk

& Wales
C/O Hafal   47 Duckpool Road   Newport NP19 8FL
Tel: 01633 264 625
Email via website
www.mentalhealth.org.uk

Mental Welfare Commission for Scotland
Protects the rights and interests of people with a mental illness or learning disability in Scotland
Thistle House 91 Haymarket Terrace
Edinburgh EH12 5HE
Freephone: 0800 389 6809
Tel: 0131 313 8777
Email Via Website
www.mwcscot.org.uk

Mentoring and Befriending Foundation
Provides assistance and support for the development of mentoring
Suite 1, 4th Floor, Building 3 Universal Square Devonshire Street North Manchester M12 6JH
Tel: 03300 882877
info@mandbf.org
www.mandbf.org

Mercy Corps
To alleviate suffering, poverty and oppression by helping people all over the world
40 Sciennes Edinburgh EH9 1NJ
To give: 0800 066 5766
email via website
www.mercycorps.org.uk

MERLIN
Provides emergency healthcare to people affected by wars, epidemics and natural disasters
12th Floor, 207 Old Street London EC1V 9NR
Tel: 020 7014 1600
hq@merlin.org.uk
www.merlin.org.uk

Mermaids
Family and individual support for teenagers and children with gender identity issues
BM Mermaids London WC1N 3XX
Information line: 0208 1234819
email via website
www.mermaidsuk.org.uk

Message Home see also Missing People and Runaway Helpline
Helps missing people who feel unable to make direct contact with the people they have left behind, by forwarding a message on their behalf. They will only pass on the message and will not tell the family any other information
Freefone: 116 000
116000@missingpeople.org.uk
www.missingpeople.org.uk/areyoumissing/message-home/

Met Office
UK's national weather service
FitzRoy Road Exeter Devon EX1 3PB
Tel: 0870 900 0100
Tel: 01392 885680
enquiries@metoffice.gov.uk
education@metoffice.gov.uk
www.metoffice.gov.uk
www.metoffice.gov.uk/education

Metabolic Diseases see Climb

Meteorological Organization (World)
7 bis, avenue de la Paix, Case postale No.
2300, CH 1211 Geneva 2   Switzerland
Tel: 00 41 22 730 8111
Email Via Website
www.wmo.int

Meteorological Society (Royal)
Advancing the understanding of weather
and climate, the science and its applications
for the benefit of all
104 Oxford Rd   Reading RG1 7LL
Tel: 0118 956 8500
chiefexec@rmets.org
www.rmets.org

Meteorology see Met Office

Methodist Association of Youth Clubs see
Methodist Children & Youth

Methodist Children & Youth
Discipleship & Ministries Cluster   The
Connexional Team   Methodist Church House
25 Marylebone Road   London NW1 5JR
Helpdesk: 020 7486 5502
childrenandyouthteam@methodistchurch.
org.uk
www.childrenandyouth.org.uk

Methodist Church
25 Marylebone Road   London NW1 5JR
Tel: 020 7486 5502
helpdesk@methodistchurch.org.uk
www.methodist.org.uk

Metropolitan Police
New Scotland Yard   Broadway   London SW1H
0BG
Anti-Terrorist Hotline: 0800 789 321
Tel: 0300 123 1212
For Victims of Human Trafficking: 0800 7
Email via website
www.met.police.uk

Michael Palin Centre see Stammering
Children (Michael Palin Centre for)

Midi Music Company
Uses arts to bring groups of young
disadvantaged people together. Provides
a range of music and midi technology
activities
77 Watsons St   Deptford   London SE8 4AU
Tel: 020 8694 6093
Email Via Website
www.themidimusiccompany.co.uk

Midwives UK (Independent)
Working outside the NHS to give
individualised care to women
PO Box 539   Abingdon OX14 9DF
Tel: 0845 4600 105
information@independentmidwives.org.uk
www.independentmidwives.org.uk

Migraine Action Association
4th Floor   27 East Street   Leicester LE1 6NB
Tel: 0116 275 8317
Email via website
www.migraine.org.uk
www.migraineadventure.org.uk

Migraine Trust
Patient support and medical research charity
providing information and support
52-53 Russell Square   London WC1B 4HP
Tel: 020 7631 6970
info@migrainetrust.org
www.migrainetrust.org

Migration Policy Group
Independent organisation committed to
policy development on mobility, migration,
diversity, equality and anti-discrimination
205 Rue Belliard, Box 1   1040 Brussels
Belgium
Tel: 32 2 230 59 30
info@migpolgroup.com
www.migpolgroup.com

Millennium Seed Bank
Aims to safeguard over 24,000 plant species
worldwide & to secure the future of UK
native flowering plants
Wakehurst Place   Ardingly   Haywards Heath
W. Sussex RH17 6TN
Tel: 01444 894066
wakehurst@kew.org
www.kew.org/science-conservation/save-
seed-prosper/millennium-seed-bank/

MIND National Association for Mental Health
Leading mental health charity in England
and Wales
15-19 Broadway   Stratford   London E15 4BQ
Infoline: 0300 123 3393
Tel: 020 8519 2122
contact@mind.org.uk
www.mind.org.uk

Mine Action Service (UN) now see E-MINE

Mine Information Network (Electronic) see
E-MINE

Mines see also Action on Armed Violence,
HALO Trust, Landmines (International
Campaign to Ban)

Mines Advisory Group MAG
Mine clearance & awareness programmes
68 Sackville Street   Manchester M1 3NJ
Tel: 0161 236 4311
info@maginternational.org
www.maginternational.org

Mining Museum (National) Scotland
Lady Victoria Colliery   Newtongrange
Midlothian EH22 4QN
Tel: 0131 663 7519
enquiries@scottishminingmuseum.com
www.scottishminingmuseum.com

Ministry of Defence see Defence (Ministry of)

Minority Rights Group International
Working to secure the rights of ethnic, linguistic and religious minorities and indigenous peoples worldwide
54 Commercial Street London E1 6LT
Tel: 020 7422 4200
minority.rights@mrgmail.org
www.minorityrights.org

Miracles
Crisis funding to alleviate situations of dire and multiple distress; positive thinking; a listening ear, and practical support for those with nowhere else to turn.
PO Box 3003 Littlehampton West Sussex BN16 1SY
Tel: 01903 775673
miracles@fastnet.co.uk
www.miraclesthecharity.org

Miscarriage Association
Provides support and information on pregnancy loss
17 Wentworth Terrace Wakefield WF1 3QW
Tel: 01924 200 799
Tel: 01924 200795 (admin)
email via website
www.miscarriageassociation.org.uk

Missing Children website
www.missingkids.co.uk

Missing People see also Runaway Helpline and Message Home
Search on behalf of those left behind and provide specialised support
284 Upper Richmond Road West London SW14 7JE
Freefone: 116 000
Tel: 020 8392 4590
info@missingpeople.org.uk
www.missingpeople.org.uk/

Mobilise now see Disabled Motoring UK

MoD see Defence (Ministry of)

Monetary Justice (Christian Council for)
Campaigning for democratic control of the monetary system
Tel: 020 7207 0509
info@ccmj.org
www.ccmj.org

Money Advice Service
Work with partners from a wide range of industries, government and other sectors to find new ways of making money matters and financial choices clearer for everyone
Holborn Centre, 120 Holborn, London, EC1N 2TD
Money Advice Line: 0300 500 5000
Tel: 020 7943 0593
enquiries@moneyadviceservice.org.uk
www.moneyadviceservice.org.uk

Money Claim Online
Electronic service can be used by individuals, solicitors, businesses and government departments to sue for money owing, subject to conditions
Online helpdesk: 0845 601 5935
  or 01604 619 402
www.direct.gov.uk/en/
MoneyTaxAndBenefits/ManagingDebt/
Makingacourtclaimformoney/DG_195688

Moneysavingexpert.com
Tips on how to save money and get the best deals
www.moneysavingexpert.com

Mongabay.com
Environmental science and conservation news sites
www.mongabay.com

Monopolies and Mergers Commission now see Competition Commission

Montessori Centre
Training college for those wishing to train in the Montessori method of teaching young children
18 Balderton St London W1K 6TG
Tel: 020 7493 8300
centre@montessori.org.uk
www.montessori.org.uk

Monuments see Public Monuments & Sculpture Association

Morris Federation
Association of self-governing Morris clubs
www.morrisfed.org

Mosac
Supports all non-abusing parents and carers whose children have been sexually abused, providing advocacy, information and advice, befriending, counselling, play therapy and support groups following alleged child sexual abuse
141 Greenwich High Road London SE10 8JA
Helpline: 0800 980 1958
Tel: 020 8293 9990
enquiries@mosac.org.uk
www.mosac.org.uk

MOSI Museum of Science & Industry
Liverpool Road Castlefield Manchester M3 4FP
Tel: 0161 832 2244
email via website
www.mosi.org.uk

Most Wanted (UK)
Website aimed at tracking Britain's most wanted crime suspects
Crimestoppers: 0800 555 111
email via website
wanted.crimestoppers-uk.org

Mothers see also MATCH

Mothers at home Matter formerly Full Time Mothers
Supports full time mothers and campaigns for policy changes
PO Box 43690 London SE22 9WN
info@mothersathomematter.co.uk
www.mothersathomematter.co.uk

Mothers' Union Christian care for families
Mary Sumner House 24 Tufton St London SW1P 3RB
Tel: 020 7222 5533
email via website
www.themothersunion.org

Motor Manufacturers and Traders Ltd. (Society of)
Encouraging and promoting in the UK and abroad, the interests of the motor industry
71 Great Peter Street London SW1P 2BN
advice line 0800 692 0825
Tel: 020 7235 7000
Email via website
www.smmt.co.uk

Motor Neurone Disease Association
Provides support and advice to people affected by Motor Neurone Disease and funds research
PO Box 246 Northampton NN1 2PR
Helpline: 08457 626262
Tel: 01604 250505
enquiries@mndassociation.org
www.mndassociation.org

Mountain Leader Training England
Administers the training programme and qualifications for leaders of groups hill walking and rock climbing in mountainous country
Siabod Cottage Capel Curig Conwy LL24 0ES
Tel: 01690 720314
info@mlte.org
www.mlte.org

Mountaineering Council (British)
Governing body for sport of mountaineering in Britain
The Old Church 177-179 Burton Rd Manchester M20 2BB
Tel: 0161 445 6111
office@thebmc.co.uk
www.thebmc.co.uk

Mountaineering Council of Scotland
Representative body for mountaineers and walkers
The Old Granary West Mill Street Perth PH1 5QP
Tel: 01738 493942
email via website
www.mcofs.org.uk

Mousetrap Theatre Projects ...inspiring young people
Charity dedicated to creating theatre access and education programme for young people with limited resources or support
23-24 Henrietta Street Covent Garden London WC2E 8ND
Tel: 020 7836 4388
info@mousetrap.org.uk
www.mousetrap.org.uk

Mouth Cancer Foundation
Supporting people with mouth, throat and other head & neck cancer
C/O Media Ambitions (Enterprises) Limited Top Floor,1 Victoria Parade Sandycombe Road Kew, Richmond, Surrey TW9 3NB
Helpline: 01924 950 950
email via website
www.mouthcancerfoundation.org

Movie Review Query Engine
Allows access to reviews of over 30,000 film titles
www.mrqe.com

MRC see Medical Research Council

MS see Multiple Sclerosis

Multiple Births see also Twins & Multiple Births Association

Multiple Births Foundation
Hammersmith House Level 4 Queen Charlotte's and Chelsea Hospital Du Cane Rd London W12 0HS
Tel: 020 3313 3519
mbf@imperial.nhs.uk
www.multiplebirths.org.uk

Multiple Sclerosis Society
MS National Centre 372 Edgware Rd London NW2 6ND
Helpline: 0808 800 8000
Tel: 020 8438 0700
helpline@mssociety.org.uk
www.mssociety.org.uk

& Scotland
Ratho Park 88 Glasgow Road Ratho Station Newbridge EH28 8PP
Tel: 0131 335 4050

& Wales/Cymru
Temple Court Cathedral Road Cardiff CF11 9HA
Tel: 029 2078 6676

& Northern Ireland
The Resource Centre 34 Annadale Avenue Belfast BT7 3JJ
Tel: 02890 802 802

Multiple Sclerosis Therapy Centres (National)
PO Box 126 Whitchurch SY14 7WL
Tel: 0845 3670977
info@msntc.org.uk
www.msntc.org.uk

Multiple Sclerosis Trust
Spirella Building Bridge Road Letchworth
Garden City Herts SG6 4ET
Free Phone Information Service: 0800 032 3839
Tel: 01462 476700
info@mstrust.org.uk
www.mstrust.org.uk

Mumsnet
Product reviews and parenting advice given by parents
www.mumsnet.com

Murder see SAMM

Muscular Dystrophy Campaign
Provides support and information
61 Southwark Street London SE1 0HL
Tel: 0800 652 6352 (freephone)
Tel: 020 7803 4800
info@muscular-dystrophy.org
www.muscular-dystrophy.org

Musculoskeletal Medicine (British Institute of)
PO Box 1116 Bushey Herts WD23 9BY
Tel: 020 8421 9910
deena@bimm.org.uk
www.bimm.org.uk

Museum Net
Search for museums throughout the UK by keyword or name
www.museums.co.uk

Museum of London Docklands
No 1 Warehouse London E14 4AL
Tel: 020 7001 9844
info.docklands@museumoflondon.org.uk
www.museumoflondon.org.uk/docklands

Museum of London Archaeology and Archaeological Archive
Mortimer Wheeler House 46 Eagle Wharf Road London N1 7ED
Tel: 020 7410 2200 (archaeology)
Tel: 020 7490 8447/020 7566 9317 (archive)
email via website
www.museumoflondon.org.uk/archaeology

Museum of Science & Industry see MOSI

Museum of Scotland (National)
Chambers St Edinburgh EH1 1JF
Tel: 0300 123 6789
www.nms.ac.uk

Museums (International Council of) ICOM
Secretariat
Maison de l'UNESCO 1 rue Miollis 75732 Paris Cedex 15 France
Tel: 00 33 1 47 34 05 00
email via website
icom.museum

Museums, Libraries & Archives Council
now see Arts Council England

Music (Royal Academy of) see Royal Academy of Music

Music and the Deaf
Helping deaf people access music and the performing arts through workshops, schools projects & signed theatre performances
7 Northumberland St Huddersfield HD1 1RL
Tel: 01484 483115
Textphone: 01484 483117
email via website
www.matd.org.uk

Music Council (National)
c/o BASCA British Music House 26 Berners Street London W1T 3LR
info@nationalmusiccouncil.org.uk
www.nationalmusiccouncil.org.uk

Music Educators (National Association of) NAME
Supports its members in development of highest quality music education accessible to all
Gordon Lodge Snitterton Road Matlock Derbyshire DE4 2JG
tel. 01629 760791
admin@name.org.uk
www.name.org.uk

Music for Youth MFY
Organises the National Festival of Music for Youth, Regional Festivals and the Schools Proms and promotes performance opportunities for young people.
3rd Floor, South Wing Somerset House Strand London WC2R 1LA
Tel: 020 7759 1830
mfy@mfy.org.uk
www.mfy.org.uk

Music Freedom Day
3rd March annually - marked with events, seminars, exhibitions, radio programmes and newspaper articles on the subject of freedom of expression for musicians all over the world
www.musicfreedomday.org

Music Publishers Association
Trade Association supporting UK based music publishers
6th Floor British Music House 26 Berners Street London W1T 3LR
Tel: 020 7580 0126
email via website
www.mpaonline.org.uk

Music Societies (National Federation Of)
see Making Music

Music Therapy (British Association for)
BAMT
Professional body for music therapists. Music therapy is an established clinical discipline which is widely used to help people whose lives have been affected by injury, illness or disability
24-27 White Lion Street London N1 9PD
Tel: 020 7837 6100
info@bamt.org
www.bamt.org

Musicians (Incorporated Society of)
Professional body for musicians
10 Stratford Place London W1C 1AA
Tel: 020 7629 4413
membership@ism.org
www.ism.org

Musicians Union
Trade Union for professional musicians
60-62 Clapham Road London SW9 0JJ
Tel: 020 7582 5566
info@theMU.org
www.musiciansunion.org.uk

Muslim Schools UK (Association of)
Supports & develops excellence in full-time Muslim schools & acts as a voice for Islamic education with government bodies & the media. Gives advice to new Muslim schools
PO Box 14109 Birmingham B6 9BN
Tel: 0844 482 0407
email via website
www.ams-uk.org

Muslim Welfare House
Provides marriage counselling, courses in English for Speakers of Other Languages, IT, crafts, careers, business advice, out of school care for children for whole community
233 Seven Sisters Rd Finsbury Park London N4 2DA
Tel: 020 7263 3071
email via website
www.mwht.org.uk

My Supermarket
Supermarket price comparison website
www.mysupermarket.co.uk

My World of Work formerly learndirect Scotland
Helpline: 0808 100 1050
myworldofwork@sds.co.uk
www.myworldofwork.co.uk

Myalgic Encephalomyelitis see also ME
(Action for), ME Association, Young People with ME (Association of)

MyBnk My money, our future
Provides young people with the skills to manage their money effectively.
MyBnk @ Unit 4 Huguenot Place, Heneage Street London E1 5LN
Tel: 020 7377 8770
info@mybnk.org
www.mybnk.org

Mycological Society (British)
Promotes study of fungi in all its aspects
City View House 5 Union Street Ardwick Manchester M12 4JD
Tel: 0161 277 7638 / 7639
email via website
www.britmycolsoc.org.uk

Mydaughter.co.uk
Providing information, expert opinion and useful advice on all aspects of raising and educating happy, fulfilled girls
Girls' Schools Association 130 Regent Road Leicester LE1 7PG
Tel: 0116 254 1619
email via website
www.mydaughter.co.uk

N

NAACE National Association of Advisers for Computers in Education
Advancing education through ICT
PO Box 6511 Nottingham NG11 8TN
Tel: 0115 945 7235
office@naace.co.uk
www.naace.co.uk

NABSS National Association of Black Supplementary Schools
Central resource for parents, helpers and members of the Afrikan/Caribbean community to find help with their children's education in their locality
43 Cherwell House Church Street Estate Penfold Street London NW8 8PT
Tel: 07958 348 558
info@nabss.org.uk
www.nabss.org.uk

Nacro The Crime Reduction Charity
Runs crime reduction projects including housing, training, prison projects and youth work
Park Place 10-12 Lawn Lane London SW8 1UD
Tel: 020 7840 7200
Email via website
www.nacro.org.uk/

NAKMAS National Association of Karate and Martial Art Schools
National Governing Body for Traditional and Modern Martial Arts
PO Box 262 Herne Bay Kent CT6 9AW
Tel: 01227 370055
email via website
www.nakmas.org.uk

NAME see Music Educators (National Association of)

NAN (National Advocacy Network) see Advocacy Resource Exchange

NAPE National Association for Primary Education
Independent voice to represent and raise the profile of the primary phase of education
Moulton College Management Centre
Moulton Northampton NN3 7RR
Tel 01604 647646
nationaloffice@nape.co.uk
www.nape.org.uk

NAPS see Premenstrual Syndrome (National Association for)

Narcolepsy UK
Narcolepsy causes excessive daytime sleepiness and attacks of paralysis
PO Box 13842 Penicuik EH26 8WX
Tel: 0845 4500 394
info@narcolepsy.org.uk
www.narcolepsy.org.uk

Narcotics Anonymous UK
A fellowship of recovering addicts who meet regularly to help each other stay clean
Helpline: 0300 999 1212
email via website
www.ukna.org

NATE see Teaching of English (National Association for the)

National Advocacy Network see Advocacy Resource Exchange

National Archives
UK national archives with records from 11th century to today. Includes link to the UK Government Web Archive
Kew Richmond TW9 4DU
Tel: 020 8876 3444
Textphone: 020 8392 9198
email via website
www.nationalarchives.gov.uk

National Archives of Scotland (NAS)
From 1 April 2011, the General Register Office for Scotland merged with the National Archives of Scotland to become the National Records of Scotland (NRS). This website will remain active until it is replaced in due course by a new website for NRS
HM General Register House 2 Princes St Edinburgh EH1 3YY
Tel: 0131 535 1314
enquiries@nas.gov.uk
www.nas.gov.uk

National Childbirth Trust NCT
Information & support for all pregnant women & parents of young children
Alexandra House Oldham Terrace London W3 6NH
Tel: 0300 330 0700
Tel: 0844 243 6000
email via website
www.nct.org.uk

National Churches Trust
31 Newbury Street London EC1A 7HU
Tel: 0207 600 6090
email via website
www.nationalchurchestrust.org

National Debtline
National telephone helpline for people with debt problems in England, Wales & Scotland. Free, confidential, independent
Tricorn House 51-53 Hagley Road Edgbaston Birmingham B16 8TP
Helpline: 0808 808 4000
Email via website
www.nationaldebtline.co.uk

National Drama
Professional association for drama educators
asknd@nationaldrama.org.uk
www.nationaldrama.co.uk

National Energy Action
Develops and promotes energy efficiency to
tackle the heating and insulation problems
of low income households
West 1 Forth Banks
Newcastle-upon-Tyne NE1 3PA
Tel: 0191 261 5677
www.nea.org.uk

National Extension College
Specialises in distance learning courses,
training materials, open learning packs, open
and distance learning consultancy services
Michael Young Centre Purbeck Rd
Cambridge CB2 8HN
Tel: 0800 389 2839
Tel: 01223 400 200
info@nec.ac.uk
www.nec.ac.uk

National Forest Company
A project, blending new and maturing
woodland, transforming 200 square miles of
central England
Enterprise Glade Bath Yard Moira
Swadlincote Derbyshire DE12 6BA
Tel: 01283 55121
enquiries@nationalforest.org
www.nationalforest.org

National Foundation for Educational
Research see NFER

National Gallery
Trafalgar Square London WC2N 5DN
Tel: 020 7747 2885
Education: 020 7747 2424
information@ng-london.org.uk
www.nationalgallery.org.uk

National Gallery (Scottish)
The Mound Edinburgh EH2 2EL
Tel: 0131 624 6200
nginfo@nationalgalleries.org
www.nationalgalleries.org/visit/introduction
www.nationalgalleries.org

National Gallery of Modern Art (Scottish)
75 Belford Road Edinburgh EH4 3DR
Tel: 0131 624 6200
gmainfo@nationalgalleries.org
www.nationalgalleries.org

National Institute for Health and Clinical
Excellence NICE
MidCity Place 71 High Holborn
London WC1V 6NA
Tel: 0845 003 7780
nice@nice.org.uk
www.nice.org.uk

National Libraries (Friends of the)
Gives grants to libraries, record offices etc
for rare books and manuscripts and archival
acquisitions
c/o Dept of Manuscripts The British Library
96 Euston Rd London NW1 2DB
Tel: 020 7412 7559
email via website
www.friendsofnationallibraries.org.uk

National Library of Scotland
George IV Bridge Edinburgh EH1 1EW
Tel: 0131 623 3700
enquiries@nls.uk
www.nls.uk

National Library of Wales
Aberystwyth Ceredigion SY23 3BU
Tel: 01970 632 800
Email via website
www.llgc.org.uk

National Media Museum
Bradford West Yorkshire BD1 1NQ
Tel: 0844 856 3797(General & Box Office)
Groups & schools: 0844 856 3799
talk@nationalmediamuseum.org.uk
www.nationalmediamuseum.org.uk

National Museum Cardiff
Cathays Park Cardiff CF10 3NP
Tel: 029 2039 7951
Email via website
www.museumwales.ac.uk

National Museum of Labour History see
People's History Museum

National Opera Studio
The Clore Building 2 Chapel Yard
Wandsworth High Street London SW18 4HZ
Tel: 020 8874 8811
info@nationaloperastudio.org.uk
www.nationaloperastudio.org.uk

National Parks (Campaign for)
Campaigning environmental charity
6-7 Barnard Mews London SW11 1QU
Tel: 020 7924 4077
info@cnp.org.uk
www.cnp.org.uk

National Portrait Gallery
St Martin's Place London WC2H 0HE
Tel: 020 7306 0055
www.npg.org.uk

National Portrait Gallery (Scottish)
1 Queen Street Edinburgh EH2 1JD
Tel: 0131 624 6200
enquiries@nationalgalleries.org
www.nationalgalleries.org

National Records of Scotland (NRS)

formerly Register Office for Scotland (General)
Responsible for registration of births,
marriages, deaths, divorces & adoptions,
censuses of population
New Register House 3 West Register Street
Edinburgh EH1 3YT
Tel: 0131 334 0380
Email via website
www.gro-scotland.gov.uk

National Society for the Prevention of Cruelty to Children see NSPCC

National Theatre

South Bank London SE1 9PX
Tel: 020 7452 3000 (Box Office)
Tel: 020 7452 3400 (Info Desk)
info@nationaltheatre.org.uk
www.nationaltheatre.org.uk

National Tidal and Sea Level Facility

Tidal predictions for selected UK and Irish
ports
Proudman Oceanographic Laboratory
Joseph Proudman Building 6 Brownlow
Street Liverpool L3 5DA
Tel: 0151 795 4800
Email via website
www.pol.ac.uk/ntslf/

National Trust

The National Trust,
PO Box 574, Manvers,
Rotherham, S63 3FH
Tel: 0844 800 1895
enquiries@nationaltrust.org.uk
www.nationaltrust.org.uk

National Trust for Ireland see An Taisce

National Trust for Scotland

Conservation charity that protects and
promotes Scotland's natural and cultural
heritage
Hermiston Quay 5 Cultins Road Edinburgh
EH11 4DF
Tel: 0844 493 2100
information@nts.org.uk
www.nts.org.uk

National Trust Holiday Cottages

PO Box 536 Melksham Wiltshire SN12 8SX
Tel: 0844 8002070 (Booking Line)
cottages@nationaltrust.org.uk
www.nationaltrustcottages.co.uk

National Trust Volunteering

Heelis Kemble Drive Swindon SN2 2NA
Tel: 0844 800 1895
enquiries@nationaltrust.org.uk
www.nationaltrust.org.uk/main/w-trust/w-
volunteering.htm

National Trust Working Holidays

Working holidays in beautiful locations
undertaking countryside conservation (min.
age 18)
www.nationaltrust.org.uk/workingholidays

National Union of Students see NUS

National Youth Ballet of Great Britain

An amateur ballet company for young
people of 8-18 years
The Old Dairy Wintersell Farm Dwelly Lane
Edenbridge TN8 6QD
Tel: 01732 864 781
info@nyb.org.uk
www.nyb.org.uk

Natural Death Centre

Info on green, inexpensive, DIY & woodland
funerals and living wills
In The Hill House Watley Lane Twyford
Winchester SO21 1QX
Tel: 01962 712 690
email via website
www.naturaldeath.org.uk

Natural England

Working for people, places and nature now
and in the future
Foundry House 3 Millsands Riverside
Exchange Sheffield S3 8NH
Tel: 0845 600 3078 (enquiries)
enquiries@naturalengland.org.uk
www.naturalengland.gov.uk

Natural Environment Research Council

Polaris House North Star Ave Swindon SN2
1EU
Tel: 01793 411500
email via website
www.nerc.ac.uk

Natural Heritage (Scottish)

Concerned with all environmental issues in
Scotland
Great Glen House Leachkin Road Inverness
IV3 8NW
Tel: 01463 725000
email via website
www.snh.gov.uk

Natural History Museum

Cromwell Road London SW7 5BD
Tel: 020 7942 5000
Tel: 020 7942 5011 (Main info desk)
Tel: 020 7942 5511 (Customer services)
email via website
www.nhm.ac.uk

Natural Voice Practitioners' Network

Umbrella organisation for local singing
groups that aim to recreate the sense that
singing is natural and open to all
Tel: 0114 230 9439
admin@naturalvoice.net
www.naturalvoice.net

Naturewatch Campaigning Against Animal Cruelty
Campaigns for vital changes in the law to help stop animal abuse
14 Hewlett Road Cheltenham GL52 6AA
Tel: 01242 252871
email via website
www.naturewatch.org

Navigation (Royal Institute of)
To unite in one body those interested in the science and art of navigation
1 Kensington Gore London SW7 2AT
Tel: 020 7591 3130
admin@rin.org.uk
www.rin.org.uk

Navy (US)
Official information site
www.navy.mil

NAWE see Writers in Education (National Association of)

NBCS National Blind Children's Society
Bradbury House Market Street Highbridge Somerset TA9 3BW
Freephone: 0800 781 1444 (Family Support
Tel: 01278 764764
enquiries@nbcs.org.uk
www.nbcs.org.uk

NCB National Children's Bureau
Promotes interests and wellbeing of all children and young people
8 Wakley St London EC1V 7QE
Tel: 020 7843 6000
enquiries@ncb.org.uk
www.ncb.org.uk

NCDL see Dogs Trust

NCDT see Drama Training (National Council for)

NCF see Sports Coach UK

NCH (National Children's Homes) now see Action for Children

NCT see National Childbirth Trust

Neonatal Death see SANDS

NESTA see Science, Technology & the Arts (National Endowment for)

Netdoctor
Online health advice
www.netdoctor.co.uk

Nethouseprices
Access to the latest house prices for England, Scotland and Wales
www.nethouseprices.com

Netmums
Online parenting organisation offering information, advice, chat and support
www.netmums.com

Network 81
For parents of children with special educational needs
10 Boleyn Way West Clacton Essex CO15 2NJ
Tel: 0845 077 4055
Mobile: 0777 956 3849
www.network81.org
www.sen-training.co.uk

Neuro Foundation UK
Provides help, support and advice to those affected by Neurofibromatosis, their families and the professionals working with them
Quayside House 38 High Street Kingston on Thames Surrey KT1 1HL
Tel: 020 8439 1234
info@nfauk.org
www.nfauk.org

New Bridge Foundation
Befriending service for prisoners (prison visiting and writing) & resettlement service
27a Medway Street London SW1P 2BD
Tel: 020 7976 0779
info@newbridgefoundation.org.uk
www.newbridgefoundation.org.uk

New Economics Foundation
Works to put people and the environment at the centre of economic thinking
3 Jonathan St London SE11 5NH
Tel: 0207 820 6300
info@neweconomics.org
www.neweconomics.org

New Internationalist
New Internationalist Publications is a communications co-operative. It exists to report on issues of world poverty and inequality. Publishes New Internationalist magazine, films, books and other materials
www.newint.org

New Opportunities Fund now see Big Lottery Fund

Newlife Foundation for Disabled Children
Action to help disabled and terminally ill children in the UK
Newlife Centre Hemlock Way Cannock Staffordshire, WS11 7GF
Tel: 01543 462 777
email via website
www.newlifecharity.co.uk

Newspaper Library (British Library)
UK National Newspaper Archive. Only available to over 18 years with proof of I.D.
newspapers.bl.uk/blcs/

NFER National Foundation for Educational Research
Independent educational research body
The Mere Upton Park Slough SL1 2DQ
Tel: 01753 574123
enquiries@nfer.ac.uk
www.nfer.ac.uk

NHS Blood and Transplant
Information and statistics on blood and how to register as a blood or bone marrow donor
Customer Services Collindale Avenue Collindale London NW9 5BG
Tel: 0300 123 2323
Minicom: 0845 730 0106
Email via website
www.blood.co.uk

NHS Careers
Tel: 0345 60 60 655
Email via website
www.nhscareers.nhs.uk

NHS Confederation
Dedicated to improving health policy and practice
29 Bressenden Place London SW1E 5DD
Tel: 020 7074 3200
enquiries@nhsconfed.org
www.nhsconfed.org

NHS Confederation (Welsh)
Unit 3 Waterton Park Bridgend CF31 1PH
Tel: 0845 33 00 499
tegan.williams@welshconfed.org
www.nhsconfed.org

NHS Direct
Helpline provides direct contact with a trained nurse
Helpline: 0845 4647
www.nhsdirect.nhs.uk

NHS Health Scotland
Woodburn House Canaan Lane Edinburgh EH10 4SG
Tel: 0131 536 5500
Textphone: 0131 536 5503
nhs.healthscotland-generalenquiries@nhs.net
www.healthscotland.com

NHS Support Federation
A campaign by NHS staff and the public to ensure the survival of a comprehensive and adequately funded NHS
www.nhscampaign.org

NIACE National Institute of Adult Continuing Education
Promoting adult learning
Chetwynd House, 21 De Montfort Street Leicester, LE1 7GE,
Tel: 0116 204 4200/1
enquiries@niace.org.uk
www.niace.org.uk

Nicaragua Solidarity Campaign
86 Durham Road London N7 7DT
Tel: 020 7561 4836
email via website
www.nicaraguasc.org.uk

NICON - Northern Ireland Confederation
Dedicated to improving health policy and practice
The Beeches 12 Hampton Manor Drive Belfast BT7 3EN
Tel: 028 90 644811
info@niconfdhss.org
www.nhsconfed.org

Nil by Mouth
Campaign against sectarianism in Scotland
c/o SCVO 3rd Floor Brunswick House 51 Wilson Street Glasgow G1 1UZ
Tel: 0141 559 5008
mail@nilbymouth.org
www.nilbymouth.org

NIPPA now see Early Years

No candidate deserves my vote
Political party whose presence on a ballot paper allows voters to abstain positively
8 Belmont Court Belmont Hill St Albans AL1 1RB
Tel: 01727 847370
admin@nocandidate.org.uk
www.nocandidate.org.uk

No Panic
Help on panic attacks, phobias & obsessive/compulsive disorders
Unit 3 Prospect House Halesfield 22 Telford - Shropshire TF7 4QX
helpline 0800 138 8889
Tel: 01952 680460
ceo@nopanic.org.uk
www.nopanic.org.uk

No Sweat
Campaigning against sweatshop bosses, in solidarity with workers, worldwide
5 Caledonian Road London N1 9DX
Tel: 07904 431959
admin@nosweat.org.uk
www.nosweat.org.uk

NOAH National Organization for Albinism and Hypopigmentation
Volunteer self-help organisation for research and education. It does not diagnose, treat or provide genetic counselling
www.albinism.org

Nobel Prize Internet Archive
List of prizewinners
www.almaz.com/nobel/peace/

NODA National Operatic & Dramatic Association
15 The Metro Centre Woodston Peterborough PE2 7UH
Tel: 01733 374 790
info@noda.org.uk
www.noda.org.uk

Noise Abatement Society

Raises awareness of noise pollution and helps to relieve the physical and mental distress and ill health which noise and related pollutants cause
The Courtyard Shoreham Road Upper Beeding,Steyning West Sussex BN44 3TN
Free advice helpline: 01273 823850
email via website
www.noiseabatementsociety.com

Nominet UK

National registry of all Internet Domain Names ending in .uk
Tel: 01865 332244
Tel: 01865 332211
nominet@nominet.org.uk
www.nominet.org.uk

Non-smokers see also Cleanair, QUIT

Northern Ballet

Professional touring ballet company with the most widespread touring programme of any UK company
Quarry Hill Leeds LS2 7PA
Tel: 0113 220 8000
info@northernballet.com
northernballet.com

Northern Broadsides

National touring theatre company presenting classic texts
Dean Clough Halifax HX3 5AX
Tel: 01422 369704
www.northern-broadsides.co.uk

Northern Ireland Environment Link

89 Loopland Drive Belfast BT6 9DW
Tel: 028 9045 5770
iona@nienvironmentlink.org
www.nienvironmentlink.org

Northern Ireland Executive

Stormont Castle Stormont Estate Belfast BT4 3TT
Tel: 028 9052 8400
www.northernireland.gov.uk

Northern Ireland Office

Stormont House Stormont Estate Belfast BT4 3SH & 11 Millbank London SW1P 4PN
Tel: 028 9052 0700
Textphone: 028 9052 7668
Email via website
www.nio.gov.uk

Northern Ireland Ombudsman

Progressive House 33 Wellington Place Belfast BT1 6HN Or Freepost BEL1478 Belfast BT1 6BR
Helpline: 0800 343424
Tel: 028 9023 3821
Textphone: 028 90897789
ombudsman@ni-ombudsman.org.uk
www.ni-ombudsman.org.uk

Northern Stage

Producing theatre company
Barras Bridge Newcastle upon Tyne NE1 7RH
Tel: 0191 230 5151
info@northernstage.co.uk
www.northernstage.co.uk

Norwood

Supports people with learning disabilities and children and families in need in the Jewish community and in the wider community, in London and the South East
Broadway House 80-82 The Broadway Stanmore Middlesex HA7 4HB
Tel: 020 8809 8809
info@norwood.org.uk
www.norwood.org.uk

Not Dead Yet UK

A network of disabled people who oppose the legalised killing of disabled people
www.notdeadyetuk.org

NSPCC National Society for the Prevention of Cruelty to Children
Help for adults concerned about a child:0808 800 5000
Tel: 020 7825 2500 (headquarters)
Childline: 0800 1111
info@nspcc.org.uk
www.nspcc.org.uk

Nuclear Disarmament see CND, CND (Scottish)

Nuclear Society (European)

Largest nuclear society for science and industry
www.euronuclear.org

Nuclear Tourist (Virtual)

Independent website on nuclear power & nuclear power stations
www.nucleartourist.com

Nursing & Midwifery Council

23 Portland Place London W1B 1PZ
Tel:020 7637 7181
email via website
www.nmc-uk.org

& Scotland
Ground Floor 114-116 George Street Edinburgh EH2 4LH
Tel: 0131 624 5000
scotland@nmc-uk.org
www.nmc-uk.org

Nurture Group Network Helping young people
International umbrella organisation for nurture groups. Supports members in their work to improve the life chances of the most vulnerable and disadvantaged children and young people
CAN Mezzanine 49-51 East Road Old Street London N1 6AH
info@nurturegroups.org
www.nurturegroups.org

NUS National Union of Students
4th Floor 184-192 Drummond Street London NW1 3HP
Tel: 0845 5210 262
Text phone: 0207 380 6600
nusuk@nus.org.uk
www.nus.org.uk

& Scotland
29 Forth Street Edinburgh EH1 3LE
Tel: 0131 556 6598
mail@nus-scotland.org.uk
www.nus.org.uk/scotland

& Ireland NUS-USI
42 Dublin Road Belfast BT2 7HN
Tel: 028 90 244 641
info@nistudents.org
www.nistudents.org

& Wales
2nd floor Cambrian Buildings Mount Stuart Square Cardiff CF10 5FL
Tel: 02920 435 390
office@nus-wales.org.uk
www.nus.org.uk/en/About-NUS/Who-We-Are/Nations/NUS-Wales/

Nutrition Foundation (British)
High Holborn House 52-54 High Holborn London WC1V 6RQ
Tel: 020 7404 6504
postbox@nutrition.org.uk
www.nutrition.org.uk

Nutrition Society
Aims to advance the scientific study of nutrition and its application to the maintenance of human and animal health
10 Cambridge Court 210 Shepherds Bush Road London W6 7NJ
Tel: 0207 602 0228
office@nutsoc.org.uk
www.nutritionsociety.org

NWR see Women's Register (National)

NYAS see Youth Advocacy Service (National)

O

OASIS Overseas Adoption Support and Information Service
For people who want to adopt children from orphanages abroad
email via website
www.adoptionoverseas.org

Obesity see also International Association for the Study of Obesity

Obesity (International Association for the Study of) & Obesity TaskForce (International) IASO & IOTF
Works with WHO to alert the world to the growing problem of obesity
Charles Darwin House 12 Roger Street London WC1N 2JU
Tel: 020 7685 2580
enquiries@iaso.org
www.iaso.org

Obesity Forum (National)
Raises awareness of the growing impact of obesity and being overweight on patients and our National Health Service
c/o Unit 1.03 Enterprise House 1/2 Hatfields London SE1 9PG
Tel: 02076 271510
nof@sbcommunicationsgroup.com
www.nationalobesityforum.org.uk

Occupational Hygiene Society (British)
5-6 Melbourne Business Court Millennium Way Pride Park Derby DE24 8LZ
Tel: 01332 298101
admin@bohs.org
www.bohs.org

Occupational Safety & Health (Institution of) IOSH
Professional body
The Grange Highfield Drive Wigston Leics LE18 1NN
Tel: 0116 257 3100
email via webite
www.iosh.co.uk

OCD Action
Promoting recovery from obsessive compulsive disorders
Suite 506-509 Davina House 137-149 Goswell Road London EC1V 7ET
Support & information helpline: 0845 390 6232
Tel: 020 7253 5272 (Office)
support@ocdaction.org.uk
email via website
www.ocdaction.org.uk

Ocean Mammal Institute
Helps individuals understand and feel their connection to nature and give them courage to act responsibly for the planet and its inhabitants
www.oceanmammalinst.com

Ocean Youth Trust Adventure under Sail
Offshore sail training
www.oyt.org.uk

OCR/Oxford Cambridge and RSA Examinations
1 Hills Road Cambridge CB1 2EU
Tel: 01223 553311
email via website
www.cambridgeassessment.org.uk

ODL QC see Open & Distance Learning Quality Council

OFCOM
Regulator of UK communication Industries encompassing television, radio, telecommunications & wireless communication services
Riverside House 2A Southwark Bridge Rd
London SE1 9HA
Tel: 020 7981 3040
Tel: 0300 123 3333
Textphone: 020 7981 3043
www.ofcom.org.uk/

Offenders see UNLOCK, Nacro, SACRO

Office for National Statistics ONS
Room 1.101 Government Buildings Cardiff Road Newport South Wales NP10 8XG
Tel: 0845 601 3034
info@statistics.gov.uk
www.ons.gov.uk

Official Residences of the Queen now see British Monarchy (The official website of)

Ofgem Gas & Electricity Markets (Office of)
Regulatory body for gas and electricity markets, protects customers' interests and encourages competition. Independent advisors to the UK Government on tackling and preparing for climate change
9 Millbank London SW1P 3GE
Tel: 020 7901 7295
consumeraffairs@ofgem.gov.uk
www.ofgem.gov.uk

Ofqual Office of Qualifications and Examinations Regulation
Regulates general and vocational qualifications in England and vocational qualifications in Northern Ireland
Spring Place Coventry Business Park Herald Avenue Coventry CV5 6UB
Helpline: 0300 303 3346
Tel: 0300 303 3344
Textphone: 0300 303 3345
info@ofqual.gov.uk
www.ofqual.gov.uk

Ofsted Office for Standards in Education
Inspection of schools, local education authorities, teacher training institutions and youth work and registration of early years childcare
Piccadilly Gate Store Street Manchester M1 2WD
Tel: 0300 123 4234 (education or adult skills)
general helpline: 0300 123 1231
Textphone/Minicom: 0161 618 8524
enquiries@ofsted.gov.uk
www.ofsted.gov.uk

OFWAT see Water Services (Office of)

Old Bailey, London (Proceedings of) 1674 to 1834
Accounts of over 100,000 criminal trials held at London's central criminal court
www.oldbaileyonline.org

Olympic Association (British)
60 Charlotte Street London W1T 2NU
Tel: 0207 842 5700
boa@boa.org.uk
www.olympics.org.uk

Olympic Committee (International) see International Olympic Committee

Ombudsman Public Services Ombudsman for Wales
1 Ffordd yr Hen Gae Pencoed CF35 5LJ
Tel: 0845 601 0987
email via website
www.ombudsman-wales.org.uk

Ombudsman Association
Lists the ombudsmen and other complaint-handling bodies
PO Box 308 Twickenham London TW1 9BE
Tel: 020 8894 9272
secretary@ombudsmanassociation.org
www.ombudsmanassociation.org

ONE International
Aims to raise awareness about, and spark response to the crises swamping Africa: unpayable Debts, uncontrolled spread of AIDS, and unfair Trade rules which keep Africans poor
151 Wardour Street London W1F 8WE
Tel: 0207 434 7550
email via website
www.one.org

One parent families see also Families Need Fathers, Friendship Works, Gingerbread, HELP, One Plus One

One Plus One
To enhance understanding of how family relationships contribute to the well being of adults and children
1 Benjamin Street London EC1M 5QG
Tel: 020 7553 9530
email via website
www.oneplusone.org.uk

Onekind
Campaigns against all animal abuse
10 Queensferry St Edinburgh EH2 4PG
Tel: 0131 225 6039
email via website
www.onekind.org

ONS see Office for National Statistics

Open & Distance Learning Quality Council
Accreditation of open and distance learning
providers
79 Barnfield Wood Road Beckenham Kent
BR3 6ST
Tel: 020 8658 83373
email via website
www.odlqc.org.uk

Open College of the Arts
Providing high quality arts courses by
distance learning
Michael Young Arts Centre Redbrook
Business Park Wilthorpe Rd Barnsley S75
1JN
Freephone: 0800 731 2116
enquiries@oca-uk.com
www.oca-uk.com

Open Museum
Offers a free service that allows groups,
venues and community event organisers
in Glasgow to borrow museum objects and
create displays
200 Woodhead Road South Nitshill Industrial
Estate Glasgow G53 7NN
Tel: 0141 276 9368
Text Phone: 0141 276 9428
OpenMuseumEnquiries@glasgowlife.org.uk
www.glasgowlife.org.uk/museums/our-
museums/open-museum/Pages/home.aspx

Open Spaces Society
Preserves commons & protects footpaths
and public open spaces
25A Bell St Henley-on-Thames RG9 2BA
Tel: 01491 573535
hq@oss.org.uk
www.oss.org.uk

Open University
PO Box 197 Milton Keynes MK7 6BJ
Tel: 0845 300 6090
email via website
www.open.ac.uk

Open-City
Architectural education charity
44-46 Scrutton Street London EC2A 4HH
Tel: 020 3006 7008
admin@open-city.org.uk
www.open-city.org.uk

Opera see English National Opera, NODA,
Royal Opera, Scottish Opera, Welsh National
Opera, Youth Opera (British)

Operation Black Vote
To raise the profile of the democratic rights
of the black community in the UK
18A Victoria Park Square Bethnal Green
London E2 9PB
Tel: 020 8983 5430/5426
info@obv.org.uk
www.obv.org.uk

Operation Smile UK
Medical charity providing reconstructive
surgery to young people with facial
disfigurements in developing countries
Unit 15, The Coda Centre 189 Munster Road
London SW6 6AW
Tel: 0844 581 1110
Tel: 020 7386 9386
info@operationsmile.org.uk
www.operationsmile.org.uk

Opportunity International UK
A charity working to create income-raising
opportunities with the world's poor people
Angel Court 81 St Clements Oxford OX4
1AW
Tel: 01865 725304
impact@opportunity.org.uk
www.opportunity.org.uk

& Scottish Office
A charity working to create income-raising
opportunities with the world's poor people
43 Charlotte Square Edinburgh EH2 4HQ
scotland@opportunity.org.uk
www.opportunity.org.uk

Opportunity Now
Business-led campaign for recruitment,
retention and development of women
employees
137 Shepherdess Walk London N1 7RQ
Tel: 0207 566 8650
email via website
www.bitcdiversity.org.uk/

Optimum Nutrition (Institute for)
Educational trust for the study, research &
practice of nutritional therapy
Avalon House 72 Lower Mortlake Road
Richmond Surrey TW9 2JY
Tel: 020 8614 7800
email via website
www.ion.ac.uk

Oral History Society
Unit 8, The Old Silk Mill Brook Street Tring
Herts HP23 5EF
Tel: 01422 820585
ohs@webscribe.co.uk
www.ohs.org.uk

Orangutan Foundation
7 Kent Terrace London NW1 4RP
Tel: 020 7724 2912
email via website
www.orangutan.org.uk

Orchestras (Association of British)
32 Rose Street London WC2E 9ET
Tel: 020 7557 6770
info@abo.org.uk
www.abo.org.uk

Orchid Cancer Appeal
Dedicated to funding research into
diagnosis, prevention and treatment of
prostate and testicular cancer as well as
promoting awareness of these previously
neglected diseases.
St Bartholomew's Hospital London EC1A
7BE
Tel: 0203 465 5766
info@orchid-cancer.org.uk
www.orchid-cancer.org.uk

Ordnance Survey
National mapping organisation
Adanac Drive Southampton SO16 0AS
Tel: 08456 050505
Textphone: 023 8005 6146
email via website
www.ordnancesurvey.co.uk

Organ Donation
NHS Blood and Transplant Organ Donation
and Transplantation Directorate Fox Den Rd
Stoke Gifford Bristol BS34 8RR
Organ Donor Line: 0300 123 2323
Tel: 0117 975 7575
email via website
www.organdonation.nhs.uk

**Organ Donation and Transplantation
(International Registry of)** IRODAT
A complete database that provides
the annual values of the donation and
transplantation activity from the countries
that dispose of them
www.tpm.org/secciones/irodat.swf

Organic Research Centre
Organic farming centre, advisory & research
body
Elm Farm Hamstead Marshall   Newbury
Berks RG20 0HR
Tel: 01488 658298
elmfarm@organicresearchcentre.com
www.efrc.com

Orienteering Federation (British)
8a Stancliffe House Whitworth Road Darley
Dale Matlock DE4 2HJ
Tel: 01629 734 042
email via website
www.britishorienteering.org.uk

Ornithology (British Trust for)
The Nunnery Thetford Norfolk IP24 2PU
Tel: 01842 750050
info@bto.org
www.bto.org

Osteopathic Council (General)
Statutory regulatory body for osteopaths
176 Tower Bridge Rd London SE1 3LU
Tel: 020 7357 6655
contactus@osteopathy.org.uk
www.osteopathy.org.uk

Osteoporosis Society (National)
Camerton Bath BA2 0PJ
Helpline: 0845 450 0230
Tel: 01761 471 771 / 0845 130 3076
info@nos.org.uk
www.nos.org.uk

Our Dynamic Earth
Interactive visitor attraction showing the
story of the Earth
Holyrood Rd Edinburgh EH8 8AS
Tel: 0131 550 7800
Email via website
www.dynamicearth.co.uk

Out of Joint
Theatre company touring primarily new
work nationally and internationally
7 Thane Works Thane Villas London N7 7NU
Tel: 020 7609 0207
ojo@outofjoint.co.uk
www.outofjoint.co.uk

Out of trouble
Prison Reform Trust campaign working to
reduce the number of children and young
people who are imprisoned in the UK
Prison Reform Trust 15 Northburgh Street
London EC1V 0JR
outoftrouble@prisonreformtrust.org.uk
www.outoftrouble.org.uk

Outdoor Learning (Institute for)
Learning through outdoor experience
Warwick Mill Business Centre Warwick
Bridge Carlisle CA4 8RR
Tel: 01228 564 580
email via website
www.outdoor-learning.org

Outward Bound Trust
Inspiring young people through challenging
outdoor experiences
Hackthorpe Hall Hackthorpe Penrith
Cumbria CA10 2HX
Tel: 01931 740000
enquiries@outwardbound.org.uk
www.theoutwardboundtrust.org.uk

& Scotland
Inspiring young people through challenging
outdoor experiences
2 Buchanan Gate Cumbernauld Road
Stepps G33 6FB
Tel: 07776 177468
martin.davidson@outwardbound.org.uk
www.theoutwardboundtrust.org.uk

Overeaters Anonymous of Great Britain
483 Green Lanes London N13 4BS
Tel: 07000 784985
email via website
www.oagb.org.uk

Overseas Adoption Support and Information Service see OASIS

Overseas Development Institute
Independent think-tank on international
development and humanitarian issues
111 Westminster Bridge Rd London SE1 7JD
Tel: 020 7922 0300
odi@odi.org.uk
www.odi.org.uk

Oxfam
Oxfam House John Smith Drive Cowley
Oxford OX4 2JY
Tel: 0300 200 1292
Email via website
www.oxfam.org.uk

Oxfam International
www.oxfam.org/en

P

PACE
Lesbian and gay counselling, groups,
advocacy, employment, HIV prevention and
youthwork services and family therapy
34 Hartham Rd London N7 9JL
Tel: 020 7700 1323
info@pacehealth.org.uk
www.pacehealth.org.uk

PACT (Parents & Abducted Children Together)
To fight parental child abduction across
borders and to locate and retrieve missing
children
22 The Vineyard Richmond Surrey TW10 6AN
Tel: 07506 448 116
support@pact-online.org
www.pact-online.org

PACT (Parents and Children Together)
7 Southern Court South Street Reading
Berkshire RG1 4QS
Tel: 0800 731 1845 (freephone)
Tel: 0118 938 7600
info@pactcharity.org
www.pactcharity.org

PACT (Prison Advice & Care Trust)
Works with prisoners who have mental
health needs and support prisoners' families
Park Place 12 Lawn Lane Vauxhall London
SW8 1UD
Offenders family helpline:
0808 808 200
Tel: 020 7735 9535
info@prisonadvice.org.uk
www.prisonadvice.org.uk

Pain Relief Foundation
Researches the causes & treatment of chronic
pain
Clinical Sciences Centre University Hospital
Aintree Lower Lane Liverpool L9 7AL
Tel: 0151 529 5820
secretary@painrelieffoundation.org.uk
www.painrelieffoundation.org.uk

Pain Society (British)
3rd Floor, Churchill House 35 Red Lion
Square London WC1R 4SG
Tel: 020 7269 7840
info@britishpainsociety.org
www.britishpainsociety.org

Pain Support
www.painsupport.co.uk

Palliative Care (National Council for)
Umbrella body
The Fitzpatrick Building 188-194 York Way
London N7 9AS
Tel: 020 7697 1520
enquiries@ncpc.org.uk
www.ncpc.org.uk

Panos Institute
Non-profit institute providing information on global issues with a developing country perspective
9 White Lion St London N1 9PD
Tel: 020 7278 1111
info@panos.org.uk
www.panos.org.uk

Paperboy
Web site with links to more than 5,000 newspapers worldwide
www.thepaperboy.com

Papworth Trust
Helps disabled people progress to greater independence
Bernard Sunley Centre Papworth Everard Cambridge CB23 3RG
Freephone 0800 952 5000
Tel: 01480 357200
info@papworth.org.uk
www.papworth.org.uk

PAPYRUS Prevention of young suicide
Founded by parents who have lost a young person through suicide & wish to reduce such tragedies in the future
67 Bewsey Street Warrington Cheshire WA2 7JQ
HOPELineUK 0800 068 41 41
Tel: 01925 572 444
admin@papyrus-uk.org
www.papyrus-uk.org

Parachute Association (British)
Governing body of sport parachuting (skydiving) in UK
5 Wharf Way Glen Parva Leicester LE2 9TF
Tel: 0116 2785271
skydive@bpa.org.uk
www.bpa.org.uk

Paralympic GB
Organisation responsible for GB Team competing at Paralympic Games
60 Charlotte Street, London W1T 2NU
Tel: 020 7842 5789
info@paralympics.org.uk
www.paralympics.org.uk

Parent Teacher Associations (National Confederation of) now see PTA-UK

Parenting UK
The national organisation for people working with parents
Unit 431 Highgate Studios 53-79 Highgate Road London NW5 1TL
Tel: 020 7284 8370
email via website
www.parentinguk.org

Parentline Plus now see Family Lives

Parents & Abducted Children Together see
PACT (Parents & Abducted Children Together)

Parents and Children Together see PACT
(Parents and Children Together)

Parents for Inclusion
Supports parents of disabled children who want to be included in mainstream school & society as a whole
336 Brixton Road London SW9 7AA
Helpline: 0800 652 3145
Tel: 020 7738 3888
info@parentsforinclusion.org
www.parentsforinclusion.org

Parkinson's Disease Society
215 Vauxhall Bridge Road London SW1V 1EJ
Helpline: 0808 800 0303
Tel: 020 7931 8080
hello@parkinsons.org.uk
www.parkinsons.org.uk

Parliament
UK parliament website - includes all aspects of Westminster
www.parliament.uk/

Parliamentary and Health Service Ombudsman
Carries out independent investigations into complaints about UK government departments and their agencies, and the NHS in England
Millbank Tower Millbank London SW1P 4QP
Complaints Helpline: 0345 015 4033
Tel: 07624 813 005 'call back' with your Textphone (Minicom)0300 061 4298
phso.enquiries@ombudsman.org.uk
www.ombudsman.org.uk

Parliamentary Education Unit
Information about the work of parliament for students & teachers
www.parliament.uk/education

Parliaments (Websites of National)
Portal opening to worldwide parliaments
www.ipu.org/english/parlweb.htm

Partially Sighted Society
Provides information, advice, equipment and clear print material to Help visually impaired people make the best use of their remaining vision
7-9 Bennetthorpe Doncaster DN2 6AA
Tel: 0844 477 4966
info@partsight.org.uk
www.partsight.org.uk

Passenger Focus
Official, independent watchdog for rail passengers
FREEPOST (RRRE-ETTC-LEET)
PO Box 4257 Manchester M60 3AR
Tel: 0300 123 2350
info@passengerfocus.org.uk
www.passengerfocus.org.uk

Passenger Transport UK (Confederation of) CPT
National trade association for bus, coach & light rail operators
Drury House 34-43 Russell Street London WC2B 5HA
Tel: 020 7240 3131
www.cpt-uk.org

Passion for Jazz
History of Jazz music origins, styles and musicians featuring timeline, photos, festivals, glossary, guitar & piano chords, scales & online lessons.
www.apassion4jazz.net

Passport Office now see Identity & Passport Service

Pastoral Care in Education (National Association for)
PO Box 6005 Nuneaton CV11 9GY
Tel: 07531 453 670
Email via website
www.napce.org.uk

Patent Office (European)
www.epo.org

Pathfinder International
Promotes the right of women and families throughout the world to have reproductive health and family planning services
Email via website
www.pathfind.org

Patient UK
Medical website
www.patient.co.uk

Patients Association
Represents the needs & wishes of patients in the NHS
PO Box 935 Harrow Middlesex HA1 3YJ
Helpline: 0845 608 4455
Tel: 020 8423 9111 (Admin)
helpline@patients-association.com
www.patients-association.com

Paul Mellon Centre for Studies in British Art see Studies in British Art (Paul Mellon Centre for)

Paul's Cancer Support Centre
Providers of information and support, complementary therapies and educational programmes
1st Floor Woburn House 20-22 York Road London SW11 3QA
Tel: 020 7924 3924
email via website
www.paulscancersupportcentre.org.uk

Pax Christi International Catholic Movement for Peace
International workcamps, peace education, campaigning on arms trade and nuclear disarmament issues
Christian Peace Education Centre St Joseph's Watford Way Hendon London NW4 4TY
Tel: 020 8203 4884
info@paxchristi.org.uk
www.paxchristi.org.uk

Payplan
A not-for-profit organisation which works closely with charities who are involved in assisting individuals who have unmanageable debts
Kempton House Dysart Road Grantham NG31 7LE
Freephone: 0800 280 2816
Email via website
www.payplan.com

PC David Rathband's Blue Lamp Foundation
Raises money to relieve the financial hardship that some personnel of the emergency services may face afer being criminally injured whilst on duty
PO Box 96 Blyth Northumberland NE24 1AA
Tel: 0871 2345 999
email via website
bluelamp-foundation.org

PDSA People's Dispensary for Sick Animals
Free veterinary services for sick & injured animals of needy owners
Whitechapel Way Priorslee Telford TF2 9PQ
Helpline: 0800 7312502
Tel: 01952 290999
Email via website
www.pdsa.org.uk

Peace & Freedom (Women's International League for) WILPF
Works for peace, disarmament and gender equality
1 rue de Varembe Case Postale 28 1211 Geneva 20 Switzerland
Tel: 00 41 22 919 7080
infoquest@wilpf.ch
www.wilpfinternational.org

Peace Alliance
Independent voluntary organisation working to reduce crime and the fear of crime and promote peace
Tottenham Town Hall Town Hall Approach London N15 4RY
Tel: 0208 808 9439
email via website
www.peacealliance.org.uk

Peace Brigades International
Humanitarian organisation working for non-violent transformation of conflict & to raise awareness of human rights
Development House 56-64 Leonard Street London EC2A 4LT
Tel: 020 7065 0775
Email via website
www.peacebrigades.org

Peace Pledge Union
Provides a wide range of teaching and study resources on peace and war
1 Peace Passage London N7 0BT
Tel: 020 7424 9444
email via website
www.ppu.org.uk
www.learnpeace.org.uk

Pedestrians see Living Streets

PEN see English PEN

Penal Reform see also Howard League for Penal Reform

Penal Reform International
Works for penal reform and against the death penalty
60-62 Commercial Street London E1 6LT
Tel: 020 7247 6515
info@penalreform.org
www.penalreform.org

Pensioners Convention (National)
Campaigns for better pensions, health services and other services for older people
Walkden House 10 Melton Street London NW1 2EJ
Tel: 020 7383 0388
info@npcuk.org
www.npcuk.org

Pensions Ombudsman
Investigates and decides complaints and disputes concerning occupational & personal pension schemes
11 Belgrave Rd London SW1V 1RB
Tel: 020 7630 2200
enquiries@pensions -ombudsman.org.uk
www.pensions-ombudsman.org.uk

People & Planet
Network of UK students campaigning on issues of world poverty, human rights and the environment
16-17 Turl Street Oxford OX1 3DH
Tel: 01865 264 180
email via website
www.peopleandplanet.org

People First
Run for and by people with learning difficulties to help them speak up for themselves
F173 Riverside Business Park Haldane Place London SW18 4UQ
Tel: 0208 874 1377
email via website
www.peoplefirstltd.com

People for the Ethical Treatment of Animals see PETA Foundation

People with Learning Disabilities (National Development Team for) now see Inclusion (National Development Team for)

People's Dispensary for Sick Animals see PDSA

People's History Museum
Left Bank
 Spinningfields Manchester M3 3ER
Tel: 0161 838 9190
email via website
www.phm.org.uk

People's Network
Access to a wide range of software and digital content, in public libraries already with a trained and supportive staff
The Museums, Libraries and Archives Council Grosvenor House 14 Bennetts Hill Birmingham B2 5RS
Tel: 0121 345 7300
info@mla.gov.uk
www.peoplesnetwork.gov.uk

People's Palace and Winter Gardens
Tells the story of the people and city of Glasgow from 1750 to the end of the 20th century
Glasgow Green Glasgow G40 1AT
Tel: 0141 276 0788
Text Phone: 0141 276 0795
museums@glasgowlife.org.uk
www.glasgowlife.org.uk/museums/our-museums/peoples-palace/Pages/home.aspx

People's Trust for Endangered Species
Ensures a future for endangered species throughout the world
15 Cloisters House 8 Battersea Park Road London SW8 4BG
Tel: 020 7498 4533
enquiries@ptes.org
www.ptes.org

Performing Arts and Technology see BRIT School for Performing Arts and Technology

Performing Arts Medicine (British Association for)

Diagnosis and treatment for medical problems encountered by performers of all kinds
Totara Park House, 4th Floor 34-36 Gray's Inn Road London WC1X 8HR
Tel: 020 7404 5888
Tel: 020 7404 8444 (Clinic)
enquiries@bapam.org.uk
www.bapam.org.uk

Performing Rights Society see PRS for music

Permaculture Association (Britain)

Provides information about courses, groups and projects concerned with a sustainable life style
BCM Permaculture Association London WC1N 3XX
Tel: 0845 458 1805
Email via website
www.permaculture.org.uk

Personal Finance Education Group pfeg

Helps schools to teach personal finance
Fifth Floor 14 Bonhill Street London EC2A 4BX
 advisory service:0300 6660 127
Tel: 020 7330 9470
Tel: 0845 241 0925
info@pfeg.org
www.pfeg.org

Personal Injury Lawyers (Association of)

APIL
Dedicated to improving the service provided to victims of accidents and clinical negligence
3 Alder Court Rennie Hogg Road Nottingham NG2 1RX
Tel: 0115 958 0585
Email via website
www.apil.org.uk

Personnel & Development (Chartered Institute of)

Professional body
151 The Broadway London SW19 1JQ
Tel: 020 8612 6200
email via website
www.cipd.co.uk

Pesticide Action Network UK

Independent health and ecological charity working to eliminate the hazards of pesticides
54-64 Leonard Street Development House London EC2A 4LT
Tel: 020 7065 0905
Email via website
www.pan-uk.org

Pet Advisory Committee

Makes recommendations to central and local government to encourage responsible pet ownership in society
PO Box 574 Dorking RH4 9GW
Tel: 01306 628136
email via website
www.petadvisory.org.uk

Pet Behaviour Counsellors (Association of)

PO Box 46 Worcester WR8 9YS
Tel: 01386 751151
email via website
www.apbc.org.uk

Pet Care Trust

Association promoting responsible pet ownership and professionalism in the trade
Pet Care Trade Association Bedford Business Centre 170 Mile Rd Bedford MK42 9TW
Tel: 01234 273933
Email via website
www.petcare.org.uk

Pet Health Council

Promotes health & welfare of pet animals
4th Floor 6 Catherine Street London WC2B 5JJ
enquiries@pethealthcouncil.co.uk
www.pethealthcouncil.co.uk

Pet Month (National)

Encourages responsible pet ownership via National Pet Week annually
3 Crossfield Chambers Gladbeck Way Enfield EN2 7HF
Tel: 020 8370 3688
info@nationalpetmonth.org.uk
www.nationalpetmonth.org.uk

PETA Foundation People for the Ethical Treatment of Animals

UK-based charity dedicated to establishing and protecting the rights of all animals through public education, research, legislation, special events, celebrity involvement and protest campaigns
PO Box 36678 London SE1 1YE
Tel: 020 7357 9229
info@peta.org.uk
www.peta.org.uk

PetLog Database (National)

The National Pet Identification Scheme using microchips
The Kennel Club
4A Alton House Gatehouse Way Aylesbury Bucks HP19 8XU
Tel: 0844 4633 999
Minicom: 01296 337 517
petlogadmin@thekennelclub.org.uk
www.petlog.org.uk

Pets as Therapy
Provides therapeutic visits to hospitals, hospices, nursing and care homes, special needs schools etc by volunteers with their own friendly temperament tested and vaccinated dogs and cats
14a High Street Wendover Aylesbury Buckinghamshire HP22 6EA
Tel: 01844 345 445
reception@petsastherapy.org
www.petsastherapy.org

Phab Physically Disabled & Able Bodied (England)
Brings together people with & without physical disabilities
Summit House 50 Wandle Rd Croydon CR0 1DF
Tel: 020 8667 9443
info@phab.org.uk
www.phab.org.uk

Pharmaceutical Society (Royal)
Professional, regulatory and statutory body of Britain's practising pharmacists
1 Lambeth High St London SE1 7JN
Tel: 0207 572 2737
Tel: 0845 257 2570
support@rpharms.com
www.rpharms.com

& Scottish Office
Holyrood Park House 106 Holyrood Road Edinburgh EH8 8AS
Tel: 0131 556 4386
scotinfo@rpharms.com

Pharmaceutical Society (Royal) Welsh Office
Unit 2, Ashtree Court Woodsy Close Cardiff Gate Business Park Cardiff CF23 8RW
Tel: 029 2073 0310
wales@rpharms.com
www.rpharms.com

Philip Lawrence Awards Network PLAnet
Award scheme which acclaims and rewards outstanding achievements in good citizenship by young people of 11-20 years
c/o Nacro Park Place 10-12 Lawn Lane London SW8 1UD
Tel: 020 7840 7222
philiplawrenceawards@nacro.org.uk
www.philiplawrenceawards.net

Phonebrain
Interactive website providing a young person's guide to the real cost of premium phone lines
www.phonebrain.org.uk

Phonepay Plus formerly Independent
Committee for the Supervision of Standards of Telephone Information Services
Regulates the premium rate goods and services that you can buy by charging the cost to your phone bill and pre-pay account
Clove Building 4 Maguire Street London SE1 2NQ
Free Helpline: 0800 500212
Tel: 020 7940 7474
email via website
www.phonepayplus.org.uk

Photographic Society (Royal)
Fenton House 122 Wells Road Bath BA2 3AH
Tel: 01225 325733
reception@rps.org
www.rps.org

photoLondon
Archive collection and gateway to London's public photographic collections
www.photolondon.org.uk

Physical Education (Association for)
Professional association for teachers of physical education
Room 117 Bredon University of Worcester Henwick Grove Worcester WR2 6AJ
Tel: 01905 855 584
enquiries@afpe.org.uk
www.afpe.org.uk

Physical Recreation (Central Council of)
see Sport & Recreation Alliance

Physically Disabled & Able Bodied (England) see Phab

Physics (Institute of)
76 Portland Place London W1B 1NT
Tel: 020 7470 4800
physics@iop.org
www.iop.org

Physiotherapy (Chartered Society of)
Professional, educational and trade union body for chartered physiotherapists, students and assistants
14 Bedford Row London WC1R 4ED
Tel: 020 7306 6666
Email via website
www.csp.org.uk

Pilates Foundation
Promotes & develops body awareness
PO Box 51186 London SE13 9DA
Tel: 020 7033 0078
admin@pilatesfoundation.com
www.pilatesfoundation.com

Pipedown
Campaigns for the right to freedom from piped music in public places
1 The Row Berwick St James Salisbury SP3 4TP
Tel: 01722 790622
Tel: 07971 518976
Email via website
www.pipedown.info

Pituitary Foundation
Provides information and support to sufferers of pituitary disorders and their relatives, friends and carers
PO Box 1944 Bristol BS99 2UB
Tel: 0845 450 0375 (Support and Information)
Tel: 0845 450 0376
Email via website
www.pituitary.org.uk

Placement Survival Guide
Skills for life for 14-19 years, comprising work experience, community involvement and personal challenge
www.placementsurvivalguide.com

Plaid Cymru - The Party of Wales
Ty Gwynfor Anson Court Atlantic Wharf Cardiff CF10 4AL
Tel: 029 2047 2272
post@plaidcymru.org
www.plaidcymru.org

Plain English Campaign
Campaigning for clarity of official communications, edits documents & does training in plain English
PO Box 3 New Mills High Peak SK22 4QP
Tel: 01663 744409
info@plainenglish.co.uk
www.plainenglish.co.uk

Plan UK
Humanitarian child-focused organisation working with families and their communities to meet the needs of children around the world
Finsgate 5-7 Cranwood Street London EC1V 9LH
Tel: 0300 777 9777
email via website
www.plan-uk.org

Planned Parenthood Federation (International) IPPF
Global network of family planning associations in 182 countries
4 Newhams Row London SE1 3UZ
Tel: 020 7939 8200
info@ippf.org
www.ippf.org

Plantlife
The UK's leading plant conservation charity
14 Rollestone Street Salisbury Wiltshire SP1 1DX
Tel: 01722 342730
enquiries@plantlife.org.uk
www.plantlife.org.uk

Plantlife Cymru
Unit 14, Llys Castan Ffordd Y Parc Parc Menai Bangor LL57 4FD
Tel: 01248 670691
cymru@plantlife.org.uk
www.plantlife.org.uk

Plantlife Scotland
Balallan House Allan Park Stirling FK8 2QG
Tel: 01786 478509/479382
scotland@plantlife.org.uk
www.plantlife.org.uk

Platform see GFS Platform for Young Women

Platform 51
Supports girls and women as they take control of their lives
New Barclay House 234 Botley Road Oxford OX2 OHP
Tel: 01865 304200
info@platform51.org
www.platform51.org

Play see also thematic guide - Children & Young People

Play England
Aims for all children and young people in England to have regular access to and opportunity for free, inclusive, local play provision and play space
8 Wakley St London EC1V 7QE
Tel: 020 7843 6300
playengland@ncb.org.uk
www.playengland.org.uk

Play Wales
Aims to influence the policy of all organisations that have an interest in children's play
Baltic House Mount Stuart Sq Cardiff CF10 5FH
Tel: 029 2048 6050
email via website
www.playwales.org.uk

Playbus Association (National) now see Working on Wheels

PLAYLINK
Works to improve opportunities for children's free play in quality environments
72 Albert Palace Mansions Lurline Gardens London SW11 4DQ
Tel: 020 7720 2452
info@playlink.org
www.playlink.org

Plus
Voluntary social activities organisation for
18-36 year olds
Email via website
www.plusgroups.org.uk

PMS see Premenstrual Syndrome (National
Association for)

Pod Charitable Trust
Magicians, musicians, puppeteers,
storytellers and clowns give monthly
shows in children's hospitals, hospices and
children's wards throughout the UK
Mount Hall Llanfair Caereinion Welshpool
SY21 0BH
Tel: 01938 810374
pod@podcharity.org.uk
www.podcharity.org.uk

Podiatrists see Chiropodists & Podiatrists

Poetry Library
The most comprehensive and accessible
collection of poetry from 1912 in Britain and
home to a full-text database for UK poetry
magazines of the 20th and 21st centuries
Level 5 Royal Festival Hall London SE1 8XX
Tel: 020 7921 0943/0664
Email via website
www.poetrylibrary.org.uk
www.poetrymagazines.org.uk

Poetry Society
22 Betterton St London WC2H 9BX
Tel: 020 7420 9880
info@poetrysociety.org.uk
www.poetrysociety.org.uk

Police see also Ask The Police, Black Police
Association (National), Human Independent
Police Complaints Commission, INQUEST,
Metropolitan Police

Police Federation (Scottish) The Voice of
Scotland's Police Service
5 Woodside Place Glasgow G3 7QF
Tel: 0141 332 5234
gensec@spf.org.uk
www.spf.org.uk

Police Federation of England & Wales
Federation House Highbury Drive
Leatherhead Surrey KT22 7UY
Tel: 01372 352000
gensec@polfed.org
www.polfed.org

Policy on Ageing (Centre for)
Policy formation, library and information
services on all aspects of aging and later life
28 Great Tower Street London EC3R 5AT
Tel: 020 7553 6500
cpa@cpa.org.uk
www.cpa.org.uk

Policy Studies (Centre for)
Centre-right independent think tank
57 Tufton St London SW1P 3QL
Tel: 020 7222 4488
tim@cps.org.uk
www.cps.org.uk

Policy Studies Institute
Non-politically affiliated independent
research institute concerned with
government policy
50 Hanson Street London W1W 6UP
Tel: 020 7911 7500
website@psi.org.uk
www.psi.org.uk

Polio Fellowship (British)
Eagle Office Centre The Runway South
Ruislip HA4 6SE
Freephone: 0800 018 0586
info@britishpolio.org.uk
www.britishpolio.org.uk

Political Studies Association
Links academics in political science and
current affairs, theorists and practitioners,
policy-makers, journalists, researchers and
students in higher education
Department of Politics University of
Newcastle Newcastle-upon-Tyne NE1 7RU
Tel: 0191 222 8021
psa@ncl.ac.uk
www.psa.ac.uk

Polka Theatre World-class theatre for children
240 The Broadway Wimbledon London
SW19 1SB
Box Office: 020 8543 4888
www.polkatheatre.com

Pony Club
International youth organisation for those
interested in ponies & riding
Stoneleigh Park Kenilworth Warwicks CV8
2RW
Tel: 02476 698300
enquiries@pcuk.org
www.pcuk.org

Pool Association (English)
www.epa.org.uk

Poppy Project
Eaves project which provides
accommodation and support to women
who have been trafficked into prostitution or
domestic servitude
Tel: 020 7735 2062
www.eaves4women.co.uk/POPPY_Project/
POPPY_Project.php

Popular Astronomy (Society for) SPA
Aims to help beginners, and those who like
a less technical approach, to learn about
astronomy
www.popastro.com

Population Concern see Interact Worldwide

Population Services International PSI
Global health organisation targeting malaria, child survival, HIV, reproductive health and non-communicable disease to help the most vulnerable populations lead healthier lives
www.psi.org

Port of London Authority
Ensuring navigational safety along the Tidal Thames, promoting use of the River and safeguarding the environment.
London River House Royal Pier Road Gravesend Kent DA12 2BG
Tel: 01474 562200
Email via website
www.pla.co.uk

Portman Group
Funded by the drinks industry to promote responsible drinking
4th Floor, 20 Conduit Street London W1S 2XW
Tel: 020 7290 1460
info@portmangroup.org.uk
www.portmangroup.org.uk

Positively UK
National charity championing the rights of people living with HIV
347-349 City Road London EC1V 1LR
Peer support helpline: 020 7713 0222
Tel: 020 7713 0444
info@positivelyuk.org
www.positivelyuk.org

Post Natal Illness
Community site and forum offering support and information
www.pni.org.uk

Post Office
Tel: 08457 223344
Textphone: 08457 22 33 55
Email via website
www.postoffice.co.uk

Post-Adoption Centre
Offers support, counselling, family work & advice to anyone involved in adoption
5 Torriano Mews Torriano Avenue London NW5 2RZ
Advice Line: 020 7284 5879
Tel: 020 7284 0555
advice@pac.org.uk
www.postadoptioncentre.org.uk

Post-Natal Illness (Association for)
145 Dawes Rd Fulham London SW6 7EB
Tel: 020 7386 0868
Email via website
www.apni.org

Postcode Finder
Find postcodes online, or find addresses if you only have the postcode and other useful information about postal services
www.royalmail.com

Postwatch now see Consumer Focus

Practical Action
Specialises in helping people to use technology for practical answers to poverty
The Schumacher Centre Bourton on Dunsmore Rugby CV23 9QZ
Tel: 01926 634400
enquiries@practicalaction.org.uk
www.practicalaction.org

Prader-Willi Syndrome Association UK
PWSA (UK)

Pre-school Learning Alliance
Educational charity providing support, information & training for people working with under 5s & their families
The Fitzpatrick Building 188 York Way London N7 9AD
Tel: 020 7697 2500
email via website
www.pre-school.org.uk

Pre-school Play Association (Scottish)
SPPA
Works to improve pre-school provision
21-23 Granville Street Glasgow G3 7EE
Tel: 0141 221 4148
info@sppa.org.uk
www.sppa.org.uk

Pre-School Providers Association (Wales)
Educational charity. Largest provider of community based pre-school childcare in Wales
Unit 1 The Lofts 9 Hunter Street Cardiff Bay Cardiff CF10 5GX
Tel: 029 2045 1242
info@walesppa.org
www.walesppa.org

Premenstrual Syndrome (National Association for) NAPS
Information, advice & support for PMS sufferers & their families
41 Old Rd East Peckham Kent TN12 5AP
Tel: 0844 8157311
email via website
www.pms.org.uk

Preservation Trusts (UK Association of)
APT
Representative body for building preservation trusts in UK, offering support and advice
9th Floor, Alhambra House 27-31 Charing Cross Road London WC2H 0AU
Tel: 020 7930 1629
email via website
www.ukapt.org.uk

President USA see White House

Press and Broadcasting Freedom (Campaign for)
Campaigns for a diverse, democratic & accountable media
2nd Floor, Vi & Garner Smith House 23 Orford Rd Walthamstow London E17 9NL
Tel: 07729 846146.
freepress@cpbf.org.uk
www.cpbf.org.uk

Press Association
UK national news agency
292 Vauxhall Bridge Rd London SW1V 1AE
Tel: 0870 120 3200
Email via website
www.pressassociation.com

Press Association Ireland
Scottish Provident Building 7 Donegall Square West Belfast BT1 6JH
Tel: 028 9024 5008
Email via website
www.pressassociation.com

Press Association Scotland
One Central Quay Glasgow G3 8DA
Tel: 0870 830 6725
Email via website
www.pressassociation.com

Press Complaints Commission
Investigates written complaints concerning the editorial content of newspapers & magazines in the UK
Halton House 20/23 Holborn London EC1N 2JD
Tel: 020 7831 0022
Textphone: 020 7831 0123
complaints@pcc.org.uk
www.pcc.org.uk

Prevention of Accidents (Royal Society for the) see RoSPA

Prevention of Cruelty to Animals see RSPCA and Scottish SPCA

Prevention of Cruelty to Children see CHILDREN 1ST, NSPCC

Primary Education (Association for the Study of) see ASPE

Primary Education (National Association for) see NAPE

Primary School Science see SCIcentre

Primate Protection League (International) see IPPL (UK)

Prince's Trust - Cymru
Baltic House Mount Stuart Square Cardiff CF10 5FH
Freephone: 0800 842 842
Tel: 029 2043 7000
webinfowa@princes-trust.org.uk
www.princes-trust.org.uk

Prince's Trust - Northern Ireland
Block 5, Jennymount Court North Derby Street Belfast BT15 3HN
Freephone: 0800 842 842
Tel: 028 9074 5454
webinfoni@princes-trust.org.uk
www.princes-trust.org.uk

Prince's Trust - Pembrokeshire Adventure Centre
Offers a wide range of adventure sports, based on both land and water
Cleddau Reach Pembroke Dock Pembrokeshire SA72 6UJ
Tel: 01646 622013
adventure@princes-trust.org.uk
www.princes-trust.org.uk/pembrokeshire_adventure_centre/centre.aspx

Prince's Trust - Scotland
6th Floor Portland House 17 Renfield Street, Glasgow G2 5AH
Freephone: 0800 842 842
Tel: 0141 204 4409
webinfosc@princes-trust.org.uk
www.princes-trust.org.uk

Prince's Trust (Head Office)
Practical solutions to help young people get their lives working
18 Park Square East London NW1 4LH
Freephone: 0800 842 842
Tel: 020 7543 1234
Minicom: 020 7543 1374
webinfops@princes-trust.org.uk
www.princes-trust.org.uk

Princess Royal Trust for Carers now see Carers Trust

Prison Advice & Care Trust see PACT (Prison Advice & Care Trust)

Prison Reform Trust
Wide range of publications on penal issues and information and advice to prisoners and their families & campaign for reform
15 Northburgh St London EC1V 0JR
Tel: 020 7251 5070
email via website
www.prisonreformtrust.org.uk

Prison Service NI
Dundonald House Upper Newtownards Road Belfast BT4 3SU
Tel: 028 9186 3028 / 028 9186 3063
info@niprisonservice.gov.uk
www.niprisonservice.gov.uk

Prison Studies (International Centre for)
ICPS
Seeks to assist governments & other relevant agencies to develop appropriate policies on prisons & the use of imprisonment
1st Floor, The Merchant Centre 1 New Street Square London EC4A 3BF
Tel: 020 7842 8505
admin@icps.essex.ac.uk
www.prisonstudies.org

Prison Visitors (National Association of Official)
info@naopv.com
www.naopv.com

Prisoners Abroad
Charity providing practical support to British Citizens imprisoned abroad. Also provide assistance to those affected by imprisonment, and help ex-prisoners start a new life free of crime after their release
89-93 Fonthill Rd Finsbury Park London N4 3JH
Family freephone 0808 172 0098
Tel: 020 7561 6820
info@prisonersabroad.org.uk
www.prisonersabroad.org.uk

Prisoners of Conscience Appeal Fund
Helps those persecuted for conscientiously-held beliefs, provided they have not used or advocated violence
PO Box 61044 London SE1 1UP
Tel: 020 7407 6644
info@prisonersofconscience.org
www.prisonersofconscience.org

Prisoners' Advice Service
Provides free and confidential legal advice to all adult prisoners in England & Wales
PO Box 46199 London EC1M 4XA
Tel: 0207 253 3323
email via website
www.prisonersadvice.org.uk

Prisoners' Families (Action for)
Info on local support services and lobby on behalf of prisoners' families
Unit 21, Carlson Court 116 Putney Bridge Road London SW15 2NQ
Tel: 020 8812 3600
email via website
www.prisonersfamilies.org.uk

Prisoners' Families & Friends Service
Independent voluntary agency providing support, friendship and advice to the families and friends of anyone sentenced to imprisonment or remanded in custody
20 Trinity St London SE1 1DB
Freephone helpline: 0808 808 3444
Tel: 020 7403 4091 (Admin)
email via website
www.pffs.org.uk

Prisons and Probation Ombudsman for England and Wales
Investigates complaints from prisoners, people on probation and immigration detainees held at immigration removal centres and deaths of prisoners, residents of probation service Approved Premises, and those held in immigration removal centres
Ashley House 2 Monck St London SW1P 2BQ
Tel: 020 7035 2876 or 0845 010 7938
mail@ppo.gsi.gov.uk
www.ppo.gov.uk

Privacy International
Human rights group formed as a watchdog on surveillance by governments & corporations
46 Bedford Row London WC1R 4LR,
Tel: 020 7242 2836
info@privacy.org
www.privacyinternational.org

Probation Service (National) now see
directgov for public information or Justice for practitioner or corporate information

Professional and Career Development Loans see Career Development Loans

Professional Footballers Association
The union for professional footballers
www.givemefootball.com

Professional Golfers' Association
Centenary House The Belfry
Sutton Coldfield West Midlands B76 9PT
Tel: 01675 470 333
email via website
www.pga.info

Professional Music Therapists (Association of) now see Music Therapy (British Association for)

Professional Theatre for Children and Young People (Association of) now
see Theatre for Children and Young People (International Association of)

Project Gutenberg
American website providing texts of literature which is out of copyright
www.gutenberg.org

Project Trust
Gap year placements abroad, teaching or social projects
The Hebridean Centre Isle of Coll Argyll PA78 6TE
Tel: 01879 230444
info@projecttrust.org.uk
www.projecttrust.org.uk

Proofreaders see Editors and Proofreaders (Society for)

Prospects
UK's official graduate careers website
www.prospects.ac.uk

Prostate Cancer Charity
Research, support, information and
campaigning work
Cambridge House 100 Cambridge Grove
London W6 0LE
Confidential Helpline: 0800 074 8383
Tel: 020 8222 7622
info@prostatecanceruk.org
www.prostatecanceruk.org

Protection of Animals (World Society for)
see WSPA

Protection of Birds see RSPB

**Protection of Horses (International
League for the)** now see World Horse Welfare

**Protection of Rural Wales (Campaign for
the)** Ymgyrch Diogelu Cymru Wledig
Ty Gwyn 31 High St Welshpool Powys SY21 7YD
Tel: 01938 552 525 / 556 212
info@cprwmail.org.uk
www.cprw.org.uk

Provands Lordship
Dating from the Middle Ages, this museum
gives a glimpse of historical Scotland
3 Castle Street Glasgow G4 0RB
Tel: 0141 276 1625
museums@glasgowlife.org.uk
www.glasgowlife.org.uk/museums/our-
museums/provands-lordship/Pages/home.aspx

PRS for Music Performing Rights Society
Copyright House 29-33 Berners St London
W1T 3AB
Tel: 020 7580 5544
Email via website
www.prsformusic.com

Psoriasis Association
Help & support for sufferers
Dick Coles House 2 Queensbridge
Northampton NN4 7BF
Tel: 01604 251620
Local rate: 0845 676 0076
mail@psoriasis-association.org.uk
www.psoriasis-association.org.uk

Psychiatrists (Royal College of)
17 Belgrave Square London SW1X 8PG
Tel: 020 7235 2351
email via website
www.rcpsych.ac.uk

Psychical Research (Society for) SPR
For anyone interested in the paranormal.
Library, journal and funding university
research.
49 Marloes Rd London W8 6LA
Tel: 020 7937 8984
Email via website
www.spr.ac.uk

Psychological Society (British)
Professional and regulatory body of
psychologists
St Andrews House 48 Princess Rd East
Leicester LE1 7DR
Tel: 0116 254 9568
enquiries@bps.org.uk
www.bps.org.uk

Psychotherapists (British Association of)
37 Mapesbury Rd London NW2 4HJ
Tel: 020 8452 9823
email via website
www.bap-psychotherapy.org

Psychotherapy see thematic guide -
Counselling & Mental Health

Psychotherapy (UK Council for) UKCP
Umbrella body & voluntary regulatory
organisation. Provides a register of suitably
trained psychotherapists
2nd Floor Edward House 2 Wakley Street
London EC1V 7LT
Tel: 020 7014 9955
info@ukcp.org.uk
www.psychotherapy.org.uk

PTA-UK
Encourages formation of PTAs and
involvement of parents in their children's
education
39 Shipbourne Road Tonbridge Kent TN10 3DS
Advice Line: 0845 850 5460
info@pta.org.uk
www.pta.org.uk

Public Art Forum now see IXIA

Public Concern at Work
Leading authority on whistleblowing in
the workplace offering advice/services to
employees and organisations
3rd Floor, Bank Chambers 6 - 10 Borough
High Street London SE1 9QQ
Tel: 020 7404 6609
whistle@pcaw.co.uk
www.pcaw.co.uk

Public Health Agency
Supports those working in the areas of
health promotion and public health in
Northern Ireland
Linenhall Street Unit 12-22 Linenhall Street
Belfast, BT2 8BS
Tel: 0289032 1313
email via website
www.publichealth.hscni.net

**Public Management and Policy
Association** PMPA
Networking organisation for workers in
central & local government
3 Robert St London WC2N 6RL
Tel: 0207 543 5679
info.pmpa@cipfa.org
www.cipfa.org.uk/pmpa/

Public Monuments & Sculpture Association

For the promotion and protection of public monuments and sculpture in UK. Website contains details of National Recording Project which is surveying all public monuments & sculpture in the UK
70 Cowcross Street London EC1M 6EJ
Tel: 020 7490 5001
pmsa@btconnect.com
www.pmsa.org.uk

Public Policy Research (Institute for) see IPPR

Public Record Office now see National Archives

Public Sector Information (Office of) now see legislation.gov.uk

Public Service Excellence (Association for)

Advises local councils on best practice in delivery of public services
2nd Floor, Washbrook House Lancastrian Office Centre Talbot Rd Old Trafford Manchester M32 0FP
Tel: 0161 772 1810
enquiries@apse.org.uk
www.apse.org.uk

Public Services Ombudsman (Scottish)

SPSO
Investigates complaints about maladministration and service failure in public services in Scotland
4 Melville Street Edinburgh EH3 7NS or Freepost EH641 Edinburgh EH3 0BR
Tel: 0800 377 7330
Text: 0790 049 4372
Email via website
www.spso.org.uk

Public Whip

A searchable site providing the complete voting record of every MP
www.publicwhip.org.uk/

PWSA (UK) Prader-Willi Syndrome Association UK

Supports those affected by this chromosomal disorder
125a London Road Derby DE1 2QQ
Tel: 01332 365 676
email via website
www.pwsa.co.uk

Pyramid

Helps primary-school children build self-esteem and confidence
www.continyou.org.uk/children_and_families/pyramid/home

Q

Quaker Voluntary Action

Volunteer projects in the UK and abroad
1 Holt Lane Holmfirth West Yorkshire HD9 3BW
Tel: 01484 687139
mail@qva.org.uk
www.qva.org.uk

Quakers in Britain

Friends House 173-177 Euston Rd London NW1 2BJ
Tel: 020 7663 1000
enquiries@quaker.org.uk
www.quaker.org.uk

Qualifications Authority (Scottish) see Scottish Qualifications Authority

Quality in Study Support and Extended Services

Provides consultancy, professional development and an accredited recognition scheme for study support
Email Via Website
www.canterbury.ac.uk/education/quality-in-study-support

Queen's House

The 17th-century House showcases the Museum's fine-art collection and provides a unique venue for weddings, corporate and private events
Greenwich London SE10 9NF
Museum switchboard: 020 8858 4422
Recorded information line: 020 8312 6565
Bookings;: 020 8312 6608
bookings@nmm.ac.uk
www.nmm.ac.uk/places/queens-house/

Questionpoint

US virtual reference service and set of administrative tools for libraries of all sizes
questionpoint.org

Quilters' Guild of the British Isles

Independent registered educational charity which is dedicated to preserving the heritage and craft of quilting and patchwork in the UK
St Anthony's Hall York YO1 7PW
Tel: 01904 613 242
info@quiltersguild.org.uk
www.quiltersguild.org.uk

QUIT National Society of Non Smokers

Helping smokers to quit
20 Curtain Rd London, Greater London EC2A 3NF
Quit line: 0800 002200
Tel: 0207 539 1700
stopsmoking@quit.org.uk
www.quit.org.uk

R

Rabbit Council (British)
Governing body for exhibition rabbit
fancying
Purefoy House 7 Kirkgate Newark Notts
NG24 1AD
Tel: 01636 676042
info@thebrc.org
www.thebrc.org

RAC
Motoring services
www.rac.co.uk

Race Equality Foundation
Seeks to explore what is known about
discrimination and disadvantage, and to use
this evidence to develop interventions that
overcome barriers and promote race equality
in health, housing and social care
Unit 17 Deane House Studios Greenwood
Place London NW5 1LB
Tel: 0207 428 1880
Support Line: 0207 428 1891
email via website
www.raceequalityfoundation.org.uk/

Race Relations (Institute of)
2-6 Leeke St London WC1X 9HS
Tel: 020 7837 0041
Tel: 020 7833 2010
info@irr.org.uk
www.irr.org.uk

Racial Equality (Commission for) now see
Equality and Human Rights Commission

Racism see also thematic guide Race

RAD see Royal Academy of Dance

RADA Royal Academy of Dramatic Art
Vocational training for actors and theatre
technicians
62-64 Gower St London WC1E 6ED
Tel: 020 7636 7076
enquiries@rada.ac.uk
www.rada.org

RADAR now see Disability Rights UK

Radio see also BBC

Radio Authority now see OFCOM

Radio Communications Agency now see
OFCOM

Radio Society of Great Britain
Supports and promotes amateur (or ham)
radio
3 Abbey Court Fraser Road Priory Business
Park Bedford MK44 3WH
Tel: 01234 832 700
email via website
www.rsgb.org

Rail Enquiries (National)
Rail timetables, fares etc for all national rail
services in UK
www.nationalrail.co.uk

Rail Europe
Information for travellers and rail fans. Gives
links to national timetables
34 Tower View Kings Hill West Malling Kent
ME19 4ED
General Reservations: 08448 484 064
email via website
www.raileurope.co.uk

Rail Regulation (Office of)
One Kemble Street London WC2B 4AN
Tel: 020 7282 2000
contact.cct@orr.gsi.gov.uk
www.rail-reg.gov.uk

Railfuture
Independent campaign for a better
passenger and freight rail network
www.railfuture.org.uk

Railway Children
Helps runaway and abandoned children in
the UK & internationally
1st Floor 1 The Commons Sandbach
Cheshire CW11 1EG
Tel: 01270 757596
enquiries@railwaychildren.org.uk
www.railwaychildren.org.uk

Railway Crime (Partners Against) now see
Trackoff

Railway Museum (National)
Leeman Road York YO26 4XJ
Tel: 08448 15 3 139
School bookings enquiries: 01904 686230
nrm@nrm.org.uk
www.nrm.org.uk

Railways see also Better Transport (Campaign
for), Community Rail Partnerships (Association
of), Rail Europe, Heritage Railway Association,
Passenger Focus, Passenger Transport UK
(Confederation of), Sustrans, Trainline,
WalesRails

Rainer now see Catch22

Rainforest see also thematic guide
Environment & Countryside

Rainforest Concern
Conservation & protection of rainforests in
Central and South America & Asia
73 Great Pulteney Street Bath BA2 4DL
Tel: 020 7229 2093
info@rainforestconcern.org
www.rainforestconcern.org

Rainforest Foundation

Protects the world's rainforests and their inhabitants
233A Kentish Town Road, London NW5 2JT
Tel: 020 7485 0193
info@rainforestuk.com
www.rainforestfoundationuk.org

Raleigh International

Youth development charity running community, environmental and adventure projects in developing countries
3rd Floor 207 Waterloo Road London SE1 8XD
Tel: 020 7183 1270
info@raleighinternational.org
www.raleighinternational.org

Rambert Dance Company

Contemporary dance with education and community units
94 Chiswick High Rd London W4 1SH
Tel: 020 8630 0600
rdc@rambert.org.uk
www.rambert.org.uk

Ramblers

Britain's biggest charity working on behalf of walkers
2nd Floor Camelford House 87-90 Albert Embankment London SE1 7TW
Tel: 020 7339 8500
ramblers@ramblers.org.uk
www.ramblers.org.uk

Ramblers Scotland

Ramblers Scotland is the representative body for walkers in Scotland.
Kingfisher House Auld Mart Business Park Milnathort Kinross KY13 9DA
Tel: 01577 861222
scotland@ramblers.org.uk
www.ramblers.org.uk/scotland

Ramblers' Association Wales Cymdeithas y Cerddwyr

Representative body for walkers in Wales. Aims to encourage walking and public understanding of the outdoors
3 Coopers Yard Curran Road Cardiff CF10 5NB
Tel: 029 2064 4308
cerddwyr@ramblers.org.uk
www.ramblers.org.uk/wales

Rape see also Crossroads Women's Centre, Mankind UK, Roofie Foundation, SurvivorsUK

Rape Crisis England and Wales

Gives contact information about rape crisis centres throughout the UK
BCM Box 4444 London WC1N 3XX
freephone helpline 0808 802 9999
info@rapecrisis.org.uk
www.rapecrisis.co.uk

RAPt Rehabilitation for Addicted Prisoners Trust

Works to help people with drug and alcohol dependence, both in prison and in the community, move towards, achieve and maintain positive and fulfilling drug-free and crime-free lives
Riverside House 27-29 Vauxhall Grove London SW8 1SY
Tel: 0207 582 4677
info@rapt.org.uk
www.rapt.org.uk

Rare Breeds Survival Trust RBST

Works to conserve endangered breeds of British farm livestock
Stoneleigh Park Nr Kenilworth Warwickshire CV8 2LG
Tel: 024 7669 6551
email via website
www.rbst.org.uk

Rathbone

Charity helping people with special educational and training needs. Helpline advises parents on special education procedures
4th Floor Churchgate House 56 Oxford St Manchester M1 6EU
Free Phone: 0800 731 5321
Tel: 0161 236 5358
Email via website
www.rathboneuk.org

Raw Material

Getting young Londoners active in professional music, creative arts and media development
2 Robsart St London SW9 0DJ
Tel: 0207 737 6103
hello@rawmusicmedia.co.uk
www.rawmusicmedia.co.uk

Raynaud's & Scleroderma Association

Offers support to sufferers of both conditions and raises funds for research and welfare
112 Crewe Rd Alsager Cheshire ST7 2JA
Tel: 01270 872776
Tel: 0800 9172494
info@raynauds.org.uk
www.raynauds.org.uk

RDA see Riding for the Disabled Association

RE Today Services

Works nationally and internationally to support religious education in schools
1020 Bristol Rd Selly Oak Birmingham B29 6LB
Tel: 0121 472 4242
admin@retoday.org.uk
www.natre.org.uk

Re-Cycle Bicycle Aid for Africa
Collects secondhand bicycles to send to
Africa, some help health/AIDS workers
reach remote villages and even provide an
ambulance service
Unit A Global Park   Moorside (off East Street)
Colchester   Essex CO1 2TJ
Telephone:01206 863111
Email: info@re-cycle.org
www.re-cycle.org

Reach Skilled volunteers
Job placement for managerial and
professional people available to offer
part-time services as unpaid volunteers to
voluntary organisations
89 Albert Embankment   London SE1 7TP
Tel: 020 7582 6543
email via website
www.reachskills.org.uk

React Rapid Effective Assistance for Children
with Potentially Terminal illness
Helps families facing the financial burden of
caring for a potentially terminally ill child
St Luke's House   270 Sandycombe Rd   Kew
Surrey TW9 3NP
Tel: 020 8940 2575
Email via website
www.reactcharity.org

Read The Reading Agency
A charity aiming to inspire a reading nation
by working with readers, writers, libraries
and their partners
60 Farringdon Road   London EC1R 3GA
Tel: 0207 324 2544
info@readingagency.org.uk
www.readingagency.org.uk

Reading see also BookCrossing, BOOKTRUST,
Listening Books, Literacy Association (National),
People's Network, Volunteer Reading Help

Reading Agency now see Read

Real Ale (Campaign for) see CAMRA

Real Education (Campaign for)
For higher standards and more choice in
state schools
18 Westlands Grove   York YO31 1EF
Tel: 01904 424134
cred@cre.org.uk
www.cre.org.uk

Recording Association (Professional) see
APRS – The Professional Recording Association

Recycle for London
Helpline: 0845 600 0323
Email:recycleforlondon@london.gov.uk
www.recycleforlondon.com

recycle more
Encourages homes, businesses and schools
to recycle more waste
Valpak Ltd   Stratford Business Park   Banbury
Road
Stratford-Upon-Avon CV37 7GW
Tel: 08450 682 572
recycle-more@valpak.co.uk
www.recycle-more.co.uk

Recycle-IT! Ethical solutions
Community Interest Company providing
training, paid work experience and real
jobs for homeless and other long term
unemployed people
Unit 8 Unit 8, Parkway Trading Estate,
Longbridge Rd, Trafford Park, Manchester
M17 1SN
Tel: 0161 226 0637
info@recycle-it.uk.com
www.recycle-it.uk.com

RecycleNow
Helpline: 0845 600 0323
Email via website
www.recyclenow.com

Recycling see also Access Space, Aluminium
Packaging Recycling Organisation, Computer
Aid International, Freecycle, Furniture Re-use
Network, Garden Organic, Save A Cup, Steel
Can Recycling Information Bureau, Waste
Watch, WRAP

Recycling Appeal
Collects mobile phones, PDAs and printer
cartridges for reuse and recycling, raising
funds and helping the environment.
31-37 Etna Road   Falkirk FK2 9EG
Tel: 08451 30 20 10
info@recyclingappeal.com
www.recyclingappeal.com

Red Cross (British)
44 Moorfields   London EC2Y 9AL
Tel: 0844 871 1111
Tel: 0844 412 2804
Textphone: 020 7562 2050
information@redcross.org.uk
www.redcross.org.uk

**Red Cross (International Committee of
the)**
19 Avenue de la Paix CH-1202 Geneva
Tel: 00 41 22 734 6001
email via website
www.icrc.org

Red List of Endangered Species
The World Conservation Union assesses the
threat to species
www.iucnredlist.org

Red Ribbon International see AIDS Trust
(National)

REDRESS
Charity seeking reparation for torture survivors
87 Vauxhall Walk London SE11 5HJ
Tel: 020 7793 1777
info@redress.org
www.redress.org

Redwings Horse Sanctuary
To provide and promote the welfare, care
and protection of horses, ponies, donkeys
and mules
Hapton Norwich NR15 1SP
Tel: 01508 481000
info@redwings.co.uk
www.redwings.org.uk

Reflexology Association (British)
Representative body for reflexology
practitioners and students
Monks Orchard Whitbourne Worcester WR6
5RB
Tel: 01886 821207
bra@britreflex.co.uk
www.britreflex.co.uk

Reform Judaism (Movement for)
The Sternburg Centre 80 East End Road
London N3 2SY
Tel: 020 8349 5640
Email via website
www.reformjudaism.org.uk

Reformed Offenders (National Association
of) see UNLOCK

Refuge
Provides safe accommodation for women
& children experiencing domestic violence.
Support, advice and referrals
4th Floor International House 1 St
Katharine's Way London E1W 1UN
24 hr national domestic violence helpline
0808 2000 247
Tel: 020 7395 7700
info@refuge.org.uk
www.refuge.org.uk
www.womensaid.org.uk

Refugee Agency (United Nations) see UNHCR

Refugee Council
Promotes refugees' rights in the UK and
abroad and advocate on their behalf
PO Box 68614 London E15 9DQ
Advice Line: 0808 808 2255
Tel: 020 7346 6700
Text phone: 0808 808 2259
email via website
www.refugeecouncil.org.uk

Refugees (Student Action for) STAR
Network of students and young people aged
16-25 supporting refugees
356 Holloway Road London N7 6PA
Tel: 0207 697 4130
email via website
www.star-network.org.uk

Refugees (US Committee for)
www.refugees.org

Refugees and Exiles (European Council on)
Umbrella organisation of over 70 agencies
working in 30 countries to assist refugees
Secretariat Rue Royale 146, 1st Floor 1000
Brussels Belgium
Tel: +32 (0)2 234 3800
ecre@ecre.org
www.ecre.org

Register Office for Northern Ireland (General)
Administers marriage law and the
registration of births, deaths, marriages, civil
partnerships and adoption
Oxford House 49-55 Chichester St Belfast
BT1 4HL
Tel: 028 9151 3101
GRO_NISRA@dfpni.gov.uk
www.nidirect.gov.uk/gro

Register Office for Scotland (General) now
see National Records of Scotland (NRS)

Registering life events
Order birth, marriage, death, civil
partnership, stillbirth or adoption certificates
through the General Register Office
www.direct.gov.uk/en/
Governmentcitizensandrights/
Registeringlifeevents/index.htm

Relate The relationship people
Supports family life. Provides counselling
& therapy for couples with relationship
problems
Tel: 0300 100 1234
www.relate.org.uk

Relationships Scotland
Helps separating and divorcing parents,
children, young people and families
18 York Place Edinburgh EH1 3EP
Tel: 0845 1192020
email via website
www.relationships-scotland.org.uk

Relatives & Residents Association
Promotes the well being of older people in
homes and long stay hospitals
1 The Ivories 6-18 Northampton Street
London N1 2HY
Advice Line: 020 7359 8136
Tel: 020 7359 8148 (Admin)
info@relres.org
www.relres.org

Release National drugs and legal helpline
124-128 City Road London EC1V 2NJ
Advice Line: 0845 4500 215
Tel: 020 7324 2989
ask@release.org.uk
www.release.org.uk

Religious Education (Professional Council for) now see Teachers of Religious Education (National Association of)

Religious Society of Friends see Quakers in Britain

REMAP
UK-wide charity with panels of local voluntary engineers who help disabled people by making specialist equipment for free
D9 Chaucer Business Park Kemsing Sevenoaks TN15 6YU
Tel: 0845 1300 456
email via website
www.remap.org.uk

Remploy
Provides employment services and employment to people with disabilities and complex barriers to work
18c Meridian East Meridian Business Park
Leicester LE19 1WZ
Tel:0845 155 2700
Minicom: 0845 155 0532
info@remploy.co.uk
www.remploy.co.uk

RenewableUK
Professional body for the UK wind industry
Greencoat House Francis Street London SW1P 1DH
Tel: 020 7901 3000
info@renewable-uk.com
www.bwea.com

REonline
Providing information for all those working and interested in religious education in England
www.reonline.org.uk

Reporters sans Frontières see Reporters Without Borders

Reporters Without Borders
Defends jailed journalists and press freedom throughout the world. Fights against censorship and laws and works to improve the safety of journalists, especially those reporting in war zones
en.rsf.org

Republic Campaigning for a democratic alternative to the monarchy
Suite 14040 145-157 St John Street London EC1V 4PY
Tel: 0207 608 5742
email via website
www.republic.org.uk

Research Into Ageing now see Age Cymru, Age UK, Age NI, Age Scotland

Resolution First for family law
Organisation of lawyers who believe in a constructive, non-confrontational approach to family law matters. Also campaigns for improvements to the family justice system
PO Box 302 Orpington BR6 8QX
Tel: 01689 820272
info@resolution.org.uk
www.resolution.org.uk

ReSolv The Society for the Prevention of Solvent & Volatile Substance Abuse
National charity solely dedicated to the prevention of solvent and volatile substance abuse
30A High St Stone Staffs ST15 8AW
Tel:01785 810762
Tel: 01785 817885
information@re-solv.org
www.re-solv.org

Resource Information Service now see Homeless Link

Respect
UK membership association for domestic violence perpetrator programmes and associated support services
4th Floor, Development House 56-64 Leonard Street London EC2A 4LT
Respect Phoneline 0808 802 4040 free
Tel: 020 7549 0578
textphone: 18001 0808 802 4040
info@respect.uk.net
www.respect.uk.net

Respect for Animals
Campaign against the international fur trade
PO Box 6500 Nottingham NG4 3GB
Tel: 0115 952 5440
info@respectforanimals.org
www.respectforanimals.co.uk

Restless Development
An international development charity that recruits and trains young adults as volunteer Peer Educators, to lead programmes that address urgent health and environmental issues in Africa and Asia
7 Tufton Street London SW1P 3QB
Tel: 020 7976 8070
info@restlessdevelopment.org
www.restlessdevelopment.org

Restricted Growth Association
Support and information for people with restricted growth, families, professionals and other interested parties
PO Box 15755 Solihull B93 3FY
RGA Office & Helpline: 0300 111 1970
office@restrictedgrowth.co.uk
www.restrictedgrowth.co.uk

Rethink Severe Mental Illness Charity
Working to improve the lives of everyone
affected by schizophrenia and other severe
mental illnesses
15th Floor 89 Albert Embankment London
SE1 7TP
Tel: 020 7840 3188 (advice)
Tel: 0300 5000 927
info@rethink.org
www.rethink.org

Retired and Senior Volunteer Programme
RSVP
Enables people aged 50+ to become actively
involved in voluntary work of their choice
237 Pentonville Rd London N1 9NJ
Tel: 020 7643 1385
rsvpinfo@csv.org.uk
www.csv-rsvp.org.uk

reunite International Child Abduction Centre
Information & support for parents who fear
or have experienced the abduction of a child
PO Box 7124 Leicester LE1 7XX
Advice Line: 01162 556 234
Tel: 01162 555 345 (Admin)
reunite@dircon.co.uk
www.reunite.org

Revision see Bitesize: BBC revision web site

RIBA see Architects (Royal Institute of British)

Ricability
Provides consumer information for elderly
and disabled consumers about useful
products and services
Unit G03 The Wenlock Business Centre 50-
52 Wharf Road London N1 7EU
Tel: 020 7427 2460 (voice)
Textphone: 020 7427 2469
mail@ricability.org.uk
www.ricability.org.uk

**Richard Dawkins Foundation for Reason
and Science**
Supports scientific education, critical
thinking and evidence-based understanding
of the natural world in the quest to
overcome religious fundamentalism,
superstition, intolerance and suffering
PO Box 866 Oxford OX1 9NQ
UKcontact@richarddawkins.net
richarddawkinsfoundation.org

RICS see Chartered Surveyors (Royal Institute
of)

Riding for the Disabled Association RDA
Norfolk House 1A Tournament Court
Edgehill Drive Warwick CV34 6LG
Tel: 0845 658 1082
info@rda.org.uk
www.rda.org.uk

**Rifle Association (National) of United
Kingdom**
Bisley Brookwood Surrey GU24 0PB
Tel: 01483 797777
info@nra.org.uk
www.nra.org.uk

Rights of Women
Research into the law affecting women & free
legal advice line for women
52-54 Featherstone St London EC1Y 8RT
Advice line: 020 7251 6577
Tel: 020 7251 6575 (Admin)
Textphone: 020 7490 2562
info@row.org.uk
www.rightsofwomen.org.uk

Rising Tide
UK coalition of groups committed to a
grassroots approach to fighting climate
change
62 Fieldgate Street London E1 1ES
Tel:+44 (0)7708 794665
info@risingtide.org.uk
www.risingtide.org.uk

**Riverside Museum: Scotland's Museum of
Transport and Travel**
100 Pointhouse Place Glasgow G3 8RS
Tel: 0141 287 2720
museums@glasgowlife.org.uk
www.glasgowlife.org.uk/museums/our-
museums/riverside-museum/Pages/default.
aspx

RNIB
UK's leading charity offering information,
support and advice to almost two million
people with sight loss
RNIB Headquarters 105 Judd Street London
WC1H 9NE
Helpline: 0303 123 9999
Tel: 020 7388 1266
email via website
www.rnib.org.uk

RNID now see Action on Hearing Loss

Road Haulage Association
Roadway House Bretton Way Bretton
Peterborough PE3 8DD
email via website
www.rha.uk.net

Road Runners Club
Represents road runners nationwide
www.roadrunnersclub.org.uk

RoadPeace UK National Charity for Road Crash
Victims
For bereaved & injured road traffic victims
Shakespeare Business Centre 245a
Coldharbour Lane Brixton London SW9 8RR
Helpline: 0845 4500355
Tel: 020 7733 1603
info@roadpeace.org
www.roadpeace.org

Roller Hockey (England)
42 Croft Avenue Letchworth Hertfordshire
SG6 1AP
email via website
www.englandrollerhockey.com

Roller Hockey Association (National) now
see Roller Hockey (England)

Roller Skating see Artistic Roller Skating
(Federation of)

Roman Legion Museum (National)
Researches, preserves and displays half a
million objects from Roman fortresses
High Street Caerleon NP18 1AE
Tel: 01633 423134
email via website
www.museumwales.ac.uk/en/roman/

Rona Sailing Project
Provides voyages for underprivileged and
disadvantaged youngsters aged 14-25 years
and for young people and adults with special
needs
Universal Marina Crableck Lane Sarisbury
Green Southampton SO31 7ZN
Tel: 01489 885098
email via website
www.ronasailingproject.org

Roofie Foundation
For people who have been drug raped or
sexually abused through drink spiking
1 Prime Parkway Prime Enterprise Park
Derby DE1 3QB
Tel: 01723 367251
email via website
www.roofie.com

Room to Read World Change Starts with
Educated Children
Seeks to transform the lives of millions of
children in developing countries by focusing
on literacy and gender equality in education
www.roomtoread.org

RoSPA Royal Society for the Prevention of
Accidents
RoSPA House 28 Calthorpe Road Edgbaston
Birmingham B15 1RP
Tel: 0121 248 2000
help@rospa.co.uk
www.rospa.com

Roundhouse
Performing arts venue
Chalk Farm Rd London NW1 8EH
Tel: 0844 482 8008
Tel: 020 7424 9991
info@roundhouse.org.uk
www.roundhouse.org.uk

Rowing see British Rowing

Rowntree see Joseph Rowntree Foundation

Roy Castle Lung Cancer Foundation
The only charity in the world wholly
dedicated to defeating lung cancer, the
biggest cancer killer in the world
Enterprise Way Wavertree Technology Park
Liverpool L13 1FB
Tel: 0333 323 7200
foundation@roycastle.org
www.roycastle.org

Royal Academy of Arts
independent, privately funded institution.
Promotes the creation, enjoyment and
appreciation of the visual arts through
exhibitions, education and debate
Burlington House Piccadilly London W1J 0BD
Tel: 020 7300 8000
Education: 020 7300 5995
Tickets: 0844 209 0051
email via website
www.royalacademy.org.uk

Royal Academy of Dance
Exists to promote knowledge, understanding
and practice of dance internationally
36 Battersea Sq London SW11 3RA
Tel: 020 7326 8000
info@rad.org.uk
www.rad.org.uk

Royal Academy of Dramatic Art see RADA

Royal Academy of Music
Britain's senior music conservatoire, training
performers and composers. Part of the
University of London
Marylebone Rd London NW1 5HT
Tel: 020 7873 7373
email via website
www.ram.ac.uk

Royal Air Force
www.raf.mod.uk

Royal Airforce Museum Cosford
Shifnal Shropshire TF11 8UP
Tel: 01902 376 200
cosford@rafmuseum.org
www.rafmuseum.org.uk/cosford/

Royal Airforce Museum London
Grahame Park Way London NW9 5LL
Tel: 020 8205 2266
Tel:020 8358 4964 (24Hr info line)
london@rafmuseum.org
www.rafmuseum.org.uk/london/

Royal Armouries National museum of arms
and armour Fort Nelson
Trace the development of artillery from pre-
gunpowder siege machines to modern-day
super guns. There are over 350 big guns on
display
Portsdown Hill Road Fareham PO17 6AN
Tel: 01329 233 734
fnenquiries@armouries.org.uk
www.royalarmouries.org

Royal Armouries HM Tower of London
Trace the development of artillery from pre-gunpowder siege machines to modern-day super guns. There are over 350 big guns on display
London EC3N 4AB
Tel: 020 3166 6660
www.royalarmouries.org

Royal Armouries Museum National Museum of Arms and Armour Leeds
Armouries Drive Leeds LS10 1LT
Tel: 0113 220 1999
enquiries@armouries.org.uk
www.royalarmouries.org

Royal Ballet
Royal Opera House Covent Garden London WC2E 9DD
Tel: 020 7240 1200 (Admin)
Tel: 020 7304 4000 (Box Office & Info)
Email via website
www.roh.org.uk

Royal Botanic Garden Edinburgh
Made up of four gardens, together representing one of the world's largest living collection of plants
20a Inverleith Row Edinburgh EH3 5LR
Tel: 0131 552 7171
Email via website
www.rbge.org.uk

Royal Botanic Gardens, Kew
Saving plants for life
Richmond Surrey TW9 3AB
Tel: 020 8332 5655
Tel: 020 8332 5655 (24-hour visitor info
info@kew.org
www.kew.org

Royal College of Veterinary Surgeons RCVS
Belgravia House 62-64 Horseferry Rd
London SW1P 2AF
Tel: 020 7222 2001
info@rcvs.org.uk
www.rcvs.org.uk

Royal Geographical Society with The Institute of British Geographers
Promotes, supports and enhances geographical research, education, fieldwork and expeditions and the professional accreditation of geographers
1 Kensington Gore London SW7 2AR
Tel: 020 7591 3000
Email via website
www.rgs.org

Royal Horticultural Society
The UK's leading gardening charity dedicated to promoting good gardening
80 Vincent Square London SW1P 2PE
Tel: 0845 260 5000
Email via website
www.rhs.org.uk

Royal Institution of Great Britain
Independent charity dedicated to connecting people with the world of science. Also an events space and museum
21 Albemarle Street London W1S 4BS
Tel: 020 7409 2992
ri@ri.ac.uk
www.rigb.org

Royal Mail see Post Office

Royal Mint (British)
World's leading export mint. Makes and distributes United Kingdom coins as well as supplying blanks and official medals
Freepost NAT23496 PO Box 500 Llantrisant Pontyclun CF72 8YT
Tel: 01443 222111
Email via website
www.royalmint.com

Royal National Lifeboat Institution
Charity that saves lives at sea and provides sea safety and educational resources
West Quay Road Poole Dorset BH15 1HZ
Tel: 0845 045 6999
email via website
www.rnli.org.uk

Royal Naval Museum
Making the story of the Royal Navy and its people, from earliest times to the present, accessible to all
HM Naval Base (PP66) Portsmouth PO1 3NH
023 9272 7562
email via website
www.royalnavalmuseum.org

Royal Navy
www.royalnavy.mod.uk

Royal Observatory, Greenwich
Home of Greenwich Mean Time and the Prime Meridian of the World, making it the official starting point for each new day and year. Also home to London's only planetarium, the Harrison timekeepers and the UK's largest refracting telescope
Blackheath Avenue Greenwich SE10 8XJ
National Maritime Museum switchboard: 020 8858 4422
Recorded information line: 020 8312 6565
Bookings: 020 8312 6608
www.rmg.co.uk/royal-observatory

Royal Opera
Royal Opera House Covent Garden London WC2E 9DD
Tel: 020 7240 1200 (Admin)
Tel: 020 7304 4000 (Box Office & Info)
email via website
www.roh.org.uk

Royal Parks
Locations and history
The Old Police House Hyde Park London
W2 2UH
Tel: 0300 061 2000
hq@royalparks.gsi.gov.uk
www.royalparks.org.uk

Royal School for the Blind see SeeAbility

Royal Scottish Academy
Promotes living artists in Scotland through
its annual and student shows, scholarships,
awards and other exhibitions
The Mound Edinburgh EH2 2EL
Tel: 0131 225 6671
Email via website
www.royalscottishacademy.org

Royal Shakespeare Theatre see RSC

Royal Society
Fellowship of the world's most eminent
scientists and is the oldest scientific academy
in continuous existence. Aims to expand the
frontiers of knowledge by championing the
development and use of science, mathematics,
engineering and medicine for the benefit of
humanity and the good of the planet
6-9 Carlton House Terrace London SW1Y
5AG
Tel: 020 7451 2500
email: specific addresses listed on website
royalsociety.org

Royal Society of Medicine RSM
Educational activities and opportunities for
doctors, dentists, veterinary surgeons and
allied professions
1 Wimpole Street London W1G 0AE
Tel: 020 7290 2900
www.rsm.ac.uk

Royalty see British Monarchy (The official
website of)

RSA Royal Society for the Encouragement of
Arts, Manufactures and Commerce
To develop and promote new ways of
thinking about human fulfilment and social
progress
8 John Adam St London WC2N 6EZ
Tel: 020 7930 5115
general@rsa.org.uk
www.thersa.org

RSA Exams see OCR/Oxford Cambridge and
RSA Examinations

RSC Royal Shakespeare Company
Royal Shakespeare Theatre Waterside
Stratford-upon-Avon Warwickshire CV37 6BB
Tel: 0844 800 1110 (General and tickets)
Tel: 0844 800 1113 (School tickets)
Email via website
www.rsc.org.uk

RSM see Royal Society of Medicine

RSPB Royal Society for the Protection of Birds
The Lodge Potton Road Sandy Bedfordshire
SG19 2DL
Tel: 01767 680551
Email via website
www.rspb.org.uk

RSPCA Royal Society for the Prevention of
Cruelty to Animals
Animal welfare charity
Wilberforce Way Southwater Horsham West
Sussex RH13 9RS
Cruelty Line: 0300 1234 999 (24 hrs)
Advice Line: 0300 1234 555
www.rspca.org.uk

RSSPCC see CHILDREN 1ST

RSVP see Retired and Senior Volunteer
Programme

RTPI see Town Planning Institute (Royal)

Rugby see also Scrum.com, World Rugby
Museum

Rugby Football League
Red Hall Red Hall Lane Leeds LS17 8NB
Tel: 0844 477 7113
enquiries@rfl.uk.com
www.rfl.uk.com

Rugby Football Union
Rugby House Twickenham Stadium 200
Whitton Road Twickenham Middlesex TW2 7BA
Tel: 0871 222 2120
enquiries@therfu.com
www.rfu.com

Rugby Football Union (Irish)
10/12 Lansdowne Rd Dublin 4 Ireland
Tel: 00 353 1 647 3800
info@irishrugby.ie
www.irishrugby.ie

Rugby Football Union for Women
Co-ordinating body for women's rugby in
the UK
Rugby House Twickenham Stadium 200
Whitton Road Twickenham
Middlesex TW2 7BA
Tel: 0871 222 2120
enquiries@therfu.com
www.rfu.com/womensRugbyPortal/

Runaway Helpline see also Missing People
and Message Home
National, free, confidential service, provided
by the charity Missing People, for anyone
who has run away from home or care, or
been forced to leave home
Helpline: 116 000 (free, confidential and
24/7)
Text 116 000 (can text even if no credit left
on your mobile phone)
General enquiries: 020 8392 4590
116000@missingpeople.org.uk
www.runawayhelpline.org.uk

Runnymede Trust

Conducts research & policy analysis in racial equality and cultural diversity
7 Plough Yard Shoreditch London EC2A 3LP
Tel: 020 7377 9222
info@runnymedetrust.org
www.runnymedetrust.org

Rural affairs see CLA, Communities in Rural England (Action with), Countryside Alliance, CPRE: Campaign to Protect Rural England, Defra, Natural England, Protection of Rural Wales (Campaign for the), Self Unlimited

Rural Communities (Commission for)

To promote awareness of the social and economic needs of people who live and work in rural areas and help decision-makers across and beyond government identify how those needs can best be addressed
Unit 1 Saw Mill End Corinium Avenue
Gloucester GL4 3DE
Defra Helpline: 08459 33 55 77
Tel: 01452 627508
info@ruralcommunities.gov.uk
www.ruralcommunities.gov.uk

Rural Research (Centre for)

An academic research unit specialising in economic, social, agricultural and environmental change in the countryside
Institute of Science and the Environment
University of Worcester Henwick Road
Worcester WR2 6AJ
Tel: 01905 855185
crr@worc.ac.uk
www.worc.ac.uk/crr

Rural Scotland (Association for the Protection of) APRS

Scotland's countryside champion
Gladstone's Land (3rd Floor) 483
Lawnmarket Edinburgh EH1 2NT
Tel: 0131 225 7012
info@ruralscotland.org
www.ruralscotland.btik.com

Ruskin College

To enable mature students with little or no qualifications to study
Walton St Oxford OX1 2HE
Tel: 01865 759600
enquiries@ruskin.ac.uk
www.ruskin.ac.uk

RYA Sailability

National body for all forms of boating, including dinghy and yacht racing, motor and sail cruising, sports boats, powerboat racing, windsurfing, inland cruising and narrowboats. Offers training, advice and support to those with disabilities to take up the sport
RYA House Ensign Way Hamble
Southampton SO31 4YA
Tel: 0844 556 9550
Text: 07823559018
sailability@rya.org.uk
www.rya.org.uk/programmes/ryasailability/Pages/RYASailability.aspx

S

S4C
Welsh fourth TV channel
Parc Ty Glas Llanishen Cardiff CF14 5DU
Tel: 0870 600 4141
Email via website
www.s4c.co.uk
www.s4c.co.uk/e_index.shtml

SACRO Safeguarding Communities - Reducing Offending in Scotland
Services to reduce conflict and offending, to make communities safer
29 Albany Street Edinburgh EH1 3QN
Tel: 0131 624 7270
info@national.sacro.org.uk
www.sacro.org.uk

SAD see Seasonal Affective Disorder Association

Safe Standing see Football Supporters' Federation

Safer Medicines Campaign
Scientists and medical professionals who question the value of testing human drugs on animals
PO Box 62720 London SW2 9FQ
Tel: 020 8265 2880
info@safermedicines.org
www.safermedicines.org

Saferworld
Independent foreign affairs think tank working for prevention of armed conflict
The Grayston Centre 28 Charles Square
London N1 6HT
Tel: 020 7324 4646
general@saferworld.org.uk
www.saferworld.co.uk

Safety Council (British)
Corporate membership organisation that provides health, safety and environmental training, auditing, information and publications
70 Chancellors Rd London W6 9RS
Tel: 020 8741 1231
info@britsafe.org
www.britsafe.org

Sailing see also Cirdan Sailing Trust, Ellen MacArthur Trust, Historical Maritime Society, Jubilee Sailing Trust, Marine Leisure Association, Ocean Youth Trust, Rona Sailing Project, RYA Sailability, Sea Ranger Association, Tall Ships Youth Trust

Salvation Army
101 Newington Causeway London SE1 6BN
Tel: 020 7367 4500
Email via website
www.salvationarmy.org.uk

SALVO Architectural Salvage Listings
www.salvo.co.uk

Samaritans
See website for local branches. Samaritans offer 24 hour emotional support to anyone in distress in the UK and Republic of Ireland. See Befrienders Worldwide for international centres and support
PO Box 9090 Stirling FK8 2SA
Tel: 08457 909090
jo@samaritans.org
www.samaritans.org

Samaritans International
Charitable non-profit corporation whose sole purpose is feeding and helping destitute children
www.samaritansinternational.org

SAMH see Mental Health (Scottish Association for)

SAMM Support After Murder & Manslaughter
Offers support and understanding to families bereaved through murder and manslaughter
Pershore Road Edgbaston
Birmingham B5 7RN
Hotline: 0845 872 3440
Tel: 0121 471 1200 (enquiries)
info@samm.org.uk
www.samm.org.uk

Sand & Land Yacht Clubs (British Federation of)
www.bfslyc.org.uk

SANDS Stillbirth & Neonatal Death Charity
Supporting anyone affected by the death of a baby and promoting research to reduce the loss of babies' lives
28 Portland Place London W1B 1LY
Helpline: 020 7436 5881
Tel: 020 7436 7940
support@uk-sands.org
www.uk-sands.org

SANE Meeting the challenge of mental illness
Works to raise mental health awareness; combat stigma and increase understanding
First Floor Cityside House 40 Adler St
London E1 1EE
Helpline: 0845 767 8000
Tel: 020 7375 1002
Email via website
www.sane.org.uk

Sargent Cancer Care for Children now see CLICSargent

Save A Cup
Scheme set up to collect and recycle used plastic vending cups.
Falcon Point Park Plaza Heath Hayes
Cannock Staffs WS12 2DE
Tel: 01543 505210
sales@save-a-cup.co.uk
www.save-a-cup.co.uk

Save the Children UK
Emergency relief runs alongside long-term development & prevention work
1 St John's Lane London EC1M 4AR
Tel: 020 7012 6400
supporter.care@savethechildren.org.uk
www.savethechildren.org.uk

Saving Faces
Raises awareness about facial disfigurement through art. Fundraising charity for research into the causes of facial cancers and other conditions leading to disfigurement
St Bartholomew's Hospital West Smithfield London EC1A 7BE
Tel: 0203 46 55755
Email via website
www.savingfaces.co.uk

Scarlet Centre
Eaves project providing advice and drop-in support to women who are affected by domestic violence, rape or sexual abuse, homelessness, prostitution, mental health and/or substance misuse problems
Tel; 020 7840 7142 from Tuesdays-Saturday
www.eaves4women.co.uk/Scarlet_Centre/Scarlet_centre.php

Schizophrenia see also Rethink

School Councils UK
Charity training teachers & pupils to set up effective structures for pupil involvement
The Old Dairy Victoria Street Felixstowe IP11 7EW
Tel: 0845 4569428
email via website
www.schoolcouncils.org

School Food Trust
National charity and specialist adviser to government on school meals, children's food and related skills
3rd Floor
1 East Parade Sheffield S1 2ET
Tel: 0114 2996901
info@childrensfoodtrust.org.uk
www.schoolfoodtrust.org.uk

School Governors (National Association of) see Governors' Association (National)

School Journey Association
Educational tours for school groups and young people
48 Cavendish Rd London SW12 0DH
Tel: 020 8675 6636
thesja@btconnect.com
www.sjatours.org

School Librarianship (International Association of) IASL
Provides an international forum for those interested in promoting school library programmes worldwide
www.iasl-online.org

School Library Association
Committed to promotion and development of libraries and information literacy in schools
1 Pine Court Kembrey Park Wanborough Swindon SN2 8AD
Tel: 01793 530166
info@sla.org.uk
www.sla.org.uk

Schools Adjudicator (Office of the)
Decides on schools organisation issues & admission arrangements which can't be resolved locally
via website
www.education.gov.uk/schoolsadjudicator

Schools Health Education Unit
3 Manaton Court Manaton Park Exeter EX2 8PF
Tel: 01392 667272
sheu@sheu.org.uk
www.sheu.org.uk

Schools Music Association of Great Britain
SMA provides a vital link between school music teachers and the education policy makers
24 Royston Street Potton Bedfordshire SG19 2LP
email via website
www.schoolsmusic.org.uk

Schumacher see also Practical Action

Schumacher UK
Promotes human scale sustainable development "as though people matter" in the UK and abroad
Create Environment Centre Smeaton Rd Bristol BS1 6XN
Tel: 0117 903 1081
email via website
www.schumacher.org.uk

SCIAF Scottish Catholic International Aid Fund
Works in over 16 countries across Asia, Africa and Latin America, to help some of the poorest people in the world, regardless of religion, to work their way out of poverty
19 Park Circus Glasgow G3 6BE
Tel: 0141 354 5555
sciaf@sciaf.org.uk
www.sciaf.org.uk

SCIcentre The National Centre for Initial Teacher Training in Primary School Science
Produces resources to help with the training of student teachers in the teaching of science
School of Education University of Leicester 21 University Road Leicester LE1 7RF
Tel: 0116 252 3659
iab6@le.ac.uk
www.le.ac.uk/se/centres/sci/SCIcentre.html

Science Association (British)
Nationwide organisation dedicated to public engagement with science through programmes and membership
Wellcome Wolfson Building 165 Queen's Gate London SW7 5HD
Tel: 0870 770 7101
email via website
www.britishscienceassociation.org

Science Centre (Glasgow)
Visitor attraction presenting concepts of science and technology in unique and inspiring ways
50 Pacific Quay Glasgow G51 1EA
Tel: 0141 420 5000
Email via website
www.gsc.org.uk

Science Education (Association for)
The subject association for teachers, technicians and others involved in science education
College Lane Hatfield Herts AL10 9AA
Tel: 01707 283000
info@ase.org.uk
www.ase.org.uk

Science Education (Centre for)
Sheffield Hallam University City Campus Howard St Sheffield S1 1WB
Tel: 0114 225 4870
email via website
www.shu.ac.uk/research/cse/

Science in the Public Interest (Center for)
US organisation that focuses on food and alcohol & on reducing the carnage caused by alcoholic beverages
www.cspinet.org

Science Museum
Exhibition Road London SW7 2DD
Tel: 0870 870 4868
Email via website
www.sciencemuseum.org.uk

Science, Technology & the Arts (National Endowment for) NESTA
Promotes talent, innovation and creativity
1 Plough Place London EC4A 1DE
Tel: 020 7438 2500
information@nesta.org.uk
www.nesta.org.uk

Scientific Exploration Society
Expeditions for ordinary people to do extraordinary things for conservation and the environment
Expedition Base Motcombe Shaftesbury Dorset SP7 9PB
Tel: 01747 853353
Email via website
www.ses-explore.org

Scientists for Global Responsibility
Promotes ethical science and technology
Ingles Manor Castle Hill Avenue Folkestone CT20 2RD
Tel: 01303 851965
info@sgr.org.uk
www.sgr.org.uk/

Scoliosis Association (UK)
Links sufferers from curvature of the spine
4 Ivebury Court 325 Latimer Rd London W10 6RA
Helpline: 020 8964 1166
Tel: 020 8964 5343
info@sauk.org.uk
www.sauk.org.uk

Scope
Disability organisation whose focus is people with cerebral palsy
6 Market Rd London N7 9PW
Helpline: 0808 800 3333
Switchboard: 020 7619 7100
response@scope.org.uk
www.scope.org.uk

Scotland Office
Dover House Whitehall London SW1A 2AU
Tel: 020 7270 6754
Email via website
www.scotlandoffice.gov.uk

Scotland Street School Museum
Tells the story of education in Scotland over a hundred years, from the late 19th century to the late 20th century
225 Scotland Street Glasgow G5 8QB
Tel: 0141 287 0500
Text Phone: 0141 287 0513
museums@glasgowlife.org.uk
www.glasgowlife.org.uk/museums/our-museums/scotland-street-school/Pages/home.aspx

Scots Language Centre
A K Bell Library York Place Perth PH2 8EP
Tel: 01738 440199
info@scotslanguage.com
www.scotslanguage.com

Scottish Arts Council now see Creative Scotland

Scottish Awards Agency now see Student Awards Agency for Scotland

Scottish Ballet
Scotland's National Dance Company
Tramway 25 Albert Drive Glasgow G41 2PE
Tel: 0141 331 2931
email via website
www.scottishballet.co.uk

Scottish Canals
Looking after Scottish canals and conserving their heritage
Canal House 1 Applecross Street Glasgow G4 9SP
Tel: 0141 332 6936
enquiries@scottishcanals.co.uk
www.scottishcanals.co.uk

Scottish Cultural Resources Access Network now see SCRAN

Scottish Cycle Union now see Scottish Cycling

Scottish Cycling
Caledonia House South Gyle Edinburgh EH12 9DQ
Tel: 0131 317 9704
info@scottishcycling.org.uk
www.britishcycling.org.uk/scotland

Scottish Environment LINK
Umbrella organisation providing forum and network for voluntary environmental groups
2 Grosvenor House Shore Rd Perth PH2 8BD
Tel: 01738 630804
Email via website
www.scotlink.org

Scottish Government
St Andrew's House Regent Road Edinburgh EH1 3DG
Tel: 0131 556 8400
Tel: 08457 741 741
Minicom: 0131 244 1829
ceu@scotland.gsi.gov.uk
www.scotland.gov.uk

Scottish National Disability Information Service see UPDATE

Scottish National Gallery
The Mound Edinburgh EH2 2EL
Tel: 0131 624 6200
nginfo@nationalgalleries.org
www.nationalgalleries.org

Scottish National Gallery of Modern Art
Collection of modern and contemporary art
75 Belford Rd Edinburgh EH4 3DR
Tel: 0131 624 6200
gmainfo@nationalgalleries.org
www.nationalgalleries.org

Scottish National Party see SNP

Scottish Opera
39 Elmbank Crescent Glasgow G2 4PT
Tel: 0141 248 4567
information@scottishopera.org.uk
www.scottishopera.org.uk

Scottish Parliament
Edinburgh EH99 1SP
Tel: 0131 348 5000
Tel: 0800 092 7500
Textphone: 0800 092 7100
sp.info@scottish.parliament.uk
www.scottish.parliament.uk

Scottish Qualifications Authority SQA
Main body in Scotland, responsible for all qualifications except degrees and some professional qualifications
Lowden, 24 Wester Shawfair Dalkeith Midlothian EH22 1FD
Tel: 0845 279 1000
customer@sqa.org.uk
www.sqa.org.uk

Scottish SPCA
Animal welfare charity
Kingseat Road Halbeath Dunfermline KY11 8RY
Tel: 03000 999 999
Email via website
www.scottishspca.org

Scottish Tourist Board now see VisitScotland

Scottish Youth Theatre
Scotland's national theatre 'for and by' young people
The Old Sheriff Court 105 Brunswick Street Glasgow G1 1TF
Tel: 0141 552 3988
info@scottishyouththeatre.org
www.scottishyouththeatre.org

scottishathletics
Governing body for athletics in Scotland
Caledonia House South Gyle Edinburgh EH12 9DQ
Tel: 0131 539 7320
admin@scottishathletics.org.uk
www.scottishathletics.org.uk

Scout Association
Gilwell Park Chingford London E4 7QW
Tel: 0845 300 1818
info.centre@scouts.org.uk
www.scouts.org.uk

SCRAN
Part of the Royal Commission on the Ancient and Historical Monuments of Scotland - aims to provide educational access to digital materials representing our material culture and history
John Sinclair House 16 Bernard Terrace Edinburgh EH8 9NX
Tel: 0131 662 1456
Email via website
www.scran.ac.uk

Scrum.com
Rugby website
www.espnscrum.com/

Sea Ranger Association
For girls aged 10-21, all forms of boating
'Lord Amory' 631 Manchester Road Dollar
Bay London E14 3NU
info@searangers.org.uk
www.searangers.org.uk

Seafish
Supports the seafood industry for a
sustainable, profitable future
18 Logie Mill Logie Green Rd Edinburgh
EH7 4HS
Tel: 0131 558 3331
seafish@seafish.co.uk
www.seafish.org

Sealed Knot Ltd
Charity teaching about the 17th century by
re-enacting civil war battles
Burlington House Botleigh Grange Business
Park Southampton SO30 2DF
Email via website
www.thesealedknot.org.uk

Searchlight Magazine Ltd
Anti-racism and fascism monthly magazine
PO Box 1576 Ilford IG5 0NG
email via website
www.searchlightmagazine.com

Seasonal Affective Disorder Association
SAD
Advises sufferers. Informs public & health
professions
PO Box 989 Steyning West Sussex BN44
3HG
Tel: 01903 814942
www.sada.org.uk

SEBDA Social, Emotional & Behavioural
Difficulties Association
c/o Goldwyn School Godinton Lane, Great
Chart Ashford TN23 3BT
Tel: 01233 622958
admin@sebda.org
www.sebda.org

Secular Society (National)
Fights religious privilege & upholds the
rights of those without religion. Works for
separation of Church and State
25 Red Lion Square London WC1R 4RL
Tel: 020 7404 3126
enquiries@secularism.org.uk
www.secularism.org.uk

SeeAbility
Supports adults who are visually impaired
with multiple disabilities including; learning,
physical and mental health disabilities,
acquired brain injuries and degenerative
conditions, to explore their potential
SeeAbility House 1a Hook Rd Epsom Surrey
KT19 8SQ
Tel: 01372 755 000
enquiries@seeability.org
www.seeability.org

Self Unlimited
Maintains a network of support services
for people with learning disabilities across
the country. Assisting people to live as
independently as possible and to realise
their full potential
14 Nursery Court Kibworth Business Park
Harborough Road Kibworth Leicester LE8
0EX
Tel: 0116 279 3225
info@selfunlimited.co.uk
www.selfunlimited.co.uk

Self-Injury Guidance & Network Support
see FirstSigns

Sense For deafblind people
National charity that supports and
campaigns for children and adults. Gives
advice, information and specialist services to
deafblind people, their families, carers and
the professionals who work with them
101 Pentonville Road London N1 9LG
Tel: 0845 127 0060
Textphone: 0845 127 0066
info@sense.org.uk
www.sense.org.uk

Sense about Science
Equips people to make sense of scientific
and medical claims in public discussion
14a Clerkenwell Green   London EC1R 0DP
Tel: 020 7490 9590
enquiries@senseaboutscience.org
www.senseaboutscience.org

Sentencing, prison and probation
www.direct.gov.uk/en/
CrimeJusticeAndTheLaw/
Sentencingprisonandprobation/index.htm

SEPA see Environment Protection Agency
(Scottish)

Serene now see Cry-sis

Serious Fraud Office
Elm House 10-16 Elm St London WC1X 0BJ
Tel; 0300 123 2040 (Report a fraud)
Tel: 020 7239 7272
Email via website
www.sfo.gov.uk

Seven Stories

Exhibitions, activities and events based on children's books
30 Lime Street Ouseburn Valley Newcastle upon Tyne NE1 2PQ
Tel: 0845 271 0777 ext 715
info@sevenstories.org.uk
www.sevenstories.org.uk

Sex Education Forum

Information and support for teachers and other professionals
National Children's Bureau 8 Wakley St London EC1V 7QE
Tel: 020 7843 6000
enquiries@ncb.org.uk
www.ncb.org.uk/sef

Sexual Abuse see SurvivorsUK

Sexual Advice Association

Provides advice & information on male and female sexual problems
Suite 301 Emblem House London Bridge Hospital 27 Tooley Street London SE1 2PR
Helpline: 0207 486 7262
info@sexualadviceassociation.co.uk
www.sda.uk.net

SFA see Football Association (Scottish)

SFL see Football League (Scottish)

Shakespeare see also Folger Shakespeare Library, RSC

Shakespeare Association (British)

Professional association of teachers, researchers, theatre practitioners, writers and anyone who regularly works with Shakespeare's plays and poems
www.britishshakespeare.ws

Shakespeare at the Tobacco Factory

Theatre company producing large-cast professional Shakespeare
The Tobacco Factory Raleigh Rd Bristol BS3 1TF
Tel: 0117 963 3054
email via website
www.sattf.org.uk

Shakespeare Birthplace Trust

Lectures, workshops, day schools, courses & library with archive of Royal Shakespeare Company
The Shakespeare Centre Henley St Stratford-upon-Avon CV37 6QW
Tel: 01789 204016
info@shakespeare.org.uk
www.shakespeare.org.uk

Shakespeare Schools Festival

Largest youth drama festival in the UK
140 London Wall Road London EC2Y 5DN
Tel: 020 7601 1800
enquiries@ssf.uk.com
www.ssf.uk.com

Shakespeare's Globe Theatre

21 New Globe Walk Bankside London SE1 9DT
Tel: 020 7902 1400
info@shakespearesglobe.com
www.shakespearesglobe.com

Shared Experience

Theatre company with a distinctive performance style that celebrates the union of physical and text-based theatre
Oxford Playhouse 11-12 Beaumont Street Oxford OX1 2LW
Tel: 01865 305321
email via website
www.sharedexperience.org.uk

Shared Interest Society Ltd

Ethical investment - finance for fair trade
2 Cathedral Square The Groat Market Newcastle-upon-Tyne NE1 1EH
Tel: 0191 233 9100
info@shared-interest.com
www.shared-interest.com

Shared Parenting Information Group SPIG

To encourage and promote the continuation of parenting by both parents after family breakdown.
www.spig.clara.net

ShareGift

Charity share donation scheme exists to make it easy to give any number of shares to charity
17 Carlton House Terrace London SW1Y 5AH
Telephone: 020 7930 3737
help@sharegift.org.uk
www.sharegift.org

Shark Alliance

Restoring and conserving shark populations by improving shark conservation policies
www.sharkalliance.org

Shelter
Works to alleviate the distress caused by homelessness and bad housing by giving advice, information and advocacy to people in housing need, and by campaigning for lasting political change
88 Old St London EC1V 9HU
Housing Advice Helpline: 0808 800 4444
Tel: 0844 515 2000
info@shelter.org.uk
www.shelter.org.uk

& Cymru
25 Walter Road Swansea SA1 5NN
Housing Support: 0845 075 5005
Email via website
www.sheltercymru.org.uk

& Scotland
4th Floor, Scotiabank House 6 South Charlotte Street Edinburgh EH2 4AW
Housing Advice Helpline: 0808 800 4444
Tel: 0344 515 2000
email via website
scotland.shelter.org.uk/

Shiatsu Society (UK)
Complementary therapy based on oriental medicine
PO Box 4580 Rugby CV21 9EL
Tel: 0845 130 4560
Email via website
www.shiatsusociety.org

Shine Association for Spina Bifida & Hydrocephalus
Europe's largest organisation dedicated to supporting individuals and families as they face the challenges arising from spina bifida and hydrocephalus
42 Park Road Peterborough PE1 2UQ
Tel: 01733 555988
email via website
www.shinecharity.org.uk

Shine a Light
Helping young homeless people via grassroots organisations in Latin America
www.shinealight.org

Shingles Support Society
Enclose sae for information on all aspects of herpes virus infections
41 North Rd London N7 9DP
Helpline: 0845 123 2305
info@shinglessupport.org.uk
www.shinglessupport.org

Shoplifting see Crisis Counselling for Alleged Shoplifters

Shopmobility (National Federation of)
NFSUK
Aims to promote equality of access and to encourage independence of people with disabilities (permanent or temporary), through the provision of mobility equipment such as scooters, wheelchairs and power chairs
PO Box 6641 Christchurch BH23 9DQ
Tel: 0844 41 41 850
info@shopmobilityuk.org
www.shopmobilityuk.org

Short Persons Support
www.shortsupport.org

Show Jumping Association (British)
National Agricultural Centre Stoneleigh Park Kenilworth CV8 2LR
Tel: 024 7669 8800
email via website
www.britishshowjumping.co.uk

Show Racism the Red Card
Against racism in football
PO Box 141 Whitley Bay Tyne & Wear NE26 3YH
Tel: 0191 257 8519
info@theredcard.org
www.srtrc.org

Sibs For brothers and sisters of disabled children and adults
Support siblings of all ages who are growing up with or who have grown up with a brother or sister with any disability, long term chronic illness, or life limiting condition
Meadowfield Oxenhope West Yorkshire BD22 9JD
Tel: 01535 645453
info@sibs.org.uk
www.sibs.org.uk

Sick Children (Action for)
Aims to improve standards in children's healthcare
32b Buxton Rd, High Lane Stockport SK6 8BH
Helpline: 0800 0744 519
Tel: 01663 763 004
Email via website
www.actionforsickchildren.org

Sickle Cell Society
Provides info, counselling & care for people with sickle cell disorder
54 Station Rd London NW10 4UA
Tel: 020 8961 7795
info@sicklecellsociety.org
www.sicklecellsociety.org

Sightsavers
Projects to prevent & cure blindness in the developing world and train incurably blind people
Grosvenor Hall Bolnore Rd Haywards Heath RH16 4BX
Tel: 01444 446600
info@sightsavers.org
www.sightsavers.org

Signature Excellence in communication with deaf people
Promotes communication between deaf & hearing people. National examination board of British Sign Language
Mersey House Mandale Business Park Belmont Durham DH1 1TH
Tel: 0191 383 1155
Tel: 0191 383 7915 (Textphone Answerphone)
durham@signature.org.uk
www.signature.org.uk

Signed Performances in Theatre see SPIT

Sikh Organisations (Network of) NSO
Addresses issues of common concern and organises celebration of Sikh activities
Suite 405 Highland House 165 The Broadway Wimbledon SW19 1NE
Tel: 020 8544 8037
sikhmessenger@aol.com
www.nsouk.co.uk

Simon Community
Provides caring & campaigns for London's street homeless
St. Joseph's House 129 Malden Road London NW5 4HS
Tel: 020 7485 6639
Tel: 020 7482 0447
info@simoncommunity.org.uk
www.simoncommunity.org.uk

Simon Jones Memorial Campaign
Campaigned against the dangers of casualisation of the workforce, following the death of Simon Jones in 1998. Now acts as archive and link to other campaigns.
action@simonjones.org.uk
www.simonjones.org.uk

Simon Wiesenthal Centre
International Jewish human rights organisation dedicated to preserving the memory of the Holocaust
www.wiesenthal.com

Simple Free Law Advisor
www.sfla.co.uk

Siobhan Dowd Trust
Bringing books and reading to disadvantaged young people in the UK through the legacy of an award winning writer
c/o 46b Vanbrugh Park Blackheath London SE3 7JQ
Email via website
www.siobhandowdtrust.com/

Ski Club of Great Britain
The White House 57-63 Church Rd Wimbledon London SW19 5SB
Tel: 0845 45 807 80
Tel: 020 8410 2000
skiers@skiclub.co.uk
www.skiclub.co.uk

Skills for Care
Aiming to modernise adult social care in England, by ensuring qualifications and standards continually adapt to meet the changing needs of people who use care services
West Gate 6 Grace Street Leeds LS1 2RP
Tel: 0113 245 1716
info@skillsforcare.org.uk
www.skillsforcare.org.uk

Skills for Justice Developing skills for safer communities
Works with employers to raise skills across the Justice Sector
Centre Court Atlas Way Sheffield S4 7QQ
Tel: 0114 261 1499
info@skillsforjustice.com
www.skillsforjustice.com

Skills Funding Agency
Funds and regulates adult further education and skills training in England
Cheylesmore House Quinton Road Coventry CV1 2WT
Tel: 0845 377 5000
info@skillsfundingagency.bis.gov.uk
skillsfundingagency.bis.gov.uk

Skillshare International
Development agency working in Africa and Asia
Imperial House St Nicholas Circle Leicester LE1 4LF
Tel: 0116 254 1862
info@skillshare.org
www.skillshare.org

Skin Care Campaign SCC
Working to improve the quality of life for more than 15 million people in the UK with skin conditions
www.skincarecampaign.org

Skin Foundation (British)
Tel: 0207 391 6341
email via website
www.britishskinfoundation.org.uk

Sky British Sky Broadcasting
www.sky.com

Skylight Circus Arts
Circus skills workshops and projects for
young people, can lead to performances
email via website
www.skylightcircusarts.com

Slate Museum (National)
Llanberis Gwynedd LL55 4TY
Tel: 029 2057 3700
email via website
www.museumwales.ac.uk/en/slate/

Slavery see Anti-Slavery International

Slavery Museum (International)
Hear the untold stories of enslaved people
and learn about historical and contemporary
slavery
Dock Traffic Office Albert Dock Liverpool
L3 4AX
Tel: 0151 478 4499
email via website
www.liverpoolmuseums.org.uk/ism

Sleep Council
Promotes the benefits to health of a good
night's sleep. Non-profit organisation funded
by bed manufacturers & retailers.
High Corn Mill Chapel Hill Skipton
N Yorkshire BD23 1NL
Freephone leaflet line: 0800 018 7923
Tel: 0845 058 4595
info@sleepcouncil.org.uk
www.sleepcouncil.org.uk

Slivers of Time
Social enterprise running online
marketplaces where anyone can sell spare
hours, on their own terms, to multiple
employers.
www.sliversoftime.com

Slow Food UK
To save & protect small-scale quality
specialist food production from industrial
standardisation & to list & protect threatened
varieties of foodstuffs
6 Neal's Yard Covent Garden London WC2H
9DP
Tel: 020 7099 1132
info@slowfood.org.uk
www.slowfood.org.uk

**Small Animal Veterinary Association
(British)**
Woodrow House 1 Telford Way Waterwells
Business Park Quedgeley Gloucester GL2
2AB
Tel: 01452 726700
administration@bsava.com
www.bsava.com

Small Businesses (Federation of)
UK's largest campaigning pressure group
promoting and protecting the interests of
the self-employed and owners of small firms
Sir Frank Whittle Way Blackpool Business
Park Blackpool FY4 2FE
Tel: 01253 336000
email via website
www.fsb.org.uk

Smallpeice Trust
Engineering awareness courses for students
13 - 18 years old
Holly House 74 Upper Holly Walk
Leamington Spa Warwickshire CV32 4JL
Tel: 01926 333200
info@smallpeicetrust.org.uk
www.smallpeicetrust.org.uk

Smith Institute
Independent think-tank undertaking
research/education in issues arising from
interaction of equality and enterprise
Somerset House South Wing Strand
London WC2R 1LA
Tel: 020 7845 5845
info@smith-institute.org.uk
www.smith-institute.org.uk

Smokefree (NHS)
NHS Smoking Helpline: 0800 022 4332
smokefree.nhs.uk

Snow and Ice Data Center (National)
Support scientific research that informs the
world about our planet and our climate
systems
nsidc.org

SNP Scottish National Party
Gordon Lamb House 3 Jackson's Entry
Edinburgh EH8 8PJ
Tel: 0800 633 5432
info@snp.org
www.snp.org

SOCA Serious Organised Crime Agency
Tackles crime that affects the UK and our
citizens including Class A drugs, people
smuggling and human trafficking, major gun
crime, fraud, computer crime and money
laundering
PO Box 8000 London SE11 5EN
Tel: 0370 496 7622
www.soca.gov.uk

Social & Economic Research (Institute for)
Production and analysis of longitudinal data
- evidence tracking changes in the lives of
the same individuals over time
University of Essex Wivenhoe Park
Colchester CO4 3SQ
Tel: 01206 872957
iser@essex.ac.uk
www.iser.essex.ac.uk

Social Care Association
Professional membership association for all staff in the social care service
350 West Barnes Lane Motspur Park New Malden KT3 6NB
Tel: 020 8949 5837
email via website
www.socialcareassociation.co.uk

Social Democratic & Labour Party
121 Ormeau Rd Belfast BT7 1SH
Tel: 028 9024 7700
info@sdlp.ie
www.sdlp.ie

Social Entrepreneurs (School for)
Provide training and opportunities to enable people to use their creative and entrepreneurial abilities more fully for social benefit. Supports individuals to set up new charities, social enterprises and social businesses across the UK
2nd Floor, The Fire Station 139 Tooley Street London SE1 2HZ
Tel: 020 7089 9120
email via website
www.the-sse.org

Social Issues Research Centre
Independent, non-profit organisation conducting research on social & lifestyle issues
27/28 St Clements Oxford OX4 1AB
Tel: 01865 262255
group@sirc.org
www.sirc.org

Social Market Foundation
Social policy think tank
11 Tufton St Westminster London SW1P 3QB
Tel: 020 7222 7060
enquiries@smf.co.uk
www.smf.co.uk

Social Sciences (Association for the Teaching of the) ATSS
Voluntary group of teachers who have joined together to further the interests of Social Science teaching in secondary schools
C/o The British Sociological Association Bailey Suite, Palatine House Belmont Business Park Durham DH1 1TW
Tel: 0191 383 0839
Email via website
www.atss.org.uk

Social Workers (British Association of)
16 Kent St Birmingham B5 6RD
Tel: 0121 622 3911
email via website
www.basw.co.uk

Socialism see also Christian Socialist Movement

Socialist Health Association
Campaigning membership organisation which promotes health and well-being and the eradication of inequalities
22 Blair Road Manchester M16 8NS
Tel: 0161 286 1926
admin@sochealth.co.uk
www.sochealth.co.uk

Socialist Labour Party
Aims to end capitalism & replace it with socialism
PO Box 706 Barnsley S70 9LE
Tel: 01226 212951
slpscot@btinternet.com
www.socialist-labour-party.org.uk

Soil Association
Campaigning for organic food and farming and sustainable forestry
South Plaza Malborough Street Bristol BS1 3NX
Tel: 0117 314 5000
email via website
www.soilassociation.org

Sojourner Project
Eaves project for women with no recourse to public funds, who entered the UK on a spousal or partner visa and are eligible to apply for Indefinite Leave to Remain (ILR) under the Domestic Violence Rule
Tel: 020 7735 2062
www.eaves4women.co.uk/Sojourner/Sojourner.php

Solar Energy Society UK-ISES
PO Box 489 Abingdon OX14 4WY
Tel: 0776 016 3559
info@uk-ises.org
www.uk-ises.org

Solicitors Family Law Association see
Resolution

Solicitors for the Elderly
National association committed to providing high quality legal services for older people, their family and carers
Suite 17 Conbar House Mead Lane Hertford SG13 7AD
admin@solicitorsfortheelderly.com
www.solicitorsfortheelderly.com

Solidar
Lobbying for trade union rights, development and humanitarian aid
Rue de Commerce 22 B-1000 Brussels Belgium
Tel: 00 322 500 1020
email via website
www.solidar.org

Solo Clubs (National Federation of)

For widowed, divorced, separated and single people
PO Box 2278 Nuneaton CV11 5PA
Tel: 02476 736 499
national@federation-solo-clubs.co.uk
www.federation-solo-clubs.co.uk

Songwriters, Composers and Authors (British Academy of) see BASCA

SOS Children's Villages

A child welfare organisation providing families for orphaned and abandoned children
Terrington House 13-15 Hills Road
Cambridge CB2 1NL
Tel: 01223 365589
info@soschildrensvillages.org.uk
www.soschildrensvillages.org.uk

Sound and Music SAM

UK's landmark agency for new music and sound
3rd Floor, South Wing Somerset House, The Strand London WC2R 1LA
Tel: 020 7759 1800
Email via website
www.soundandmusic.org

Sound Seekers Improving the lives of the hearing impaired

Charity supporting the needs of deaf children in the developing countries of the Commonwealth
34 Buckingham Palace Rd London SW1W 0RE
Tel: 020 7233 5700
admin@sound-seekers.org.uk
www.sound-seekers.org.uk

Sound Sense

Offers comprehensive advice and information on all aspects of community music and music and disability
www.soundsense.org

SoundJunction

Interactive site about exploring, discovering and creating music. Produced by the Associated Board of the Royal Schools of Music
www.soundjunction.org

Southall Black Sisters

Challenges domestic and gender-related violence locally and nationally
21 Avenue Road Southall Middlesex UB1 3BL
Helpline Tel: 020 8571 0800
Tel: 020 8571 9595
email via website
www.southallblacksisters.org.uk

Southbank Centre

Largest single-run arts centre in the world and includes Royal Festival Hall, Haywards Gallery, Queen Elizabeth Hall, Purcell Room, Poetry Library and 21 acres of creative arts
Belvedere Road London SE1 8XX
Tel: 020 7960 4200
www.southbankcentre.co.uk

SOVA Supporting Others Through Volunteer Action

Recruits & supports volunteers working with offenders and socially excluded people
Unit 201 Lincoln House 1-3 Brixton Road
London SW9 6DE
Tel: 020 7793 0404
email via website
www.sova.org.uk

Space Agency (European)

www.esa.int

Space Agency (UK)

At the heart of the UK efforts to explore and benefit from space
Polaris House North Star Avenue Swindon Wiltshire SN2 1SZ
Tel: 020 7215 5000
email via website
www.ukspaceagency.bis.gov.uk

Space Centre (National)

Exploration Drive Leicester LE4 5NS
Information Line,Äì 0845 605 2001
Tel: 0116 2610261
info@spacecentre.co.uk
www.spacecentre.co.uk

Spanish Embassy Education Office

Spanish-language website with information for students and teachers.
www.educacion.gob.es

Spanish Institute Instituto Cervantes

Spanish courses, lectures, cultural activities and library
102 Eaton Sq London SW1W 9AN & 326/330 Deansgate Campfield Avenue Arcade Manchester M3 4FN
Tel: 020 7235 0353 (London)
Tel: 0161 661 4201 (Manchester)
cenlon@cervantes.es
cenman@cervantes.es
londres.cervantes.es
manchester.cervantes.es

Sparks

The Children's Medical Research Charity. Funds pioneering research that has a practical and positive impact on the lives of babies and children
6th Floor, Westminster Tower 3 Albert Embankment London SE1 7SP
Tel: 0207 091 7750
info@sparks.org.uk
www.sparks.org.uk

Spartacus Educational

History website
www.spartacus.schoolnet.co.uk

Speakability Rebuilding communication
National charity dedicated to supporting and
empowering people with Aphasia and their
carers
1 Royal Street London SE1 7LL
Tel: 080 8808 9572
Tel: 020 7261 9572
speakability@speakability.org.uk
www.speakability.org.uk

Speakers Clubs (Association of)

Exists to promote effective speaking,
communication, and the conduct of
meetings
www.the-asc.org.uk

Speaking up now see Voiceability

Special Educational Advice (Independent Parental) see IPSEA

Special Educational Needs (National Association for) nasen

nasen House 4/5 Amber Business Village
Amber Close Amington Tamworth B77 4RP
Tel: 01827 311500
welcome@nasen.org.uk
www.nasen.org.uk

Special Educational Needs & Disability Tribunal now see Justice

Special Needs Education (European Agency for Development in)

Ostre Stationsvej 33 DK-5500 Odense C
Denmark
Tel: 00 45 64 41 00 20
secretariat@european-agency.org
www.european-agency.org

Special Olympics

The world's largest sports organization for
people with intellectual disabilities: with
nearly 4 million athletes in more than 170
countries -- and millions more volunteers
and supporters
info@specialolympics.org
www.specialolympics.org

Special Olympics Great Britain

Year-round sport training and competition
opportunities and is open to all people with
intellectual (learning) disabilities regardless
of their ability
Corinthian House 1st Floor 6-8 Great Eastern
Street London EC2A 3NT
Tel: 020 7247 8891
email via website
www.specialolympicsgb.org.uk

Specialist Schools and Academies Trust
SSAT

Charity working with schools throughout
England, and in 36 countries across the
world, to raise achievement for all students
(3-19 years)
5th Floor 142 Central Street London EC1V
8AR
Tel: 020 7802 2300
info@ssatuk.co.uk
www.ssatuk.co.uk

Speech see also Afasic, Cued Speech
Association UK, Stammering Association
(British), Stammering Children (Michael Palin
Centre for)

Speech and Language Therapists (Royal College of)

Professional body for UK speech and
language therapists. Sets standards of
practice. Provides careers information to the
public
2 White Hart Yard London SE1 1NX
Tel: 020 7378 1200
info@rcslt.org
www.rcslt.org

Spelling Society (The English) TESS
Raising awareness of the problems caused
by the irregularity of English spelling and
to promote remedies to improve literacy,
including spelling reform
www.spellingsociety.org

Spina Bifida see Shine

Spinal Injuries Association SIA
Represents spinal cord injured people
regardless of how the impairment occurred
SIA House 2 Trueman Place Oldbrook
Milton Keynes MK6 2HH
Freephone advice line: 0800 980 0501
Tel: 0845 678 6633
email via website
www.spinal.co.uk

Spinal injury see Aspire

SPIT Signed Performances in Theatre
Charity promoting BSL interpreted
performances of mainstream theatre
6 Thirlmere Drive Lymm Cheshire WA13 9PE
email via website
www.spit.org.uk

Sport & Recreation Alliance

Umbrella organisation to which all sport &
recreation governing bodies in the UK are
affiliated
14 Burwood House Caxton Street London
SW1H 0QT
Tel: 020 7976 3900
info@sportandrecreation.org.uk
www.sportandrecreation.org.uk

Sport England
To lead the development of sport in England
3rd Floor Victoria House Bloomsbury Square
London WC1B 4SE
Tel: 08458 508508
info@sportengland.org
www.sportengland.org

Sport Northern Ireland
House of Sport 2a Upper Malone Rd Belfast
BT9 5LA
Tel: 028 90 381 222
info@sportni.net
www.sportni.net

Sport Wales
Fostering excellence and quality in both
grassroots and elite sports provision
Sophia Gardens Cardiff CF11 9SW
Tel: 0845 045 0904
info@sportwales.co.uk
www.sportwales.org.uk/

Sports Aid Foundation now see SportsAid

Sports Association for People with
Learning Disability (UK) UKSA
Co-ordinates and develops sporting
opportunities
1st Floor, 12 City Forum 250 City Road
London EC1V 2PU
Tel: 020 7490 3057
info@uksportsassociation.org
www.uksportsassociation.org

Sports Centre (Lilleshall National)
Sports and conference centre run on behalf
of Sport England
Lilleshall National Sports & Conferencing
Centre Near Newport Shropshire TF10 9AT
Tel: 01952 603003
email via website
www.lilleshallnsc.co.uk

Sports Coach UK National Coaching
Foundation
To help develop sports coaching
Chelsea Close Off Amberley Road, Armley
Leeds LS12 4HP
Tel: 0113 274 4802
email via website
www.sportscoachuk.org

Sports Council (Northern Ireland) now see
Sport Northern Ireland

Sports Council UK see UK Sport

Sports Leaders UK
Funds and administers the Sports Leader
awards
The British Sports Trust 23-25 Linford Forum
Rockingham Drive Linford Wood Milton
Keynes MK14 6LY
Tel: 01908 689180
contact@sportsleaders.org
www.sportsleaders.org

SportsAid
Charity for sports people, helping the next
generation of young British sportsmen and
women to succeed
3rd Floor Victoria House Bloomsbury Square
London WC1B 4SE
Tel: 020 7273 1975
email via website
www.sportsaid.org.uk

sportscotland
National agency for sport
Doges Templeton on the Green 62
Templeton Street Glasgow G40 1DA
Tel: 0141 534 6500
sportscotland.enquiries@sportscotland.org.
uk
www.sportscotland.org.uk

sportscotland Avalanche Information
Service
Daily forecasts on web of avalanche and
climbing conditions in 5 main Scottish
climbing areas from mid December - mid
April
www.sais.gov.uk

SPPA see Pre-school Play Association (Scottish)

SPR see Psychical Research (Society for)

SQA see Scottish Qualifications Authority

Squatters (Advisory Service for)
Angel Alley 84b Whitechapel High Street
London E1 7QX
Tel: 020 3216 0099
advice@squatter.org.uk
www.squatter.org.uk

St Fagans: National History Museum
Open-air museum and heritage attraction
Cardiff CF5 6XB
Tel: 029 2057 3500
email via website
www.museumwales.ac.uk/en/stfagans/

St Giles Trust
Supports offenders who want to change
64-68 Camberwell Church Street London
SE5 8JB
Tel: 020 7703 7000
info@stgilestrust.org.uk
www.stgilestrust.org.uk

St John Ambulance
27 St. John's Lane London EC1M 4BU
Tel: 08700 10 49 50
Email via website
www.sja.org.uk

St Mungo Museum of Religious Life and Art
Explores the importance of religion in peoples' lives. Aims to promote understanding and respect between people of different faiths and of none
2 Castle Street Glasgow G4 0RH
Tel: 0141 276 1625
Text Phone: 0141 276 1629
museums@glasgowlife.org.uk
www.glasgowlife.org.uk/museums/our-museums/st-mungo-museum

Stakeholder Forum
International organisation working to advance sustainable development and promote democracy at a global level
3 Whitehall Court London SW1A 2EL
Tel: 0207 930 8752
info@stakeholderform.org
www.stakeholderforum.org

Stammering Association (British)
15 Old Ford Rd London E2 9PJ
Helpline:
0845 603 2001
Tel: 020 8983 1003
mail@stammering.org
www.stammering.org

Stammering Children (Michael Palin Centre for) The Association for Research into Stammering in Childhood
Provides a specialist advice and assessment service for children from all over the UK
Finsbury Health Centre Pine St London EC1R OLP
Tel: 020 7530 4238
email via website
www.stammeringcentre.org

STAR see Refugees (Student Action for)

State Education (Campaign for)
Campaigns for the best in state education for all children
98 Erlanger Road London SE14 5TH
Tel: 07932 149942
contact@campaignforstateeducation.org.uk
www.campaignforstateeducation.org.uk

State of the Ocean (International Programme on the)
Established by scientists with the aim of saving the Earth and all life on it
Tel: 020 7449 6669
email via website
www.stateoftheocean.org

Statewatch
Monitors the state and civil liberties in the UK and the EU
PO Box 1516 London N16 0EW
Tel: 020 8802 1882
office@statewatch.org
www.statewatch.org

Statistics see also Australian Bureau of Statistics, Education Statistics (National Center for), General Register Office, Indian Census, National Archives, National Records of Scotland (NRS), Office for National Statistics, Register Office for N. Ireland, World Gazetteer, Worldometers

Statistics New Zealand
www.stats.govt.nz

Steel Can Recycling Information Bureau
Offers free resources to everyone, supporting the development of steel can recycling and environmental awareness. Aligned with the curriculum, the Recycling Matters publication is an aid to teaching and learning
c/o Tata Steel Packaging Recycling Trostre Llanelli Carmarthenshire SA14 9SD
Tel: 01554 741111
admin@scrib.org.uk
www.scrib.org
www.tatasteeleurope.com

Steiner Waldorf Education (European Council for) ECSWE
Comprises 26 national Waldorf Associations, representing over 680 schools in Europe. Work in active partnership with other organisations who are concerned with the social emotional education and well being of children
Kidbrooke Park Forest Row East Sussex RH18 5JA
ecswe@waldorf.net
www.steinerwaldorfeurope.org

Steiner Waldorf Schools Fellowship
Serving Steiner Education in the UK & Ireland
11 Church Street Stourbridge DY8 1LT
Tel: 01342 374116
admin@steinerwaldorf.org
www.steinerwaldorf.org.uk

Stephen Lawrence Charitable Trust
Established in memory of Stephen Lawrence to provide young black people with opportunities to study architecture and associated arts
39 Brookmill Road London SE8 4HU
Tel: 020 8100 2800
information@stephenlawrence.org.uk
www.stephenlawrence.org.uk/

STEPS Centre
STEPS (Social Technological and Environmental Pathway to Sustainability) links environmental sustainability and technology with poverty reduction and social justice
Institute of Development Studies University of Sussex Brighton BN1 9RE
Tel: 01273 915673
steps-centre@ids.ac.uk
www.steps-centre.org

Stillbirth & Neonatal Death Charity see SANDS

Stock Exchange (London)
10 Paternoster Square London EC4M 7LS
Tel: 020 7797 1000
www.londonstockexchange.com

Stonewall
Equality and justice for lesbians, gay men and bisexuals
Tower Building York Road London SE1 7NX
Tel: 08000 50 20 20
Minicom: 020 7633 0759
info@stonewall.org.uk
www.stonewall.org.uk

Stop Climate Chaos Coalition
The UK's largest group of people dedicated to action on climate change and limiting its impact on the world's poorest communities
c/o Oxfam 232-242 Vauxhall Bridge Road London SW1V 1AU
Tel: 020 7802 9989
admin@stopclimatechaos.org
www.stopclimatechaos.org

Stop Climate Chaos Scotland
Ground Floor 2 Lochside View Edinburgh EH12 9DH
Tel: 0131 317 4112
info@stopclimatechaosscotland.org
www.stopclimatechaos.org/scotland

Storytelling (Society for)
Morgan Library Aston St Wem SY4 5AU
Tel: 07534 578 386
email via website
www.sfs.org.uk

Stress Management Association UK (International) ISMA UK
Promotes sound knowledge and best practice
PO Box 108 Caldicot Monmouthshire NP26 9AP
Tel: 01179 697284
Tel: 0845 680 7 083
stress@isma.org.uk
www.isma.org.uk

Stroke Association
Helps stroke sufferers and their families to fight stroke which is the third biggest killer and most serious disabler in the UK
Stroke Association House 240 City Road London EC1V 2PR
Helpline: 0303 303 3100
Tel: 020 7566 0300
Textphone: 020 7251 9096
info@stroke.org.uk
www.stroke.org.uk

Strokes see also Different Strokes

Student Awards Agency for Scotland
Processes applications from Scottish students for higher education courses throughout the UK
Gyleview House 3 Redheughs Rigg Edinburgh EH12 9HH
Tel: 0300 555 0505
Email via website
www.saas.gov.uk

Student Drama Festival (National)
Britain's premier festival of the finest student theatre
Woolyard 54 Bermondsey Street London SE1 3UD
Tel: 020 7036 9027
info@nsdf.org.uk
www.nsdf.org.uk

Student Loans Company Ltd
Administers the Government's student loans schemes for undergraduates in the UK
100 Bothwell Street Glasgow G2 7JD
Tel: 0141 306 2000 (Admin)
www.slc.co.uk

Students see also thematic guide - Education

Students in Europe see ESU

Students Partnership Worldwide now see Restless Development

Studies in British Art (Paul Mellon Centre for)
16 Bedford Sq London WC1B 3JA
Tel: 020 7580 0311
info@paul-mellon-centre.ac.uk
www.paul-mellon-centre.ac.uk

Study Support see Quality in Study Support and Extended Services

Sub Aqua Club (British)
Telford's Quay South Pier Road Ellesmere Port CH65 4FL
Tel: 0151 350 6200
info@bsac.com
www.bsac.com

Substance abuse see thematic guide for Addiction, Alcohol and for Drugs and Substance Abuse

Sudley House
Explore a Victorian merchant's house with its period furniture and beautiful paintings
Mossley Hill Road Aigburth Liverpool L18 8BX
Tel: 0151 478 4016
email via website
www.liverpoolmuseums.org.uk/sudley

Suicide see PAPYRUS (Prevention of Suicides), Survivors of Bereavement by Suicide

Sundial Society (British)
Concerned with art & science of gnomonics
www.sundialsoc.org.uk

SunSmart Campaign
Australian website providing sun protection advice
www.sunsmart.com.au

Support After Murder & Manslaughter see
SAMM

Support Dogs
Trains dogs for people with epilepsy, physical disabilities and other specific medical conditions
21 Jessops Riverside Brightside Lane Sheffield S9 2RX
Tel: 0114 261 7800
info@support-dogs.org.uk
www.support-dogs.org.uk

Surf Life Saving GB
Teaching, sport & patrolling of surf beaches
1st Floor 19 Southernhay West Exeter EX1 1PJ
Tel: 01392 218007
mail@slsgb.org.uk
www.slsgb.org.uk

Surfers Against Sewage
Campaigns for cessation of marine sewage and toxic waste discharge
Unit 2 Wheal Kitty Workshops St Agnes Cornwall TR5 0RD
Tel: 01872 553001
email via website
www.sas.org.uk

Surgery Door
UK health website
www.surgerydoor.co.uk

Surname Profiler
Maps the distribution of surnames in Great Britain and the rest of the world, both current and historic
www.publicprofiler.org/index.php

Survival International
Supports tribal peoples and helps them protect their lives, lands and human rights
6 Charterhouse Buildings London EC1M 7ET
Tel: 020 7687 8700
info@survivalinternational.org
www.survivalinternational.org

Survivors of Bereavement by Suicide
Charity. Self-help organisation. Offers emotional and practical support to those bereaved by the suicide of a close relative or friend
The Flamsteed Centre Albert Street Ilkeston Derby DE7 5GU
National Helpline: 0844 561 6855
Tel: 0115 944 1117
sobs.admin@care4free.net
www.uk-sobs.org.uk

SurvivorsUK
Counselling for male rape and sexual abuse
Ground Floor 34 Great James St London WC1N 3HB
Helpline: 0845 122 1201
Tel: 0207 404 6234
info@survivorsuk.org
www.survivorsuk.org/

Sustain The Alliance for Better Food & Farming Promoting food and agriculture policies and practices that enhance the health and welfare of people and animals.
94 White Lion St London N1 9PF
Tel: 020 7837 1228
sustain@sustainweb.org
www.sustainweb.org

SustainAbility
Specialises in business strategy & sustainable development
20-22 Bedford Row London WC1R 4EB
Tel: 020 7269 6900
email via website
www.sustainability.com

Sustrans
UK charity enabling people to travel by foot, bike or public transport for more of the journeys we make every day
2 Cathedral Square College Green Bristol BS1 5DD
Infoline: 0845 113 0065
Tel: 0117 926 8893
info@sustrans.org.uk
www.sustrans.org.uk

Sustrans Cymru
123 Bute Street Cardiff CF10 5AE
Tel: 029 2065 0602
sustranscymru@sustrans.org.uk
www.sustrans.org.uk

Sustrans Northern Ireland
Ground Floor Premier Business Centres 20 Adelaide Street Belfast BT2 8GD
Tel: 028 9043 4569
belfast@sustrans.org.uk
www.sustrans.org.uk

Sustrans Scotland
Rosebery House 9 Haymarket Terrace Edinburgh EH12 5EZ
Tel: 0131 346 1384
scotland@sustrans.org.uk
www.sustrans.org.uk

Suzuki Institute (British)
Charity promoting the Suzuki method of music education
Unit 1.01 The Lightbox 111 Power Road Chiswick London W4 5PY
Tel: 020 3176 4170
info@britishsuzuki.com
www.britishsuzuki.com

Suzy Lamplugh Trust

Aims to raise awareness of the importance of personal safety and to provide solutions that effect change in order to help people to avoid violence and aggression and live safer, more confident lives
National Centre for Personal Safety 218 Strand London WC2R 1AT
Tel: 020 7091 0014
info@suzylamplugh.org
www.suzylamplugh.org

Swimming

Also gives access to British Swimming, Amateur Swimming Association and the Institute of Swimming
www.swimming.org

Swimming see also Lifeguard Skills, Lifesavers, Surf Life Saving GB

Swimming Clubs for people with Disabilities (National Association for)

The Willows Mayles Lane Wickham Hants PO17 5ND
Tel: 01329 833689
naschswim-willows@yahoo.co.uk
www.nasch.org.uk

SYHA Hostelling Scotland

Provider of budget accommodation across all of Scotland from rural areas to cities
7 Glebe Crescent Stirling FK8 2JA
Tel: 01786 891400
info@syha.org.uk
www.syha.org.uk

T

Table Tennis Association (English)

via website
www.englishtabletennis.org.uk

TACT The Adolescent and Children's Trust
Finds new families for adoption & fostering of children with special needs
The Courtyard 303 Hither Green Lane Hither Green London SE13 6TJ
Tel: 020 8695 8142
Tel: 0800 232 1157
Email via website
www.tactcare.org.uk

Tai Chi Finder

Locates classes and organisations
www.taichifinder.co.uk

Tai Chi Union for Great Britain

5 Corrunna Drive Horsham West Sussex RH13 5HG
Tel: 01403 257918
email via website
www.taichiunion.com

Talk Adoption

Telephone helpline for any young person who has any issues about adoption
Unit 5 Citygate 5 Blantyre Street Manchester M15 4JJ
Helpline: 0800 0568 578
Tel: 0161 839 4932
information@afteradoption.org.uk
www.afteradoption.org.uk

Talking Newspapers and Magazines (National)

Subscription service supplying, in alternative format, newspapers and magazines to blind, visually impaired and disabled people
National Recording Centre Browning Road Heathfield East Sussex TN21 8DB
Tel: 01435 866102
info@tnauk.org.uk
www.tnauk.org.uk

Tall Persons Club (GB & Ireland)

Promotes interest of tall people and gives practical, medical and social information
88-90 Hatton Gardens London EC1N 8PN
Tel: 07000 825512
email via website
www.tallclub.co.uk

Tall Ships Youth Trust

Dedicated to the personal development of young people aged 12 to 25 through the crewing of their vessels
2A The Hard Portsmouth PO1 3PT
Tel: 023 9283 2055
info@tallships.org
www.tallships.org

Tampon Alert (Alice Kilvert)
Provides information about tampon related toxic shock syndrome and support for those affected
16 Blinco Rd Urmston Manchester M41 9NF
Tel: 0161 748 3123
enquiries@tamponalert.org.uk
www.tamponalert.org.uk

Tandem Club
To promote and help tandem riding
email via website
www.tandem-club.org.uk

TAPOL The Indonesia Human Rights Campaign
Campaigns to expose human rights violations in Indonesia, East Timor, West Papua and Aceh
111 Northwood Rd Thornton Heath Surrey CR7 8HW
Tel: 020 8771 2904
info@tapol.org
www.tapol.org

Taskforce for the Rural Poor (International)
Network of development workers, researchers and organisations working for the rural poor in the Third World
12 Eastleigh Ave Harrow Middlesex HA2 0UF
Tel: 020 8864 4740
Email via website
www.ivcs.org.uk/intaf

Tate Britain
Millbank London SW1P 4RG
Tel: 020 7887 8888
visiting.britain@tate.org.uk
www.tate.org.uk

Tate Liverpool
One of the largest galleries of modern art outside London
Albert Dock Liverpool L3 4BB
Tel: 0151 702 7400
visiting.liverpool@tate.org.uk
www.tate.org.uk/liverpool

Tate Modern
Bankside London SE1 9TG
Tel: 020 7887 8888
visiting.modern@tate.org.uk
www.tate.org.uk/modern

Tate St Ives
Porthmeor Beach St Ives Cornwall TR26 1TG
Tel: 01736 796226
visiting.stives@tate.org.uk
www.tate.org.uk/stives

Tax see also Conscience, HM Revenue and Customs

TaxAid
Charity providing free tax advice to people in financial need
Room 304, Linton House 164-180 Union Street Southwark SE1 0LH
Helpline: 0345 120 3779
email via website
www.taxaid.org.uk

TB Alert
FREEPOST LON12815 London NW10 1YS
Helpline: 0845 456 0995
Tel: 01273 234029
info@tbalert.org
www.tbalert.org

Tea Council (UK) Ltd.
Suite 10, 4th Floor Crown House One Crown Square Woking GU21 6HR
Tel: 01483 750599
info@teacouncil.co.uk
www.tea.co.uk

Teacher Support Network
Counselling, support and services for trainees, working teachers and retired teachers, plus free and confidential 24hr telephone support line
Support lines: England & Scotland - 08000 562 561
Wales - 08000 855 088
email via website
www.teachersupport.info

Teacher Training in Primary School Science see SCIcentre

TeacherNet now see Education (Department for)

Teachers of Mathematics (Association of)
Unit 7 Prime Industrial Park Shaftesbury St Derby DE23 8YB
Tel: 01332 346599
admin@atm.org.uk
www.atm.org.uk

Teachers of Religious Education (National Association of) NATRE
For RE professionals in primary and secondary schools and higher education
1020 Bristol Rd Selly Oak Birmingham B29 6LB
Tel: 0121 472 4242
admin@natre.org.uk
www.natre.org.uk

Teaching Council for Wales (General)
Ensures that teachers are appropriately qualified and that they maintain high standards of conduct and practice. Advises government and others.
9th Floor Eastgate House 35-43 Newport Road Cardiff CF24 0AB
Tel: 029 20 46 00 99
information@gtcw.org.uk
www.gtcw.org.uk

Teaching English & Other Community Languages to Adults (National Association for) NATECLA
National forum and professional organisation for ESOL teachers
South Birmingham College Room HA205, Hall Green Campus Cole Bank Road Hall Green Birmingham B28 8ES
Tel: 0121 688 8121
info@natecla.org.uk
www.natecla.org.uk

Teaching of Drama (National Association for the) NATD
www.natd.eu

Teaching of English (National Association for the) NATE
50 Broadfield Rd Sheffield S8 0XJ
Tel: 0114 255 5419
info@nate.org.uk
www.nate.org.uk

Tearfund
Evangelical Christian relief and development charity
100 Church Rd Teddington Middlesex TW11 8QE
Tel: 0845 355 8355
enquiry@tearfund.org
www.tearfund.org

Technology Colleges Trust now see
Specialist Schools and Academies Trust

Teenage Cancer Trust
Helping young people fight cancer
3rd Floor 93 Newman Street London W1T 3EZ
Tel: 020 7612 0370
email via website
www.teenagecancertrust.org

Telecommunications Action Group now
see TAG

Telephone Directories On Web
Telephone directories of various types for most countries of the world, including UK
www.infobel.com/en/world

Telephone Preference Service TPS
Free opt-out facility to avoid cold-call phone sales
DMA House 70 Margaret St London W1W 8SS
Tel: 020 7291 3300
Resgistration Line: 0845 070 0707
tps@dma.org.uk
www.tpsonline.org.uk

Telephone Standards see Phonepay Plus

Telescope (Bradford Robotic)
Collection of telescopes and other instruments on Mount Teide, Tenerife
www.telescope.org/

Television see also thematic guide - Media

Telework Association
Encourages take up of telework - providing information and advice to employers and employees
61 Charterhouse Road Orpington Kent BR6 9EN
Tel: 0800 616008
email via website
www.telework.org.uk

Temperance League (British National) now
see BNTL-Freeway

Tenant Participation Advisory Service for England
Non-profit organisation providing information, advice, training on all aspects of involving tenants in their housing management
Suite 4b Trafford Plaza 73 Seymour Grove Manchester M16 0LD
Tel: 0161 868 3500
info@tpas.org.uk
www.tpas.org.uk

Tenovus
Helps patients and their families with essential support
Gleider House Ty Glas Road Cardiff CF14 5BD
Cancer support line: 0808 808 10 10
Tel: 029 2076 8850
post@tenovus.org.uk
www.tenovus.org.uk

Terrence Higgins Trust
Largest HIV and sexual health charity in the UK
314-320 Gray's Inn Rd London WC1X 8DP
Helpline: 0808 802 1221
Tel: 020 7812 1600
info@tht.org.uk
www.tht.org.uk
www.myhiv.org.uk

Theatre de Complicite
14 Anglers Lane London NW5 3DG
Tel: 020 7485 7700
email@complicite.org
www.complicite.org

Thalidomide Society (UK)
User-led organisation offering support, information and advice to people affected by Thalidomide and similarly disabled
Tel: 01462 438212
info@thalsoc.demon.co.uk
www.thalidomidesociety.co.uk

The Adolescent and Children's Trust see TACT

The Deep
Aquarium telling the story of the world's oceans
Tower Street Hull HU1 4DP
Tel: 01482 381000
info@thedeep.co.uk
www.thedeep.co.uk

The Sikh Way
To raise cultural awareness of Sikh people through workshops and educational activities
Sikh Education Council 27 Old Gloucester Street London WC1N 3XX
Tel: 07870 138 616
Email via website
www.thesikhway.com

The Survivors Trust
Umbrella agency for agencies providing support to women, men and children who are victims/survivors of rape, sexual violence and sexual abuse
Unit 2, Eastlands Court Business Centre St Peter's Road Rugby Warwickshire CV21 3QP
Tel: 01788 550554
info@thesurvivorstrust.org
www.thesurvivorstrust.org

Theatre see also thematic guide - Arts, Dance & Music. Refer also to the Dance, Drama, Music & Performing Arts Schools section

Theatre Council (Independent)
Management association for performing arts organisations
12 The Leathermarket Weston St London SE1 3ER
Tel: 020 7089 6821
email via website
www.itc-arts.org

Theatre for Children and Young People (International Association of)
Networking, training, advocacy, conferences
www.assitej-international.org

Theatre Network (The Amateur)
Promotes amateur theatre
email via website
amdram.co.uk

Theatrenet
News, events and links
www.theatrenet.com

Theatres Trust
Protecting our theatres and making them better. Charitable trust.
22 Charing Cross Rd London WC2H 0QL
Tel: 020 7836 8591
info@theatrestrust.org.uk
www.theatrestrust.org.uk

Thesite.org Your guide to the real world
Aims to be the first place all young adults turn to when they need support and guidance through life. Provides factsheets and articles on all the key issues facing young people including: sex and relationships; drinking and drugs; work and study; housing, legal and finances; and health and wellbeing
www.thesite.org

TheyWorkForYou.com
Not for profit organisation to help keep tabs on MPs
www.theyworkforyou.com

Think Global Development Education Association
Membership based charity. Works to educate and engage the UK public on global issues
Can Mezzanine 32-36 Loman Street London SE1 0EH
Tel: 020 7922 7930
info@think-global.org.uk
www.think-global.org.uk

Third Age Trust University of the Third Age (U3A)
National representative body. Self-help, self-managed lifelong learning for older people no longer in full time work, pursuing learning not for qualifications, but for fun
National Office Old Municipal Buildings 19 East Street Bromley BR1 1QE
Tel: 020 8466 6139
email via website
www.u3a.org.uk

Third World First now see People & Planet

This is abuse
Website providing help and advice about abuse in relationships
thisisabuse.direct.gov.uk

Thrive
Research, educate and promote the use and advantages of gardening for people with a disability
The Geoffrey Udall Centre Beech Hill Reading RG7 2AT
Tel: 0118 988 5688
email via website
www.thrive.org.uk
www.carryongardening.org.uk

Tibet see also Free Tibet

Tibet Society UK
Works for the freedom of the Tibetan people
Unit 9 139 Fonthill Road Finsbury Park London N4 3HF
Tel: 020 7272 1414
info@tibetsociety.com
www.tibetsociety.com

Tibetan Nuns Project
Helps to support 3 nunneries in NW India through sponsorship and fundraising in the UK
www.tnp.org

Tim Parry and Johnathan Ball see
Foundation for Peace

Time for God
Christian organisation arranging volunteering opportunities for 18-25 year olds in the UK, Europe and worldwide
Community House 46-50 East Parade Harrogate N Yorkshire HG1 5RR
Tel: 01423 536248
office@timeforgod.org
www.timeforgod.org

Time to change
Campaigns to end the stigma and discrimination that people with mental health problems face
15-19 Broadway London E15 4BQ
info@time-to-change.org.uk
www.time-to-change.org.uk

Tinnitus Association (British)
Support and information for people with tinnitus in the UK to help them achieve an improved quality of life
Ground Floor Unit 5 Acorn Business Park Woodseats Close Sheffield S8 0TB
Enquiry Line: 0800 018 0527
Tel: 0114 250 9922
Minicom: 0114 258 5694
info@tinnitus.org.uk
www.tinnitus.org.uk

Toc H
International Christian movement whose members seek to ease the burdens of others through acts of service, to promote reconciliation and work to bring disparate sections of society together.
PO Box 15824 Birmingham B13 3JU
Tel: 0121 4433552
info@toch.org.uk
www.toch.org.uk

Tommy's, the baby charity
Funds medical research on causes and prevention of miscarriage, stillbirth, premature birth and pregnancy health.
Nicholas House 3 Laurence Pountney Hill London EC4R 0BB
PregnancyLine information service: 0800 0147 800
Tel: 0207 398 3400
mailbox@tommys.org
www.tommys.org

Tools for Self Reliance
Volunteers throughout the UK collect and refurbish handtools for grassroots development projects in Africa
Ringwood Road Netley Marsh Southampton SO40 7GY
Tel: 023 8086 9697
info@tfsr.org
www.tfsr.org

Topmarks
Free website to help teachers, parents and pupils to use the internet effectively for learning
contact@topmarks.co.uk
www.topmarks.co.uk

Torture see Amnesty International UK, Freedom from Torture, REDRESS

Torture (Association for the Prevention of)
Independent non-governmental organisation committed to working internationally to tackle the global problem of torture and ill-treatment
PO Box 137 CH-1211 Geneva 19
Tel: 00 41 22 919 2170
apt@apt.ch
www.apt.ch

Torture (The World Organisation Against)
PO Box 21 8, rue du Vieux-Billard CH-1211 Geneva 8 Switzerland
Tel: 00 41 22 809 4939
omct@omct.org
www.omct.org

Tour de France
This official website is multilingual
www.letour.fr

Tour Operators (Association of Independent) AITO
Represents around 160 specialist tour operators
133A St Margaret's Rd Twickenham Middlesex TW1 1RG
Tel: 020 8744 9280
info@aito.com
www.aito.co.uk

Tourism Concern
Campaigning for fairly traded and ethical tourism.
Stapleton House 277-281 Holloway Rd London N7 8HN
Tel: 020 7133 3800
email via website
www.tourismconcern.org.uk

Tourism for All
Provides information to the public, especially to older or disabled people, on where their specific access needs can be met so that they can fully participate in travel and leisure
7A Pixel Mill 44 Appleby Road Kendal Cumbria LA9 6ES
Tel: 0845 124 9971
info@tourismforall.org.uk
www.tourismforall.org.uk

Tourism Offices Worldwide Directory
Provides information about tourist offices in most countries of the world
www.towd.com

Town & Country Planning Association
Registered charity providing independent comment on planning and environmental policy in the UK and Europe
17 Carlton House Terrace London SW1Y 5AS
Tel: 020 7930 8903
tcpa@tcpa.org.uk
www.tcpa.org.uk

Town Planning Institute (Royal) RTPI
Chartered professional body for town planning in the UK
41 Botolph Lane London EC3R 8DL
Tel: 020 7929 9494
www.rtpi.org.uk

Trackoff
Britain's rail industry initiative to help educate children and teenagers about safe conduct on the railway
0800 40 50 40
email via website
www.trackoff.org

Trade Union see also European Trade Union Confederation, Friedrich Ebert Foundation, Liberal Democrat Trade Unionists (Association of), Simon Jones Memorial Campaign, Solidar

Trade Union Confederation (International) ITUC
Boulevard du Roi Albert II, 5, 1210 Brussels Belgium
Tel: 00 32 2 224 0211
info@ituc-csi.org
www.ituc-csi.org

Trade Union Rights (International Centre for)
UCATT House 177 Abbeville Rd London SW4 9RL
Tel: 020 7498 4700
ictur@ictur.org
www.ictur.org

Trades Union Congress
Congress House Great Russell St London WC1B 3LS
Tel: 020 7636 4030
email via website
www.tuc.org.uk

Trading Standards Institute
A one stop shop for consumer protection information
www.tradingstandards.gov.uk

Traffic Statistics (Global) from UK Road Safety Ltd
Live updating road safety statistics
www.uk-roadsafety.co.uk/Rs_Documents/accident_count.htm

Traffic Victims see Roadpeace

Traidcraft
Fighting poverty through fair trade with the developing world. Mail order catalogue available free
Kingsway Team Valley Trading Estate Gateshead NE11 0NE
Tel: 0191 491 0591
email via website
www.traidcraft.co.uk

Trainline
Website providing information about train times and tickets for routes on mainland UK and a booking service
www.thetrainline.com

Tranquillisers, Antidepressants and Painkillers (Council for Information on)
National helpline, support and information service
The JDI Centre 3-11 Mersey View Waterloo Liverpool L22 6QA
Helpline: 0151 932 0102
Tel: 0151 474 9626
cita@citap.org.uk
www.citawithdrawal.org.uk

Transform Drug Policy Foundation
Advocates an effective system of regulation and control of drugs at national & international levels
9-10 King Street Bristol BS1 4EQ
Tel: 0117 325 0295
info@tdpf.org.uk
www.tdpf.org.uk

Transforming Conflict
Citizenship and human rights education
National Centre for Restorative Justice in Youth Settings Mortimer Hill Mortimer Berkshire RG7 3PW
Tel: 0118 933 1520
info@transformingconflict.org
www.transformingconflict.org

Transparency International
Fights bribery & corruption worldwide. Collects and makes available information about corruption and anti-corruption measures
International Secretariat Alt Moabit 96 10559 Berlin Germany
Tel: 00 49 30 3438 20 0
email via website
www.transparency.org

Transport (Department for)
Great Minster House 76 Marsham St London SW1P 4DR
Tel: 0300 330 3000
Email via website
www.dft.gov.uk

Transport & Environment (European Federation for)
Co-ordinates European groups on transport related environmental campaigning
Rue d'Edimbourg, 26 B-1050 Brussels Belgium
Tel: 0032 2 893 0841
Email via website
www.transportenvironment.org

Transport for London
London Travel 24hr Info Line: 0843 222 1234
Textphone: 020 7918 3015
email via website
www.tfl.gov.uk

Transport Safety (Parliamentary Advisory Council for)
Registered charity advising parliament on air, rail and road safety issues
Clutha House 10 Storey's Gate London SW1P 3AY
Tel: 020 7222 7732
admin@pacts.org.uk
www.pacts.org.uk

Travel advice see Foreign and Commonwealth Office Travel Advice

Travel and Tourism (Institute of)
PO Box 217 Ware Herts SG12 8WY
Tel: 0844 4995 653
enquiries@itt.co.uk
www.itt.co.uk

Travel Warnings (US State Department)
www.travel.state.gov

Travellers see Foreign and Commonwealth Office Travel Advice, Friends, Families and Travellers, MASTA

Treasury see HM Treasury

Tree Council
Promotes improvement of environment through planting and conservation of trees
71 Newcomen Street London SE1 1YT
Tel: 020 7407 9992
info@treecouncil.org.uk
www.treecouncil.org.uk

Treloar Trust
Provides residential education, care & independence training for young people aged 7-25 with severe physical disabilities
Upper Froyle Alton Hampshire GU34 4JX
Tel: 01420 547 477
email via website
www.treloar.org.uk

Triathlon Association (British)
PO Box 25 Loughborough Leicestershire LE11 3WX
Tel: 01509 226161
info@britishtriathlon.org
www.britishtriathlon.org

Triumph over Phobia (TOP UK)
Network of self-help groups for phobia and obsessive compulsive disorder sufferers
PO Box 3760 Bath BA2 3WY
Tel: 0845 6009601
info@topuk.org
www.topuk.org

Trócaire
Irish Catholic agency for world development
Maynooth Co. Kildare Ireland
Tel: 00 353 1 6293333
email via website
www.trocaire.org

Tropical Diseases (Hospital for)
Travel health advice
Mortimer Market Building Capper Street Tottenham Court Road London WC1E 6JB
Tel: 020 7388 9600 (Travel clinic)
email via website
www.thehtd.org

Tuberous Sclerosis Association UK
Group of parents, affected individuals and doctors interested in promoting greater understanding of the condition and providing mutual support for affected families
www.tuberous-sclerosis.org

Turn2us To access benefits & grants
Helps people in financial need gain access to welfare benefits, charitable grants and other financial help
www.turn2us.org.uk

Turning Point
Drug, alcohol-related & mental health
problems & learning disabilities
Standon House 21 Mansell Street London
E1 8AA
Tel: 020 7481 7600
info@turning-point.co.uk
www.turning-point.co.uk

Twentieth Century Society
Exists to safeguard the heritage of
architecture & design in Britain from 1914
onwards
70 Cowcross St London EC1M 6EJ
Tel: 020 7250 3857
caseworker@c20society.org.uk
www.c20society.org.uk

Twins & Multiple Births Association
(TAMBA)
Information and support for families with
twins, triplets and more and for professionals
involved with their care
2 The Willows Gardner Rd Guildford Surrey
GU1 4PG
Twinline: 0800 138 0509
Tel: 01483 304 442
enquiries@tamba.org.uk
www.tamba.org.uk

U

U3A see Third Age Trust

UCAS
Handles all applications for entry to UK
universities and other higher education
institutions
Rosehill New Barn Lane Cheltenham GL52
3LZ
Customer services: 0871 468 0 468
Tel: 01242 222 444
enquiries@ucas.ac.uk
www.ucas.com

UEFA
Route de Genève 46 Case postale CH-1260
Nyon 2 Switzerland
Tel: 00 41 848 00 2727
www.uefa.com

UJIA United Jewish Israel Appeal
Strengthening Jewish Identity, regenerating
the Galil through education and connecting
the UK and Israel
37 Kentish Town Road London NW1 8NX
Tel: 020 7424 6400
central@ujia.org

UK Border Agency
Responsible for securing the United
Kingdom borders and controlling migration
www.ind.homeoffice.gov.uk

UK Climate Projections UKCP09
Provide UK climate information designed
to help those needing to plan how they will
adapt to a changing climate
ukclimateprojections.defra.gov.uk

UK New Citizen
Promotes the social integration of refugees,
immigrants and their descendants through
citizenship and a sense of democracy
Tel: 07946 80 89 76
info@uknewcitizen.org
www.uknewcitizen.org

UK Parents Lounge
Online magazine and forum for parents
www.ukparents.co.uk

UK Sport
Governing body for whole of UK for elite
athletics
40 Bernard St London WC1N 1ST
Tel: 020 7211 5100
info@uksport.gov.uk
www.uksport.gov.uk

UK Theatre Web
Database of information on people, plays,
venues, performances etc. and extensive
archive
www.uktw.co.uk

UK Youth
National youth work charity, helping young people to develop skills and interests
7 Heron Quays Canary Wharf London E14 4JB
Tel: 01425 672347
info@ukyouth.org
www.ukyouth.org

UKDPC see Disabled People's Council (UK)

UKERNA see JANET

UKRC Advancing Gender Equality in Science, Engineering and Technology
Provision of advice, services and policy consultation regarding the under-representation of women in science, engineering, technology and the built environment (SET)
Athlone Wing, Old Building Great Horton Road Bradford, BD7 1AY
Tel: 01274 436485
email via website
www.theukrc.org

UN High Commissioner for Human Rights (Office of the)
www.ohchr.org

unbiased.co.uk
Promotes the value and accessibility of independent financial advice to the public
1 Sekforde Street London EC1R 0BE
Tel: 0330 1000 755
contact@unbiased.co.uk
www.unbiased.co.uk

Unborn Children (Society for the Protection of)
Defending human life, through education and political lobbying, from conception until natural death
3 Whitacre Mews Stannary Street London SE11 4AB
Tel: 020 7091 7091
information@spuc.org.uk
www.spuc.org.uk

Uncaged Campaigns
Pressure group campaigning to abolish animal experiments and for animal rights
PO Box 4823 Sheffield S36 0BE
Tel: 0114 283 1155
info@uncaged.co.uk
www.uncaged.co.uk

Undercurrents
Video support and training and archive materials for the use of social and environmental groups
Old Exchange Pier Street Swansea SA1 1RY
Tel: 01792 455900
hello@undercurrents.org
www.undercurrents.org

Understanding Animal Research
Information about the use of animals in medical research
Charles Darwin House London WC1N 2JU
Tel: 020 7685 2670
Email via website
www.understandinganimalresearch.org.uk

UNESCO United Nations Educational, Scientific & Cultural Organisation
1 rue Miollis 75732 Paris Cedex 15 France
Tel: 00 331 45 68 1000
Email via website
www.unesco.org

UNHCR The UN Refugee Agency
Safeguards the rights and well-being of refugees
Strand Bridge House 138 - 142 Strand London WC2R 1HH
Tel: 020 7759 8090
gbrloea@unhcr.org
www.unhcr.org.uk

Uni4me
Answers questions about what it is like to be a university student. Website developed by all the universities in Greater Manchester
www.uni4me.com

UNICEF UK
United Nations children's fund
2 Kingfisher House Woodbrook Crescent Billericay CM12 0EQ
Tel: 0844 801 2414
Email via website
www.unicef.org.uk

Unicorn Theatre for Children
147 Tooley Street More London Southwark London SE1 2HZ
Tel: 020 7645 0500
admin@unicorntheatre.com
www.unicorntheatre.com

Union Cycliste Internationale see Cycling Union (International)

Unistats
Brings information about universities and their courses together in one place
unistats.direct.gov.uk/

Unite
Unite was formed by a merger between two of Britain's' leading unions, the T&G and Amicus
128 Theobald's Road Holborn London WC1X 8TN
Tel: 020 7611 2500
email via website
www.unitetheunion.org

Unite Against Fascism
New national campaign against the extreme right
PO Box 68229 London SW1P 9WZ
Tel: 020 7801 2782
email via website
www.uaf.org.uk

United Nations Association of the UK
Membership organisation, campaigning and educating to turn the ideals of the UN into a reality
3 Whitehall Court London SW1A 2EL
Tel: 020 7766 3454
Email via website
www.una-uk.org

United Nations Development Programme
(UNDP)
The UN's global development network
www.undp.org

United Nations Educational, Scientific & Cultural Organisation see UNESCO

United Nations Environment Programme
www.unep.org

United Nations High Commissioner for Refugees see UNHCR

United Nations Volunteers
Volunteer arm of the United Nations
www.unvolunteers.org

United Reformed Church
86 Tavistock Place London WC1H 9RT
Tel: 020 7916 2020
urc@urc.org.uk
www.urc.org.uk

Universities and Colleges Sport (British)
Organises inter-university championships and GB team for World University Championships
20-24 Kings Bench Street London SE1 0QX
Tel: 020 7633 5080
email via website
www.bucs.org.uk

University of the First Age
National educational charity working in partnership to develop the confidence and achievement of young people
St Paul's Cottages 59-60 Water Street The Jewellery Quarter Birmingham B3 1EP
Tel: 0121 212 9838
ufa@ufa.org.uk
www.ufa.org.uk

University of the Third Age Trust see Third Age Trust

UNLOCK National Association of Reformed Offenders
Aims to overcome the social exclusion and discrimination which currently exists and which prevents reformed offenders from re-integrating into society and leading crime-free lives
35A High St Snodland Kent ME6 5AG
Tel: 01634 247350
enquiries@unlock.org.uk
www.unlock.org.uk

Unlock Democracy incorporating Charter 88
Campaigns for a modern democracy and human rights
37 Grays Inn Road London WC1X 8PQ
Tel: 020 7278 4443
info@unlockdemocracy.org.uk
www.unlockdemocracy.org.uk

UPDATE Disability Information Scotland
Hays Community Business Centre 4 Hay Avenue Edinburgh EH16 4AQ
Helpline: 0131 669 1600
info@update.org.uk
www.update.org.uk

Urban Saints
Christian youth organisation with weekly groups and summer holidays
Kestin House 45 Crescent Rd Luton LU2 0AH
Tel: 01582 589 850
email@urbansaints.org
www.urbansaints.org

US Department of State
www.state.gov

US Educational Advisory Service see Fulbright Commission

V

Values Education for Life (The Collegiate Centre for)
The centre exists to access and provide further increasing knowledge and understanding about the importance of values in the development of young people
College House Albion Place Hockley Hill Birmingham B18 5AQ
Tel: 0121 523 0222
info@vefl.org.uk
vefl.org.uk

Vatican
Website giving information on many aspects of the Vatican in many European languages
www.vatican.va

Vatican Museums & Sistine Chapel
Information on various Vatican museums including opening dates and times
www.christusrex.org/www1/vaticano/0-Musei.html

Vegan Society
Advocating lifestyle free from animal products
21 Hylton Street Hockley Birmingham B18 6HJ
Tel: 0121 523 1730
email via website
www.vegansociety.com

Vegetarian & Vegan Foundation
Provides free information on becoming vegetarian/vegan. Researches health & nutrition issues relating to diet
8 York Court Wilder St Bristol BS2 8QH
Tel: 0117 970 5190
info@vegetarian.org.uk
www.vegetarian.org.uk

Vegetarian Society
Parkdale Dunham Rd Altrincham Cheshire WA14 4QG
Tel: 0161 925 2000
info@vegsoc.org
www.vegsoc.org

Vegetarians International Voice for Animals see Viva!

Venice in Peril Fund
British charity for restoration and preservation of Venice
Unit 4, Hurlingham Studios Ranelagh Gardens London SW6 3PA
Tel: 020 7736 6891
info@veniceinperil.org
www.veniceinperil.org

Venture Trust A chance for change...
Exploring new ways to help young people make positive changes in their lives
6d Bruntsfield Terrace Edinburgh EH1 4EX
Tel: 0131 228 7700
info@venturetrust.org.uk
www.venturetrust.org.uk

Venuemasters
Offers free venue finding service for meeting and accommodation facilities at UK academic venues
Enquiry hotline: 0114 249 3090
info@venuemasters.co.uk
www.venuemasters.co.uk

Victim Support
National charity providing help and information to people affected by crime
Supportline: 0845 30 30 900
supportline@victimsupport.org.uk
www.victimsupport.org

Victorian Society
Provides advice to owners and public authorities regarding preservation and repair of Victorian and Edwardian buildings. Aims to involve and educate the public to increase the likelihood of conserving buildings
1 Priory Gardens London W4 1TT
Tel: 020 8994 1019
admin@victoriansociety.org.uk
www.victoriansociety.org.uk

Video Standards Council
Advises shops on legality of video sales and rental
Kinetic Business Centre Theobald St Borehamwood Herts WD6 4PJ
Tel: 020 8387 4020
vsc@videostandards.org.uk
www.videostandards.org.uk

Vision Aid Overseas
Provides spectacles and training in eye care in developing countries.
12 The Bell Centre Newton Rd Crawley W Sussex RH10 2FZ
Tel: 01293 535016
info@visionaidoverseas.org
www.visionaidoverseas.org

Visit London
The official tourism organisation for London
2 More London Riverside London SE1 2RR
Tel: 08701 566 366
email via website
www.visitlondon.com

Visit Wales
Tel: 08708 300 306
Minicom: 08701 211255
info@visitwales.co.uk
www.visitwales.com

VisitBritain
Marketing Britain overseas and developing the visitor economy
Headquarters 1 Palace Street London SW1E 5HX
Tel: 020 7578 1000
email via website
www.visitbritain.org
www.visitbritain.com

VisitEngland The England Tourist Board
National organisation for marketing England overseas and in the UK
1 Palace Street London SW1E 5HX
Tel: 020 7578 1400
email via website
www.enjoyengland.com

VisitScotland
The official site of Scotland's national tourism organisation
Ocean Point One 94 Ocean Drive Edinburgh EH6 6JH
Tel: 0845 859 1006 (brochures)
info@visitscotland.com
www.visitscotland.com

Visual Arts & Galleries Association
Network & voice for the visual arts world
Camden Arts Centre Arkwright Road London NW3 6DG
Tel: 07841 481 883
admin@vaga.co.uk
www.vaga.co.uk

Vitiligo Society
Promotes and funds research projects
125 Kennington Road London SE11 6SF
Freephone: 0800 018 2631
www.vitiligosociety.org.uk/

Viva! Vegetarians International Voice for Animals
Campaigning organisation working to end factory farming and educate people on vegetarian and vegan diets
8 York Court Wilder St Bristol BS2 8QH
Tel: 0117 944 1000
info@viva.org.uk
www.viva.org.uk

Vivisection see also Anti-Vivisection Society (National), BUAV, Humane Research Trust, PETA Foundation, Respect for Animals, Uncaged Campaigns, Viva!

Vivisection (British Union for the Abolition of) see BUAV

Voice Getting young voices heard
Working and campaigning for children and young people in public care
320 City Road London EC1V 2NZ
Freefone: 0808 800 5792
Tel: 020 7833 5792
info@voiceyp.org
www.voiceyp.org

Voice for Choice
Campaigning for abortion on request throughout the UK
www.vfc.org.uk

Voice of the Listener and Viewer
Represents the citizen and consumer on all broadcasting issues and works for quality and diversity
PO Box 401 Gravesend Kent DA12 9FY
Tel: 01474 338711 or 01474 338716
info@vlv.org.uk
www.vlv.org.uk

Voice UK
National charity supporting people with learning disabilities and other vulnerable people who have experienced crime or abuse
Rooms 100-106 Kelvin House RTC Business Centre London Road Derby DE24 8UP
Helpline: 0808 802 8686
email via website
www.voiceuk.org.uk

VoiceAbility
Gives a voice to vulnerable people and supports them to take control of their lives
Mount Pleasant House Huntingdon Road Cambridge CB3 0RN
Tel: 01223 555800
Textphone: 18001 01223 555800
Email via website
www.voiceability.org

Voices Foundation Transforming children through singing
Music education
34 Grosvenor Gardens London SW1W 0DH
Tel: 020 7730 6677
vf@voices.org.uk
www.voices.org.uk

Volleyball Association (English)
SportPark Loughborough University 3 Oakwood Drive Loughborough LE11 3QF
Tel: 01509 227722
info@volleyballengland.org
www.volleyballengland.org

Volleyball Association (Scottish)
48 The Pleasance Edinburgh EH8 9TJ
Tel: 0131 556 4633
www.scottishvolleyball.org

Voluntary Action (Wales Council for) see WCVA Δ

Voluntary Agencies (International Council of) ICVA
Advocacy network of non-governmental organisations
26-28 avenue Guiseppe Motta 1202 Geneva Switzerland
Tel: 00 41 22 950 96 00
secretariat@icva.ch
www.icva.ch

Voluntary and Community Action (National Association for) NAVCA

The England-wide organisation which provides services to local councils for voluntary service
The Tower 2 Furnival Square Sheffield S1 4QL
Tel: 0114 2786636
Textphone: 0114 278 7025
navca@navca.org.uk
www.navca.org.uk

Voluntary Arts Network VAN

To help people, irrespective of age, participate in the arts
121 Cathedral Road Pontcanna Cardiff CF11 9PH
Tel: 029 20 395395
info@voluntaryarts.org
www.voluntaryarts.org

Voluntary Euthanasia Society see Dignity in Dying

Voluntary Organisations (National Council for) (NCVO)

Umbrella body. Giving voice and support to civil society
Regent's Wharf 8 All Saints St London N1 9RL
Tel: 020 7713 6161
ncvo@ncvo-vol.org.uk
www.ncvo-vol.org.uk

Voluntary Organisations (Scottish Council for)

Umbrella body for all voluntary organisations in Scotland
Mansfield Traquair Centre 15 Mansfield Place Edinburgh EH3 6BB
Freephone: 0800 169 0022
Tel: 0131 474 8000
enquiries@scvo.org.uk
www.scvo.org.uk

Voluntary Service Overseas see VSO

Voluntary Youth Services (National Council for)

Represents voluntary organisations working with young people and volunteers
3rd Floor Lancaster House 33 Islington High Street London N1 9LH
Tel: 020 7278 1041
mail@ncvys.org.uk
www.ncvys.org.uk

Volunteer Action for Peace

UK based charity organisation that works towards creating and preserving international peace, justice and human solidarity for people and their communities
16 Overhill Road East Dulwich
London SE22 0PH
Tel: 0844 20 90 927
action@vap.org.uk
www.vap.org.uk

Volunteer Development Scotland

Support organisations in Scotland who involve volunteers
Jubilee House Forthside Way Stirling FK8 1QZ
Tel: 01786 479593
vds@vds.org.uk
www.vds.org.uk

Volunteer Now

Promotes and develops volunteering in Northern Ireland
129 Ormeau Road Belfast Northern Ireland BT7 1SH
Tel: 028 9023 2020
info@volunteernow.co.uk
www.volunteernow.co.uk

Volunteer Reading Help

Supports volunteers to help primary school children
14-15 Perseverance Works 38 Kingsland Rd London E2 8DD
Tel: 020 7729 4087
info@vrh.org.uk
www.vrh.org.uk

Volunteering England

Promotes volunteering as a force for change for volunteers and the community as a whole
Regent's Wharf 8 All Saints St London N1 9RL
Tel: 020 7520 8900
volunteering@volunteering.org.uk
www.volunteering.org.uk

Volunteers For Rural India VRI

DRIVE scheme - opportunity to live in rural India
12 Eastleigh Avenue South Harrow HA2 0UF
Tel: 020 8864 4740
enquiries@vri-online.org.uk
www.vri-online.org.uk

VSO (Voluntary Service Overseas)

International development charity that works through volunteers
Carlton House 27A Carlton Drive Putney London SW15 2BS
Volunteering advice line: 020 8780 7500
enquiry@vso.org.uk
www.vso.org.uk

W

W.I. see Women's Institutes (National Federation of)

Wales Environment Link
27 Pier Street Aberystwyth Ceredigion SY23 2LN
Tel: 01970 611621
Email via website
www.waleslink.org

Wales Office
Discovery House Scott Harbour Cardiff CF10 4PJ
Tel: 020 7270 0534
wales.office@walesoffice.gsi.gov.uk
www.walesoffice.gov.uk

Wales PPA see Pre-School Providers Association (Wales)

WalesRails
Independent survey of railways & the attractions they serve
www.walesrails.co.uk

Walk to School see Living Streets

Walker Art Gallery
William Brown Street Liverpool L3 8EL
Tel: 0151 478 4199
email via website
www.liverpoolmuseums.org.uk/walker

Walking see also Backpackers Club, Byways & Bridleways Trust, Long Distance Walkers Association

Walking Federation (British)
Member clubs organising events designed for people of all ages and abilities
Ground Floor 5 Windsor Square Silver Street Reading RG1 2TH
info@bwf-ivv.org.uk
www.bwf-ivv.org.uk

Walkit
The urban walking route planner
www.walkit.com

WalkScotland
Scottish outdoor & countryside news updated weekly
www.walkscotland.com

WAMT see Women and Manual Trades

War on Want
Campaign against world poverty
44-48 Shepherdess Walk London N1 7JP
Tel: 020 7324 5040
support@waronwant.org
www.waronwant.org

War Resisters League
339 Lafayette St New York NY 10012
Tel: 001 212 228 0450
wrl@warresisters.org
www.warresisters.org

Waste Watch
Deals with methods of reduction, reuse and recycling of waste
56-64 Leonard Street London EC2A 4LT
Tel: 020 7549 0300
email via website
www.wastewatch.org.uk

WATCh? see What about the Children?

Water Aid
Sustainable provision of safe water, sanitation and hygiene education to the world's poorest
2nd Floor, 47-49 Durham Street London SE11 5JD
Tel: 020 7793 4594
Email via website
www.wateraid.org

Water Services (Office of) OFWAT
Protecting consumers, promoting value and safeguarding the future
Centre City Tower 7 Hill St Birmingham B5 4UA
Tel: 0121 644 7500
enquiries@ofwat.gsi.gov.uk
www.ofwat.gov.uk

Water Ski & Wakeboard (British)
Governing body
Unit 3 The Forum Hanworth Lane Chertsey Surrey KT16 9JX
Tel: 01932 560 007
Email via website
www.britishwaterski.org.uk

Waterfront Museum (National)
Industry and innovation in Wales, now and over the last 300 years
Oystermouth Road Maritime Quarter Swansea SA1 3RD
Tel: 029 2057 3600
email via website
www.museumwales.ac.uk/en/swansea/

Waterway Recovery Group
Restores derelict canals
Island House Moor Road Chesham HP5 1WA
Tel: 01494 783 453
enquiries@wrg.org.uk
www.wrg.org.uk

Waterways (British) now see Canal & River Trust and Scottish Canals

Waterways Museum (National)
South Pier Road Ellesmere Port Cheshire CH65 4FW
Tel: 0151 355 5017
ellesmereport@thewaterwaystrust.org.uk
www.nwm.org.uk

WCVA Voluntary Action (Wales Council for)
Voice of the voluntary sector
Baltic House Mount Stuart Square Cardiff
CF10 5FH
Helpdesk: 0800 2888 329
Minicom: 0808 1804 080
help@wcva.org.uk
www.wcva.org.uk

We Are What We Do
Not-for-profit behaviour change company
that creates ways for millions of people to do
more small, good things
71 St John Street London EC1M 4NJ
Tel: 020 7148 7666
info@wearewhatwedo.org
www.wearewhatwedo.org

Weather Centre (BBC Online)
www.bbc.co.uk/weather

Weights & Measures Association (British)
Promotion of traditional weights and
measures and opposition to compulsory
metrication
98 Eastney Road Croydon Surrey CR0 3TE
bwma@email.com
www.bwmaonline.com

Wellbeing of Women
Medical research charity concerned with
women's reproductive health
27 Sussex Place Regent's Park London NW1
4SP
Tel: 020 7772 6400
wellbeingofwomen@rcog.org.uk
www.wellbeingofwomen.org.uk

Welsh Government Llywodraeth Cymru
Cathays Park Cardiff CF10 3NQ
Tel: 0300 0603300 or 0845 010 3300
Tel: Welsh: 0300 0604400 or 0845 010 440
wag-en@mailuk.custhelp.com
www.wales.gov.uk

Welsh Athletics
Official governing body for athletics in Wales
Cardiff International Sports Stadium
Leckwith Road Cardiff CF11 8AZ
Tel: 02920 644870
office@welshathletics.org
www.welshathletics.org

Welsh Cycling
Wales National Velodrome Newport
International Sport Village Velodrome Way
Newport South Wales NP19 4RB
Tel: 01633 670540
info@welshcycling.co.uk
www.britishcycling.org.uk/wales

Welsh Language Board (Bwrdd yr Iaith Gymraeg)
Site contains the archive of the Welsh
Language Board. The board was abolished
on 31 March 2012
www.welsh-language-board.org.uk

Welsh Language Society see Cymdeithas yr Iaith Gymraeg

Welsh National Opera
Wales Millennium Centre Bute Place Cardiff
CF10 5AL
Tel: 029 2063 5000
email via website
www.wno.org.uk

Welsh Sports Council see Sport Wales

Wessex Cancer Trust
Independent charity. Supports many
aspects of cancer care, including leading
edge research, the improvement of patient
facilities, purchase of much needed
equipment, patient grants, complementary
therapy and counselling services
Bellis House 11 Westwood Road
Southampton Hampshire SO17 1DL
Tel: 023 8067 2200
wct@wessexcancer.org
www.wessexcancer.org

Whale & Dolphin Conservation Society
Brookfield House 38 St Paul St Chippenham
Wiltshire SN15 1LY
Tel: 01249 449 500
info@wdcs.org
www.wdcs.org

What About The Children?
National charity. Information, research
& education on the emotional needs of
children under 3
Feldon House Chapel Lane Newbold on
Stour CV37 8TY
Tel: 0845 602 7145
enquiries@whataboutthechildren.org.uk
www.whataboutthechildren.org.uk

Wheelchair Sports Foundation (British)
see WheelPower

WheelPower
British wheelchair sport. Promotes and
develops sports for both adults and children
with disabilities
Stoke Mandeville Stadium Guttmann Rd
Stoke Mandeville Bucks HP21 9PP
Tel: 01296 395995
info@wheelpower.org.uk
www.wheelpower.org.uk

Wheels for All see Cycling Projects

Which?
Campaign to protect consumer rights, review
products and offer independent advice
Castlemead Gascoyne Way Hertford SG14
1LH
Tel: 01992 822800
email via web
www.which.co.uk

White House

1600 Pennsylvania Avenue NW Washington
DC 20500
Tel: 001 202 456 1414
email via website
www.whitehouse.gov

White Ribbon Alliance For safe motherhood

Aims to ensure that pregnancy and
childbirth are safe for all women and
newborns in every country around the world.
2nd Floor, 138 Portobello Road London W11
2DZ
Tel: 0207 965 6060
info-uk@whiteribbonalliance.org
www.whiteribbonalliance.org

Whizz-Kidz

Provides mobility equipment to disabled
children
4th Floor Portland House Bressenden Place
London SW1E 5BH
Tel: 020 7233 6600
Email via website
www.whizz-kidz.org.uk

Who Cares? Trust

Improving education, employment, health,
counselling & information services for young
people in public care
Kemp House 152-160 City Rd
London EC1V 2NP
Tel: 020 7251 3117
mailbox@thewhocarestrust.org.uk
www.thewhocarestrust.org.uk

Wild Flower Society

Identifies and records wild flowers in Britain
www.thewildflowersociety.com

Wildfowl & Wetlands Trust (WWT) Saving

wetlands for wildlife & people
Leading conservation organisation saving
wetlands for wildlife and people across the
world
Slimbridge Gloucs GL2 7BT
Tel: 01453 891900
enquiries@wwt.org.uk
www.wwt.org.uk

Wildlife Aid

Rescue, rehabilitation, care of sick, injured
and orphaned British wildlife and strong
educational emphasis
Randalls Farmhouse Randalls Rd
Leatherhead Surrey KT22 OAL
Helpline: 09061 800 132
Tel: 01372 377332 (Admin only)
Email via website
www.wildlifeaid.org.uk

Wildlife and Countryside Link

Brings together voluntary organisations
in the UK to protect and enhance wildlife,
landscape and the marine environment,
and to further the quiet enjoyment and
appreciation of the countryside
89 Albert Embankment London SE1 7TP
Tel: 020 7820 8600
enquiry@wcl.org.uk
www.wcl.org.uk

Wildlife Trusts (Royal Society of)

Administers lottery funding to provide grants
to communities for various environmental
projects. The 47 regional Wildlife Trusts are
dedicated to protecting wildlife for the
future
The Kiln Waterside Mather Road Newark
NG24 1WT
Tel: 01636 677711
enquiry@wildlifetrusts.org
www.wildlifetrusts.org

Williams Syndrome Foundation (UK)

Supports those affected by this non-
hereditary chromosomal disorder
161 High Street Tonbridge Kent TN9 1BX
Tel: 01732 365152
email via website
www.williams-syndrome.org.uk

Willow Foundation

Charity dedicated to improving the quality of
life of seriously ill young people aged 16-40
through the provision of special days
Willow House 18 Salisbury Square Hatfield
Hertfordshire AL9 5BE
Tel: 01707 259777
info@willowfoundation.org.uk
www.willowfoundation.org.uk

WILPF see Peace & Freedom (Women's
International League for)

Wimbledon

Official site of the tennis tournament
www.wimbledon.com

Wind Energy Association (European) EWEA

Rue d'Arlon 80 B-1040 Brussels Belgium
Tel: 0032 2 213 1811
ewea@ewea.org
www.ewea.org

Wind Sand & Stars

School journeys and expeditions to the
desert and mountains of Sinai, Egypt
PO Box 4322 Bath BA1 2BU
Tel: 01225 320 839
office@windsandstars.co.uk
www.windsandstars.co.uk

Windsurfing Association (UK) UKWA
Organises & provides first class national competition
PO Box 703 Haywards Heath RH16 9EE
admin@ukwindsurfing.com
www.ukwindsurfing.com

Winston Churchill Memorial Trust
Offers Fellowships to acquire knowledge and experience abroad.
South Door 29 Great Smith Street London SW1P 3BL
Tel: 0207 799 1660
office@wcmt.org.uk
www.wcmt.org.uk

Winston's Wish The charity for bereaved children
Offers practical support and guidance to families, professionals and anyone concerned about a grieving child
3rd Floor Cheltenham House Clarence Street Cheltenham Gloucestershire GL50 3JR
Helpline: 08452 03 04 05
Tel: 01242 515157
info@winstonswish.org.uk
www.winstonswish.org.uk

Winvisible (Women with visible & invisible disabilities) contact Crossroads Women's Centre
www.allwomencount.net

Wired Safety
Dedicated to helping protect children in cyberspace
www.wiredsafety.org

Wireless for the Blind Fund (British)
Provides radio equipment on free permanent loan to registered blind & partially-sighted people in need
10 Albion Place Maidstone Kent ME14 5DZ
Tel: 01622 754 757
Email via website
www.blind.org.uk

Womankind Worldwide
Working with women in the developing world and the UK in the field of human rights
2nd Floor, Development House 56-64 Leonard Street London EC2A 4LT
Tel: 020 7549 0360
info@womankind.org.uk
www.womankind.org.uk

Women (National Assembly of)
Campaigning for full social, economic, legal, political & cultural equality for women
naw@sisters.org.uk
www.sisters.org.uk

Women and Manual Trades WAMT
The national organisation for tradeswomen and women training in skilled craft trades
52-54 Featherstone Street London EC1Y 8RT
Tel: 020 7251 9192
info@wamt.org
www.wamt.org

Women Entrepreneurs (British Association of) BAWE
British Affiliate to the World Association of Women Entrepreneurs (FCEM) with 40 countries and 80,000 members founded in France 1945
Tel: 01827 312 812
president@bawe-uk.org
www.bawe-uk.org

Women in Prison
Campaigns on issues affecting women in prison and provides education, support and welfare. NB Does not have the capacity to respond to enquiries from students and researchers. Please refer to website
Unit 10, The Ivories 6 Northampton Street London N1 2HY
Freephone advice line: 0800 953 0125 (offenders and ex-offenders seeking help on Tel: 020 7359 6674
Email via website
www.womeninprison.org.uk

Women in Publishing
Website of information designed to promote the status of women working in publishing
info@womeninpublishing.org.uk
www.womeninpublishing.org.uk

Women Into Science & Engineering (WISE)
The UKRC Athlone Wing, Old Building Great Horton Road Bradford, BD7 1AY
Tel: 01274 436485
email via website
www.wisecampaign.org.uk

Women living under Muslim laws
An international network that provides information, solidarity and support for all women whose lives are shaped, conditioned or governed by laws and customs said to derive from Islam
PO Box 28455 London N19 5JT
www.wluml.org

Women of Great Britain (National Council of) Giving women a voice
Work nationally and internationally on issues of concern to women
72 Victoria Road Darlington Co. Durham DL1 5JG
Tel: 01325 367375
info@ncwgb.org
www.ncwgb.org

Women Solicitors (Association of)

Network helping to promote the potential and success of each women solicitor at every stage of her career
Email via website
www.womensolicitors.org.uk

Women Working Worldwide

Supports the struggles of women workers throughout the world
MMU Manton Building Rosamond Street West Manchester M15 6LL
Tel: 0161 247 1760
Or: 0161 247 6171
contact@women-ww.org
www.women-ww.org

Women's Aid (Scottish)

National office for 40 affiliated Women's Aid groups in Scotland who provide information, refuge and support for women, children and young people experiencing domestic abuse
2nd Floor 132 Rose Street Edinburgh EH2 3JD
24 hr Domestic Abuse Helpline: 0800 027 1234
Tel: 0131 226 6606
contact@scottishwomensaid.org.uk
www.scottishwomensaid.org.uk

Women's Aid (Welsh)

National umbrella organisation for women's aid groups throughout Wales
Wales Domestic Abuse Helpline: 0808 80 10 800
email via website
www.welshwomensaid.org

Women's Aid Federation (N. Ireland)

Provides help for women and children experiencing domestic violence in N. Ireland
129 University St Belfast BT7 1HP
Helpline: 0800 917 1414
Tel: 028 9024 9041
Email via website
www.womensaidni.org

Women's Aid Federation of England

National charity working to end domestic violence against women and children. We support a network of over 500 domestic and sexual violence services across the UK
PO Box 391 Bristol BS99 7WS
24hr National Domestic Violence Helpline 0808 2000 247
Tel: 0117 944 4411 (general enquiries only)
info@womensaid.org.uk helpline@womensaid.org.uk
www.womensaid.org.uk
www.thehideout.org.uk

Women's Archive of Wales

Collecting, preserving and publicising sources for women's history in Wales
South Wales Miners' Library Hendrefoelan Campus Gower Road Swansea SA2 7NB
info@womensarchivewales.org
www.womensarchivewales.org

Women's Bowling Federation (English)

www.fedbowls.co.uk

Women's Clubs (National Association of)

Clubs to promote education, recreation and friendship for the benefit of women
5 Vernon Rise King's Cross Rd London WC1X 9EP
Tel: 020 7837 1434
www.nawc.org.uk

Women's Cricket see Cricket Board (England & Wales)

Women's Engineering Society

Inspiring women as engineers, scientists and technical leaders
The IET Michael Faraday House Six Hills Way Stevenage Hertfordshire SG1 2AY
Tel: 01483 765506
Email via website
www.wes.org.uk

Women's Environmental Network

Campaigns on issues which link women, the environment and health
Ground Floor 20 Club Row London E2 7EY
Tel: 020 7481 9004
info@wen.org.uk
www.wen.org.uk

Women's Food & Farming Union

Cargill plc Witham St Hughs Lincoln LN6 9TN
Tel: 0844 3350 342
secretary@wfu.org.uk
www.wfu.org.uk

Women's Golf Association (English) now see Golf UK

Women's Institutes (National Federation of) NFWI

Largest voluntary organisation for women in the UK
104 New Kings Road London SW6 4LY
Tel: 020 7371 9300
Email via website
www.thewi.org.uk

Women's Library Celebrating and recording women's lives
The most extensive collection of women's history in the UK
London Metropolitan University 25 Old Castle Street Aldgate London E1 7NT
Tel: 020 7320 2222
moreinfo@thewomenslibrary.ac.uk
www.thewomenslibrary.ac.uk

Women's Register (National)

Coordinates women's groups to enable women to find new friends and widen their horizons
Unit 23 Vulcan House Vulcan Rd North Norwich NR6 6AQ
Tel: 0845 450 0287
Email via website
www.nwr.org

Women's Resource Centre

Co-ordinating and support body for non-profit groups working for and with women
Ground Floor East 33-41 Dallington Street London EC1V 0BB
Tel: 020 7324 3030
Email via website
www.wrc.org.uk

Women's Royal Voluntary Service see WRVS

Women's Sports & Fitness Foundation

Charity that campaigns to make physical activity an everyday part of life for women and girls. Aims to create a nation of active women
Victoria House Bloomsbury Square London WC1B 4SE
Tel: 0207 273 1740
email via website
www.wsf.org.uk

Women's Therapy Centre

Individual and group psychotherapy advice and information, training and education to professionals
10 Manor Gardens London N7 6JS
Tel: 020 7263 6200
Tel: 020 7263 7860 (General enquiries)
enquiries@womenstherapycentre.co.uk
www.womenstherapycentre.co.uk

Wood Green Animal Shelters

Take in unwanted and lost animals, provide shelter and care, find secure and loving homes, provide advice, support and guidance for pet owners and increase the public's awareness of its responsibility towards animals in society
601 Lordship Lane Wood Green London N22 5LG
Tel: 0844 248 8181
email via website
www.woodgreen.org.uk

Woodcraft Folk

Develop children's self-confidence and build their awareness of society around them, through activities, outings and camps. Help members understand important issues like the environment, world debt and global conflict etc
Units 9-10 83 Crampton Street London SE17 3BQ
Tel: 020 7703 4173
info@woodcraft.org.uk
www.woodcraft.org.uk

Woodland Trust

Protects native woodland heritage
Kempton Way Grantham Lincolnshire NG31 6LL
Tel: 01476 581111
enquiries@woodlandtrust.org.uk
www.woodlandtrust.org.uk

Woodworking Federation (British)

Trade association for the woodworking and joinery manufacturing industry in the UK
The Building Centre 26 Store Street London WC1E 7BT
Tel: 0844 209 2610
bwf@bwf.org.uk
www.bwf.org.uk

Wool Museum (National)

Dre-Fach Felindre Llandysul Carmarthenshire SA44 5UP
Tel: 029 2057 3070
email via website
www.museumwales.ac.uk/en/wool/

Work & Pensions (Department for) DWP

Government agency responsible for benefit & pension claims
www.dwp.gov.uk

Work Foundation

Campaign to make a better working life for employees
21 Palmer Street London SW1H 0AD
Tel: 020 7976 3565
email via website
www.theworkfoundation.com

Workaholics Anonymous

Self help groups with international coverage
www.workaholics-anonymous.org

Workers Educational Association WEA

Provides education for adults who are not full-time students
4 Luke Street London EC2A 4XW
Tel: 020 7426 3450
national@wea.org.uk
www.wea.org.uk

Working Class Movement Library

A unique collection capturing the stories and struggles of ordinary people's efforts to improve their world - Access by appointment only
51 The Crescent Salford M5 4WX
Tel: 0161 736 3601
Email via website
www.wcml.org.uk

Working Families

Information & support & campaigns on issues of concern for working parents
1-3 Berry St London EC1V 0AA
Helpline: 0800 013 0312
Tel: 020 7253 7243
advice@workingfamilies.org.uk
www.workingfamilies.org.uk

Working For A Charity

Offers training courses aimed at people wanting to move into the voluntary sector
NCVO Regent's Wharf 8 All Saints Street London N1 9RL
Tel: 020 7520 2512
www.workingforacharity.org.uk

Working Men's College for Women & Men
Europe's longest established college for adult learning
44 Crowndale Rd London NW1 1TR
Tel: 020 7255 4700
info@wmcollege.ac.uk
www.wmcollege.ac.uk

Working on Wheels
Promotes effective use of community work on converted vehicles throughout the UK
Brunswick Court Brunswick Square Bristol BS2 8PE
Tel: 0117 916 6580
info@workingonwheels.org
www.workingonwheels.org

& Scotland
Promotes effective use of community work on converted vehicles throughout the UK
Gilmerton Community Centre 4 Drum Street Edinburgh EH17 8QG
Tel: 0131 664 4922
lesley@workingonwheels.org
www.workingonwheels.org

Working with men
Develops support projects that benefit the development of men and boys. Raises awareness of issues impacting upon men and boys.
Unit K308 Tower Bridge Business Complex 100 Clements Road London SE16 4DG
Tel: 020 7237 5353
info@workingwithmen.org
www.workingwithmen.org

WorkLife Support Limited
Provides employee assistance programmes for LEAs and schools and also programmes where staff feedback to management ideas of what works in a school to improve its atmosphere and culture
Suite G, Maples Business Centre 144 Liverpool Road London N1 1LA
Tel: 0845 873 5680
Email via website
www.worklifesupport.com

World AIDS Day
Takes place on 1st December every year
www.worldaidsday.org

World Bank
Committed to helping achieve the MDGs. Source of financial and technical assistance to developing countries around the world. Fighting poverty and helping people help themselves and their environment by providing resources and sharing knowledge
www.worldbank.org

World Cancer Research Fund International
WCRF International - Stopping cancer before it starts
Not-for-profit umbrella association that leads a global network of cancer charities based in the US, UK, Netherlands, Hong Kong and France. Dedicated to funding research and education programmes into the link between food, nutrition, physical activity, weight maintenance and cancer risk
22 Bedford Square London WC1B 3HH
Tel: 020 734 34200
info@wcrf.org
wcrf.org

World Challenge Expeditions
Provides leadership, teamwork & personal development training for young people
17-21 Queens Road High Wycombe Buckinghamshire HP13 6AQ
Tel: 01494 427600
email via website
www.world-challenge.co.uk

World Cup
The official site for the Football World Cup
www.fifa.com

World Development Movement
Campaigns to tackle the root causes of poverty
66 Offley Road London SW9 0LS
Tel: 020 7820 4900
wdm@wdm.org.uk
www.wdm.org.uk

World Food Programme (United Nations)
Via C.G.Viola 68 Parco dei Medici 00148 Rome Italy
Tel: 00 39 06 65131
Email via website
www.wfp.org

World Gazetteer
World population statistics
www.world-gazetteer.com

World Health Organisation
Avenue Appia 20 1211 Geneva 27 Switzerland
Tel: 00 41 22 791 21 11
email via website
www.who.int

World Horse Welfare
Charity dedicated to giving abused and neglected horses a second chance in life
Anne Colvin House Ada Cole Avenue Snetterton Norwich NR16 2LR
UK Welfare Hotline: 08000 480180
Tel: 01953 498682
info@worldhorsewelfare.org
www.worldhorsewelfare.org

World Jewish Relief
Acts on behalf of the UK Jewish community
to provide emergency and development
aid to those in need throughout the world
regardless of race, religion or ethnic origin
Oscar Joseph House 54 Crewys Road
London NW2 2AD
Tel: 020 8736 1250
info@wjr.org.uk
www.wjr.org.uk

World Ju-Jitsu Federation (Ireland)
The Dojo Unit 7, No. 1 Woodside Industrial
Estate Woodside Road Ballymena BT42 4QJ
Tel: 028 2563 8511
wjjf@jujitsuireland.com
www.jujitsuireland.com

World Land Trust
Purchases and protects critically threatened
wilderness areas
Blyth House, Bridge Street Halesworth
Suffolk, IP19 8AB
Tel: 0845 054 4422
info@worldlandtrust.org
www.worldlandtrust.org

World Monuments Fund Britain
Charity that promotes on-site conservation
of cultural landmarks and supports
educational activities
70 Cowcross Street London EC1M 6EJ
Tel: 0207 251 8142
enquiries@wmf.org.uk
www.wmf.org.uk

World Museum
Discover treasures from around the world,
explore outer space and meet live creatures!
William Brown Street Liverpool L3 8EN
Tel: 0151 478 4393
Learning department: 0151 478 4296
email via website
www.liverpoolmuseums.org.uk/wml

World Rugby Museum
Twickenham Stadium Rugby Road
Twickenham Middlesex TW1 1DZ
Tel: 020 8892 8877
Email via website
www.rfu.com/microsites/museum

**World Society for the Protection of
Animals** see WSPA International

World Space Week
The Largest Public Space Event on Earth -
celebrated in over 55 Nations every October 4-10
www.worldspaceweek.org

World Tourism Organization WTO
Inter-governmental body for the promotion
and development of tourism
Capitán Haya 42 28020 Madrid Spain
Tel: 00 34 91 567 81 00
omt@unwto.org
www.world-tourism.org

World Trade Organization WTO
Administers multilateral trade agreements,
acts as a forum for negotiations, and handles
international trade disputes
www.wto.org

World Travel & Tourism Council
1-2 Queen Victoria Terrace Sovereign Court
London E1W 3HA
Tel: 020 7481 8007
email via website
www.wttc.org

World Vision UK
Humanitarian aid and development agency
Opal Drive Fox Milne Milton Keynes MK15
0ZR
Tel: 01908 84 10 00
info@worldvision.org.uk
www.worldvision.org.uk

World Wide Fund for Nature see WWF-UK

**World Wide Opportunities on Organic
Farms** see WWOOF

Worldometers
World statistics updated in real time
www.worldometers.info

WorldWide Volunteering
Search and match database of 350,000 UK
and worldwide volunteering opportunities
for all ages
7 North Street Workshops Stoke sub
Hamdon Somerset TA14 6QR
Tel: 01935 825588
email via website
www.wwv.org.uk

WRAP
Works in partnership, helping businesses
and the general public to reduce waste, to
use more recycled material and recycle more
things more often
The Old Academy 21 Horse Fair Banbury
OX16 0AH
Resource Efficiency Helpline: 0808 100 2040
Switchboard: 01295 819 900
Envirowise advice line: 0800 585 794
Email via website
www.wrap.org.uk

**Writers in Education (National Association
of)** NAWE
Supports development of creative writing
PO Box 1 Sheriff Hutton York YO60 7YU
Tel: 01653 618 429
Email via website
www.nawe.co.uk

Writers' Guild of Great Britain
40 Rosebery Avenue London EC1R 4RX
Tel: 020 7833 0777
erik@writersguild.org.uk
www.writersguild.org.uk

WriteToThem.com
Allows you to contact your MP even if you don't know their name or your constituency
Email via website
www.writetothem.com

WRVS
Registered charity helping people maintain independence and dignity in their homes and communities, particularly in later life
Beck Court Cardiff Gate Business Park Cardiff CF23 8RP
Tel: 0845 600 5885
Email via website
www.wrvs.org.uk

WSPA International World Society for the Protection of Animals
Promoting animal welfare. Concentrate on regions of the world where few, if any, measures exist to protect animals
5th Floor 222 Grays Inn Road   London WC1X 8HB
Tel: 0800 316 9966
Tel: 020 7587 0500
wspa@wspa.org.uk
www.wspa.org.uk

WWF-UK
Charity conserving and protecting endangered species & habitats, for the benefit of people & nature
Panda House Weyside Park Godalming Surrey GU7 1XR
Tel: 01483 426 444
Email via website
www.wwf.org.uk
www.panda.org

WWOOF UK World Wide Opportunities on Organic Farms
Membership charity teaching people about organic growing and low-impact lifestyles through hands-on experience in the UK. Holds a list of organic farms, gardens and smallholdings, all offering food and accommodation in exchange for practical help on their land
PO Box 2154 Winslow Buckinghamshire MK18 3WS
Email via website
www.wwoof.org.uk
www.wwoof.org (international)

Y

Y Care International
YMCA's international relief and development agency. Work in partnership with YMCAs across the developing world to respond to the needs of the most disadvantaged young people
Kemp House 152-160 City Road London EC1V 2NP
Tel: 020 7549 3150
enquiries@ycareinternational.org
www.ycareinternational.org

Yachting Association (Royal)
National body for all forms of boating, including dinghy and yacht racing, motor and sail cruising
RYA House Ensign Way Hamble Southampton SO31 4YA
Tel: 023 8060 4100
enquiries@rya.org.uk
www.rya.org.uk

Year Out Group
Provides a total reference and resource for all that is needed to make the most of a Year Out (Gap Year).
Queensfield 28 Kings Road Easterton Wiltshire SN10 4PX
email via website
www.yearoutgroup.org

YHA Youth Hostel Association (UK)
Accommodation and activity provider. All ages, families and groups welcome
Trevelyan House Dimple Road Matlock Derbyshire DE4 3YH
Tel: 01629 592600 or 0800 0191700
customerservices@yha.org.uk
www.yha.org.uk

YMCA England
Committed to helping young people, particularly at times of need
29-35 Farringdon Road London, EC1M 3JF
Tel: 020 7186 9500
enquiries@ymca.org.uk
www.ymca.org.uk

Ymgyrch Diogelu Cymru Wledig see Protection of Rural Wales (Campaign for the)

Yoga (British Wheel of)
25 Jermyn St Sleaford Lincs NG34 7RU
Tel: 01529 306851
office@bwy.org.uk
www.bwy.org.uk

Yoga (Iyengar Institute)
223a Randolph Avenue Maida Vale London W9 1NL
Tel: 020 7624 3080
office@iyi.org.uk
www.iyi.org.uk

Young Christian Workers

St Josephs, off St Joseph's Grove (Watford Way) Hendon London NW4 4TY
Tel: 020 8203 6290
info@ycwimpact.com
www.ycwimpact.com

Young Concert Artists Trust

Identifies, nurtures and promotes outstanding young classical soloists and chamber ensembles trained in the UK
23 Garrick St London WC2E 9BN
Tel: 020 7379 8477
info@ycat.co.uk
www.ycat.co.uk

Young Engineers

National network of engineering, electronics & technology clubs and run engineering competitions in schools and colleges
Chiltlee Manor Liphook Hampshire GU30 7AZ
Tel: 01428 727265
Email via website
www.youngeng.org

Young Enterprise

Practical enterprise activities for young people aged 4-25, supported by business and industry volunteers
Peterley House Peterley Rd Oxford OX4 2TZ
Tel: 01865 776845
info@young-enterprise.org.uk
www.young-enterprise.org.uk

Young Farmers' Clubs (National Federation of)

YFC Centre 10th Street Stoneleigh Park Kenilworth Warwickshire CV8 2LG
Tel: 024 7685 7200
post@nfyfc.org.uk
www.nfyfc.org.uk

Young Fathers Initiative

Information and advice about fatherhood
Working with Men Unit K401 Tower Bridge Business Complex London SE16 4DG
Tel: 020 7237 5353
info@workingwithmen.org
www.young-fathers.org.uk

Young Men's Christian Association see
YMCA England

Young People in Focus

The organisation has closed but the site retains an archive of its work including information resources.
www.youngpeopleinfocus.org.uk

Young People with ME (Association of)

AYME

Offers cheerful support for all children and young people with ME aged 5 to 25. Free membership to eligible applicants
10 Vermont Place Tongwell Milton Keynes MK15 8JA
Tel: 08451 232389
info@ayme.org.uk
www.ayme.org.uk

Young Scot

Scottish youth information for 11 - 26 year olds
InfoLine: 0808 801 0338 or text 'callback' to 87023
infoline@youngscot.org
www.youngscot.org

Young Women's Christian Association now
see Platform 51

YoungMinds

National charity committed to improving the mental health of all children and young people
Suite 11, Baden Place Crosby Row London SE1 1YW
Parents helpline: 0808 802 5544
Tel: 020 7089 5050
Email via website
www.youngminds.org.uk

Your Life

Accurate information related to reproductive and sexual health
www.your-life.com

Youth Access

Provides referral service to youth information, advice & counselling services across the country
1 - 2 Taylors Yard 67 Alderbrook Rd London SW12 8AD
Tel: 020 8772 9900
admin@youthaccess.org.uk
www.youthaccess.org.uk

Youth Advocacy Service (National) NYAS

Help and guidance for all young people
Egerton House Tower Road Birkenhead Wirral CH41 1FN
Tel: 0300 330 3131
Tel: 0151 649 8700
help@nyas.net
www.nyas.net

Youth Agency (National)

Aims to advance youth work to promote young people's development and their voice in public life
Eastgate House 19-23 Humberstone Road Leicester LE5 3GJ
Tel: 0116 242 7350
Email via website
www.nya.org.uk

Youth Arts Network (English National) see ENYAN

Youth Arts Wales (National)
Representing the National Youth Brass Band, Chamber Ensemble, Choir, Orchestra and Theatre of Wales and National Youth Dance, Wales
245 Western Ave Cardiff CF5 2YX
Tel: 02920 265 060
nyaw@nyaw.co.uk
www.nyaw.co.uk

Youth at Risk
Support and mentors for disadvantaged 15 -19 year olds
The Old Warehouse 31 Upper King Street Royston Herts SG8 9AZ
Tel: 01763 241120
Email via website
www.youthatrisk.org.uk

Youth Award Scheme see ASDAN

Youth Cancer Trust
Provides free, fun activity based holidays for young people (aged 14 to 30) suffering with cancer or any malignant disease, from anywhere in the UK and the Irish Republic, or who are patients of any UK hospital
Tracy Ann House 5 Studland Road Alum Chine Bournemouth BH4 8HZ
Tel: 01202 763591
admin@yct.org.uk
www.yct.org.uk

Youth Choir of Great Britain (National)
NYCBG
Nurtures exceptional young musical talent. Offers residential courses and concerts
Pelaw House University of Durham Leazes Road Durham DH1 1TA
Tel: 0191 3348110
office@nycgb.net
www.nycgb.net

Youth Clubs (UK) see UK Youth

Youth Council (British)
National voice for young people in the UK
CAN Mezzanine 49-51 East Road London N1 6AH
Tel: 0845 458 1489
email via website
www.byc.org.uk

Youth Council for Northern Ireland
Advisory body on quality of life for children and young people
Forestview Purdy's Lane Belfast BT8 7AR
Tel: 028 9064 3882
info@ycni.org
www.ycni.org

Youth for Christ
Christian outreach
Business Park East Unit D2, Coombswood Way Halesowen West Midlands B62 8BH
Tel: 0121 502 9620
email via website
www.yfc.co.uk

Youth Hostel see also Hostelling International, Hostelling International (N. Ireland), Hostels.com, SYHA Hostelling Scotland

Youth Hostel Association (N. Ireland) now see Hostelling International (N. Ireland)

Youth Hostel Association (UK) see YHA

Youth Hostel Federation (International) now see Hostelling International

Youth Hostels Association (Scottish) now see SYHA Hostelling Scotland

Youth in Action
UK National Agency for the European Commission's YOUTH programme eg youth exchange, voluntary service etc
British Council 10 Spring Gardens London SW1A 2BN
Tel: 0116 242 7400 (England)
Tel: 0131 313 2488 (Scotland)
Tel: 0289 064 3882 (Northern Ireland)
Tel: 02920 575 705 (Wales)
yia@nya.org.uk
www.britishcouncil.org/youthinaction

Youth Information The information toolkit for Young People
Information for young people from the National Youth Agency
www.youthinformation.com

Youth Justice Board for England and Wales now see Justice

Youth Music
UK charity using music to transform the lives of disadvantaged children and young people
Suites 3-5, Swan Court 9 Tanner Street London SE1 3LE
Tel: 020 7902 1060
info@youthmusic.org.uk
www.youthmusic.org.uk

Youth Music Theatre (National)
Adrian House 27 Vincent Square London SW1P 2NN
Tel: 020 7802 0386
enquiries@nymt.org.uk
www.nymt.org.uk

Youth Opera (British)
LSBU 103 Borough Road London SE1 0AA
Tel: 020 7815 6090
info@byo.org.uk
www.byo.org.uk

Youth Orchestra (National of GB)
Somerset House South Building London
WC2R 1LA
Tel: 020 7759 1880
info@nyo.org.uk
www.nyo.org.uk

Youth Sport Trust
Quality physical education and sport
programmes for all young people
SportPark Loughborough University
3 Oakwood Drive Loughborough LE11 3QF
Tel: 01509 226600
info@youthsporttrust.org
www.youthsporttrust.org

Youth Theatre see Scottish Youth Theatre,
Youth Music Theatre (National)

Youth Theatre of GB (National)
Acting, administration, costume making,
lighting and sound, scenery and prop
making or stage management for 14 - 21
year olds
Woolyard 52 Bermondsey Street London
SE1 3UD
Tel: 020 7281 3863
info@nyt.org.uk
www.nyt.org.uk

Youth Theatres (National Association of)
NAYT
Umbrella organisation for youth theatres
c/o York Theatre Royal St Leonard's Place
York YO1 7HD
Tel: 01325 363 330
Email via website
www.nayt.org.uk

Youthhealthtalk
Young people's real life experiences of health
and lifestyle
DIPEx PO Box 428 Witney Oxon OX28 9EU
Tel: 01865 201330
info@youthhealthtalk.org
www.youthhealthtalk.org

YouthNet UK
Website directs young people to where they
can obtain information about organisations
and publications
First Floor 50 Featherstone Street London
EC1Y 8RT
Tel: 020 7250 5700
email via website
www.youthnet.org

YWCA now see Platform 51

Z

Zoo Check see Born Free Foundation

Zoological Society of London
London Zoo Outer Circle Regent's Park
London NW1 4RY
& Whipsnade Zoo Dunstable
Bedfordshire LU6 2LF
Tel: 0844 225 1826
Email via website
www.zsl.org

Universities & Colleges

The majority of institutions accept applications via UCAS, but some, particularly specialist dance, drama, music and art institutions, require a direct application.

The institutions are arranged in alphabetical order by place name wherever possible.

UCAS
(Universities & Colleges Admissions Service)
www.ucas.ac.uk

Unistats
unistats.direct.gov.uk

Aberdeen
www.abdn.ac.uk/sras

Abertay
www.abertay.ac.uk

Aberystwyth
www.aber.ac.uk

Accrington & Rossendale College
www.accrosshighereducation.co.uk

American InterContinental University - London
www.aiulondon.ac.uk

Anglia Ruskin University
www.anglia.ac.uk

Anglo-European College of Chiropractic
www.aecc.ac.uk

Askham Bryan College
www.askham-bryan.ac.uk

Aston
Birmingham
www.aston.ac.uk

Bangor
www.bangor.ac.uk

Barking and Dagenham College
www.barkingdagenhamcollege.ac.uk

Barony College
now see Scotland's Rural College – SRUC

Basingstoke College of Technology
www.bcot.ac.uk

Bath
www.bath.ac.uk

Bath College (City of)
www.citybathcoll.ac.uk

Bath Spa
www.bathspa.ac.uk

Bedford College
www.bedford.ac.uk

Bedfordshire
www.beds.ac.uk

Belfast
see Queen's University, St. Mary's University College & Stranmillis University College

Birkbeck
University of London
www.bbk.ac.uk

Birmingham
www.birmingham.ac.uk

Birmingham (South & City College)
www.citycol.ac.uk

Birmingham City University
www.bcu.ac.uk

Birmingham Metropolitan College
www.bmetc.ac.uk

Birmingham, University College
www.ucb.ac.uk

Bishop Burton College
Beverley, East Yorkshire
www.bishopburton.ac.uk

Bishop Grosseteste College
Lincoln
www.bishopg.ac.uk

Blackburn College
www.blackburn.ac.uk

Blackpool and The Fylde College
www.blackpool.ac.uk

Bolton
www.bolton.ac.uk

Bournemouth
www.bournemouth.ac.uk

Bournemouth
The Arts University College at
www.aucb.ac.uk

BPP University College
www.bpp.com

Bradford
www.bradford.ac.uk

Bradford College
www.bradfordcollege.ac.uk

Bridgwater College
www.bridgwater.ac.uk

Brighton
www.brighton.ac.uk

Brighton & Sussex Medical School
www.bsms.ac.uk

Bristol
www.bristol.ac.uk

Bristol College (City of)
www.cityofbristol.ac.uk

Bristol Filton College
www.filton.ac.uk

British Institute of Technology & E-commerce
London
www.bite.ac.uk

British School of Osteopathy
www.bso.ac.uk

Brooklands College
www.brooklands.ac.uk

Brooksby Melton College
www.brooksbymelton.ac.uk

Brunel University
www.brunel.ac.uk

Buckingham
www.buckingham.ac.uk

Buckinghamshire New University
www.bucks.ac.uk

Cambridge
www.cam.ac.uk

Canterbury Christ Church University
www.canterbury.ac.uk

Cardiff
www.cardiff.ac.uk

Cardiff Metropolitan University
www3.cardiffmet.ac.uk

Carmarthenshire College
see Coleg Sir Gar

Castle College Nottingham
now see Central College Nottingham

Central College Nottingham
www.snc.ac.uk

Central Lancashire
www.uclan.ac.uk

Central School of Speech & Drama
www.cssd.ac.uk

Chester
www.chester.ac.uk

Chichester
www.chiuni.ac.uk

Chichester College
www.chichester.ac.uk

City University London
www.city.ac.uk

Cleveland College of Art and Design
www.ccad.ac.uk

Cliff College
www.cliffcollege.ac.uk

Colchester Institute
www.colchester.ac.uk

Coleg Llandrillo, Cymru
www.llandrillo.ac.uk

Coleg Menai
www.menai.ac.uk

Coleg Sir Gar/Carmarthenshire College
www.colegsirgar.ac.uk

College of Agriculture, Food and Rural Enterprise
Antrim
www.cafre.ac.uk

Cornwall College
www.cornwall.ac.uk

Courtauld Institute of Art
(University of London)
www.courtauld.ac.uk

Coventry
www.coventry.ac.uk

Coventry (City College)
www.covcollege.ac.uk

Craven College
www.craven-college.ac.uk

Creative Arts, University for the
www.ucreative.ac.uk

Croydon College
www.croydon.ac.uk

Cumbria University
www.cumbria.ac.uk

Dartington College of Arts
Now see Falmouth

Dearne Valley College
www.dearne-coll.ac.uk

Derby
www.derby.ac.uk

Dewsbury College
now see Kirklees College

Doncaster College
www.don.ac.uk

Duchy College
www.duchy.ac.uk

Dudley College of Technology
www.dudleycol.ac.uk

Dundee
www.dundee.ac.uk

Durham
www.dur.ac.uk

Durham (New College)
www.newdur.ac.uk

Ealing, Hammersmith & West London College
www.wlc.ac.uk

East Anglia
www.uea.ac.uk

East London
www.uel.ac.uk

Easton College
www.easton-college.ac.uk

East Riding College
www.eastridingcollege.ac.uk

East Surrey College
(Incorporating Reigate School of Art, Design & Media)
www.esc.ac.uk

Edge Hill University
www.edgehill.ac.uk

Edinburgh
www.ed.ac.uk

Edinburgh
see also Heriot-Watt, Napier, Queen Margaret

Edinburgh College of Art
www.eca.ac.uk

Edinburgh: Queen Margaret University
www.qmu.ac.uk

Essex
www.essex.ac.uk

European Business School, London
www.ebslondon.ac.uk

European School of Economics
www.eselondon.ac.uk

European School of Osteopathy
www.eso.ac.uk

Exeter
www.exeter.ac.uk

Exeter College
www.exe-coll.ac.uk/HE

Exeter Medical School (University of)
www.exeter.ac.uk/medicine

Falmouth (University College)
www.falmouth.ac.uk

Farnborough College of Technology
www.farn-ct.ac.uk

Glamorgan
www.glam.ac.uk

Glasgow
www.gla.ac.uk

Glasgow Caledonian University
www.gcu.ac.uk

Glasgow School of Art
www.gsa.ac.uk

Gloucestershire
www.glos.ac.uk

Gloucestershire College
www.gloscol.ac.uk

Glyndwr University
formerly North East Wales Institute of Higher Education
www.glyndwr.ac.uk

Goldsmiths College

(University of London)
www.gold.ac.uk

Gower College Swansea
www.gowercollegeswansea.ac.uk

Greenmount and Enniskillen Colleges
see College of Agriculture, Food and Rural Enterprise

Greenwich
www2.gre.ac.uk

Greenwich School of Management
www.greenwich-college.ac.uk

Grimsby Institute and University Centre
www.grimsby.ac.uk

Guildford College of Further and Higher Education
www.guildford.ac.uk

Harper Adams University College
www.harper-adams.ac.uk

Havering College of Further and Higher Education
www.havering-college.ac.uk

Hereford College of Arts
www.hca.ac.uk

Heriot-Watt
www.hw.ac.uk

Hertfordshire
www.herts.ac.uk

Heythrop College
(University of London)
www.heythrop.ac.uk

Highbury College
www.highbury.ac.uk

Highlands & Islands
www.uhi.ac.uk

Holborn College
www.holborncollege.ac.uk

Hopwood Hall College
www.hopwood.ac.uk

Huddersfield
www.hud.ac.uk

Huddersfield Technical College
now see Kirklees College

Hull
www2.hull.ac.uk

Hull College
www.hull-college.ac.uk/higher-education

Hull York Medical School
www.hyms.ac.uk

ifs School of Finance
www.ifslearning.ac.uk

Imperial College
(University of London)
www.imperial.ac.uk

Islamic College for Advanced Studies
www.islamic-college.ac.uk

Keele
www.keele.ac.uk

Kensington College of Business
www.kensingtoncoll.ac.uk

Kent
www.kent.ac.uk

Kent Institute of Art and Design
see Creative Arts, University for the

King's College London
www.kcl.ac.uk

Kingston
www.kingston.ac.uk

Kirklees College
www.kirkleescollege.ac.uk

LCA Business School
London
www.lcabusinessschool.com

Lakes College West Cumbria
www.lcwc.ac.uk

Lampeter
now see Trinity Saint David

Lancaster
www.lancs.ac.uk

Leeds
www.leeds.ac.uk

Leeds City College
www.leedscitycollege.ac.uk

Leeds College of Art
www.leeds-art.ac.uk

Leeds College of Music
www.lcm.ac.uk

Leeds Metropolitan University
www.leedsmet.ac.uk

Leeds: Trinity University
www.leedstrinity.ac.uk

Leicester
www.le.ac.uk

Leicester College
www.leicestercollege.ac.uk

Leicester: De Montfort
www.dmu.ac.uk

Lincoln
www.lincoln.ac.uk

Lincoln College (including Newark & Gainsborough Colleges)
www.lincolncollege.ac.uk

Liverpool
www.liv.ac.uk

Liverpool Community College
www.liv-coll.ac.uk

Liverpool Hope University College
www.hope.ac.uk

Liverpool Institute for Performing Arts
www.lipa.ac.uk

Liverpool John Moores University
www.ljmu.ac.uk

Llandrillo College
see Coleg Llandrillo

London College, UCK
www.lcuck.ac.uk

London Electronics College
www.lec.org.uk

London Guildhall University
see London Metropolitan University

London Metropolitan University
www.londonmet.ac.uk

London: Queen Mary
(University of London)
www.qmul.ac.uk

London School of Commerce
www.lsclondon.co.uk

London School of Economics and Political Science
(University of London)
www.lse.ac.uk

London School of Science and Technology
www.lsst.com

London South Bank University
www.lsbu.ac.uk

London: University of West London
www.uwl.ac.uk

Loughborough
www.lboro.ac.uk

Loughborough College
www.loucoll.ac.uk

Manchester
www.manchester.ac.uk

Manchester College, The
www.themanchestercollege.ac.uk

Manchester Metropolitan University
www.mmu.ac.uk

Medway School of Pharmacy
www.msp.ac.uk

Menai
see Coleg Menai

Mid-Cheshire College
www.midchesh.ac.uk

Middlesex
www.mdx.ac.uk

Moulton College
www.moulton.ac.uk

Mountview Academy of Theatre Arts
www.mountview.org.uk

Myerscough College
www.myerscough.ac.uk

Napier
Edinburgh
www.napier.ac.uk

Nazarene Theological College
www.nazarene.ac.uk

Neath Port Talbot College
www.nptc.ac.uk

NESCOT
North East Surrey College of Technology
www.nescot.ac.uk

New College Telford
www.nct.ac.uk

Newcastle
www.ncl.ac.uk

Newcastle College
www.ncl-coll.ac.uk

Newham College London
www.newham.ac.uk

Newman University College Birmingham
www.newman.ac.uk

Newport
www.newport.ac.uk

North East Surrey College of Technology
see NESCOT

North East Worcestershire College
www.ne-worcs.ac.uk

North Glasgow College
www.northglasgowcollege.ac.uk

North Lindsey College
www.northlindsey.ac.uk

North London
see London Metropolitan University

North Warwickshire and Hinckley College
www.nwhc.ac.uk

Northampton
www.northampton.ac.uk

Northbrook College Sussex
www.northbrook.ac.uk

Northumberland College
www.northumberland.ac.uk

Northumbria
www.northumbria.ac.uk

Norwich: City College
www.ccn.ac.uk

Norwich University College of the Arts
www.nuca.ac.uk

Nottingham
www.nottingham.ac.uk

Nottingham (New College)
www.ncn.ac.uk

Nottingham Trent University
www.ntu.ac.uk

Open University
www.open.ac.uk

Oxford
www.ox.ac.uk

Oxford and Cherwell Valley College
www.ocvc.ac.uk

Oxford Brookes
www.brookes.ac.uk

Paisley
now see West of Scotland

Paris (University of London Institute in)
www.ulip.lon.ac.uk

Pembrokeshire College
www.pembrokeshire.ac.uk

Peninsula College of Medicine and Dentistry
now see University of Exeter Medical School
or Plymouth University Peninsula Schools of
Medicine and Dentistry

Peterborough - University Centre
www.anglia.ac.uk/ucp

Petroc
www.petroc.ac.uk

Plymouth
www.plymouth.ac.uk

Plymouth College of Art
www.plymouthart.ac.uk

Plymouth University Peninsula Schools of Medicine and Dentistry
www1.plymouth.ac.uk/peninsula

Portsmouth
www.port.ac.uk

Queen's University
Belfast
www.qub.ac.uk

Ravensbourne
www.rave.ac.uk

Reading
www.reading.ac.uk

Regents Business School London
www.rbslondon.ac.uk

Richmond, The American International University in London
www.richmond.ac.uk

Riverside College Halton
Widnes
www.riversidecollege.ac.uk

270

Robert Gordon
Aberdeen
www.rgu.ac.uk

Roehampton
(University of Surrey)
www.roehampton.ac.uk

Rose Bruford
Sidcup
www.bruford.ac.uk

Rotherham College of Arts and Technology
www.rotherham.ac.uk

Royal Academy of Dance
London
www.rad.org.uk

Royal Agricultural College
Gloucester
www.rac.ac.uk

Royal College of Art
London (Post graduate only)
www.rca.ac.uk

Royal Holloway
London
www.rhul.ac.uk

Royal Veterinary College
London
www.rvc.ac.uk

Royal Welsh College of Music & Drama
Cardiff
www.rwcmd.ac.uk

Ruskin College Oxford
www.ruskin.ac.uk

SAE Institute
(School of Audio Engineering) Glasgow,
Liverpool & London
www.sae.edu

Salford
www.salford.ac.uk

Salisbury College
now see Wiltshire College

Sandwell College
www.sandwell.ac.uk

School of Oriental and African Studies
(University of London)
www.soas.ac.uk

School of Pharmacy
(University of London)
www.pharmacy.ac.uk

Scotland's Rural College – SRUC
www.sruc.ac.uk

Sheffield
www.sheffield.ac.uk

Sheffield College
www.sheffcol.ac.uk

Sheffield Hallam
www.shu.ac.uk

Solihull College
www.solihull.ac.uk

Somerset College of Arts and Technology
www.somerset.ac.uk

South Cheshire College
www.s-cheshire.ac.uk

South Devon College
www.southdevon.ac.uk

South Downs College
www.southdowns.ac.uk

South Essex College
www.southessex.ac.uk

South Tyneside College
www.stc.ac.uk

Southampton
www.southampton.ac.uk

Southampton Solent University
www.solent.ac.uk

Southport College
www.southport-college.ac.uk

Sparsholt College Hampshire
www.sparsholt.ac.uk

St Andrews
Fife
www.st-andrews.ac.uk

St George's University of London
www.sgul.ac.uk

St Helens College
www.sthelens.ac.uk

St Mary's University College
Twickenham
www.smuc.ac.uk

St Mary's University College
Belfast
www.smucb.ac.uk

Staffordshire
www.staffs.ac.uk

Stamford New College
www.stamford.ac.uk

Stephenson College Coalville
www.stephensoncoll.ac.uk

Stirling
www.stir.ac.uk

Stockport College
www.stockport.ac.uk

Stourbridge College
www.stourbridge.ac.uk

Stranmillis University College
Belfast
www.stran.ac.uk

Stratford upon Avon College
www.stratford.ac.uk

Strathclyde
www.strath.ac.uk

Suffolk, University Campus
www.ucs.ac.uk

Sunderland
www.sunderland.ac.uk

Sunderland College (City of)
www.citysun.ac.uk

Surrey
www.surrey.ac.uk

Sussex
www.sussex.ac.uk

Swansea
www.swansea.ac.uk

Swansea Metropolitan University
www.smu.ac.uk

Swindon College
www.swindon-college.ac.uk

Tameside College
www.tameside.ac.uk

Teesside
www.tees.ac.uk

Trinity St David
(University of Wales)
www.trinitysaintdavid.ac.uk

Truro and Penwith College
www.trurocollege.ac.uk

Tyne Metropolitan College
www.tynemet.ac.uk

UCP Marjon
St Mark and St John (The College of), Plymouth
www.marjon.ac.uk

UHI Millennium Institute
www.uhi.ac.uk

Ulster
www.ulster.ac.uk

University College London
www.ucl.ac.uk

University of the Arts London
Camberwell College of Arts, Central Saint
Martins College of Art and Design, Chelsea
College of Art and Design, London College of
Communication, London College of Fashion,
Wimbledon College of Art
www.arts.ac.uk

University of Wales Institute, Cardiff (UWIC)
see Cardiff Metropolitan University

Uxbridge College
www.uxbridgecollege.ac.uk

Wakefield College
www.wakefield.ac.uk

Walsall College
www.walsallcollege.ac.uk

Warrington Collegiate
www.warrington.ac.uk

Warwick
www.warwick.ac.uk

Warwickshire College
www.warwickshire.ac.uk

West Anglia (College of)
www.col-westanglia.ac.uk

West Cheshire College
www.west-cheshire.ac.uk

West of England
Bristol
www.uwe.ac.uk

West of Scotland
www.uws.ac.uk

West London
www.uwl.ac.uk

West Thames College
www.west-thames.ac.uk

Westminster
www.westminster.ac.uk

Westminster Kingsway College
www.westking.ac.uk

Wigan and Leigh College
www.wigan-leigh.ac.uk

Wiltshire College
www.wiltshire.ac.uk

Winchester
www.winchester.ac.uk

Wirral Metropolitan College
www.wmc.ac.uk

Wolverhampton
www.wlv.ac.uk

Worcester
www.worcester.ac.uk

Worcester College of Technology
www.wortech.ac.uk

Writtle College
www.writtle.ac.uk

York
www.york.ac.uk

York College
www.yorkcollege.ac.uk

York St John University College
www.yorksj.ac.uk

Yorkshire Coast College Scarborough
www.yorkshirecoastcollege.ac.uk

Dance, drama, music & performing arts

The institutions listed offer post-16 vocational training. This is different from the theatre, dance, drama and performing arts degrees offered by many universities.

Some institutions accept applications through UCAS but for the majority application will be direct.

Those listed as DADA are accredited to offer Dance and Drama (DADA) Awards. These cover most of the tuition fees for their courses, which are at National Certificate or National Diploma level. For 2013 entry, awards will be income assessed.

Drama UK, formed from the merger of the National Council for Drama Training (NCDT) and the Conference of Drama Schools (CDS), accredits vocational courses and acts as a voice for the sector, linking industry and training organisations.

The Council for Dance Education and Training (CDET) is the national standards body of the professional dance industry. It accredits programmes of training in vocational dance schools.

There are also prestigious institutions which function outside of other systems and administer their own admissions and funding.

Academy of Live and Recorded Arts (Alra)
Studio 24
Royal Victoria Patriotic Building
John Archer Way
London SW18 3SX
Tel: 020 8870 6475
email via website
www.alra.co.uk
ALRA North:
Turner Street
Wigan
WN1 3SU
Telephone, email and website as above
Drama UK

Arts Ed London
Cone Ripman House
14 Bath Rd
London W4 1LY
Tel: 020 8987 6666
email via website
www.artsed.co.uk
CDET DADA Drama UK

Bird College – Dance and Drama Theatre Performance
The Centre
27 Station Rd
Sidcup DA15 7EB
Tel: 020 8300 6004
For range of email addresses see website
www.birdcollege.co.uk
CDET DADA

Birmingham School of Acting
Millennium Point
Curzon Street
Birmingham B4 7XG
Tel: 0121 331 7220
info@bsa.bcu.ac.uk
www.bcu.ac.uk/pme/school-of-acting
Drama UK

Bristol Old Vic Theatre School
2 Downside Road
Clifton
Bristol BS8 2XF
Tel: 0117 973 3535
enquiries@oldvic.ac.uk
www.oldvic.ac.uk
Drama UK
Conservatoire for Dance and Drama

Cambridge Performing Arts at Bodyworks
Bodywork Dance Studios
25-29 Glisson Rd
Cambridge CB1 2HA
Tel: 01223 314461
Email via website
www.bodywork-dance.co.uk
CDET DADA

Central School of Ballet
10 Herbal Hill
Clerkenwell Road
London EC1R 5EG
Tel: 020 7837 6332
info@csbschool.co.uk
www.centralschoolofballet.co.uk
Conservatoire for Dance and Drama

Central School of Speech and Drama
Eton Avenue
London NW3 3HY
Tel: 020 7722 8183
admissions@cssd.ac.uk
www.cssd.ac.uk
Drama UK

Circus Space
Coronet Street
London, N1 6HD
Tel: 020 7729 9522
info@circusspace.co.uk
www.circusspace.co.uk

Conservatoire for Dance and Drama
Tavistock House,
Tavistock Square
London
WC1H 0JJ
Tel: 020 7387 5101
info@cdd.ac.uk
www.cdd.ac.uk
The Conservatoire is a Higher Education
Institution comprising eight small, specialist
institutions with international reputations for
high quality delivery in their respective fields:
Bristol Old Vic Theatre School
Central School of Ballet
Circus Space
London Academy of Music and Dramatic Art
London Contemporary Dance School
Northern School of Contemporary Dance
Rambert School of Ballet and Contemporary
Dance

CPA College
The Studios
219b North Street
Romford,
Essex
RM1 4QA
Tel: 01708 766 007
Email via website
www.cpastudios.co.uk
CDET

Drama Centre London
Central Saint Martins College of Arts and Design
University of the Arts London
Granary Building
1 Granary Square
King's Cross
London
N1C 4AA
Tel: 020 7514 8760
drama@arts.ac.uk
www.csm.arts.ac.uk
Drama UK

Drama Studio London
Grange Court
1 Grange Rd
Ealing
London W5 5QN
Tel: 020 8579 3897
admin@dramastudiolondon.co.uk
www.dramastudiolondon.co.uk
DADA Drama UK

East 15 Acting School
Loughton campus:
Hatfields
Rectory Lane
Loughton
Essex IG10 3RY
Tel: 020 8508 5983
Southend Campus:
Elmer Approach
Southend-on-Sea SS1 1LW, UK
Tel: 01702 328200
east15@essex.ac.uk
www.east15.ac.uk
Drama UK

Elmhurst School for Dance (in association with
Birmingham Royal Ballet)
249 Bristol Rd
Edgbaston
Birmingham B5 7UH
Tel: 0121 472 6655
enquiries@elmhurstdance.co.uk
www.elmhurstdance.co.uk
CDET DADA

English National Ballet School
Carlyle Building
Hortensia Road
London SW10 0QS
Tel: 020 7376 7076
info@enbschool.org.uk
www.enbschool.org.uk
CDET, DADA

Guildford School of Acting
Stag Hill Campus,
Guildford
Surrey GU2 7X
Tel: 01483 560701
www.gsauk.org
Drama UK

Guildhall School of Music & Drama
Silk Street
Barbican
London EC2Y 8DT
Tel: 020 7628 2571
registry@gsmd.ac.uk
www.gsmd.ac.uk
Drama UK

Hammond School
Mannings Lane
Chester CH2 4ES
Tel: 01244 305350
info@thehammondschool.co.uk
www.thehammondschool.co.uk
CDET, DADA

Italia Conti Academy of Theatre Arts Ltd
For BA (Hons) Acting:
'Avondale'
72 Landor Road
London, SW9 9PH
Tel: 020 7733 3210
For Theatre Arts School:
Italia Conti House
23 Goswell Road
London EC1M 7AJ
Tel: 020 7608 0044
admin@italiaconti.com
www.italiaconti.com
CDET DADA Drama UK

Laban see Trinity Laban Conservatoire of Music and Dance

Laine Theatre Arts
The Studios
East Street
Epsom
Surrey KT17 1HH
Tel: 01372 724 648
info@laine-theatre-arts.co.uk
www.laine-theatre-arts.co.uk
CDET DADA

LAMDA see London Academy of Music & Dramatic Art

Leeds College of Music
3 Quarry Hill
Leeds LS2 7PD
Tel: 0113 222 3400
enquiries@lcm.ac.uk
www.lcm.ac.uk

Liverpool Institute for Performing Arts
Mount Street
Liverpool L1 9HF
Tel: 0151 330 3000
reception@lipa.ac.uk
www.lipa.ac.uk
CDET

Liverpool Theatre School and College
Performing Arts Centre
19 Aigburth Road
Liverpool L17 4JR
Tel: 0151 728 7800
info@liverpooltheatreschool.co.uk
www.liverpooltheatreschool.co.uk
CDET DADA

London Academy of Music & Dramatic Art (LAMDA)
155 Talgarth Road
London W14 9DA
Tel: 020 8834 0510
enquiries@lamda.org.uk
www.lamda.org.uk
Drama UK
Conservatoire for Dance and Drama

London Contemporary Dance School
The Place
17 Dukes Road
London WC1H 9PY
Tel: 020 7121 1000
lcds@theplace.org.uk
www.theplace.org.uk
Conservatoire for Dance and Drama

London Studio Centre
artsdepot
5 Nether Street
Tally Ho Corner
North Finchley
London N12 0GA
Tel: 020 7837 7741
info@londonstudiocentre.org
www.london-studio-centre.co.uk
CDET

Manchester School of Theatre
Manchester Metropolitan University
Mabel Tylecote Building
Cavendish Street
Manchester
M15 6BG
Tel: 0161 247 1751
artdes.fac@mmu.ac.uk
www.theatre.mmu.ac.uk
Drama UK

Midlands Academy of Dance and Drama

Century House, Building B
428 Carlton Hill
Nottingham
NG4 1QA
Tel: 0115 911 0401
admin@maddcollege.supanet.com
www.maddcollege.co.uk
CDET

Millennium Performing Arts

29 Thomas Street
Woolwich
London SE18 6HU
Tel: 020 8301 8744
info@md2000.co.uk
www.md2000.co.uk
CDET, DADA

Mountview Academy of Theatre Arts

Ralph Richardson Memorial Studios
Kingfisher Place
Clarendon Road
London N22 6XF
Tel: 020 8881 2201
enquires@mountview.ac.uk
www.mountview.org.uk
DADA Drama UK

Northern Ballet School

The Dancehouse
10 Oxford Road
Manchester M1 5QA
Tel: 0161 237 1406
enquiries@northernballetschool.co.uk
www.northernballetschool.co.uk
CDET DADA

Northern School of Contemporary Dance

98 Chapeltown Road
Leeds LS7 4BH
Tel: 0113 219 3000
info@nscd.ac.uk
www.nscd.ac.uk
Conservatoire for Dance and Drama

Oxford School of Drama

Sansomes Farm Studios
Woodstock
Oxfordshire OX20 1ER
Tel: 01993 812 883
info@oxforddrama.ac.uk
www.oxforddrama.ac.uk
DADA Drama UK

Performers College

Southend Road
Corringham
Essex SS17 8JT
Tel: 01375 672 053
lesley@performerscollege.co.uk
www.performerscollege.co.uk
CDET DADA

Rambert School of Ballet & Contemporary Dance

Clifton Lodge
St. Margaret's Drive
Twickenham TW1 1QN
Tel: 0208 892 9960
info@rambertschool.org.uk
www.rambertschool.org.uk
Conservatoire for Dance and Drama

Rose Bruford College

Lamorbey Park
Burnt Oak Lane
Sidcup
Kent DA15 9DF
Tel: 020 8308 2600
enquiries@bruford.ac.uk
www.bruford.ac.uk
Drama UK

Royal Academy of Dance (Faculty of Education)

36 Battersea Square
London SW11 3RA
Tel: 020 7326 8000
info@rad.org.uk
www.rad.org.uk

Royal Academy of Dramatic Art (RADA)

62-64 Gower Street
London WC1E 6ED
Tel: 020 7636 7076
enquiries@rada.ac.uk
www.rada.ac.uk
Drama UK
Conservatoire for Dance and Drama

Royal Academy of Music

Marylebone Rd
London NW1 5HT
Tel: 020 7873 7373
For range of email addresses see website
www.ram.ac.uk

Royal Ballet School

Upper School:
46 Floral Street
Covent Garden, London, WC2E 9DA
Lower School:
White Lodge
Richmond Park
Richmond
Surrey TW10 5HR
Tel: 020 7836 8899 (Upper School)
Tel: 020 8392 8440 (Lower School)
enquiries@royalballetschool.co.uk
www.royal-ballet-school.org.uk

Royal College of Music

Prince Consort Rd
London SW7 2BS
Tel: 020 7591 4300
info@rcm.ac.uk
www.rcm.ac.uk

Royal Northern College of Music
124 Oxford Rd
Manchester M13 9RD
Tel: 0161 907 5200
info@rncm.ac.uk
www.rncm.ac.uk

Royal Conservatoire of Scotland
100 Renfrew St
Glasgow G2 3DB
Tel: 0141 332 4101
For range of email addresses see website
www.rcs.ac.uk
Drama UK

Royal Welsh College of Music & Drama
Castle Grounds
Cathays Park
Cardiff CF10 3ER
Tel: 029 2034 2854
admissions@rwcmd.ac.uk
www.rwcmd.ac.uk
Drama UK

SLP College Leeds
5 Chapel Lane
Garforth
Leeds LS25 1AG
Tel: 0113 286 8136
info@slpcollege.co.uk
www.slpcollege.co.uk
CDET, DADA

Stella Mann College
10 Linden Road
Bedford MK40 2DA
Tel: 01234 213331
info@stellamanncollege.co.uk
www.stellamanncollege.co.uk
CDET

Tring Park School for the Performing Arts
Tring
Hertfordshire
HP23 5LX
Tel: 01442 824 255
info@tringpark.com
www.tringpark.com
CDET DADA

Trinity Laban Conservatoire of Music and Dance
Dance Faculty
Laban
Creekside
London
SE8 3DZ
Tel: 020 8691 8600
email via website

&
Music Faculty
Trinity
King Charles Court
Old Royal Naval College
Greenwich
London SE10 9JF
Tel: 020 8305 4444
email via website
www.trinitylaban.ac.uk

Urdang Academy
The Old Finsbury Town Hall
Rosebery Avenue
London EC1R 4RP
Tel: 0207 713 7710
info@theurdangacademy.com
www.theurdangacademy.com
CDET DADA

WAC Performing Arts and Media College
Hampstead Town Hall Centre
213 Haverstock Hill
London NW3 4QP
Tel: 020 7692 5888
info@wac.co.uk
www.wac.co.uk
DADA

Theatres & touring companies

Access London Theatre
www.officiallondontheatre.co.uk/access
Guide to West End Theatres for theatregoers
with a disability

London theatres: online
www.officiallondontheatre.co.uk

Theatrenet
www.theatrenet.com

UK Theatre Web
www.uktw.co.uk/

Aberdeen: His Majesty's Theatre
Rosemount Viaduct
Aberdeen AB25 1GL
Tel: 01224 641122
www.boxofficeaberdeen.com

Action Transport
Whitby Hall
Stanney Lane
Ellesmere Port CH65 9AE
Tel: 0151 357 2120
www.actiontransporttheatre.org

Actionwork
PO Box 433
Weston Super Mare
BS24 0WY
Tel: 01934 815163
www.actionwork.com

Arc Theatre
First Floor
The Malthouse Studios
62-76 Abbey Road
Barking
Essex IG11 7BT
Tel: 020 8594 1095
www.arctheatre.com

Basingstoke: Anvil, Forge and Haymarket
Anvil Arts
Churchill Way
Basingstoke RG21 7QR
Tel: 01256 819 797
Box Office: 01256 844244
www.anvilarts.org.uk

Bath: Theatre Royal
Sawclose
Bath BA1 1ET
Box Office: 01225 448844
www.theatreroyal.org.uk

Birmingham Repertory Theatre
The REP theatre building is closed until Autumn
2013 but is performing in other Birmingham
venues.
See website for details of locations
Box Office: 0121 236 4455
www.birmingham-rep.co.uk

Blackpool: Grand Theatre
33 Church Street
Blackpool FY1 1HT
Box Office: 01253 290190
Groups: 01253 743232
www.blackpoolgrand.co.uk

Blackpool: Opera House
97 Church Street
Blackpool FY1 1HL
Box Office: 0845 856 1111
www.wintergardensblackpool.co.uk

Bolton: Octagon Theatre
Howell Croft South
Bolton BL1 1SB
Box Office: 01204 520661
www.octagonbolton.co.uk

Bradford: Alhambra Theatre
Morley Street
Bradford BD7 1AJ
Tel: 01274 432375
Box Office: 01274 432 000
www.bradford-theatres.co.uk/alhambra

Bradford: Theatre in the Mill
Off Shearbridge Rd
Bradford BD7 1NX
Box Office: 01274 233200
www.brad.ac.uk/theatre

Bristol Old Vic
King St
Bristol BS1 4ED
Tel: 0117 949 3993
Box Office: 0117 987 7877
www.bristololdvic.org.uk

Bromley: The Churchill Theatre
High Street
Bromley
Kent BR1 1HA
Box Office: 0844 871 7620
Groups: 0844 871 7636
www.atgtickets.com/The-Churchill

Buxton Opera House
Water St
Buxton SK17 6XN
Tel: 01298 72050
Box Office: 0845 1272190
www.buxtonoperahouse.org.uk

Cambridge Arts Theatre
6 St Edward's Passage
Cambridge CB2 3PJ
Box Office: 01223 503333
www.cambridgeartstheatre.com

Canterbury: Marlowe Theatre
The Friars
Canterbury, Kent CT1 2AS
Box Office: 01227 787787
www.marlowetheatre.com

Cardiff: New Theatre
Park Place
Cardiff CF10 3LN
Box Office: 029 2087 8889
www.newtheatrecardiff.co.uk

Cardiff: Sherman Theatre
Senghennydd Rd
Cardiff CF24 4YE
Box Office: 029 2064 6900
www.shermancymru.co.uk

Clwyd Theatr Cymru
Mold
Flintshire CH7 1YA
Box Office: 0845 330 3565
www.clwyd-theatr-cymru.co.uk

Colchester: Mercury Theatre
Balkerne Gate
Colchester CO1 1PT
Box Office: 01206 573948
www.mercurytheatre.co.uk

Coventry: Belgrade Theatre
Belgrade Sq
Coventry CV1 1GS
Box Office: 024 7655 3055
www.belgrade.co.uk

Darlington: Civic Theatre
Parkgate
Darlington DL1 1RR
Box Office: 01325 486555
www.darlington.gov.uk/Leisure/arts

Derby Theatre
Theatre Walk
Derby DE1 2NF
Box Office: 01332 59 39 39
www.derbytheatre.co.uk

Dundee Repertory Theatre
Tay Sq
Dundee DD1 1PB
Box Office: 01382 223530
www.dundeereptheatre.co.uk

Edinburgh: Festival Theatre
13/29 Nicolson Street
Edinburgh EH8 9FT
Tel: 0131 529 6000
www.edtheatres.com/festival

Edinburgh: Kings Theatre
2 Leven Street
Edinburgh EH3 9LQ
Tel: 0131 529 6000
www.edtheatres.com/kings

Edinburgh Playhouse
18-22 Greenside Place
Edinburgh EH1 3AA
Tickets: 0844 871 3014
www.atgtickets.com/venues/edinburgh-
playhouse/

Edinburgh: Royal Lyceum Theatre
30b Grindlay St
Edinburgh EH3 9AX
Box Office: 0131 248 4848
www.lyceum.org.uk

Edinburgh: Traverse Theatre
Scotland's New Writing Theatre
10 Cambridge St
Edinburgh EH1 2ED
Box Office: 0131 228 1404
www.traverse.co.uk

English Touring Theatre
25 Short St
London SE1 8LJ
Tel: 020 7450 1990
www.ett.org.uk

Exeter: Northcott Theatre
Stocker Rd
Exeter EX4 4QB
Box Office: 01392 493493
www.exeternorthcott.co.uk

Glasgow: Citizens Theatre
119 Gorbals St
Glasgow G5 9DS
Box Office: 0141 429 0022
www.citz.co.uk

Glasgow: Tramway
25 Albert Drive
Glasgow G41 2PE
Tel: 0845 330 3501
www.tramway.org

Glasgow: Tron Theatre
63 Trongate
Glasgow G1 5HB
Box Office: 0141 552 4267
www.tron.co.uk

Harrogate Theatre
Oxford St
Harrogate HG1 1QF
Box Office: 01423 502116
www.harrogatetheatre.co.uk

Headlong Theatre
34-35 Berwick Street
London W1F 8RP
Tel: 020 7478 0270
www.headlongtheatre.co.uk

Hornchurch: Queen's Theatre
Billet Ln
Hornchurch RM11 1QT
Box Office: 01708 443333
www.queens-theatre.co.uk

Huddersfield: Lawrence Batley Theatre
Queens Square
Queens St
Huddersfield HD1 2SP
Box Office: 01484 430528
www.thelbt.org

Hull Truck Theatre
50 Ferensway
Hull, HU2 8LB
Box Office: 01482 323638
www.hulltruck.co.uk

Ipswich: Sir John Mills Theatre
Gatacre Rd
Ipswich IP1 2LQ
Box Office: 01473 211498
www.easternangles.co.uk

Kendal: Brewery Arts Centre
122A Highgate
Kendal LA9 4HE
Box Office: 01539 725133
www.breweryarts.co.uk

Keswick: Theatre by the Lake
Lakeside
Keswick CA12 5DJ
Box Office: 01768 774411
www.theatrebythelake.co.uk

Lancaster: Duke's Cinema & Theatre
Moor Lane
Lancaster LA1 1QE
Box Office: 01524 598 500
www.dukes-lancaster.org

Leeds: Grand Theatre
46 New Briggate
Leeds LS1 6NZ
Box Office: 0844 848 2700
www.leedsgrandtheatre.com

Leeds: West Yorkshire Playhouse
Playhouse Sq
Quarry Hill
Leeds LS2 7UP
Box Office: 0113 213 7700
www.wyp.org.uk

Leicester: Curve
Rutland Street
Leicester LE1 1SB
Tel: 0116 242 3595
www.curveonline.co.uk

Lincoln: Theatre Royal
Clasketgate
Lincoln LN2 1JJ
Box Office: 01522 519999
www.lincolntheatreroyal.com

Liverpool: Empire
Lime St
Liverpool L1 1JE
Box Office: 0844 871 3017
Groups: 0844 871 3037
www.atgtickets.com/venues/liverpool-empire

Liverpool: Everyman Theatre
5-9 Hope St
Liverpool L1 9BH
Box Office: 0151 709 4776
Groups: 0151 708 3733
www.everymanplayhouse.com

Liverpool: Playhouse
Williamson Square
Liverpool L1 1EL
Box Office: 0151 709 4776
Groups: 0151 708 3733
www.everymanplayhouse.com

London: Almeida Theatre
Almeida St
Islington
London N1 1TA
Box Office: 020 7359 4404
www.almeida.co.uk

London: Barbican Centre
Silk St
London EC2Y 8DS
Box Office: 020 7638 8891
www.barbican.org.uk

London: Donmar Warehouse
41 Earlham St
Seven Dials
London WC2H 9LX
Box Office: 0844 871 7624
www.donmarwarehouse.com

London: Hampstead Theatre
Eton Ave
Swiss Cottage
London NW3 3EU
Box Office: 020 7722 9301
www.hampsteadtheatre.com

London: Lyric Theatre
King St
London W6 0QL
Box Office: 020 8741 6850
www.lyric.co.uk

London: National Theatre
South Bank
London SE1 9PX
Tel: 020 7452 3000 (Box Office)
www.nationaltheatre.org.uk

London: New Wimbledon Theatre
The Broadway
Wimbledon
London SW19 1QG
Box Office: 0844 871 7646
www.atgtickets.com/New-Wimbledon-Theatre

London: Open Air Theatre
Inner Circle
Regent's Park NW1 4NR
Box Office: 0844 826 4242
www.openairtheatre.org

London: Polka Theatre for Children
240 The Broadway
Wimbledon
London SW19 1SB
Box Office: 020 8543 4888
www.polkatheatre.com

London: Royal Court Theatre
Sloane Sq
London SW1W 8AS
Tel: 020 7565 5050
Box Office: 020 7565 5000
www.royalcourttheatre.com

London: Sadler's Wells Theatre
Rosebery Av
London EC1R 4TN
Tel: 020 7863 8198
Box Office: 0844 412 4300
www.sadlerswells.com

London: Shakespeare's Globe Theatre
21 New Globe Walk
Bankside
London SE1 9DT
Box office: 020 7401 9919
www.shakespearesglobe.com

London: Theatre Royal Stratford East
Gerry Raffles Sq
London E15 1BN
Tel: 020 8534 0310
www.stratfordeast.com

London: Tricycle Theatre
269 Kilburn High Rd
London NW6 7JR
Box Office: 020 7328 1000
www.tricycle.co.uk

London: Unicorn Theatre for Children
147 Tooley Street
London SE1 2HZ
Tel: 020 7645 0560
www.unicorntheatre.com

London: Young Vic
66 The Cut
London SE1 8LZ
Tel: 020 7922 2922
www.youngvic.org

Manchester: Contact Theatre
Oxford Rd
Manchester MI5 6JA
Box Office: 0161 274 0600
www.contactmcr.com

Manchester: Library Theatre
Cornerhouse
70 Oxford Street
Manchester M1 5NH
Lowry Box Office: 0843 208 6010
Cornerhouse Box Office: 0161 200 1500
www.librarytheatre.com

Manchester: Opera House
3 Quay Street
Manchester M3 3HP
Tel: 0844 871 3018
www.atgtickets.com/venues/opera-house-manchester

Manchester: Palace Theatre
97 Oxford Street
Manchester M1 6FT
Box Office: 0844 871 3019
www.atgtickets.com/venues/palace-theatre-manchester

Manchester: Royal Exchange Theatre Co
St Ann's Sq
Manchester M2 7DH
Box Office: 0161 833 9833
www.royalexchange.co.uk/

Manchester: The Green Room
54-56 Whitworth St West
Manchester M1 5WW
Box Office: 0161 615 0500
www.greenroomarts.org

Milford Haven: Torch Theatre
St Peter's Rd
Milford Haven SA73 2BU
Box Office: 01646 695267
www.torchtheatre.co.uk

Musselburgh: Brunton Theatre
Ladywell Way
Musselburgh EH21 6AA
Box Office: 0131 665 2240
www.bruntontheatre.co.uk

Newbury: Watermill Theatre
Bagnor
Newbury
Berks RG20 8AE
Box Office: 01635 46044
www.watermill.org.uk

Newcastle under Lyme: New Vic Theatre
Etruria Rd
Newcastle under Lyme ST5 0JG
Box Office: 01782 717962
www.newvictheatre.org.uk

Newcastle upon Tyne: Live Theatre Company
27 Broad Chare
Quayside
Newcastle upon Tyne NE1 3DQ
Box Office: 0191 232 1232
www.live.org.uk

Newcastle upon Tyne: Northern Stage
Barras Bridge
Newcastle upon Tyne NE1 7RH
Tel: 0191 230 5151
www.northernstage.co.uk

Northampton Theatres Trust: Royal & Derngate Theatre
Guildhall Rd
Northampton NN1 1DP
Box Office: 01604 624811
www.royalandderngate.co.uk

Northern Broadsides
Dean Clough
Halifax HX3 5AX
Tel: 01422 369704
www.northern-broadsides.co.uk

Norwich Playhouse
42 - 58 St. George's Street
Norwich NR3 1AB
Box office: 01603 598 598
www.norwichplayhouse.co.uk

Norwich: Theatre Royal
Theatre St
Norwich NR2 1RL
Box Office: 01603 630000
www.theatreroyalnorwich.co.uk

Nottingham Playhouse
Wellington Circus
Nottingham NG1 5AF
Box Office: 0115 941 9419
www.nottinghamplayhouse.co.uk

Nottingham: Theatre Royal
Theatre Square
Nottingham NG1 5ND
Box Office: 0115 989 5555
www.royalcentre-nottingham.co.uk

Oldham Coliseum
Fairbottom St
Oldham OL1 3SW
Box Office: 0161 624 2829
www.coliseum.org.uk

Out of Joint
7 Thane Works
London N7 7NU
Tel: 020 7609 0207
www.outofjoint.co.uk

Oxford Playhouse
11-12 Beaumont St
Oxford OX1 2LW
Box Office: 01865 305305
www.oxfordplayhouse.com

Perth Theatre
185 High St
Perth PH1 5UW
Tel: 01738 621 031
www.horsecross.co.uk

Pilot Theatre
c/o York Theatre Royal
St Leonard's Place
York YO1 7HD
Tel: 01904 635755
www.pilot-theatre.com

Plymouth: Theatre Royal
Royal Parade
Plymouth PL1 2TR
Box Office: 01752 267222
www.theatreroyal.com

Portsmouth: New Theatre Royal
20-24 Guildhall Walk
Portsmouth
Hampshire PO1 2DD
Box Office: 023 9264 9000
www.newtheatreroyal.com

Royal Opera House
Covent Garden
London WC2E 9DD
Box Office: 020 7304 4000
Switchboard: 020 7240 1200
www.roh.org.uk

Salford: The Lowry
Pier 8, Salford Quays
Manchester M50 3AZ
Tel: 0843 208 6000
www.thelowry.com

Salisbury Playhouse
Malthouse Lane
Salisbury SP2 7RA
Tel: 01722 320117
Box Office: 01722 320 333
www.salisburyplayhouse.com

Scarborough: Stephen Joseph Theatre
Westborough
Scarborough YO11 1JW
Tel: 01723 370540
Box Office: 01723 370541
www.sjt.uk.com

Shakespeare at the Tobacco Factory
Raleigh Rd
Southville
Bristol BS3 1TF
Tel: 0117 963 3054
www.sattf.org.uk

Shared Experience Theatre
Oxford Playhouse
11-12 Beaumont Street
Oxford OX1 2LW
Tel: 01865 305321
www.sharedexperience.org.uk

Sheffield: Crucible Theatre
55 Norfolk St
Sheffield S1 1DA
Tel: 0114 249 5999
Box Office: 0114 249 6000
www.sheffieldtheatres.co.uk

Sheffield: Lyceum Theatre
55 Norfolk St
Sheffield S1 1DA
Tel: 0114 249 5999
Box Office: 0114 249 6000
www.sheffieldtheatres.co.uk

Southampton: Nuffield Theatre
University Rd
Southampton SO17 1TR
Tel: 023 8031 5500
Box Office: 023 8067 1771
www.nuffieldtheatre.co.uk

Southend on Sea: Palace Theatre
Cliffs Pavillion
Station Rd
Southend-on-Sea
Essex SS0 7RA
Box Office: 01702 351135
HR & Admin: 01702 390657
www.thecliffspavilion.co.uk

Stoke-on-Trent: Regent Theatre
Piccadilly
Stoke-On-Trent ST1 1AP
Box Office: 0844 871 7649
www.atgtickets.com/Stoke-On-Trent

Stratford-upon-Avon: Royal Shakespeare Theatre
Waterside
Stratford-upon-Avon
Warwickshire CV37 6BB
Box Office: 0844 800 1110
www.rsc.org.uk

Stratford-Upon-Avon: Swan Theatre
Waterside
Stratford-Upon-Avon
Warwickshire CV37 6BB
Box Office:0844 800 1110
www.rsc.org.uk

TARA ARTS
356 Garratt Lane
Earlsfield
London SW18 4ES
Tel: 020 8333 4457
www.tara-arts.com

Théâtre de Complicité
14 Anglers Lane
London NW5 3DG
Tel: 020 7485 7700
www.complicite.org

Wakefield: Theatre Royal & Opera House
Drury Lane
Wakefield WF1 2TE
Box Office: 01924 211 311
www.wakefieldtheatres.co.uk

Watford: Palace Theatre
20Clarendon Rd
Watford WD17 1JZ
Tel: 01923 235455
Box Office: 01923 225671
www.watfordtheatre.co.uk

Worcester: Swan Theatre
The Moors
Worcester WR1 3ED
Box Office: 01905 611427
www.worcesterlive.co.uk

York Theatre Royal
St Leonards Place
York YO1 7HD
Box Office: 01904 623568
www.yorktheatreroyal.co.uk

Learning Resources
Centre